D0926396

The Origins
of Morality

The Origins
of Morality

An Evolutionary Account

Dennis L. Krebs

OXFORD
UNIVERSITY PRESS

Oxford University Press, Inc., publishes works that further Oxford University's objective of excellence in research, scholarship, and education.

Oxford   New York
Auckland   Cape Town   Dar es Salaam   Hong Kong   Karachi   Kuala Lumpur
Madrid   Melbourne   Mexico City   Nairobi   New Delhi   Shanghai   Taipei   Toronto

With offices in
Argentina   Austria   Brazil   Chile   Czech Republic   France   Greece   Guatemala   Hungary   Italy
Japan   Poland   Portugal   Singapore   South Korea   Switzerland   Thailand   Turkey   Ukraine
Vietnam

Published by Oxford University Press, Inc.
198 Madison Avenue, New York, New York 10016

www.oup.com

Oxford is a registered trademark of Oxford University Press, Inc.

Library of Congress Cataloging-in-Publication Data
Krebs, Dennis.
The origins of morality : an evolutionary account / Dennis L. Krebs.
p. cm.
Includes bibliographical references and index.
ISBN 978-0-19-977823-2 (hardcover)
1. Ethics, Evolutionary. 2. Evolutionary psychology. I. Title.
BJ1311.K74 2011
171'.7–dc22   2010051247

9 8 7 6 5 4 3 2
Printed in the United States of America on acid-free paper

This book is dedicated to my four most significant accomplishments—forming an enduring and mutually-supportive partnership with Kathy Denton, and contributing to the development of three moral and highly accomplished daughters, Danielle, Lamour, and Kaleda

PREFACE

I have spent most of my career trying to understand altruism and morality. During the past several decades, Lawrence Kohlberg's cognitive-developmental theory, which is based on the idea that people normally pass through several stages of moral development, has constituted the dominant paradigm in psychology. Without meaning any disrespect, I believe that Kohlbergian accounts of morality have outlived their usefulness and that it is time to move on. I am reinforced in this belief by other psychologists who have been guided by this approach (e.g., Lapsley, 2006).

In this book, I present an account of morality derived from the theory of evolution that I believe is equipped to serve as a framework for situating and revising psychological theories, including those advanced by cognitive-developmental theorists, and steering the study of morality in new, more productive, directions. In the past decade, there has been an explosion of theory and research on the evolution of morality, not only by psychologists, but also by biologists, neuroscientists, economists, anthropologists, political scientists, and philosophers. Cloistered in their own areas, many psychologists are missing the significance of these new developments, or worse yet, misinterpreting them. For some, the mere mention of the words "evolution," "genes," or "function" seems to conjure up images of self-seeking puppets jerked around by inexorable forces. Yet, when you ask those who equate evolution with genetic determinism whether they believe that humans evolved in the same way as other species, or whether genes play an important role in designing the brain, or whether people are motivated to survive and reproduce, most of them will answer in the affirmative.

I want to be constructive. Too often, scientists assume that there is only one valid theory out there—the one that appeals to them—and they spend their careers supporting and defending it. I try to avoid this trap. I acknowledge that the traditional accounts of morality espoused by psychologists are valid in their own explanatory realm, but argue that they tell only part of the story. In this book, I attempt to demonstrate how an evolutionary account of morality can supply a framework equipped to encompass traditional psychological accounts. My hope is that the book will help psychologists and other social scientists understand that their preferred theoretical accounts of morality are not necessarily inconsistent with an evolutionary account and that evolutionary theory supplies a basis for evaluating, correcting, and refining other approaches.

I derived the account of the evolution of morality that I advance in this book from Darwin's original model of the evolution of a moral sense, and refinements in Darwin's ideas that have been published by contemporary evolutionary theorists such as Richard Alexander, Christopher Boehm, Robert Boyd, David Buss, Leda Cosmides, Charles Crawford, Denise Cummins, Richard Dawkins, Frans de Waal, Herbert Gintis, Joshua Greene, Jonathan Haidt, Michael McCullough, Geoffrey Miller, Randolph Nesse, Peter

Richerson, Matt Ridley, Elliot Sober, John Tooby, Robert Trivers, George Williams, and David Sloan Wilson. Although I provide a first-hand account of these theorists' ideas, sometimes by quoting them extensively, my goal is to provide more than a review of the literature. I try to synthesize, integrate, and expand theory and research on the evolution of morality in a way that produces an integrated account. In view of the fact that some of the theorists whose work I review disagree quite strongly with ideas advanced by some of the other theorists, this is a challenging task.

When we write, we usually have an audience in mind. I have found myself engaging in imaginary conversations with a white-bearded Charles Darwin. The strategy I used to organize the ideas in this book was to summarize Darwin's early model of the evolution of morality (which, I argue, contains insights that have been neglected by many contemporary evolutionary theorists), then revise it in terms of modern theory and research. I would like to believe that if Darwin were alive today, he would be pleased with my attempts to update and refine his early work. However, in the main, I wrote this book for living people who are interested in expanding their understanding of evolutionary psychology and morality—not only students taking courses in evolutionary psychology, but also students in the broadest sense of the word, whether laypeople, colleagues, or pupils. I have published many of the ideas in this book in chapters and articles cited in the references at the end of the volume.

CONTENTS

Part Five: Implications and Applications

PART ONE

Setting the Stage

1

INTRODUCTION AND OVERVIEW

After many years of studying the acquisition of morality, I concluded that the theories advanced by psychologists leave a great deal unexplained. To account fully for morality, we need an overriding framework that organizes the insights in psychological models in coherent ways and resolves the differences among them. Although the theory of evolution may be the last place that many people would look for such a framework, I believe that this theory is best equipped to accomplish this task. The mental mechanisms that dispose people to behave in moral ways and the mental mechanisms that endow people with a sense of morality were not immune from natural selection; they evolved in accordance with the same principles that guided the evolution of other mental mechanisms.

In this chapter, I review my attempts to understand how children become moral. I argue that although the dominant contemporary psychological approach to morality—cognitive-developmental theory—accounts for aspects of morality that other approaches are unable to explain, it is poorly equipped to account for the ways in which people make moral decisions in their everyday lives. I explain why I decided to abandon this approach in favor of an evolutionary approach, which I believe contains significantly more explanatory power.

From the perspective of evolution, the key to understanding morality lies in identifying the adaptive functions that the mental processes that produce moral behaviors, moral norms, moral judgments, moral emotions, and moral beliefs evolved to serve. At the risk of spoiling the story by revealing its ending, I ended up concluding that the mechanisms that give rise to a moral sense evolved to help early humans solve the adaptive problems that constrained their ability to reap the benefits of sociality. The biological function of morality is to help people maximize their gains from cooperative social relations by inducing members of their groups—including themselves—to behave in mutually beneficial ways and to resist the temptation to advance their interests in ways that jeopardize the welfare of others and the social orders of their groups.

Permit me the indulgence of introducing this book in an autobiographical manner. For most of my academic career, I have attempted to understand why people sometimes behave in altruistic and moral ways and sometimes do not. Trained as a psychologist, I was guided mainly by psychological theory and research on moral development and what psychologists call "prosocial behavior." In this chapter, I trace the development of my thinking about morality, explaining why I came to decide that the folk accounts implicitly harbored by laypeople and the more formal accounts advanced by psychologists are inadequate and justifying the claim that evolutionary theory can redress their limitations. In the process, I offer an abridged version of the main issues discussed in this book, written in a way that I intend to be easy to understand on first reading.

FOLK ACCOUNTS OF THE ACQUISITION OF MORALITY

Like most other people from the Western world, I grew up believing that children acquire morals through socialization and cultural indoctrination. I assumed that infants are born fundamentally selfish and immoral but are taught to be moral by parents and other socializing agents who induce them to internalize the moral norms of their cultures. Although there is much merit in this folk account of how people acquire morals, I came to decide that it is incomplete and, therefore, misleading. It tells part of the story, but it leaves out important chapters.

One limitation of folk accounts of the acquisition of morality is that they do not begin at the beginning. Granted, they may begin at the beginning of children's lives, but they fail to explain how the moral norms that children internalize originated in the first place. When you think about it, this is a significant oversight because in these accounts moral norms constitute the content of children's sense of morality. You might say that children learn their morals from their parents, who learned them from their parents, who learned them from *their* parents, and so on back through the generations. But how did these morals originate in the first place? Who was the first person to say, "This is right, and that is wrong" and why? To account for the acquisition of a sense of morality, we need to explain how moral norms originated, why people originally created them, and why people preach them to others.

Some moral norms are universal, and others are culturally relative; some moral norms are stable, whereas others undergo changes over time. Why? For example, why do people from one era believe that slavery is right and that homosexuality is wrong; whereas people from another era believe the opposite? What causes variations in moral norms within cultures? Why, for example, do some people believe that capital punishment, abortion, and euthanasia are moral, and other people believe that they are immoral?

Perhaps the most serious limitation of folk accounts of the acquisition of morality is that they portray children as relatively passive recipients of moral ideas that are poured or stamped into them by others. Many people assume that teaching children what is moral is similar to teaching them other things, such as vocabulary, arithmetic, and history. Adults, who possess more knowledge than children do, teach them the facts of the matter; and children, who have a thirst for knowledge, are motivated to learn these facts from adults. However, as every parent knows, there is something wrong with this picture. Children do not passively accept their parents' moral injunctions.

Children challenge their parents; they argue with them, and they reject ideas that do not make sense to them. They are selective about the ideas they accept, and they advance their own points of view. Relations between children and adults involve conflicts, and a substantial portion of the energy that people devote to social relations is devoted to the resolution of conflicts.

In a book called *Evolution, Morality, and the Meaning of Life*, Murphy (1982) asks, "Is it reasonable to regard morality as nothing but a set of internalized parental commands?" (p. 65). Murphy answers:

> Surely not. Part of the moral beliefs of any mature adult will, of course, be in some sense shadowy remnants of childhood commands. But we would regard as a moral imbecile—a moral child, actually—someone whose moral outlook consisted solely of such imitative responses. It is part of our concept of a morally mature person that such a person questions some accepted prohibitions, uses his reason to inquire into justifications for them, and retains them only if he can see for himself that they have merit. . . . For most actual human beings, their morality will consist of some uncritically accepted commands (derived from parents and culture) and some critically thought out beliefs they have arrived at (or at least decided to keep) on their own by a process of critical, rational, reflection. (p. 65)

KOHLBERG'S MODEL OF MORAL DEVELOPMENT

I came to question folk accounts of the acquisition of morality in graduate school when I took a course on moral development from Lawrence Kohlberg—a scholar who ended up advancing the regnant model of morality in psychology. Building on and refining a model advanced by Jean Piaget (1932), Kohlberg objected to socialization accounts of morality, especially as formalized by early social learning theorists in psychology. Kohlberg insisted that children are not passive receptacles of moral ideas poured or pounded into them by others; children create their own conceptions of morality, interpreting the information they receive from their social worlds, thinking about it, digesting it mentally, integrating it, and constructing their own ideas.

Kohlberg did not deny that children accept some of their parents' ideas about morality, just as they accept other ideas, such as myths about Santa Claus. However, Kohlberg argued that as children grow older they get smarter, and they become increasingly inclined to think for themselves. They develop mental mechanisms, or "structures," through which they process moral information and make moral decisions. They use their heads to evaluate the ideas expressed by their parents and other people, then reach their own conclusions. In making moral decisions and resolving moral conflicts, they invoke standards of common sense, logic, and cognitive consistency.

Kohlberg was correct in insisting that children do not acquire their conceptions of morality entirely from their parents, because if they did, they would express the same ideas as their parents do, and they clearly do not. Children's conceptions of morality are significantly less sophisticated than those of their parents. For example, as observed by Piaget (1932), at early ages, children believe that a child who claims that he saw a dog as big as a cow is naughtier than a child who lies about the marks he received in school, even though their parents do not espouse such beliefs. In addition, Kohlberg pointed out that most people whom we hold up as exemplars of morality do not conform to the moral norms of their cultures; rather, they are autonomous people who advance original ideas about morality that differ from those that their parents preached to them.

Finally, Kohlberg argued that children do not acquire ideas about morality bit by bit, as learning theorists assert; instead, their ideas about morality are integrated in terms of overriding principles, and these integrated conceptions undergo several qualitative structural changes as they develop, which define stages of moral development. Kohlberg believed that the process of thinking about morality, solving moral problems, and making moral decisions induces children to develop increasingly sophisticated moral information-processing mechanisms, or as he called them, "structures of moral reasoning," which enable children to solve increasingly complex moral problems and make increasingly sophisticated moral judgments.

Kohlberg was an inspirational teacher. In part, perhaps, because of his charisma, but more so, I think, because of the hope I saw in his model of how people acquire a sense of morality, I devoted a substantial portion of my academic career to evaluating his theory. What attracted me to Kohlberg's model was its potential to redress the limitations of early socialization accounts of moral development. Clearly, there is more to morality than conformity and the passive internalization of cultural norms. People play an active role in developing their own conceptions of morality, and people tend to become increasingly moral as they develop. Models of development like the one advanced by Kohlberg foster hope in human potential. In addition, perhaps, I felt attracted to the idea that the essence of morality lies in the ability to reason. As an academic, I valued reason, and I viewed it as an ability that could—and should—be cultivated.

As I describe more fully in the last chapter of this book, my colleagues and I conducted a program of research designed to evaluate Kohlberg's model of morality. When a study failed to support some aspect of his model, we revised his model and then tested the revised model. Eventually, we patched up Kohlberg's model so much that, like a leaky boat, we decided to abandon it and construct another model that was better able to float on its own.

One of the conclusions that we reached from our research was that the structures of moral reasoning described by Kohlberg and his colleagues are one among many mental mechanisms that give rise to moral judgments and moral behaviors. If people possess the capacity to make moral decisions in a variety of ways, the challenges become to identify the full set of mental mechanisms, or sources, of moral decision making and to explain what induces people to invoke one decision-making process and not another. The results of our research suggested that people use different kinds of mental mechanisms to achieve different kinds of goals and to solve different kinds of moral problems. It is as though people acquire a chest of mental tools, or abilities, designed to perform a variety of tasks. When people face a particular moral problem, they select the tools that are best able to help them solve it. To understand the kinds of moral judgments people make (i.e., the kinds of tools they select), you need to understand the goals they are using them to achieve. People may use moral judgments to achieve moral goals, such as making decisions about how they are obliged to treat others, or they may use them to achieve immoral goals, such as justifying immoral choices and evading responsibility.

Attending to the goals that people use moral judgments (and moral behaviors) to achieve entails attending to the functions of morality. When you attend to functions, you inevitably end up in a regress toward the ultimate. People use moral judgments and moral behaviors to achieve proximate goals such as obeying rules, conforming to social norms, making a good impression, and resolving conflicts of interest. But why are people motivated to achieve these goals? Because people possess certain needs, desires, wants, and values. But how did they acquire them; where did they come from; what functions do they serve? To get along with others, perhaps, or to make themselves feel good, or to avoid punishment. But why are people motivated to get along with others, to feel good, and to avoid punishment? To make themselves happy; to survive and to reproduce? If we keep pushing back to increasingly ultimate motives, goals, and functions, we inevitably end up either in some ephemeral determining force, such as God, or in ultimate goals such as surviving and reproducing, which land us squarely in the theory of evolution.

VIEWING MORALITY FROM THE PERSPECTIVE OF EVOLUTION

When I was in graduate school working on a paper reviewing research on altruism, a young lecturer from the biology department looked me up. He said that he was writing a paper on the evolution of mechanisms that disposed animals to behave in altruistic ways and had heard that I was writing a paper on human altruism. We exchanged drafts, talked, and became friends.[1] The paper this lecturer was working on (Trivers, 1971) ended up making a monumental contribution to our understanding of social evolution. His name is Robert Trivers, and he went on to become one of the world's most eminent evolutionary biologists and one of the most innovative thinkers of our time.

Robert Trivers was a weird and wonderful person—a creative genius. He viewed social behavior in completely different ways from the ways in which I and other psychologists were trained to interpret it. He asked questions that had never occurred to me: "Why are the male members of most species larger than the female members?" (I recall him showing me pictures of lizards to illustrate this question.) "Is there any psychological research comparing people's disposition to help strangers, friends, and relatives?" "No?" "Why not?" "Aren't most people more inclined to help their friends and relatives than they are to help strangers?" "If you want to explain altruism, don't you need to attend to the most prevalent incidents, such as parents helping children?" "Is there any research comparing the amount of help mothers and fathers give their offspring?" "In some species, only one parent helps—usually, but not always, the mother; in other species both parents help." "How do humans divide this task, and why?" "In accounting for these aspects of human behavior, why would you invoke different principles from those that account for similar behaviors in other animals?"

Although the review of research on altruism that I published as a graduate student (Krebs, 1970) had an impact on the field of psychology, helping define a new area of

---

[1] Trivers (2002) offers an account of this exchange.

study, I found psychological research on altruism disappointing because it failed to address what I considered to be the most important theoretical issue: Are people naturally disposed to behave in altruistic ways, or are they capable of being altruistic or are people fundamentally selfish by nature? If you scratch an altruist, will you see a hypocrite bleed? None of the psychological research I reviewed addressed this issue. Instead, it examined proximate determinants of helping, or as it came to be called "prosocial behavior," defined as behavior that has the immediate effect of benefiting a recipient, whatever the consequences for the donor, whatever his or her reasons, or whatever the ultimate effect of the helping behavior. In contrast, Trivers's paper addressed a question with immense theoretical significance: Can any animal be altruistic by nature? Could mental mechanisms have evolved that induced animals to behave in ways that were costly to them and beneficial to recipients; and if so, how?[2]

A decade or so after I published the review of psychological research on altruism, some psychologists, most notably Dan Batson and his colleagues (whose work I review in Chapter 15), addressed what they called "the altruism question." However, in my view, the extent to which our understanding of the human capacity for altruism has been advanced by psychologists pales in comparison to the extent to which it has been advanced by evolutionary biologists.

Trivers turned me on to the explanatory power of the theory of evolution. For a psychologist to deny the impact of evolution is to deny that the brain is an evolved organ and to imply that it, or relevant aspects of it, were somehow immune to the effects of natural selection. I suppose that one could argue that humans posses some capacities such as a soul or sense of morality that originate from sources other than evolved mechanisms, but I doubt that such arguments could be evaluated scientifically, or if they could be, that they would be confirmed. In any event, in this book I argue that people's sense of morality stems from, and is structured by, evolved mental mechanisms, and I advance a great deal of evidence to support this contention.

THE EVOLUTION OF MORALITY

If the manifestations of morality stem from mental mechanisms that evolved in the human species, we need to identify these mechanisms, explain how they originated, and decipher their design. These tasks are no different from the tasks faced by any scholar motivated to account for the moral aspect of human nature, whatever his or her theoretical orientation. Psychoanalysts have attributed morality to a mechanism they call the superego; learning theorists have attributed it to the mechanisms that mediate

---

[2] Incidentally, although the title of Trivers's paper is "The Evolution of Reciprocal Altruism," the "altruistic" behaviors he accounted for were biologically selfish in the sense that they contributed to the ultimate biological welfare of those who emitted them. When I read a draft of Trivers's paper, I suggested that he drop "Altruism" from the title and call it "The Evolution of Reciprocity." As I explain in Chapter 3, I continue to believe that the term altruism is used in a misleading way by many evolutionary biologists, as is the term "selfish," such as in Dawkins's book *The Selfish Gene*.

learning; and cognitive-developmental theorists have attributed it to structures of moral reasoning. Note that each set of theorists accounts for different aspects of morality (e.g., guilt, moral behavior, and moral reasoning). Although theorists are wont to claim that the accounts advanced by theorists from other camps are wrong, I believe that all accounts contain insights that contribute to the solution of the puzzle. What is missing is a framework, or overriding umbrella, equipped to integrate them in coherent ways. The value of viewing mental mechanisms as evolved structures lies in the guidance it provides about how they are designed. If the mental mechanisms that induce people to make moral judgments and to behave in moral ways were designed by natural selection, then the products should bear the stamp of this process.[3]

Evolution is a complex process, and we need to understand its complexities to understand the ways in which it designs organisms. That physical and mental mechanisms are products of natural selection does not imply that other, more proximate, factors do not play any role in designing them and activating them. As I explain in Chapter 5, the chemical factors that affect the development of fetuses, the kinds of environments in which infants develop, and the situations that people experience in their everyday lives exert significant effects on the ways in which they behave.

Evolutionary theory encourages us to ask whether the mental mechanisms that dispose people to behave in moral ways and the mechanisms that produce a moral sense served adaptive functions in the environments of our human ancestors, and if so, what these functions were. Such eminent evolutionary theorists as George Williams (1989) have argued that at least one of the mechanisms that mediate morality—moral reasoning—evolved as a byproduct of nonmoral reasoning processes, but I do not think that this account tells the whole story, or even the most important parts. Some aspects of the moral sense—for example, ideas derived from sophisticated structures of moral reasoning—may be incidental, even maladaptive, byproducts of reasoning mechanisms that evolved to serve other adaptive purposes. However, I argue that the moral sense is rooted in mechanisms that evolved specifically to solve moral problems and that early humans who inherited genes that designed mechanisms that disposed them to behave in moral ways and endowed them with a sense of morality fared better in the struggle to survive and to reproduce than early humans who did not inherit such genes.

AN EVOLUTIONARY ACCOUNT OF MORALITY: AN OVERVIEW OF THIS BOOK

The central purpose of this book is to present an integrated account, or grand theory, of the origin and evolution of morality that synthesizes ideas published by contemporary scholars from many fields of study—one that encompasses the implicit folk models of laypeople and the more formal models advanced by psychologists. I hope that this will help psychologists and other social scientists understand that their preferred theoretical accounts of morality are not necessarily inconsistent with an evolutionary account and

---

[3] I describe this stamp, which boils down to evidence of function, in Chapter 5.

that evolutionary theory supplies a basis for evaluating, correcting, and refining other approaches.

I begin by exploring answers to the question, "What is morality?" I argue that, to define morality, we must understand what it means to people in their everyday lives. I review theory and research that has examined people's subjective conceptions of morality, including research conducted by Kohlberg and his colleagues. I advance evidence that people from all cultures share abstract conceptions of morality but that people from different cultures instantiate these ideas in different ways, and I argue that to fully understand what morality means to people, we must attend to the functions that conceptions of morality evolved to fulfill.

In Chapter 3, I remove a potential obstacle facing theories of the evolution of morality, namely the possibility, endorsed by some eminent evolutionary theorists, that the laws of natural selection dictate that all animals are selfish by nature, and because unselfishness is necessary for morality, all animals are immoral by nature. I argue that this assumption is founded on a confusion between the kind of selfishness that characterizes evolved dispositions and the kind of selfishness that characterizes immoral behaviors.

In Chapter 4, I lay the foundation for the rest of the book by outlining and evaluating the first model of how moral dispositions evolved, published by the father of evolution, Charles Darwin. Although I acknowledge that some of Darwin's ideas are outdated, and others are misguided, I argue that no one has sketched a better framework than the one Darwin sketched in the late 19th century. I devote the rest of the book to refining, extending, and updating Darwin's original account in light of new developments in theory and research on the evolution of morality, beginning in Chapter 5 by outlining three important revisions in Darwin's overriding theory of evolution.

In Part II of this book I update Darwin's ideas about how mechanisms that dispose animals to show deference to authority, to exert self-control, to care for and help members of their groups, and to engage in several forms of cooperation evolved. In Chapter 6, I explain how deference to authority can increase individuals' fitness by helping them avoid getting punished, injured, killed, or ostracized by those who are more powerful than they are and by inducing them to uphold the social orders that support the groups on which they are dependent. In Chapter 7, I review evidence that the ability to exert self-control pays off biologically by enabling animals to delay gratification and to constrain selfish urges such as those that define the Seven Deadly Sins. In Chapters 8, 9, and 10, I review accounts of the evolution of biological forms of altruism based, in turn, on kin selection, sexual selection, group selection, and imperfections in the design of evolved mental mechanisms. In Chapter 11, I review Trivers's model of the evolution of reciprocity and the refinements advanced by later evolutionary theorists. In Chapter 12, I describe the psychological and neurological mechanisms that give rise to primitive prosocial behaviors and review evidence suggesting that these mechanisms may produce genuinely altruistic motivational states. Most of the ideas discussed in these chapters are from mainstream evolutionary biology or psychology and have been discussed by others, although I have tried to organize them in original ways.

In the first two parts of the book I focus on the ways in which humans are similar to other animals. In the last three parts I focus more on the ways in which they are different. For example, although humans help their offspring and other relatives engage in simple forms of concrete reciprocity and display emotional reactions that seem similar to those of other primates, they also help people from third-world countries, participate in highly complex systems of cooperation, and communicate their thoughts and feelings symbolically. In Part III of the volume, I offer an account of how the mental mechanisms that give rise to uniquely human forms of prosocial conduct evolved. In Chapter 13, I review evidence that humans engage in expanded and refined forms of prosocial behavior that are unique in the animal kingdom, and in Chapter 14, I review accounts of how the mental mechanisms that dispose people to emit these kinds of behaviors evolved. In Chapter 15, I revise Darwin's account of the role played by uniquely human capacities such as language, perspective-taking, and high-order intelligence in the evolution of expanded and refined forms of prosocial conduct. I argue that it is important to distinguish between the cognitive competence, or capacity, to engage in complex, uniquely human behaviors and the motivation to behave in these ways.

In Part IV, I tackle a tricky issue—how humans acquired a sense of morality. Some aspects of humans' moral sense are shared by other animals; other aspects are unique to the human species. Although we would expect the uniquely human aspects to stem from mental mechanisms unique to humans, we would not expect these mechanisms to have emerged full-blown one sunny morning thousands or millions of years ago. We would expect them to have emerged from modifications in mental mechanisms shared by ancestors common to humans and other primates, and for this reason, we would expect to find precursors of the moral sense in other species.

Research that has mapped the brain regions that are activated by moral problems has demonstrated that people may derive moral judgments from "old brain" structures similar to those possessed by other animals, and from "new brain" structures unique to the human species, and that these structures may interact in a variety of ways. In some conditions old-brain and new-brain processes give rise to the same types of moral judgments; in other conditions they produce internal moral conflicts.

Building on Darwin's ideas, in Chapter 17, I attempt to explain how the primitive moral sense possessed by early humans and other primates evolved into the complex sense of morality possessed by modern humans. I suggest that the mental mechanisms that endow people with the capacity to take the perspective of others, to make moral judgments, and to engage in moral reasoning evolved in ancestral environments as tools in strategic social interactions. Although people use these tools to advance their adaptive interests, the self-serving biases inherent in them are constrained in a variety of ways, including the reactions of others.

The process of strategic social interaction and the adaptive value of resolving conflicts of interest through moral argumentation have implications for the evolution of moral norms. In Chapter 18, I revise Darwin's ideas about how moral norms evolve. Members of groups make rules to formalize their agreements about how they should behave with respect to one another, and they invoke sanctions to induce others to uphold those rules. What goes around comes around, such that the rules that members of groups create to control the behavior of others end up controlling their own behavior. Inasmuch as members of groups are more receptive to some moral prescriptions than they are to others, they serve as agents of selection, determining which ones get repeated and develop into social rules and moral norms. People are particularly receptive to moral judgments and rules that prescribe fitness-increasing forms of cooperation and to judgments that enable them to resolve conflicts of interest in mutually beneficial ways, which is why judgments and rules that uphold fair, balanced, and reversible solutions to social conflicts, such as those prescribed by the norm of reciprocity and the Golden Rule, have evolved in all cultures and constitute universal moral norms.

Several theorists have likened the acquisition of a sense of morality to the acquisition of language (e.g., Hauser, 2006; Richerson & Boyd, 2005). All people inherit the capacity to develop a moral sense that is governed by a "grammar" that induces them to sense that it is right to obey rules, to conform to moral norms, to help members of their groups, to uphold systems of cooperation, and to punish transgressors. However, like cultural variations in the content of language, the rules that enable people to accomplish these tasks may vary significantly across cultures, giving rise to cross-cultural differences in moral norms.

In the last part of the volume, I consider the implications of the evolutionary account of morality that I have fashioned for the classic question, "How moral are people by nature?" which in turn, requires taking a position on the nature of morality. Revisiting a theme introduced in Chapter 2, I argue that understanding what morality is for—the adaptive functions it evolved to serve—helps explain what it is.

In Chapter 19, I suggest that the reason that all people's sense of morality includes ideas about altruism, social contracts, rights and duties, justice, authority, punishment, resisting temptation, reconciliation, purity, and so on is because these issues inevitably arise when people who could maximize their immediate benefits by exploiting others implicitly or explicitly agree to coordinate their efforts to advance their mutual interests and long-term gains. The domain of morality pertains to the formal and informal rules and sanctions that uphold the social orders of groups in ways that increase the ability of their members to survive, to reproduce, and to propagate their genes. Some ideas and emotional reactions pertain to people's obligation to contribute to the welfare of those with whom they have formed cooperative relations (e.g., a sense of duty, responsibility, respect for authority, commitment, loyalty, and sympathy); other ideas and emotional reactions pertain to people's sense of what they deserve by virtue of their contributions; and still others pertain to the social sanctions that uphold cooperative social orders.

With respect to philosophical debates about ideal conceptions of morality, the evolutionary account that I advance in this book implies that the acquisition of a sophisticated sense of morality consists more in the acquisition of the flexibility necessary to solve moral problems in the most efficient, effective, and adaptive ways than in the ability to make highly sophisticated moral judgments in every context. When philosophers advance cardinal moral principles such as "act in a manner that produces the greatest good for the greatest number," or "treat people as ends, not as means," they are, in evolutionary terms, recommending principles that, ultimately, exhort people to interact with others in ways that promote their common welfare.

I close this volume by demonstrating how psychological models of the acquisition of morality can be organized, integrated, reframed and revised within the evolutionary framework I derived. My goal in the final chapter is not to criticize other approaches for their deficiencies, but rather to encourage adherents of other approaches to understand that there is a great deal to be gained by viewing the manifestations of morality to which they attend as products of evolved mental mechanisms.

I do not assume that all readers will read all chapters of this book. Some chapters contain reviews of theory and research that will be familiar to most developmental psychologists, and other chapters review ideas that will be familiar to those versed in evolutionary psychology. Some chapters outline the historical development of ideas; other chapters review more recent developments; and others advance some original ideas.

CONCLUSIONS

In this book, I derive the following take-home messages. To account fully for human morality, we must explain how the mechanisms that engender it evolved in the human species. The precursors of morality were dispositions that helped early humans coordinate their efforts in ways that enabled them to maximize their gains from group living, including those that endowed them with the capacity to delay gratification and to resolve conflicts of interest in adaptive ways. Early humans' capacity to behave in prosocial ways increased when they acquired the capacity for language and sophisticated forms of social intelligence. Strategic social interactions among members of groups and the social cognitive abilities that helped early humans maximize their biological and genetic gains from social exchanges were the primary factors responsible for the refinement and elaboration of the moral senses. The last aspect of a sense of morality to emerge in the human species was the kind of sophisticated deliberative moral reasoning displayed by philosophers of ethics and studied by cognitive-developmental theorists. Although this aspect of the moral sense has the potential to enable modern humans to maximize their long-term benefits from group living and to resolve their conflicts of interest in optimal ways, it plays a relatively minor role in most of the moral decisions that people make in their everyday lives. To fully understand human morality and to define the construct in psychologically meaningful ways, we must attend to the adaptive functions that the mental mechanisms that produce manifestations of morality evolved to serve.

2

WHAT IS MORALITY?

It doesn't seem appropriate to advance an account of the origins of morality without defining the construct, but this is a daunting undertaking. To my knowledge no one has yet succeeded in accomplishing it in a manner that has stood up to critical reviews.

Viewed psychologically, morality is a concept that people harbor in their heads. To understand what it means to them, we need to induce them to explicate it. The most obvious way of accomplishing this is to ask people to describe the phenomena they consider moral, then figure out what they have in common. The behaviors and traits that people consider moral tend to fit in five main categories—respect for authority, self-control, altruism, fairness, and honesty. However, people tend to conceptualize these prosocial forms of conduct in different ways, have different ideas about what makes them moral, and have difficulty explaining what they have in common.

Lawrence Kohlberg and other cognitive-developmental psychologists have employed another method of inducing people to explicate their implicit conceptions, or theories, of morality. They have asked people to decide how characters in imaginary scenarios should resolve hypothetical moral dilemmas and to justify the choices they make. After classifying the moral judgments people made to these dilemmas, Kohlberg and his colleagues concluded that people's conceptions of morality are organized in one of six systems of ideas, or implicit theories, which Kohlberg has called structures of moral reasoning. Cognitive-developmental psychologists have found that people's conceptions of morality improve as people get older, undergoing up to five qualitative changes that define stages of moral development. However, when my colleagues and I evaluated Kohlberg's model of morality, we found that people often invoke different conceptions of morality in their everyday lives from those they invoke in response to the hypothetical moral dilemmas used by Kohlberg and his colleagues.

A third approach to defining morality involves identifying the functions that people use conceptions of morality to achieve. In this approach, conceptions of morality are treated as instruments that people use to solve personal and interpersonal problems. For example, people use moral judgments to induce one another to conform to the moral norms of their cultures—obeying the rules that uphold the social orders of their groups, resisting temptation, being honest and fair, helping others in need, and so on.

Faced with different conceptions of morality, people inevitably ask whether some of these conceptions are better than others. To answer this question we need criteria to evaluate them. Candidates include (1) the cognitive sophistication of conceptions of morality, (2) the order in which people acquire different conceptions, or their place in a developmental sequence, (3) criteria used by philosophers of ethics, such as prescriptiveness, universality, and impartiality, and (4) the ability of conceptions of morality to serve the functions that they were designed to achieve.

The first challenge faced by anyone seeking to unravel the mysteries of morality is to define the phenomenon that he or she is attempting to explain. This is no easy undertaking. Although books have been devoted to defining morality (e.g., Wallace & Walace, 1970), its meaning remains obscure. As the old Harvard philosopher, R. B. Perry, once wrote, "There is something which goes on in the world which it is appropriate to give the name 'morality.' Nothing is more familiar; nothing is more obscure in its meaning" (Frankena, 1973, p. 13). Defined in some ways, it is easy for people to be moral; defined in other ways, morality is an unobtainable ideal.

It is important to recognize that in the first instance morality is a concept or an idea—or more exactly a set of ideas—that people harbor in their heads. As a psychologist I am disposed to take people's ideas about morality seriously. All normal people possess a sense of morality. Defined subjectively, morality is what people think it is, at least to them. This does not mean that everyone's conception of morality is equally adequate. There are standards on which we can evaluate people's conceptions of morality, and on these standards, some conceptions fare better than others.

THE MORAL DOMAIN

If morality is a set of ideas in people's heads, and if some people's ideas are better than other people's ideas, then it might make sense to ask those who should have the most sophisticated conceptions of morality to define the construct—experts who have considered the matter most extensively. Here is a sample of definitions derived by such experts: (1) "a normative system in which evaluative judgments . . . are made . . . from the point of view of a consideration of the effects of actions, motives, traits, etc. on the lives of persons or sentient beings as such, including the lives of others besides the person acting, being judged, or judging" (Frankena, 1980, p. 26); (2) prescriptive judgments "about welfare, justice, and rights . . . that involve concerns with dignity, worth, freedom, and treatment of persons" (Turiel, 2006, p. 10); (3) "evaluations (good vs. bad) of the actions or character of a person that are made with respect to a set of virtues held to be obligatory by a culture or subculture" (Haidt, 2001, p. 817); (4) "interlocking sets of values, practices, institutions, and evolved psychological mechanisms that work together to suppress or regulate selfishness and make social life possible" (Haidt, 2007); and (5) norms that "(1) regulate human claims and conflicts, (2) define basic human rights, (3) are culturally universal, (4) are subject to sanctions, and (5) are nonreducible" (Colby & Kohlberg, 1987, p. 49).

These definitions of morality describe the moral domain, as distinct from, for example, the legal domain and the domain of social conventions. The moral domain consists of values, norms, rules, and evaluative judgments pertaining to forms of conduct that people consider right and wrong and character traits that people consider good and bad. To flesh out these general definitions of morality—to sketch in the contents of the moral domain— we need to specify what forms of conduct and what character traits people consider moral.

FORMS OF CONDUCT THAT PEOPLE CONSIDER MORAL

Darwin (1874) took the task of defining morality more seriously than many contemporary theorists who have attempted to account for the evolution of morality have taken it. As a general characterization, he suggested that the moral sense "is summed up in that short by imperious word ought" (p. 94), and that the Golden Rule "lies at the foundation of morality" (p. 122). In addition, Darwin defined morality in terms of an ultimate "greatest good" utilitarian principle. However, if you were to peruse Darwin's writings and flag the phenomena he characterized as moral, you would find that he was most prone to conceptualize morality in terms of forms of conduct and virtues that contribute to the welfare of groups.

Darwin (1874, pp. 114–115) classified the following forms of conduct as moral: (1) **obedience** ("As soon as a tribe has a recognized leader, disobedience becomes a crime, and even abject submission is looked at as a sacred virtue"); (2) **self-command** ("No man can practice the virtues necessary for the welfare of his tribe without self-sacrifice, self-command, and the power of endurance"); (3) **altruism,** including traits such as kindness, sympathy, love, and fidelity ("risking one's life for that of a fellow-creature," "sacrificing one's life in some great cause," "faithfulness to one's comrades"); and (4) **courage** ("as . . . no man can be useful or faithful to his tribe without courage, this quality has universally been placed in the highest rank"). In addition to these group-supporting forms of conduct, Darwin included "self-regarding" virtues such as **prudence, temperance**, and **chastity** in his list of moral traits. Darwin's list of immoral behaviors included selfishness, intemperance, licentiousness, unnatural crimes, indecency, betrayal, murder, robbery, treachery, scalping, infanticide, suicide, and slavery.

Darwin's conception of morality—at least his classification of group-supporting forms of conduct—should ring true to most people. Over the years I have asked hundreds of students to explicate their conceptions of morality by identifying the phenomena that they consider moral and immoral and by explaining what it is about these phenomena that renders them such. As shown in Table 2.1, most students respond to this request by describing prosocial forms of conduct similar to those mentioned by Darwin. Although some students also include "self-regarding" forms of conduct such as chastity and temperance on their lists, these virtues tend to be less salient to students than group-supporting virtues are.

It is worth noting that the moral acts and traits that Darwin alluded to most frequently and that appear most frequently on students' lists—by far—are altruistic in nature. Many laypeople and scholars more or less equate altruism and morality. As expressed by the evolutionary biologist Richard Alexander (1987), "the concept of morality implies altruism or self-sacrifice" (pp. 179–180). However, as revealed in the list of behaviors in Table 2.1, there is more to morality than altruism.

Table 2.1 Forms of Moral Conduct

Deference, obedience, and respect for legitimate authority vs. disobedience
(obeying rules and laws vs. deviance)
Self-control vs. self-indulgence
(resisting temptation, delaying gratification vs. Seven Deadly Sins)
Altruism vs. maliciousness
(caring for, helping, loving others; upholding relationships and groups vs. hurting
and exploiting others)
Fairness vs. unfairness
(justice, sharing, reciprocating, doing one's share, equality, equity, Golden Rule vs. injustice,
selfishness, nepotism)
Honesty vs. dishonesty
(telling the truth, keeping promises vs. lying, stealing, cheating)

Some people also consider certain sexual practices, such as bestiality, homosexuality, and masturbation immoral. Interestingly, people often attach the label "dirty" to such acts, and find them disgusting. Some judgments about sexual conduct can be subsumed in the categories in Table 2.1 (for example, fidelity can be considered a form of fairness and honesty); however, other judgments cannot, even though they constitute an important aspect of some people's conceptions of morality. Researchers have found that ideas about purity (sometimes associated with divinity; sometimes not) are considered moral by many people (Shweder, Much, Mahapatra, & Park, 1997). I will offer an explanation for these findings in Chapter 16.

Finally, many people embed their conceptions of morality in religious and spiritual beliefs (Walker, Pitts, Hennig, & Matsuba, 1995). I believe that such beliefs constitute culturally provided or individually constructed frameworks for, and sources of, the sense that forms of conduct such as those in Table 2.1 are moral. If you believe that there is a God who prescribed acceptable and unacceptable forms of conduct, and that these prescriptions are explicated in books such as the Bible or Koran, then you can derive all of your moral prescriptions from deferential dispositions to obey the will of God. If you accept Jesus as an authority on morality, then you will believe that it is right to love your neighbor as yourself. If you believe that God communicated moral prescriptions and prohibitions to humans, you will possess a complete explanation of the source of morality. If, on the other hand, you view Jesus as a man who espoused an influential set of ideas, and if you believe that God is an idea created by humans, you need to explain why humans would find Jesus's ideas attractive and attribute particular prescriptions and prohibitions to God. If people from different cultures believe in different deities, yet attribute a set of identical prescriptions to them, it would suggest that these prescriptions stem from the minds of humans and are projected onto their conceptions of God.[1]

---

[1] See Atran (2004) and Boyer (2001) for analyses of the psychology of religion.

Formal Classifications of Moral Forms of Conduct

The classifications of moral and immoral forms of conduct produced by Darwin and by my students correspond quite closely to those advanced by other scholars and religious authorities. For example, one of the Ten Commandments prescribes obedience to, and respect for, authority. Others prohibit hurting others (murder), taking more than one's share (greed), cheating (adultery), and dishonesty (stealing, lying). The Seven Deadly Sins (pride, avarice, lust, envy, gluttony, wrath, and, sloth,) involve selfishness and a lack of self-control. The five virtues identified by Confucius include charity, love, honesty, uprightness (justice), and conscientiousness. In addition, Confucius preached obedience to, and respect for, authority. Hartshorne and May (1928) divided forms of moral conduct into three categories: honesty, service (altruism), and self-control. Haidt and Joseph (2004) extracted five foundations of "intuitive ethics" from the relevant literature—help/care (altruism), in-group loyalty (altruism), fairness/reciprocity (justice), authority/respect (deference), and purity/sanctity.

VIRTUES AND VICES

The categories of conduct that people consider moral and immoral are closely associated with their conceptions of virtues and vices, but when people conceptualize morality in terms of virtues and vices, the objects of their attributions tend to be people rather than forms of conduct. When we say that people are altruistic or fair or honest, we not only imply that they behave in altruistic, honest, and fair ways; we also imply that they possess internal qualities and character traits that dispose them to behave in these ways. A person may behave in helpful and fair ways without *being* an altruistic and fair person, because, for example, the person was forced to behave in these ways, or because he or she was trying to create a false impression. We tend to consider forms of conduct right and wrong, and virtuous and vicious people good and bad.

CULTURAL UNIVERSALS IN CONCEPTIONS OF MORALITY

The conceptions of morality that I have discussed to this point have been explicated by people in the Western world. Are they shared by people from other cultures? Are there species-specific commonalities in the content of people's conceptions of morality? Darwin (1874) took a position on this issue, suggesting that all people acquire moral beliefs that uphold natural, species-specific inclinations to behave in prosocial ways, but in addition, people from different cultures acquire culturally relative beliefs through social learning.

Contemporary researchers have found cultural universals in conceptions of morality. The anthropologist Brown (1991) found that people from all cultures distinguish right from wrong and that all people possess a sense of rights and obligations attached to persons and other statuses. In addition, he found that all cultures contain prohibitions against violence, rape, murder, and other acts that undermine the welfare of groups. Another anthropologist, Boehm (2008), reviewed hunter-gatherers' moral codes and found that all of them prohibited murder, incest, adultery, bullying, lying, cheating, stealing, and excessive selfishness. In addition, these moral codes promoted generosity, cooperation, and group harmony. Sober and Wilson (1998) found that all 25 cultures that they surveyed possessed norms upholding personal autonomy, mutual aid, cooperation, and group welfare, as well as norms prohibiting cheating and free-riding. Other surveys have revealed that people from all cultures consider three types of acts immoral: acts that inflict unnecessary harm on people, acts that violate people's rights, and acts that produce unjust outcomes (Miller, 2006, p. 383).

I believe that it is safe to conclude that all people possess conceptions of morality that include the idea that certain forms of conduct are right and wrong and that certain character traits are good and bad. All people everywhere, including people from non-Western cultures, consider the five forms of conduct and associated character traits and virtues described in Table 2.1 moral, and their opposites immoral (Cashdan, 1983; Gardner, 1991). It follows that to account for the origin of morality, we must account for the origin of these forms of conduct and character traits, which I attempt in ensuing chapters of this book.

There is a great deal of merit in defining morality in terms of the forms of conduct and, as Kohlberg (1984) has called them, "bags of virtues," that come most readily to people's minds when they think about morality. These ideas seem to constitute natural categories or basic intuitions about morality. However, it does not take much thought to realize that there is quite a bit more to people's conceptions of morality than the idea that certain forms of conduct are right and other forms of conduct are wrong. These ideas are like the tips of the icebergs that constitute people's conceptions of morality. There is a great deal more below the surface, and in order to understand what that is, we need to delve into the depths of people's minds and induce them to reveal their contents. As it turns out, the deeper we probe, the more complex the conceptions of morality we unearth.

DELVING MORE DEEPLY INTO PEOPLE'S CONCEPTIONS OF MORALITY

Although it might seem that people who consider such prosocial forms of conduct as altruism and fairness to be moral possess the same conception of morality, this is rarely if ever the case because different people define and instantiate these forms of conduct in different ways. When I ask students who agree on the moral status of particular forms of conduct or virtues why they consider them moral, or what makes them moral, they often give different answers. For example, some students say that virtues such as honesty and altruism are inherently moral in and of themselves—end of story. Other students say that certain acts and traits are moral because it says so in the Bible. And still other students say that prosocial behaviors and virtues are moral because they improve people's welfare and make the world a better place. At a cultural level of analysis, although all members of all cultures consider prosocial forms of conduct and prosocial character traits moral, members of different cultures may interpret, instantiate, and organize their ideas about these traits differently; and they may justify them in different ways.

Another problem with defining morality in terms of forms of conduct and virtues is that this practice does not, in itself, enable people to decide which form of conduct or which virtue to uphold when they must violate one to uphold another. Studies have found that people from different cultures prioritize different forms of moral conduct and virtues in different ways. For example, people in some cultures give preference to care-oriented virtues; whereas people from other cultures give precedence to individual rights, duties, and justice. In one study, Miller and Bersoff (1992) found that whereas most Americans said that it was wrong to steal a train ticket when it supplied the only means of attending a friend's wedding, most Indians believed that their moral obligation to attend the wedding trumped their moral obligation to refrain from stealing.

To flesh out people's conceptions of morality, we need to determine what it is about certain forms of conduct or virtues that make them seem moral, and if they differ in their moral status, what renders one type more moral than another type. Put another way, we need to determine what the forms of conduct and character traits that people consider moral have in common that entitles these forms of conduct and character traits to this status and whether some of them fill the bill better than others do. We need a standard or criterion for morality, which kind of brings us back to square one.

A COGNITIVE-DEVELOPMENTAL ANALYSIS OF CONCEPTIONS OF MORALITY

After asking students to tell me what kinds of behaviors and traits they consider moral and immoral, I ask them to explain what it is about the forms of conduct and virtues that makes them moral. This inevitably induces them to express more complex conceptions of morality. Cognitive-developmental psychologists have used a different method to induce people to explicate their implicit conceptions of morality. Let us consider this method and the conclusions it has produced.

Cognitive-developmental psychologists probe people's conceptions of morality by giving them hypothetical moral dilemmas, asking them what the protagonists in the dilemmas should do, and inducing them to justify their moral, or "deontic," choices by explaining why these choices are more moral than the choices they rejected. For example, in one of the dilemmas used by cognitive-developmental psychologists, individuals are asked to decide whether a character named Heinz should steal a drug to save his dying wife and why.

Psychologists who use this method do not care much about the specific choices that people made in response to hypothetical moral dilemmas because they do not believe that these choices reveal anything significant about their conceptions of morality. According to cognitive-developmental theorists, people's conceptions of morality are rooted in the reasons underlying their moral choices and the general principles from which they derive their moral judgments—principles that contain the kinds of standards derived by philosophers of ethics. Learning that people think that it is right to keep promises and to help others in need, and that it is wrong to lie, cheat and steal, tells you little about their conceptions of morality. To understand what morality means to people, you have to find out why they consider these forms of conduct moral and immoral.

Criticizing the "bag of virtues" approach, cognitive-developmental psychologists point out that people may believe that "vices" such as stealing and lying are moral in some contexts. In addition, they point out that people may make exactly the same choice—for example, that Heinz should steal the drug—for quite different reasons. One person could believe that Heinz should steal the drug because his wife would get mad at him if he did not steal it for her, and another person could believe that Heinz should steal the drug because he would want his wife to steal the drug for him if he were in her place. Finally, these theorists point out that people may give the same kinds of reasons to support different choices. For example, a person could derive and support the choice that Heinz should steal the drug and the choice that Heinz should not steal the drug by invoking the Golden Rule.

Structures of Moral Reasoning and Implicit Theories of Ethics

Imagine that you offered reasons and justifications for a set of choices that you considered moral. How much would they have in common? Would they reflect a bunch of ideas that existed relatively independently in your mind; would they stem from several clusters of related ideas; or would they stem from an overriding way of interpreting moral issues and resolving moral dilemmas? How are people's ideas about morality organized in their minds? At one extreme, people might possess different ideas and attitudes about different moral issues. For example, they might have one set of ideas about why abortion is right or wrong, a second set about why people should keep promises, and a third set about why people should help people in need. At the other extreme, people might possess an implicit theory of ethics that is organized in terms of overriding principles and standards, from which they derive particular moral judgments.

Some cognitive-developmental psychologists—Colby and Kohlberg (1987) prominent among them—have come down strongly on the side of the second option. These psychologists have argued that people from all cultures develop essentially the same structures of moral reasoning, which give rise to general conceptions, or implicit theories, of morality that determine how people interpret virtually all moral issues and how they derive virtually all prescriptive moral decisions. (Although these theorists do not view people's conceptions of morality as implicit theories of ethics, I believe that this is an appropriate way of characterizing them.) Kohlberg and his colleagues believe that these implicit theories produce and define people's conceptions of morality. According to them, ideas such as people should behave honestly, fairly, and altruistically are conclusions derived deductively from the general standards and principles that define their conceptions of morality (Kohlberg, 1984).

Developmental Changes in People's Implicit Theories of Morality

Anyone who seeks to derive a general definition of morality by deciphering people's subjective conceptions of the phenomenon faces two big problems. First, as discussed, different people possess different conceptions of morality. Second, people's conceptions of morality change as they develop. Cognitive-developmental psychologists have invested a great deal of effort in mapping developmental changes in the structures of moral reasoning that they assume produce people's conceptions of morality. Kohlberg and his colleagues have provided evidence that people's implicit theories of morality may undergo up to five major transformations during their life span that, these theorists argue, define the stages of moral development outlined in Table 2.2.

Table 2.2 Six Stages of Moral Judgment

Level and Stage	What is Right	Reasons for Doing Right	Sociomoral Perspective of Stage
		Content of Stage	
Level 1: Preconventional. Stage 1: Heteronomous morality	To avoid breaking rules backed by punishment, obedience for its own sake, and avoiding physical damage to persons and property.	Avoidance of punishment and the superior power of authorities.	Egocentric point of view. Doesn't consider the interests of others or recognize that they differ from the actor's; doesn't relate two points of view. Actions are considered physically rather than in terms of psychological interests of others. Confusion of authority's perspective with one's own.
Stage 2: Individualism, instrumental purpose, and exchange	Following rules only when it is to someone's immediate interest; acting to meet one's own interests and needs and letting others do the same. Right is also what is fair, what is an equal exchange, a deal, an agreement.	To serve one's own needs or interests in a world where you have to recognize that other people have their interests, too.	Concrete individualistic perspective. Aware that everybody has his own interests to pursue and these conflict, so that right is relative (in the concrete individualistic sense).
Level 2: Conventional. Stage 3: Mutual interpersonal expectations, relationships, and interpersonal conformity	Living up to what is expected by people close to you or what people generally expect of people in your role as son, brother, friend, etc. "Being good" is important and means having good motives, showing concern about others. It also means keeping mutual relationships, such as trust, loyalty, respect, and gratitude.	The need to be a good person in your own eyes and those of others. Your caring for others. Belief in the Golden Rule. Desire to maintain rules and authority that support stereotypical good behavior.	Perspective of the individual in relationships with other individuals. Aware of shared feelings, agreements, and expectations that take primacy over individual interests. Relates points of view through the concrete Golden Rule, putting yourself in the other person's shoes. Does not yet consider generalized system perspective.

Stage	What is right	Reasons for doing right	Social perspective of stage
Stage 4: Social systems and conscience	Fulfilling the actual duties to which you have agreed. Laws are to be upheld except in extreme cases where they conflict with other social duties. Right is also contributing to society, the group, or institution.	To keep the institution going as a whole, to avoid the breakdown in the system "if everyone did it," or the imperative of conscience to meet one's defined obligations.	Differentiates societal point of view from interpersonal agreement or motives. Takes the point of view of the system that defines roles and rules. Considers individual relations in terms of place in the system.
Level 3: Postconventional or principled. Stage 5: Social contract or utility and individual rights	Being aware that people hold a variety of values and opinions, that most values and rules are relative to your group. These relative rules should usually be upheld, however, in the interest of impartiality and because they are the social contract. Some nonrelative values and rights like life and liberty, however, must be upheld in any society and regardless of majority opinion.	A sense of obligation to law because of one's social contract to make and abide by laws for the welfare of all and for the protection of all people's rights. A feeling of contractual commitment, freely entered upon, to family, friendship, trust and work obligations. Concern that laws and duties be based on rational calculation of overall utility, "the greatest good for the greatest number."	Prior-to-society perspective. Perspective of a rational individual aware of values and rights prior to social attachments and contracts. Integrates perspectives by formal mechanisms of agreement, contract, objective partiality, and due process. Considers moral and legal points of view; recognizes that they sometimes conflict and finds it difficult to integrate them.
Stage 6: Universal ethical principles	Following self-chosen ethical principles. Particular laws or social agreements are usually valid because they rest on such principles. When laws violate these principles, one acts in accordance with the principle. Principles are universal principles of justice: the equality of human rights and respect for the dignity of human beings as individual persons.	The belief as a rational person in the validity of universal moral principles and a sense of personal commitment to them.	Perspective of a moral point of view from which social arrangements derive. Perspective is that of any rational individual recognizing the nature of morality or the fact that persons are ends in themselves and must be treated as such.

Source: Reprinted from Kohlberg (1976).

According to cognitive-developmental psychologists, developing conceptions of morality is more akin to developing concepts such as the logical relations among numbers than to memorizing facts. When people are young, they possess primitive conceptions, or theories, of math and morality, which are organized in terms of simple operating principles. However, as children develop, they acquire a deeper and more extensive understanding of the principles underlying these, and other, phenomena. They acquire mental abilities that they did not have before, which enable them to refine, extend, and reorganize their conceptions of morality. The new implicit theories that they develop (which define new stages of moral development) replace their older theories.

Note that each of the conceptions of morality that define the stages of moral development outlined by Kohlberg and his colleagues is defined mainly by an overriding standard or ethical principle. Morally immature people tend to assume it is right to obey authority and rules backed by punishment. More morally mature people tend to assume that it is right to meet the expectations of their groups and to uphold mutual relationships. People who have reached high stages of moral development tend to conceptualize morality in terms of the kinds of principles and standards derived by philosophers of ethics, such as upholding social orders that promote the greatest good for the greatest number.

To summarize, cognitive-developmental psychologists object to defining morality in terms of "bags of virtues," or ideas such as "you should help people in need," "you should respect authority," and "you should keep your promises." Rather, they believe that people derive moral judgments deductively from the overriding principles and standards in their implicit theories of ethics. When people derive moral judgments in this manner, they usually conclude that it is right to help others, to obey rules, to keep promises, and so on, but they sometimes conclude that it is more moral not to behave in these ways.

Limitations of Defining Morality in Terms of Justifications of Choices

Cognitive-developmental psychologists have proven beyond a doubt that as people grow older, they normally acquire the capacity to form increasingly sophisticated conceptions of morality. To account fully for the evolution of morality, we must account for the evolution of this capacity, which I will attempt in Chapter 17. However, as I will show, the structures of moral reasoning explicated by cognitive-developmental psychologists are one among many sources of moral judgment, and people usually make moral judgments in significantly less rational ways.

TOWARD A FUNCTIONAL APPROACH
TO DEFINING MORALITY

Before closing this discussion of the nature of morality, I would like to introduce an idea that I develop more fully later, namely that to understand what morality is, we must discover the purposes it originated to achieve. Consider an analogy. If someone asked you to define an automobile, you might describe what cars look like. They have a metal body, a hood, a windshield, several wheels, and so on. Alternatively, you might define an automobile by identifying the purposes it was designed to achieve, or its functions, such as transporting people from one place to another. In a similar vein, you might define a saw as a tool that was designed to cut materials; a hammer as a tool that was designed to pound and pull nails, and so on. (Note how tools that were designed for one purpose, such as pounding nails, can be used for other purposes, such as hitting people on the head, just as evolved mechanisms can be "exapted" to achieve goals that they were not originally designed to perform.)

The challenge for those who seek to define morality in terms of its functions is to identify the goals that people use morality to achieve. In the previous chapter, I suggested that the overriding function of morality is to induce individuals to behave in ways that uphold social orders that foster the adaptive interests of members of groups in cooperative ways. All conceptions of morality that we have considered so far in this chapter are consistent with this function. To uphold cooperative social orders, people must (1) respect legitimate authority and obey rules and norms that define their rights and duties, (2) resist the temptation to maximize their gains, or to freeload, at the expense of others, (3) uphold their groups, which entails helping other members, (4) coordinate their behavior with that of other members of their groups, (5) ensure that those who participate in cooperative exchanges give and take their fair share, and that cheaters and free-riders do not prosper, and (6) honor their social contracts by reciprocating, keeping their word, and so on.

The idea that the essence of morality lies in a set of dispositions and ideas designed to induce members of groups to uphold rules and norms that enable them to foster their adaptive interests in cooperative ways is consistent with the conclusions reached by theorists of other persuasions. As discussed by Rest (1983) in a review of the literature on moral development, Piaget, depicted morality as "the equilibrium of individuals in society, as individuals reciprocating with other individuals according to rules that balance the benefits and burdens of cooperation" (p. 580). According to Rest (1983), Kohlberg's hierarchy of moral development is based on a "progressive understanding of the various possibilities of cooperative relationships" (p. 558). Rest goes on to say that the philosopher

> Frankena (1970) and others regard morality . . . as standards or guidelines that govern human cooperation—in particular how rights, duties, and benefits are to be allocated. Given that people live together and that their activities affect each other, morality provides guidelines and rationales for how each person's activities should affect the others' welfare. The guidelines are not fashioned to serve any one person's interests, but are constructed with consideration for each individual's intrinsic value . . . morality, at least in principle, deals with sharable values because moralities are proposals for a system of mutual coordination of activities and cooperation among people. (p. 558)

EVALUATING CONCEPTIONS OF MORALITY

The goal of this chapter has been to define morality subjectively, by identifying the phenomena that people consider moral and explaining why they so consider. As mentioned, one of the problems with defining morality in this manner is that morality means different things to different people. People possess different conceptions of morality. Faced with such differences, an important question inevitably arises, namely are some conceptions of morality better than others? If I, or members of my culture, believe that people are morally obliged to behave in one way, but you, or people in your culture, believe people are morally obliged to behave in another way; or if I believe that altruism is the cardinal virtue and you believe that fairness trumps altruism, how can we determine whose conception is better or right?

When I ask my students questions such as these, some argue that the questions are not meaningful, because all people's conceptions of morality are equally valid. However, when this view is subjected to scrutiny, students quickly identify problems with this doctrine of moral relativism. Few people believe that an infant's conception of morality is as valid as an adult's conception, and no normal person thinks that the idea that it is right to blow up the world and exterminate all species is as valid, morally, as the idea that it is right to foster the greatest good for the greatest number.

To evaluate conceptions of morality, we need an appropriate method. One option is to assume that people's conceptions of morality become increasingly adequate as they develop, as cognitive-developmental theorists have claimed, and to treat later-developing conceptions as superior to earlier-developing conceptions. One problem with this approach is that people's conceptions of morality do not necessarily get better as they develop. For example, there is evidence that people who have developed sophisticated conceptions of morality may regress to less mature ways of thinking (Armon, 1995). Another problem is that people who have developed highly sophisticated conceptions of morality rarely reach the same conclusion.

A second approach to evaluating conceptions of morality is to use the same kind of criteria we use to evaluate conceptions of other phenomena—criteria such as how precise and encompassing the conceptions are, how accurately they represent reality, the extent to which they are organized in a coherent system, connected logically, differentiated from irrelevant considerations, and integrated with relevant considerations. The problem with this option is that cognitive superiority does not necessarily equate to moral superiority. A person could possess a highly organized, logical theory of morality based on invalid assumptions, such as, "Everyone has a right to do as he or she pleases."

A third approach to evaluating conceptions of morality, or at least the prescriptive standards in such conceptions, is to invoke the kinds of criteria used by philosophers of ethics to evaluate normative principles of morality—criteria such as prescriptiveness, universality, reversibility, and impartiality. Based on these criteria, a conception of morality that is based on a principle such as, "I deserve more than anyone else" would fare more poorly than a principle such as, "All people everywhere [should view] as equally important the interests of all people everywhere" (Alexander, 1985, p. 18).

Virtually all philosophers agree that the prescriptions in the conceptions of morality that define Kohlberg's highest two stages of moral development (see Table 2.2) fare better on such criteria than the prescriptions in the conceptions that define his four lower stages, which may have pleased Darwin, who espoused a "Stage 5" utilitarian conception of morality. However, philosophers have disagreed about whether the (deontological) principles that define Kohlberg's highest stage (Stage 6) are more adequate than the (utilitarian) principles that define the second highest stage (Stage 5). In his early writings, Kohlberg argued for the superiority of Stage 6 deontological principles of justice over Stage 5 utilitarian principles. However, in his later writings, Kohlberg and his colleagues adopted a more flexible position, allowing that any procedure that gives "equal consideration to the claims and points of view of everyone affected by a moral decision" may produce a truly moral decision (Colby & Kohlberg, 1987, p. 30). One example of such a procedure is Rawls's "veil of ignorance," in which "the chooser does not know which person in a situation or society one is to be and must choose a principle or policy with which one could best live in any position, including the position of the persons who would be most disadvantaged in the society" (Rawls, 1999, p. 31). A second example is "moral musical chairs"—a second-order application of the Golden Rule. A third example is Habermas's (1984) "dialogue among free and equal persons considering and modifying their claims in light of one another" (p. 31). A noteworthy implication of these ideas is that the adequacy of moral judgments is determined by the *procedures* people use to derive them.

There are, however, two problems with this approach. First, people may not be capable of meeting the requirements of a truly moral procedure. For example, it may not be possible for people to suppress from consciousness, or discount, information necessary to adopt a veil of ignorance. Second, a host of factors may induce different people using the same procedure to reach different conclusions. For example, free and equal people engaging in moral dialogues who have had different experiences may advance quite different arguments about the same issue.

A final criterion we could invoke to evaluate conceptions of morality is the extent to which they fulfill the functions that morality originated to serve. The better a conception of morality fulfills the purposes that morality was designed to serve, the more adequate it is. For example, if as two of the experts quoted at the beginning of this chapter imply, the function of morality is to suppress selfishness and to resolve conflicts of interest, then these outcomes could be used as criteria to evaluate the moral status of forms of conduct and virtues such as honesty, fairness, and altruism. In addition, we could use functional criteria to evaluate prescriptive principles of morality. For example, if morality evolved to uphold cooperative social orders, then we could evaluate ultimate moral principles such as the Golden Rule, the utilitarian prescription to behave in ways that maximize happiness, and Kant's categorical imperatives in terms of their potential to achieve this end. I will revisit this issue in Chapter 19.

CONCLUSIONS

My answer to the question, "What is morality?" is "a set of ideas about how people who live in groups should behave in order to meet their needs and advance their interests in cooperative ways." Conceptions of morality consist of ideas about what people have the right to expect from those with whom they interact, and what they have a duty to give in return. Conceptions of morality prescribe that people should obey the rules that uphold their groups, respect legitimate authority, resist the temptation to satisfy their needs at the expense of others, help others, do their share, take their share, reciprocate, and behave in mutually beneficial ways. The function of conceptions of morality is to induce individuals to uphold the social orders of their groups by constraining their selfish urges and biases, upholding relationships, promoting group harmony, resolving conflicts of interest in effective ways, dealing effectively with those who violate the rules, and fostering their interests in ways that, if everyone adopted them, would produce a better life for all.

3

BAD BY NATURE?

The idea that all animals, including humans, are born bad has a long and turbulent history in philosophy and the social sciences. Many scholars have argued that the dispositions that humans inherit are inherently selfish and immoral but that children may be trained to become good, or at least better, by parents and other socializing agents. It is widely assumed that the theory of evolution supports this "born bad" position, because the laws of natural selection, which favor the "survival of the fittest," seem to dictate that all animals must be selfish by nature. Although some very eminent evolutionary theorists appear to have endorsed this idea, I argue that it is misguided.

When evolutionary theorists conclude that all evolved traits are selfish, they define selfishness in a quite different way from how people define it when they make judgments about human nature. Although it may be appropriate to consider genes that prevail in competitions with other genes genetically selfish, this does not mean that the mental mechanisms that these genes design will dispose the animals that acquire them to advance their psychological interests without regard for others. The question that those who seek to understand human nature should ask is whether early humans who behaved in the ways that we consider selfish and immoral were more likely to survive, to reproduce, and to propagate their genes than early humans who behaved in ways that we consider unselfish and moral. There is good reason to expect extremely selfish people to fare poorly in most social contexts compared to people who are more cooperatively and altruistically inclined. What you see in human behavior is what you get in human nature; people are evolved to be good and to be bad, depending on the circumstances.[1]

[1] This chapter draws substantially from my chapter in H. Høgh-Olesen (Ed.) (2010) *Human morality and sociality*, pp. 13–30. Houndmills, UK: Palgrave Macmillan. Used with permission of Palgrave Macmillan.

The idea that humans are born bad has been advanced by scholars guided by a wide array of theories. For example, Anna Freud (1963) asserted that "we know that the child acts throughout the period of development [from birth to age 5] as if there was nothing more important than the gratifying of his own pleasures and fulfilling of his powerful instincts, whereas education proceeds as if the prevention of these objects was its most important task" (p. 101). In a similar vein, the colonial preacher, Jonathan Edwards, opined that children are born as "young vipers and infinitely more hateful than vipers" (Elkind & Weiner, 1978, p. 10). And Christian doctrines assert that, following Adam and Eve's fall from grace, humans became cursed with original sin, which Calvin defined as "a hereditary corruption and depravity of our nature, extending to all parts of the soul" (Calvin, 1559/1995, I: 217).

Although evolutionary biologists do not have much in common with psychoanalysts, colonial preachers, and religious scholars, many evolutionary theorists, beginning with Darwin, appear to agree that humans are bad by nature. For example, when Darwin (1874) considered the implications of his theory of evolution for the evolution of morality, he concluded that "it is extremely doubtful whether the offspring of the most sympathetic and benevolent parents, or of those which were the most faithful to their comrades, would be reared in greater number than the children of selfish and treacherous parents of the same tribe. He who was ready to sacrifice his life, as many a savage has been, rather than betray his comrades, would often leave no offspring to inherit his noble nature" (p. 127). A couple of decades later, when Darwin's cousin, Thomas Huxley (1893), considered the relation between evolution and ethics, he concluded that "the practice of that which is ethically best—what we call goodness or virtue—involves a course of conduct which, in all respects, is opposed to that which leads to success in the cosmic struggle for existence. Ethical nature may count upon having to reckon with a tenacious and powerful enemy as long as the world lasts" (p. 83).

New insights about the process of evolution do not seem to have moderated these conclusions. When the eminent contemporary evolutionary biologist, George Williams, reexamined Huxley's conclusions, he seemed to reach an even bleaker conclusion than Huxley reached. Williams (1989) concluded that, "there is no encouragement for any belief that an organism can be designed for any purpose other than the most effective pursuit of . . . self-interest. . . . Nothing resembling the Golden Rule or other widely preached ethical principles seems to be operating in living nature. It could scarcely be otherwise, when evolution is guided by a force that maximizes genetic selfishness" (pp. 195–196). And Richard Dawkins (1989), the author of one of the most influential books of our times, *The Selfish Gene*, concluded that:

> "nature red in tooth and claw" sums up our modern understanding of natural selection admirably. . . . If you look at the way natural selection works, it seems to follow that anything that has evolved by natural selection should be selfish. . . . Much as we might wish to believe otherwise, universal love and welfare of the species as a whole are concepts that simply do not make evolutionary sense. . . . Be warned that if you wish, as I do, to build a society in which individuals cooperate generously and unselfishly toward a common good, you can expect little help from biological nature. (pp. 3–4)

There are no scholars whom I admire more than Charles Darwin, George Williams, and Richard Dawkins. However, I am quite sure that the pessimistic conclusions about human nature implied in the passages I have extracted from their writings (in part, out of context) are wrong, or at least misleading. Let us examine carefully the basis for these conclusions.

THE CASE AGAINST THE EVOLUTION OF MORALITY

The conclusion that moral dispositions cannot evolve is an inference based on two premises: First, all evolved dispositions are selfish, and second, to qualify as moral, a disposition must be unselfish. Evolutionary theorists define selfishness in terms of behaviors that increase the fitness of actors at the expense of the fitness of recipients. Selfish behaviors "confer a fitness benefit on the actor, while placing a fitness cost on the recipient," and "altruism refers to interactions where the actor incurs a fitness cost while benefiting the recipient" (Kurland & Gaulin, 2005, p. 448). By fitness, modern evolutionary theorists mean the number of genes that individuals contribute to the next generation, usually by producing surviving offspring. It follows that "by definition altruists have lower fitness than the selfish individuals with whom they interact. It therefore seems inevitable that natural selection should eliminate altruistic behaviour, just as it eliminates other traits that diminish an individual's fitness" (Sober & Wilson, 1998, p. 189). With respect to the second premise, evolutionary theorists assume—usually implicitly—that selfishness violates the criteria for morality. The kinds of behaviors that people consider immoral seem selfish, and the kinds of behaviors that people consider moral seem unselfish.

"The Triumph of Selfishness"

To support the conclusion that animals are born bad, George Williams (1989) offered "obvious examples of the pursuit of self-interest as practiced in the biological cosmos," noting that, "I will need no theoretical subtleties to show their gross selfishness and moral unacceptability" (p. 197). Williams reviews evidence that, "murder" and infanticide are common in the animal kingdom. "Death from strife among neighbors tends to be recorded for any wild animal population carefully observed for a thousand hours or more" (p. 204). Although the males of most vertebrate species tend to be more blatantly aggressive than the females are, Williams argues that there is plenty of evidence of female aggression: "Females commonly deprive each other of resources in various ways, aggressively interfere with one another's reproduction, attack one another's young, and actively aggravate male competition when it serves their interests" (p. 205).

In addition to this evidence, Williams offered examples of offspring exploiting their parents and mates exploiting one another. "Recent accounts of reproductive behavior in wild animals are tales of sexual intrigue full of deception, desertion, double-dealing, and sometimes lethal violence" (p. 201). "Besides adultery and rape, just about every other kind of sexual behavior that has been regarded as sinful or unethical can be found abundantly in nature" (p. 202). Williams closes his case in support of the "triumph of selfishness" by noting that "none of the [examples of immorality] are really needed for the argument being advanced; the inescapable arithmetic of predation and parasitism should be enough to show that nature is morally unacceptable. . . . The survival of one organism is possible only at great cost to others. The moral message in this obvious fact has been recognized by many philosophers and humanists, despite the general prevalence of romanticism" (p. 229).

Although humans are different from other animals in many ways, humans also engage in beastly behaviors. Members of families compete for resources, sometimes to the point of killing one another. As documented by Daly and Wilson (1983), stepchildren are especially susceptible to abuse. People commit adultery; men rape women, and women cuckold men. Jails are bursting with people who assault others, steal their possessions, and cheat them out of their money. Infanticide is common in some cultures. Although cannibalism is rare in the human species, people kill one another at a relatively high rate, especially during wars and bouts of "ethnic cleansing."

One might argue that only a small portion of the population—the bad guys—behave badly and that there are lots of good guys in the world. It is tempting to divide people into "us," good guys, and "them," bad guys, but a great deal of evidence suggests that this dichotomy is misguided. Social psychologists such as Milgram (1974) and Zimbardo, Hane, Ganks, and Jaffe (1973) have demonstrated that it is quite easy to induce ordinary people to commit dishonest, hurtful, unfair, and irresponsible acts. On a greater scale, a large number of German people participated in the suppression and extermination of Jews in the 1930s and 1940s, and previously friendly neighbors commonly turn on one another during ethnic conflicts such as those that recently have occurred in Rwanda and Bosnia. When nations are freed from external control, people often roam the streets, looting, burning buildings, and killing one another. To some, this reveals the emergence of a previously suppressed, inherently evil human nature.

Evidence of Goodness

Let us accept the conclusion that humans and other animals sometimes—perhaps even often—behave badly. Really, it cannot be denied. This granted, evidence of depravity is only part of the story. Researchers have documented countless examples of apparently altruistic and cooperative behaviors in human beings,[2] but we do not need this evidence to establish that people frequently behave in ways that seem moral. We need only look around us. People commonly extend assistance to their friends and relatives, cooperate with members of their groups, and behave fairly. Indeed, as I show later in this book, most people from the Western world are willing to help strangers anonymously, contribute to charity, and help needy people from other countries.

---

[2] For example, see Staub (1979); Oliner, Oliner, Baron, Krebs, and Smolenska (1992); and review chapters in the handbooks of social psychology and developmental psychology.

The Challenge of Altruism to the Theory of Evolution

Evidence that animals behave in selfish ways seems consistent with the basic tenets of the theory of evolution, but evidence that animals behave in altruistic ways seems to challenge these tenets. Darwin (1874) wrote that the altruistic self-sacrifice of social insects presented "one special difficulty, which at first seemed insuperable, and actually fatal to my whole theory [of evolution]." Huxley (1893) considered it paradoxical that "ethical nature, while born of cosmic nature, is necessarily at enmity with its parent" (p. 94). And Williams (1989) asked, "how could maximizing selfishness produce an organism capable of often advocating, and occasionally practicing, charity toward strangers and even towards animals?" (p. 208). The answer, according to Williams, is that "altruistic behavior is limited to special situations in which it can be explained by . . . factors [that are not] of any use as a romantic's 'exemplar for human conduct'" (p. 209).

Explaining Altruism Away

Skeptical evolutionary theorists have accounted for the altruistic-appearing behaviors of animals in four main ways. First, they have questioned whether such behaviors are really altruistic, suggesting that, if probed deeply enough, altruistic-appearing behaviors will be exposed as disguised forms of selfishness: "Scratch an altruist and see a hypocrite bleed" (Ghiselin, 1974, p. 247). You may indeed see one animal helping another animal survive or reproduce. When viewed out of context, the helping behavior seems altruistic. However, it could be a tactic aimed at advancing the interests of the helper—a means to a selfish end. For example, it could be emitted to curry favor, to cultivate an ally, or to obtain a mate.

When examined from an evolutionary perspective, we want to know whether apparently altruistic acts ultimately produce benefits to the animals that emit them, relative both to the payoffs of other behavioral alternatives and to the benefits they bestow on recipients. (As I will explain, when examined from a psychological perspective, we want to know whether those who help others are motivated to benefit them as an end in itself or whether they are helping them in order to advance their own interests.) No one questions that animals behave in ways that have the immediate effect of helping others; however, Ghiselen, Dawkins, Williams, and other evolutionary theorists believe that most of these behaviors stem from behavioral strategies that evolved because they increased the probability that those who possessed them would survive and reproduce.

The second way in which evolutionary theorists have accounted for altruism is as a product of manipulation: As expressed by Williams (1989), "As a general rule, a modern biologist seeing one animal doing something to benefit another assumes either that it is manipulated by the other individual or that it is being subtly selfish" (p. 195). In later chapters, I argue that manipulation played an important role in the evolution of morality. When animals succeed in manipulating other animals into behaving in ways that increase their own fitness at the expense of the manipulated animals, they may induce the manipulated animals to behave in biologically altruistic ways. Although such evolutionary theorists as Williams and Dawkins acknowledge that these behaviors are biologically altruistic, they do not consider them moral, or at least up to the standards of "a romantic's exemplar for human conduct," presumably because the animals that emit them do not intend to sacrifice their interests for the sake of the recipient. The animals are tricked into behaving altruistically.

The third explanation for apparent acts of altruism advanced by skeptical evolutionary theorists is similar to the second in a certain respect, but different in another. In this explanation, altruistic and moral behaviors are viewed as incidental byproducts of mental mechanisms that evolved to suit other purposes. Mental mechanisms that induce animals to adopt *strategies* that pay off in the end may induce them to emit costly altruistic *acts* in some contexts. The short-term costs of the altruistic "mistakes" may be outweighed by the long-term benefits of the strategy. Although natural selection tends to hone the design of evolved mechanisms in increasingly fitness-increasing ways, the mechanisms that end up evolving are often far from perfect. Mechanisms that produce the greatest ultimate net gains in fitness relative to other available mechanisms in the population may induce those who inherit them to emit biologically costly altruistic behaviors in some contexts. I revisit this issue in Chapter 10.

Finally, related to all three arguments discussed above, skeptical evolutionary theorists have joined many lay people and social scientists in attributing altruistic behaviors to social learning and cultural indoctrination. For example, Dawkins (1989) wrote, "Let us try to *teach* generosity and altruism, because we are born selfish. . . . Our genes may instruct us to be selfish, but we are not necessarily compelled to obey them all our lives" (p. 3). In a similar vein, Campbell (1978) suggested that, "in man, genetic competition precludes the evolution of . . . genetic altruism. The behavioral dispositions that produce . . . self-sacrificial altruism must instead be products of culturally evolved indoctrination that has had to counter self-serving genetic tendencies" (p. 52). Campbell goes on to say that it follows that "man is profoundly ambivalent in his social role—as Freud noted. . . . The commandments, the proverbs, the religious 'law' represent social evolutionary products directed at inculcating tendencies that are in direct opposition to the 'temptations' representing, for the most part, the dispositional tendencies produced by biological evolution" (p. 53).

AN EVALUATION OF THE CASE AGAINST THE EVOLUTION OF MORAL DISPOSITIONS

To evaluate the case against the evolution of morality, we need to determine whether the two premises on which the conclusions are based are valid. Let us first examine the premise that all evolved dispositions are selfish and then turn to the premise that, to qualify as moral, a behavior must be unselfish.

Must All Evolved Dispositions Be Selfish?

If you carefully compare the excerpts from the writings of Darwin at the beginning of this chapter with the excerpts from the writings of contemporary evolutionary biologists, it should become apparent that although modern biologists seem to be saying the same thing as Darwin was, their arguments differ in several significant ways. First, Darwin viewed evolution in terms of the survival of the fittest individuals and the reproduction of offspring. (As I discuss in Chapter 10, Darwin also believed that traits could evolve through group selection.) Modern theorists view evolution in terms of the propagation of genes. Second, when Darwin alluded to "selfish and treacherous" parents, he was referring to parents who behaved in *personally* selfish ways. Modern theorists focus on *genetically* selfish behaviors. Finally, although Darwin felt that it was "*extremely doubtful*" that "the most sympathetic and benevolent parents" would produce more offspring than those who inherited more "selfish and treacherous" traits, he did not, like contemporary theorists, conclude that they *could not* produce more offspring because it would contravene the laws of evolution.

When modern evolutionary theorists define selfishness and altruism in terms of genetic fitness, the assertion that all evolved dispositions are selfish, or more exactly, *were* selfish *when they were selected*, is true by definition. To characterize a disposition as evolved is to assert that it increased the fitness of the individuals who possessed it at the expense of the fitness of individuals w ho did not possess it, which is by definition "selfish." As expressed by Randolph Nesse (2000):

> It is correct beyond question that genes shape brains that induce individuals to do whatever best gets copies of those genes into future generations. This principle follows from the logic of how natural selection works, and is not an empirical issue. When this is combined with our intuitive notion that altruism consists of costly acts that benefit others, and genes are seen as the ultimate currency, then altruism is impossible. (p. 228)

It would have been more exact for Nesse to have said "*got* copies of those genes into future generations" because the conclusion that all evolved traits are genetically selfish pertains only to the generation in which they were selected. Changes in physical, social, and cultural environments may render previously adaptive (genetically selfish) strategies maladaptive (genetically unselfish). In a book titled *Mean Genes*, Burnham and Phelan (2000) describe the maladaptive effects in the modern world of previously adaptive mechanisms governing hunger, thrill-seeking, greed, and sexual relations. The adaptiveness of social strategies often depends on their frequency in the population. Maladaptive traits can evolve in several ways.

Genetic Selfishness versus Individual Selfishness

As I discuss in Chapter 9, animals can propagate their genes in two ways. They can propagate them directly by fostering their own survival and reproductive success at the expense of the survival and reproductive success of others; and they can propagate them indirectly by fostering the survival and reproductive success of individuals who possess replicas of their genes. Although both methods are genetically selfish because they foster the propagation of genes, the second method is unselfish at the individual level, and indeed can be considered altruistic, because it entails helping others. As Dawkins (1989) has acknowledged, "there are special circumstances in which a gene can achieve its own selfish goals by fostering a limited form of altruism at the level of individual animals" (p. 6).

It follows that even if all evolved strategies were genetically selfish, they would not necessarily be individually (or biologically) selfish.

Genetic Selfishness versus Psychological Selfishness

To complicate matters further, evolutionary definitions of selfishness do not correspond to the definitions that most people invoke in their everyday lives. If you look up the word selfish in a dictionary, you will find such definitions as: "having such regard for one's own interests and advantage that the happiness and welfare of others become of less concern than is considered right or just" (Friend & Guralnik, 1960); "concerned excessively or exclusively with oneself: seeking or concentrating on one's own advantage, pleasure, or well-being without regard for others" (Merriam-Webster, 2003); and "deficient in consideration for others [and] concerned chiefly with one's own profit or pleasure" (Allen, 1984). I will label this type of selfishness *psychological selfishness.*

Psychological selfishness differs from genetic selfishness in three significant ways. First, whereas genetic selfishness is defined in terms of the consequences of behaviors (the number of replicas of one's genes that one contributes to future generations), psychological selfishness is defined in terms of a psychological state of regard, concern, caring, or consideration for oneself and a deficiency in concern for others.

Second, when individuals behave in psychologically selfish ways, they seek to obtain things such as pleasure, happiness, well-being, advantage, and profit that they want for themselves. When individuals behave in genetically selfish ways, it does not really matter whether they are motivated to obtain things for themselves or not. All that matters is whether their behaviors contribute to the propagation of their genes. Whether pursuing profit and pleasure helps individuals propagate their genes more effectively than pursuing other goals is an open question.

Finally, whereas the standard for genetic selfishness is the number of genes that one contributes to future generations relative to, or at the expense of, the genes' alleles, the standard for psychological selfishness is "excessive" or "exclusive" concern for one's own needs, desires, interests, and welfare, as well as disregard for the welfare of others. It is not necessarily psychologically selfish to be concerned about or to care for oneself, to satisfy one's own needs, to foster one's own welfare, or to seek one's own advantage, as long as one does not pursue these self-interested goals excessively without due regard for the welfare, comfort, and wishes of others.

Several theorists have pointed out that there is no necessary connection between genetic and psychological forms of selfishness and altruism. As expressed by Sober and Wilson (2000), "the automatic assumption that individualism in evolutionary biology and egoism in the social sciences must reinforce each other is as common as it is mistaken. More care is needed to connect the behaviors that evolved . . . with the psychological mechanisms that evolved to motivate those behaviors" (p. 205). Batson reports hearing Richard Dawkins make the point that alleles that rendered horses susceptible to developing bad teeth, and alleles that disposed humans to smoke cigarettes, would be genetically altruistic if they reduced individuals' prospects of surviving and reproducing. However, asserts Batson (2000), "Most people interested in the existence of altruism are not thinking about bad teeth in horses or smoking cigarettes; they are thinking about psychological altruism" (p. 208).

Making the same point in a different way, de Waal (2008, pp. 280–281) has pointed out that although evolutionary accounts of altruism are "built around the principle that all that natural selection can work with are the effects of behavior, not the motivation behind it," they persist in using motivational terms, characterizing behaviors as selfish even when actors are not motivated to benefit themselves, and characterizing behaviors that benefit others at a cost to actors as altruistic, even when the actors do not intend to produce these effects. De Waal asserts that:

> the hijacking of motivational terminology by evolutionary biologists has been unhelpful for communication about motivation per se. . . . It is not for nothing that biologists hammer on the distinction between ultimate and proximate . . . ultimate accounts stress return-benefits, i.e., positive consequences for the performer and/or its kin. Inasmuch as these benefits may be quite delayed, however, it is unclear what motivational role, if any, they play.

Whether individuals who seek to obtain benefits for themselves without regard for others fare better biologically and contribute more copies of their genes to future generations than those who behave in less psychologically selfish ways is an open question. They might, or they might not. There is nothing in the process of natural selection that dictates that individuals who are motivated to behave in psychologically selfish ways will prevail in the struggle for existence and reproduction, even though it is easy to think of circumstances in which we would expect them to. On the other side of the coin, there is no logical inconsistency in the assertion that behaving in psychologically unselfish ways may pay off biologically and genetically in the end. Cooperative individuals motivated to benefit themselves and others, and psychologically altruistic individuals motivated to help others as an end in itself could be more likely to survive, to produce offspring, and to propagate their genes than individuals who were motivated to help themselves at the expense of others.

Clearly then, the first premise in the case against the evolution of morality—that all evolved dispositions are selfish—is valid only with respect to genetic forms of selfishness in the environments in which they were selected. The process of evolution leaves the door open for the evolution of the kinds of proximate dispositions and behaviors that people commonly characterize as unselfish and moral. Inasmuch as psychologically unselfish dispositions can be genetically selfish (i.e., can increase the fitness of those who emit them), they can evolve.

Is Unselfishness Necessary for Morality?

As suggested in the previous chapter, people tend to view those who are willing to sacrifice their interests for the sake of others and those who seek to behave in fair ways as moral, and people tend to view those who seek to advance their own interests without regard for others as immoral. People tend to consider character traits that motivate people to care for others, to respect others' rights, and to do their share to be virtues, and they tend to consider those traits that motivate individuals to behave in uncaring, disrespectful, cowardly, and unfair ways to be vices. Implicit in such attributions is the assumption that to qualify as moral, a disposition must be psychologically unselfish. Most people consider those who try to get more, and to give less, than their share, and those who attempt to advance their own interests without due regard for the needs and interests of others to be selfish and immoral. In contrast, people do not necessarily consider biologically and genetically selfish behaviors immoral. Indeed, people may believe that everyone has a moral duty to preserve his or her life and to care for his or her offspring. Few people would consider it immoral to foster your genetic interests by helping your kin.

It is important to recognize that the genetic consequences of behaviors are irrelevant to most people's attributions of morality. People do not consider self-indulgent dispositions that induce individuals to eat or to drink themselves to death or to kill their offspring in fits of rage moral, even though such dispositions would be biologically and genetically altruistic if they lowered the fitness of the individuals who possessed them. In contrast, most people consider individuals who are genuinely motivated to sacrifice their profit and pleasure for the sake of others moral, even if such sacrifices end up incidentally elevating their fitness, by, for example increasing their status, or inducing those they helped to help them in return (thereby rendering the behaviors biologically and genetically selfish in effect). Morality does not pertain to individuals' success in surviving, reproducing, and propagating their genes; it pertains to how individuals go about achieving these goals—whether by trying to maximize their own profit and pleasure at others' expense or through more psychologically unselfish means. I discuss this issue more fully in the penultimate chapter of this book.

It also is important to note that concluding that psychological unselfishness is necessary for morality does not imply that psychological *altruism* is necessary for morality, or that psychological unselfishness is *sufficient*. I would argue that people can behave morally without behaving altruistically by, for example, wanting to take their fair share or striving to advance their interests in cooperative ways. People also can behave altruistically without behaving morally by, for example, seeking to help someone cheat or deciding to save the life of one friend at the expense of the lives of many strangers.

As I implied in the previous chapter, to qualify as moral, a behavior not only must be psychologically unselfish, it also must be fair. It is relatively easy to meet the first—unselfishness—criterion because it involves wanting to help individuals other than oneself. Meeting the second—fairness—criterion is more challenging because it requires individuals to seek to distribute their helping in fair and equitable ways. Philosophers of ethics such as Peter Singer (1981) have argued that when evaluated on objective criteria, the broader the range of others encompassed by a moral decision–rule (i.e., the more universal the application), the more moral the behaviors it produces.

To summarize, the case against the evolution of morality seems to be strong because the two premises on which it is based seem to be valid. It makes sense to assume that all evolved dispositions are selfish and that selfish dispositions cannot be moral. However, neither premise is valid with respect to the form of selfishness contained in the other premise. There is nothing in the process of natural selection that prevents the evolution of psychologically unselfish, cooperative, and altruistic dispositions, and there is nothing about genetically selfish dispositions that prevents them from qualifying as moral.

When one asks whether moral dispositions can evolve, it is not helpful to set genetic unselfishness as a necessary condition and then reach a negative conclusion because all evolved dispositions are genetically selfish when they are selected. When selfishness is defined in this way, there is no question to ask, because the answer is contained in the definitions of the constructs.

FROM "CAN" TO "IS"

Discrediting the idea that all evolved traits are psychologically selfish, and establishing that psychologically unselfish dispositions can evolve, opens the door for the evolution of moral dispositions, but it does not get us through. That something *could* evolve does not mean that it *has* evolved. The question we must answer is, what kinds of mental mechanisms enabled the ancestors of humans to solve the adaptive problems they encountered and to propagate their genes most effectively in the social and physical environments in which the mechanisms evolved—mechanisms that motivated them to benefit themselves at the expense of others; mechanisms that motivated them to benefit both themselves and others; or mechanisms that motivated them to benefit others even at immediate costs to themselves? I think that the best way to frame this question is in terms of a competition between psychologically selfish and psychologically unselfish strategies. What kinds of strategies were most effective at enabling early humans to propagate their genes?

Adaptive Strengths and Limitations of Psychologically Selfish Strategies

As recognized by Darwin and many other evolutionary theorists, at first glance, it seems that early humans who were naturally disposed to invoke psychologically selfish strategies (that is to say, to seek to promote their own welfare without regard for others) would have been more likely to survive and to reproduce than early humans who were naturally disposed to invoke unselfish strategies. It seems sensible to assume that individuals who are motivated to advance their interests at the expense of others fare better than individuals who are motivated to sacrifice their interests for the sake of others, and this would indeed be the case if these strategies were successful. However, when examined more closely, it becomes clear that psychologically selfish strategies suffer from some very severe shortcomings.

We would not expect an extremely selfish person who was bent on maximizing his or her profit and pleasure without regard for others to fare very well for several reasons. To begin with, the unmitigated pursuit of pleasure and other selfish excesses could be dangerous to his or her health. For example, gluttony and the unconstrained consumption of alcohol and drugs could jeopardize the person's chances of surviving and reproducing (Burnham & Phelan, 2000). Second, when two or more selfish individualists compete against one another for resources, they often do one another down, ending up with fewer individuals working together to advance their mutual interests. Third, individuals who behave in psychologically selfish ways may provoke members of their groups to punish them—by refusing to help them when they are in need, by imposing physical and material sanctions on them, by turning others against them, and by ostracizing them from their group.

Fourth, psychologically selfish attempts to maximize one's gains without regard for others may destroy beneficial relationships, undermine coalitions, and diminish the welfare of individuals' groups as a whole, thereby jeopardizing the social environment that individuals need to survive and to reproduce. And finally, although we would expect psychologically selfish strategies to evolve when they helped individuals propagate their genes at the expense of those who possessed alleles of their genes, we would not necessarily expect them to evolve when they induced individuals to behave in ways that jeopardized the genetic success of those who possessed copies of their genes.

Considering the limitations of psychologically selfish strategies, what kind of strategies should we expect to evolve? We should not expect any kind of unconditional strategy to evolve, at least in unpredictable environments. Rather, we should expect a set of conditional strategies to evolve that are designed in terms of implicit "if–then" decision rules of the form, "if the (internal or external) conditions are similar to those in which this choice paid off genetically in ancestral environments, then make it." As I document in later chapters, different "if" conditions may activate different neurological, hormonal, emotional, and motivational systems, some of which give rise to psychologically selfish motives, and some of which give rise to psychologically altruistic motives.

In closing, note that this analysis of the evolution of selfishness has an important implication for human nature. Because it is inappropriate to characterize conditional strategies as either psychologically selfish or unselfish (they may give rise to both types of behavior, depending on the conditions), it is inappropriate to characterize species in which such conditional strategies have evolved as either psychologically selfish or unselfish. They—we—are both.

CONCLUSIONS

Evolutionary theorists have implied that all species are selfish by nature, but the type of selfishness that these theorists have in mind is quite different from the type of selfishness that people have in mind when they make attributions of morality. When selfish dispositions are defined in a way that corresponds to the meaning that most people assign to the concept, such dispositions may or may not prevail in the process of natural selection. The evidence suggests that although psychologically selfish forms of conduct are adaptive in some conditions, they are maladaptive in other conditions. The mechanisms regulating selfish (and unselfish) forms of conduct are designed in terms of conditional decision rules. The key to understanding human nature and the nature of other animals lies in deciphering these decision rules, understanding how they evolved, determining the kinds of motivational states they engender, mapping the ways in which the mechanisms that produce them are shaped during development, and identifying the internal and external stimuli that activate them in everyday life.

4

DARWIN'S THEORY OF THE ORIGIN
OF MORALITY

What better place to begin an account of how moral dispositions evolved in the human species than with the father of the theory of evolution himself, Charles Darwin? A decade after publishing On the Origin of Species, *Darwin published another book, called* The Descent of Man and Selection in Relation to Sex, *that contained a chapter in which he outlined an account of the origin of morality. Darwin identified four stages in the evolution of morality. First, he suggested that, like other social animals, humans inherit social instincts that induce them to affiliate with members of their groups, to help them, and to care about their approval and disapproval. Second, he suggested that, inevitably, animals experience conflicts between selfish urges and social instincts, and in many cases, selfish urges win out. However, Darwin argued that when early humans acquired the capacity to remember what they had done and to care about the opinions of others, they ended up feeling bad about violating their social instincts and treating others poorly. This, argued Darwin, marked the origin of conscience. Third, Darwin suggested that as humans evolved, increasingly sophisticated intellectual and language abilities enabled them to expand and to refine their sense of morality. Finally, he suggested that humans' capacity for morality became honed through habits cultivated by parents and other members of their societies.*

Darwin's model of the evolution of morality is impressive in its scope. He took a position on the nature of morality and distinguished between ultimate standards such as the greatest good for the greatest number and motives that induce people to behave in ways that meet such standards. He suggested that the adaptive benefits that individuals garner from behaving in ways that uphold their groups are consistent with cardinal moral principles that prescribe group-supporting behaviors. Darwin's account offers an explanation for the evolution of behaviors that people consider moral and the psychological mechanisms that produce these considerations. Although Darwin's account is limited in many respects, he supplied a framework for the evolution of morality equipped to organize new developments in the field. In this chapter, I outline Darwin's theory of the origin of the moral sense—making use of copious quotes that capture the flavor of his thinking—then offer some evaluative comments.[1]

As mentioned in the previous chapter, Darwin was attentive to the challenge that evidence of morality presented to his theory of evolution. It seemed to him that humans behave in moral ways, and it seemed to him that they possess a sense of morality, but he struggled with the problem of identifying the mental mechanisms that produce these manifestations of morality and explaining how they evolved. In the late 19th century, in the context of comparing the mental powers of "man and the lower animals," Darwin published an account of the evolution of the moral sense. Although some of the ideas that he advanced seem shockingly misguided in the light of subsequent insights about the process of evolution, his overriding approach and basic ideas may well provide the most useful available framework for accounting for the complexities of morality. Whereas modern scholars focus on parts of the project, Darwin synthesized them into a coherent whole.

THE EVOLUTION OF A MORAL SENSE

The project that Darwin set for himself was to explain how a moral sense evolved in the human species. He theorized that this sense originated from precursors possessed by other animals, which became refined and expanded in the course of human evolution. Darwin outlined four stages in the evolution of the moral sense. First, early humans (and other primates) inherited social instincts, which "lead an animal to take pleasure in the society of its fellows, to feel a certain amount of sympathy with them, and to perform various services for them" (p. 95). Second, early humans acquired mental abilities that enabled them to develop a conscience. Third, people acquired the ability to express the wishes of the community through language, which caused "the common opinion how each member ought to act for the public good" to become the most significant guide to action (p. 96). Finally, people's disposition to obey the wishes of the community increased in strength when their social instincts became "strengthened by habit" instilled through socialization (p. 96). Let us consider each of these stages in more detail.

Stage 1: The Acquisition of Social Instincts

Darwin viewed social instincts as precursors to morality. Although Darwin did not explicitly define social instincts, he alluded to four features that characterized them: (1) feelings of pleasure when affiliating with members of one's group; (2) altruistic dispositions to perform services for members of one's group; (3) feelings of sympathy for others (by which he meant what contemporary psychologists call emotional empathy); and (4) the desire to garner others' approval and avoid their disapproval.

---

[1] All quotations are from Darwin, C. (1874). *The descent of man and selection in relation to sex.* New York: Rand McNally & Company.

With respect to the proximate goals that social instincts motivate people to pursue, Darwin argued that they dispose animals to seek the company of others and engender the desire to help others as ends in themselves, not as means of maximizing pleasure. He suggested some "instincts are persistently followed from the mere force of inheritance, without the stimulus of pleasure or pain" (p. 102). For example, he argued that it is implausible that people who rush into burning buildings to save others do so in order to maximize their pleasure or to avoid feelings of guilt. Rather, he suggested, such behaviors stem from the "impulsive power" of "the deeply planted social instinct" (p. 117) even though people may experience a "vague sense of dissatisfaction" when prevented from behaving in accordance with their social instincts (p. 102). In rooting morality in social instincts that need not necessarily be accompanied by pleasure, Darwin felt that he avoided "the reproach . . . of laying the foundation of the noblest part of our nature in the base principle of selfishness; unless, indeed, the satisfaction which every animal feels, when it follows its proper instincts, and the dissatisfaction felt when prevented, be called selfish" (p. 117).

Need for Affiliation

Darwin recognized that mental mechanisms that disposed animals to want to affiliate with others evolved because group living helped their ancestors survive and reproduce: "With those animals which were benefited by living in close association, the individuals which took the greatest pleasure in society would best escape various dangers; whilst those that cared the least for their comrades, and lived solitary, would perish in greater numbers" (p. 102). Darwin believed that need for affiliation is instinctive and that the pleasure people experience from affiliating with others (and displeasure they feel when this instinct is stifled) is "probably an extension of the parental or filial affections, since the social instinct seems to be developed by the young remaining for a long time with their parents" (p. 117).

Altruistic Dispositions

Darwin argued that in order for animals to profit from social living, they must be disposed to aid one another and uphold their groups. Darwin gave many examples of animals helping one another, some of which we would classify as cooperative, and others that seemed more biologically altruistic. With respect to humans, Darwin asserted that early humans "would from an inherited tendency be willing to defend, in concert with others, [their] fellow-men; and would be ready to aid them in any way, which did not too greatly interfere with [their] own welfare or [their] own strong desires" (p. 106). As explained by Jeffrie Murphy (1982), in Darwin's opinion "care only for self, or even care limited to one's immediate family, would not have been sufficient to promote early humans' survival. To survive, early humans would have had to possess a more generalized tendency to care for their group as a whole and, as their communities became more complex, for the rules establishing duties within the communities" (p. 73).

Sympathy

Darwin believed that sympathy (i.e., emotional empathy) was the "foundation-stone" of the social instinct (p. 96). Although he saw sympathy as one source of altruistic motivation, he did not believe that sympathetic affective states, or for that matter any affective states, were necessary for altruism. With respect to the nature of the proximate mental mechanisms that produce sympathetic reactions, Darwin rejected the idea that "the sight of another person enduring hunger, cold, fatigue, revives in us some recollection of these states . . . [and impels us] to relieve the sufferings of another, in order that our own painful feelings may be at the same time relieved," because, he argued, people feel significantly more sympathy for those they love than they feel for other people (p. 103).

Need for Approval

Darwin suggested that instinctive sympathy would have caused early humans to value, and be influenced by, "the wishes, approval, and disapproval of members of their groups" (p. 106). Indeed, he asserted that "it is . . . hardly possible to exaggerate the importance during rude times of the love of praise and the dread of blame" (p. 128).

Derivative Dispositions

In addition to the four dispositions that Darwin considered central to the social instincts, he suggested that, because "man" is an intensely social animal, "it is almost certain that he would inherit a tendency to be faithful to his comrades and obedient to the leader of his tribe for these qualities are common to most social animals. He would consequently possess some capacity for self-command" (p. 106).

The Origin of Social Instincts

Although we might expect Darwin to have believed that all social instincts evolved through natural selection, this is not, in fact, the case. Darwin was not sure how humans and other animals acquire social instincts. He felt that "it is impossible to decide in many cases whether certain social instincts have been acquired through natural selection or as the indirect result of other instincts and faculties, such as sympathy, reason, experience, and a tendency to imitation, or . . . long-continued habit" (p. 103–104).

It is easy to see how dispositions to affiliate with others, to gain their approval, and to avoid their disapproval, could evolve because it is easy to see how they could help individuals who inherited them to survive and reproduce. However, it was not clear to Darwin how sympathetic and altruistic dispositions could evolve, because it would seem that they would dispose those who inherited them to jeopardize their own welfare to increase the fitness of others. As I discuss more fully in Chapter 10, Darwin accounted for the origin of altruistic dispositions in the human species by appealing to group selection. He argued that no group could endure if its members treated one another immorally, and that "those communities, which included the greatest number of the most sympathetic members, would flourish best, and rear the greatest number of offspring" (p. 103). In addition, as I discuss in later chapters, Darwin entertained the idea that mental abilities could evolve through what contemporary evolutionary theorists call kin selection.

Stage 2: The Evolution of Conscience

Darwin believed that although social instincts are necessary for morality, they are not sufficient. Like many laypeople, Darwin located the moral sense in an agency he called *conscience*. He accounted for conscience in terms of the stability of social instincts, the mental ability to remember how one has behaved, and the tendency to compare selfish choices with more prosocial alternatives and regret the selfish choices.

Darwin believed that humans and other animals inherit all kinds of instincts that engender a primitive sense of duty, but people do not experience the sense of duty engendered by most instincts as a moral obligation. For example, humans and other animals may feel compelled to help members of their groups without experiencing a moral duty to do so. Humans and other animals may feel bad when they fail to satisfy their instinctive desires and when they fail to achieve the goals these desires motivate them to pursue, but they do not necessarily feel *guilty*. From whence, asked Darwin, does a sense of *moral* obligation and guilt originate?

Darwin began his account of the evolution of conscience by noting that animals often experience conflicts between social instincts and selfish instincts such as hunger, lust, and a desire for revenge, as well as conflicts between instincts and habits (p. 104). In some conditions, selfish instincts prevail, causing individuals to succumb to the temptation to exploit, cheat, steal from, rape, and murder members of their groups, and to behave in cowardly ways. In other conditions, such as when animals protect their offspring, social instincts may prevail (p. 108). Darwin asserted that when selfish instincts prevail, individuals suffer remorse. The question is, why? "Why should a man feel that he ought to obey one instinctive desire rather than another? Why is he bitterly regretful, if he has yielded to a strong sense of self-preservation, and has not risked his life to save that of a fellow-creature? or why does he regret having stolen food from hunger?" (pp. 106–107).

The answer, argued Darwin is that the social instincts are more enduring than other kinds of instincts. According to Darwin, after people satisfy the selfish needs engendered by instincts such as hunger and lust, these needs dissipate and lose their motivational power. In contrast, the needs engendered by social instincts such as sympathy and need for approval are "ever-present and persistent" (p. 109). When people reflect on their immoral actions, they compare the selfish choices they made, which have lost their motivational power, with the prosocial choices they neglected to make, which have left their social instincts unsatisfied, and feel bad about what they did. Darwin summarized his theory of conscience as follows:

> At the moment of action, man will no doubt be apt to follow the stronger impulse; and though this may occasionally prompt him to the noblest deeds, it will more commonly lead him to gratify his own desires at the expense of other men. But after their gratification, when past and weaker impressions are judged by the ever-enduring social instinct, and by his deep regard for the good opinion of his

fellows, retribution will surely come. He will then feel remorse, repentance, regret, or shame . . . . He will consequently resolve . . . to act differently for the future; and this is conscience; for conscience looks backwards, and serves as a guide for the future. (p. 110)

To summarize, according to Darwin, the essence of conscience lies in a mental process of reflective evaluation. Individuals reflect on the choices they have made and pass judgment on them. An "inward monitor" tells animals that "it would have been better to have followed the one impulse rather than the other. The one course ought to have been followed, and the other ought not; the one would have been right and the other wrong" (p. 97).

The Significance of Approval and Disapproval

As revealed in the passage quoted above, Darwin added what I believe to be a significant kicker to the self-reflective process that causes people to feel bad after they violate their social instincts. He suggested that when people reflect on their antisocial actions, they consider how others, or a deity, would react. The more that people care about the approval of others, the stronger their feelings of regret, shame, and remorse. Darwin summarized this idea as follows: "In order to be quite free from self-reproach, or at least of anxiety, it is almost necessary for [man] to avoid the disapprobation, whether reasonable or not, of his fellow-men . . . . He must likewise avoid the reprobation of the one God or gods in whom, according to his knowledge or superstition, he may believe; but in this case the additional fear of divine punishment often supervenes" (p. 113).

Stage 3: Refinement of the Moral Sense through Intelligence and Language

Many people believe that the moral sense stems from a human agency that is qualitatively different from any comparable agency possessed by other primates. As expressed by one of Darwin's critics, Reverend Leonard Jenyns, in a letter he wrote to Darwin in 1860, "neither can I easily bring myself to the idea that man's reasoning faculties and above all his moral sense could ever have been obtained from irrational progenitors, by mere natural selection—acting however gradually and for whatever length of time that may be required. This seems to me to be doing away with the Divine Image that forms the insurmountable distinction between man and brutes."

Darwin disagreed. Based on the evidence available to Darwin in his day, he concluded that differences among the mental abilities of humans and other primates were a matter "of degree and not of kind." He argued that humans and other primates possess the same kinds of instincts and passions—"even the more complex ones, such as jealousy, suspicion, emulation, gratitude, and magnanimity." In addition, he argued that humans and other primates possess similar mental abilities, "though in very different degrees" (p. 122). In what may be the most memorable passage of Darwin's account of the evolution of a moral sense, he wrote, "any animal whatever, endowed with well-marked social instincts . . . would inevitably acquire a moral sense or conscience as soon as its intellectual powers had become as well, or nearly as well developed, as in man" (p. 95). In this passage Darwin explicates the idea that humans' moral sense originated in primitive instincts that are similar to those possessed by other animals, but that it became refined and elaborated when humans acquired more sophisticated mental abilities—an idea I develop further in Chapters 16 and 17.

Among the mental abilities that mediated the refinement of the moral sense, Darwin emphasized cognitive abilities such as the ability to remember how one had behaved, the ability to reflect on one's behavior, the ability to compare present and past experiences, and the ability to make resolutions, or plan for the future. Darwin recognized that mental abilities such as these also enabled reciprocity. In addition, he emphasized the role that the ability to reason played in enabling people to evaluate the moral judgments of others and to appreciate the contributions that virtues make to the general welfare of groups.

Darwin believed that there was a close association between intelligence and the capacity for symbolic language. He suggested that language affects the moral sense in four main ways: by enabling humans to communicate approval and disapproval, by enabling them to communicate "the wishes of the community" (p. 96), by enabling them to create moral rules, and by enabling them to agree to follow the rules they create.

Stage 4: The Development of Moral Habits

The final source of morality discussed by Darwin was habit, or what we now call *social learning*. Darwin recognized that children's sense of morality is shaped by the ways in which their parents and other members of their cultures behave and by the ideas that adults preach to them (p. 118). Darwin fully acknowledged the effects of adult influence on children: "A belief constantly inculcated during the early years of life, whilst the brain is impressible, appears to acquire almost the nature of an instinct; and the very essence of an instinct is that it is followed independently of reason" (p. 118).

Although Darwin argued that social instincts, or dispositions to behave in group-upholding ways, evolved through natural selection, he considered it probable that children acquire such virtues as chastity, temperance, and the desire to treat animals in humane ways through social learning (p. 120). In what can only be considered an astounding anomaly in Darwin's theorizing, he entertained the idea that habits could be inherited biologically.

Interactions among Sources of Morality

Darwin recognized that the sources of morality he identified—for example, social instincts, habits, and reason—could interact with one another in antagonistic or supportive ways. On the one hand, for example, he discussed conflicts experienced by dogs between the instinct to pursue prey and the habit of obeying their masters. On the other hand, he argued that social instincts that dispose people to obey the wishes and judgments of members of their community may be strengthened by habit (p. 96), and feelings of sympathy may be strengthened by social learning and selfish desires such as those that dispose people to help others in the hope of receiving help in return (p. 103).

With respect to the relative power of different sources of moral and immoral behavior, Darwin suggested that although some instincts may be rendered stronger than others through natural selection, their strength may be increased or decreased by need for approval, social influence, reason, habit, and even self-interest. For example, he wrote, "Social instincts which must have been acquired by man in a very rude state, and probably even by his early ape-like progenitors, still give the impulse to some of his best actions; but his actions are in a higher degree determined by the expressed wishes and judgment of his fellow-men, and unfortunately very often by his own strong selfish desires" (p. 106).

Darwin's Theory of Ethics

Darwin (1874) took a stab at deriving a standard on which the morality of particular forms of conduct and virtues could be evaluated. He suggested that the quality that renders behaviors and traits moral is that they foster the "general good or welfare of the community" (p. 117). Following this line of thought, the reason that people consider most prosocial behaviors moral is that most prosocial behaviors improve the welfare of members of their communities, and the reason that people consider most antisocial behaviors immoral is that these behaviors diminish the welfare of their communities. If a seemingly prosocial behavior did not foster the general good, it would not qualify as moral (and if a seemingly antisocial behavior such as civil disobedience did improve the welfare of the community, it would render it moral). Extending this idea, the more a behavior contributes to human welfare—the more good it does—the more moral it becomes.

Although Darwin's ideas about ethics were rooted in utilitarianism, he also incorporated ideas from other ethical theories. For example, the idea that the essence of morality lies in a sense of "ought" and that reasoning is necessary for human morality converge with Kant's theory. Darwin's views about the role played by sympathy in moral judgment converge with those of Hume. His ideas about the role of habits converge with those of Aristotle, and his acceptance of the Golden Rule as a cardinal moral principle converge with those of religious authorities and many laypeople. However, he did not fully explicate the relations among these aspects of the moral sense, and in his emphasis on the social function of morality, he may have neglected other aspects of morality, such as purity and integrity. Whether such values can be subsumed under utilitarian principles such as the greatest good for the greatest number is an open question.

The utilitarian standard that Darwin invoked to define and to assess the morality of acts and traits pertains to the consequences they produce (the greatest good for the greatest number). Darwin was careful to distinguish between the standard that acts must meet to be considered moral and the motivation underlying the acts. He argued that to be considered moral, acts need not necessarily be driven by the motive to foster the welfare of the greatest number of individuals; they need only meet this standard, or achieve this effect. Darwin rejected the idea that the only acts that qualify as moral are those that are "done deliberately, after a victory over opposing desires, or when prompted by some exalted motive" (p. 107). He asserted that we should consider impulsive acts moral, as long as they foster the welfare of others, because it is impossible to determine clearly what kinds of motives impel people to behave in prosocial ways.

To flesh out Darwin's standard of morality, we need to define good and welfare. Early utilitarian theorists such as John Stuart Mill defined welfare in terms of pleasure and happiness. Darwin defined welfare more biologically as "rearing of the greatest number of individuals in full vigor and health with all their faculties perfect under the conditions to which they are subjugated" (p. 117). This said, Darwin (1874, p. 117) believed that "the welfare and the happiness of the individual usually coincide," and because "happiness is an essential part of the general good, the greatest happiness principle indirectly serves as a nearly safe standard of right and wrong." The promise in utilitarian conceptions of morality has been well expressed by Robert Wright (1994) in his book, *The Moral Animal:* "Everyone's happiness can, in principle, go up if everyone treats everyone else nicely. You refrain from cheating or mistreating me, I refrain from cheating or mistreating you; we're both better off than we would be in a world without morality" (p. 335).

The Expansion of Morality

Darwin embraced hierarchical orders. In addition to higher and lower moral norms, he believed that the process of evolution produced "higher" and "lower" forms of life. He considered nonhuman animals "lower" than humans, and among humans, he considered "savages" lower than Englishmen.[2] Most contemporary readers will find Darwin's allusions to the moral inferiority of savages distasteful and ethnocentric. However, Darwin derived his evaluation of the moral fiber of people who lived in different cultures from comparisons between their moral norms. If we can evaluate the principles of morality espoused by different individuals, then why can we not also evaluate the moral norms of different cultures? If we can say, as cognitive-developmental theorists have asserted, that one person's conception of morality is more highly developed than another person's conception of morality, and if we can say, as theorists such as Paul Bloom (2004) have asserted, that people today are more moral than people were 2000 years ago, then why can we not say that one culture's moral norms are more highly developed than another culture's moral norms?

In evaluating the quality of people's moral sense, Darwin focused on the breadth, or reach, of their morals. He believed that the growth of reason and "self-command" were primarily responsible for the expansion of morality. He wrote, "The virtues which must be practiced, at least generally, by rude men, so that they may associate in a body, are those which are still recognized as the most important. But they are practiced almost exclusively in relation to the men of the same tribe; and their opposites are not regarded as crimes in relation to the men of other tribes" (p. 113). After giving examples of "savages"

---

[2] Darwin did not go quite as far as many of his contemporaries in ordering beings in hierarchies of goodness. In a published critique of the application of natural selection to "man," the Scottish scholar William Greg wrote, "The careless, squalid, unaspiring Irishman, fed on potatoes, living in a pig-sty, doting on a superstition, multiplies like rabbits or ephemera: —the frugal, forseeing, self-respecting Scot, stern in his morality, spiritual in his faith, sagacious and disciplined in his intelligence, passes his best years in struggle and in celibacy, marries late, and leaves few behind him" (p. 361).

behaving in noble and courageous ways toward members of their own tribes, followed by examples of these people behaving in egregiously cruel ways toward members of other tribes, Darwin attributed the "low morality of savages" to three sources—"the confinement of sympathy to the same tribe," the inability to understand how virtues, especially "self-regarding" virtues, can contribute to the general welfare of their tribes, and weak self-control [due to inadequate socialization]" (pp. 115–116).

Looking into the future, Darwin asserted that, "as man advances in civilization, and small tribes are united into larger communities, the simplest reason would tell each individual that he ought to extend his social instincts and sympathies to all the members of the same nation . . . . This point being once reached, there is only an artificial barrier to prevent his sympathies extending to the men of all nations and races" (p. 119). Indeed, argued Darwin, "sympathy beyond the confines of man, that is humanity to the lower animals, seems to be one of the latest moral acquisitions . . . . This virtue, one of the noblest with which man is endowed, seems to arise incidentally from our sympathies becoming more tender and more widely diffused, until they are extended to all sentient beings" (p. 119).

Summary of Darwin's Ideas about the Evolution of Morality

Darwin advanced a model of the evolution of the moral sense based on two main assumptions. First, social instincts that induced early humans to behave in ways that were good for their communities endowed them with a sense of sympathy, sensitized them to the approval and disapproval of members of their groups, motivated them to aid their fellows, and engendered "a rude rule of right and wrong." Second, as early humans acquired intellectual abilities that enabled them to anticipate the remote consequences of their actions, reject "baneful customs and superstitions," understand how to improve the welfare and happiness of others, and develop sensible habits, their "sympathies became more tender and widely diffused, extending to men of all races, to the imbecile, maimed . . . . and finally to the lower animals" (pp. 120–121).

EVALUATION OF DARWIN'S MODEL OF MORALITY

It feels a little presumptuous to evaluate Darwin's ideas, and as expressed by one of Darwin's critics, Murphy (1982), "Darwin is not much fun to attack because he exhibits so much in the way of intellectual and academic virtue—i.e., he proceeds with great intellectual modesty and honesty, is tentative where . . . he should be tentative, and covers all that he does with a patina of personal charm and common sense" (p. 79). However, joining this critic, I will "temporarily abandon historical piety and . . . treat Charles Darwin in much the same spirit as one might treat an anonymous scholar whose article one has been assigned to referee for possible publication in a contemporary journal" (p. 79).

Truth be told, my first reaction to Darwin's account of the evolution of morality was unfavorable. I was repulsed by some of his characterizations of "savages," amazed that he would entertain the idea that habits could be inherited, and unimpressed with his account of conscience. However, over the years, as I had occasion to reread Darwin's account and study it more closely, I became increasingly impressed with his organizational approach and insights. Indeed, I grew so impressed that I ended up deciding to take on the project of refining, revising, and elaborating Darwin's account in light of contemporary theory and research, which is what this book is mainly about. In contrast to zealots who believe that the source featured in their models constitutes the sole determinant of morality—be it inherited decision-making strategies, moral emotions, social learning, moral reasoning, or whatever, Darwin derived a framework equipped to encompass them all.

It is impressive to recognize how many issues discussed by Darwin a century and a half ago are still being addressed by contemporary theorists and researchers and how insightful some of Darwin's early ideas were. Prominent among such issues and ideas, which I discuss in later chapters of this book, are those that pertain to evolutionary ethics and human nature, the evolution of sociality, group selection, kin selection, precursors of morality in other primates, the design of proximate mechanisms mediating sympathetic and empathic behaviors, the significance of need for approval, the origin of conscience, the refinement and expansion of morality mediated by the acquisition of language and the growth of intelligence, the role of social learning in the evolution of uniquely human prosocial behaviors, and the evolution of culturally specific and universal moral norms.

Multiple Sources of Morality

Most contemporary psychologists focus on one of the forms of conduct that people consider moral—for example, either altruism, or cooperation, or self-control—and attribute it to one source—for example, either automatic impulses, emotional reactions, social learning, or reason. Darwin attended to a set of moral behaviors and attributed them to a set of determinants. I believe that integrative approaches such as the one Darwin pioneered (and the revised version I advance in this book) are necessary to account for the complexities of morality.

If things were simple, each form of conduct that people consider moral would stem from a different source, enabling us to organize accounts of morality in a tidy matrix. Darwin made a start in this direction by dividing virtues into those that are "self-regarding" in nature and those that are group-supporting in nature and by attributing each to a different source (habits vs. social instincts). However, Darwin's account of the self-regarding virtues seems implausible and incomplete. In some places Darwin implies that self-regarding virtues bear no relation to fitness and that therefore we would not expect them to stem from "instinctive" processes, but in other places he implies that self-regarding virtues can increase individuals' fitness by upholding their groups. In addition, it is unclear how self-regarding virtues such as chastity and temperance relate to, or differ from, "self-command."

Types of Social Instincts

The idea that social instincts have evolved in social animals seems reasonable and consistent with modern views of sociality. However, there is reason to question the particular dispositions Darwin included in his description of social instincts and his ideas about the relations among them. Darwin's analysis would have been clearer and more helpful if he had discussed each aspect of the social instinct, or each type of social instinct, separately and explored its implications for morality more fully. Humans have a need for affiliation, and they develop attachments to others. The question is, do these psychological processes dispose them to behave morally, perhaps by motivating them to help members of their groups survive (else they would lose the objects of their attachments and have no one with whom to affiliate)? Humans sympathize with others, and they help others impulsively in emergencies. Darwin implies that sympathetic reactions give rise to impulsive helping, but researchers have found that impulsive helping stems from quite different mental mechanisms from those that produce sympathy and empathy (Piliavin, Dovidio, Gaertner, & Clark, 1981). In addition, it is unclear whether, as Darwin suggested, sympathy gives rise to the need for approval. Need for approval could stem from quite different mental mechanisms from those that induce people to sympathize with others.

The Adaptive Value of Cooperation and the Structure of Social Dilemmas

In my view, the most significant oversights in Darwin's model of the evolution of the moral sense stem from his neglect of the important role played by cooperation in the evolution of morality and his insensitivity to the moral dilemmas cooperative relations inevitably engender. This oversight is probably responsible for Darwin's failure to include fairness in his list of virtues. In the light of contemporary theory and research, it seems misguided to view reciprocity an inferior moral principle, as Darwin did, because he believed that it stemmed from and promoted selfishness (giving in order to get). Although people may reciprocate for selfish reasons, as Darwin assumed, a great deal of research (that I review in Chapter 15) suggests that people may reciprocate in order to repay favors, to "even the score," and to produce fair outcomes, as ends in themselves. In addition, in his focus on direct forms of reciprocity, Darwin neglected the more general and indirect forms of reciprocity that modern theorists such as Alexander (1987) believe underlie moral systems.

To Darwin's credit, he offered several examples of cooperative behaviors in nonhuman animals in support of his analysis of sociality. For example, he alluded to animals engaging in group hunting and baboons joining forces to move a large rock. And as mentioned, Darwin acknowledged that selfish instincts often conflict with social instincts. However, he failed to attend to the threat that selfish dispositions pose for the evolution of cooperative dispositions, or to the social and moral dilemmas that selfishness precipitates. Associated with his neglect of this adaptive problem, he failed to consider the adaptive benefits of approving and disapproving of others' behavior. Yes, humans and other animals seek approval, which as Darwin pointed out, probably stems from the benefits of social support (and the costs of losing it). However, people also use approval and disapproval as tactics of social influence to induce others to behave in ways that benefit them. Darwin neglected the dynamics of social interactions in which members of groups attempt to induce each other to behave in ways that maximize their benefits and the implications of such interactions for the evolution of morality.

An Account of the Origin of the Moral Sense

In addition to offering an explanation for how group-supporting, or prosocial, behavioral dispositions evolved—which is what most contemporary evolutionary theorists seek to explain—Darwin offered an account of the origin of the agency in people's mind that induces them to feel that they ought to behave in prosocial ways and the agency that deems these forms of conduct right and those who emit them good. Accounting for the evolution of a moral sense is more challenging than accounting for the decision-rules that induce people to behave in altruistic and cooperative ways.

Darwin offered compelling arguments in support of the idea that prosocial behavioral dispositions ("social instincts") evolved before the sense that the forms of conduct to which they give rise are morally obligatory and right. Attending to the order in which these aspects of morality evolved has important implications for a current controversy in the social sciences about relations between moral judgment and moral behavior. Darwin's account implies that humans and other animals are biologically disposed to behave in prosocial ways in certain contexts without engaging in any higher-order cognition or moral reasoning. Contemporary research on bystander intervention (Piliavin et al., 1981) and moral intuitions (Haidt, 2001) offers strong support for this view.

Role of Reason and Language in Refinement and Elaboration of the Moral Sense

Darwin claimed that higher-order reasoning is superimposed on primitive instincts to produce a true moral sense. Although this idea seems fundamentally sound, Darwin did not delve very deeply into the ways in which intelligence and language evolved and how they influenced the acquisition of a moral sense. He wrote, "Undoubtedly it would be interesting to trace the development of each separate [intellectual] faculty from the state in which it exists in the lower animals to that in which it exists in man; but neither my ability nor knowledge permits the attempt" (p. 125). Contemporary theorists have explored the evolution of intelligence and language more fully than Darwin did. Of particular significance are theories that attend to the adaptive social value of these mental abilities.

Darwin emphasized the ways in which moral reasoning supports social instincts, helps people refine their conceptions of morality, and induces them to direct their prosocial behaviors to an expanding group of recipients, but Darwin neglected the down side of reason. Reason is a tool that evolved because it helped people advance their genetic interests. On the one hand, people may, as Darwin emphasized, use this tool to understand how they and others ought to behave and how upholding their groups serves their long-term interests. However, people also may use their intelligence to figure out how to exploit others and to concoct self-serving justifications for their immoral deeds.

In a similar vein, Darwin neglected the role that language plays in strategic interaction. Although people use language to negotiate social contracts and to communicate norms that uphold the good of the community, as Darwin asserted, people also use language to deceive and to exploit others. In light of new advances in evolutionary theory and research, Darwin's failure to consider the implications of the idea that people use language and reason in the social arena to induce others to behave in ways that maximize their biological gains seems like a serious oversight.

The Evolution of Conscience

With respect to the evolution of conscience, everyone has succumbed to temptation, reflected on what he or she has done, regretted it, and resolved to behave differently in the future. However, I am not sure that attributing these processes to the enduring nature of social instincts is the most fruitful way of accounting for such manifestations of conscience. True, people experience selfish desires, which we could call instincts, and these desires conflict with social needs and social values. When the selfish desires have been satisfied, they dissipate, and people regret what they have done. The question is, what is the source of this regret? As I explain in Chapters 16 and 17, in place of "ever-enduring" social instincts, some neuroscientists attribute guilt to designated mental circuits in the brain, and many psychologists attribute it to social conditioning and fear of punishment, including the disapproval of others.

The Evolution of Cultural Norms

At best, Darwin's analysis of moral norms must be considered a promising beginning. Distinguishing between culturally universal and culturally specific moral norms, and attributing the former to species-specific social instincts supported by reason, and the later to culturally relative social learning, introduces some useful distinctions. However, we need to know more about the process through which social instincts, or evolved prosocial dispositions, give rise to universal moral norms, how culturally relative moral norms originate and spread, and what causes people to create and propagate moral norms that prescribe arbitrary or maladaptive customs. Why do people from the same culture hold different beliefs? How do evolved instincts, reason, and habit interact in the production of moral norms? To what extent are ideas that are derived from reason, and behavioral norms that are acquired through social learning, equipped to take on a life of their own independent of prosocial instincts? Do people who possess outstanding reasoning abilities really create more sensible moral norms than those who are not as well endowed intellectually, as Darwin implied?

Darwin's Theory of Ethics

Several scholars have evaluated Darwin's conception of morality and Darwin's approach to ethics. One critic, Jeffrie Murphy (1982) accused Darwin of overemphasizing social duties, neglecting individual rights, and shortchanging "the whole liberal tradition that institutions exist for individuals and not the other way around" (p. 88). I do not find this criticism valid. In the first instance, Darwin accounts for group living in terms of its biological value to individuals. Implicit in this account are the implications that individuals have the right to foster their own welfare and that these rights should be preserved. However, if individuals choose to maximize their gains by forming cooperative groups and establishing rules that specify how members of these groups should behave, they become morally obliged to follow these rules.

Other critics have reached more positive conclusions about Darwin's conception of morality. One of these critics, Robert Richards (1982), who probably has written most extensively about Darwin's work, sees a great deal of merit in Darwin's theory of ethics. Richards begins by pointing out that setting the greatest good for the greatest number as a standard of morality opens the door for the inclusion of a much broader array of forms of conduct and motivational states in the moral domain than those based on the *desire* to achieve this utilitarian effect. Even though people may not *seek* to maximize good, they may nonetheless be naturally inclined to behave in ways that produce this effect.

Richards goes on to applaud the idea implicit in Darwin's position that although "the criterion of morally approved behavior . . . will remain constant . . . the conception of what particular acts fall under the criterion will continue to change" (p. 59). When Darwin criticized other societies, he was (or at least he should have been) saying that they had not adopted as effective ways of promoting the greatest good as his society had adopted (in contrast with claiming that the means adopted by his society were the only moral ways to achieve this effect).

Richards explicates Darwin's ideas about the relation between evolved social instincts and morality by explaining that "behaviors that tended to promote the survival of the group would have been selected and become instinctive. Those moral behaviors men actually exhibited, by reason of their social instincts, in a cool hour of evaluation could also be recognized as falling under the criterion of promoting the greatest good, which, in fact, was the standard according to which social instincts were naturally selected" (p. 57).

Richards also praises Darwin's account of the role that reason plays in the derivation of principles of morality and in the refinement of moral dispositions. When humans acquired the intellectual ability to understand that the best way to foster their long-term interests was by behaving in prosocial ways that are consistent with their social instincts, they were able to derive a principle ("promote the greatest good for the greatest number") that prescribed behaviors that achieved this effect. Refining their understanding of the nature of the greatest good, the value of pursuing it, and its application to all members of the human species (and maybe to other animals as well) would, therefore, be consistent with their natural inclinations.

Finally, Richards argues that Darwin's theory of ethics solves the most challenging problem faced by ethical theories, justifying their ultimate, or cardinal, moral principles. To reach agreement about an ethical principle, the principle must ring true to most people. If, for example, I put forth the Golden Rule as a cardinal principle, and you ask me to justify it, I will end up appealing to your moral sense and to the moral sense of everyone else who evaluates the principle. According to Richards, Darwin's account "shows that the pith of every man's nature, the core by which he is constituted a social and moral being, has been created according to the same standard. Each heart must resound to the same moral cord, acting for the common good" (p. 60).

Richards's positive evaluation notwithstanding, I believe that there are several problems with Darwin's theory of ethics and his utilitarian standard of morality. To begin with, there is a significant gap between Darwin's account of the evolution of social instincts ("the pith of every man's nature") and dispositions to behave in ways that promote the greatest good for the greatest number. What Darwin explains in his account of the evolution of social instincts is the disposition to behave in ways that promote the good of *one's* community or group, not dispositions to promote the common good. There is a huge difference between evolved dispositions to behave in ways that foster the good of one's group and moral standards that prescribe fostering the welfare of groups other than one's own.

Defining the greatest good for the greatest number in terms of biological welfare, and arguing that happiness or pleasure were closely associated with biological welfare, added a new twist to the utilitarian definitions of Darwin's day. However, I see several problems with this position. To begin with, it seems unreasonable to define welfare or the general good in terms of fitness, because this would imply that people should foster the survival and reproductive success of as many people as possible, in whatever ways work best, which does not seem right. I do not see much moral goodness in overpopulating the world with humans.

Second, I question Darwin's contention that happiness and fitness covary enough to warrant equating them. Although many—perhaps even most—behaviors that increase the level of happiness in a community also increase the fitness of its members, some behaviors that increase people's happiness, such as eating to excess and masturbating, may reduce their fitness. And happiness does not seem to constitute an adequate standard for morality, because it is easy to think of behaviors that increase happiness, yet seem immoral, and of behaviors that decrease happiness, yet seem moral.

Finally, defining the morality of an act solely on the basis of the consequences it produces (the greatest good), regardless of the motives and intentions of actors, neglects an aspect of morality that most people consider very important, namely what the individuals who behaved in the good-consequence-producing ways were trying to achieve. Were these individuals trying to be fair, altruistic, or honest as an end in itself, or were they using these forms of conduct to achieve selfish goals such as exploiting others or avoiding punishment? In contrast to Darwin, who argued against defining the morality of acts in terms of the motives of actors, most people believe that to be considered moral, an individual must be guided by moral motives; he or she must *want* and *intend* to improve the welfare of others, to make fair decisions, and so on. Few, if any, people would consider a person who accidentally shot a malignant tumor out of someone he or she intended to kill moral, even though the act produced good results. Few people would consider those who help others in order to avoid punishment, to cultivate a false impression, or who mindlessly to go along with the crowd very moral.

These contentions are supported by a great deal of research. For example, studies have found that people, including children as young as three years of age, view intentional violations of moral norms as worse than accidental violations (Grueneich, 1982; Nunez & Harris, 1998; Robinson & Darley, 1995). Other studies have found that individuals who hesitate and have difficulty deciding whether to do the right thing are judged as less moral than those who form more immediate intentions, even though both end up making the same choice in the end (Tetlock et al., 2007). And neuroscientists have found that disrupting an area in the brain that affects attributions of intention (the right temporo-parietal junction) influences the kinds of moral judgments people make (Young, Camprodon, Hauser, Pascual-Leone, & Saxe, 2010). Whereas people normally make harsh moral judgments about characters in hypothetical scenarios who intend to harm others but fail to achieve this effect, people who have had their right temporo-parietal areas disrupted base their moral judgments entirely on the consequences of acts.

In conclusion, to Darwin's credit, he derived a standard of morality that accounted for the sense possessed by all people that certain forms of conduct are right and that people who practice them are good. This standard enables us to explain what the different forms of conduct and character traits that people consider moral have in common, and it enables us to decide which ones should trump others when they come into conflict. However, the particular utilitarian standard that Darwin derived does not stand up well under scrutiny.

CONCLUSIONS

Scholars become giants in their fields for a reason. I once reviewed Piaget's book, *The Moral Judgment of the Child*, which was published in 1932 (Krebs, 1979). Even though some aspects of Piaget's pioneering work have not stood up well under close scrutiny, the breadth of its reach and the depth of its insights are exceptionally impressive. As some influential developmental psychologists came to realize, contemporary psychologists such as Kohlberg who revised Piaget's early ideas about moral development steered some aspects of the field in less productive directions than those introduced by Piaget. This captures precisely my reaction to Darwin's pioneering work. Although it would be unreasonable to expect anyone to paint a perfect picture on their first attempt, Darwin proffered a broadly based sketch of the evolution of morality that offered an encompassing framework for the refinements and elaborations contributed by ensuing scholars, as I hope to demonstrate in the ensuing chapters of this book.

5

FOUNDATIONS OF A NEO-DARWINIAN APPROACH TO MORALITY

In this chapter, I lay the foundation for the approach to morality that I will develop in the remainder of this book. The first step in revising Darwin's account of the evolution of a moral sense is to review refinements in his theory of evolution that were made by later evolutionary theorists. I begin by outlining three refinements that have important implications for the evolution of morality. The first refinement stems from the recognition that genes constitute the primary unit of inheritance. It has implications for accounts of the evolution of biological forms of altruism. The second refinement stems from new developments in our understanding of the evolution of social strategies. When individuals band together to foster their interests, they inevitably experience both confluences and conflicts of interest. They experience confluences of interest because they can help each other survive and reproduce, but they also experience conflicts of interest because it is in each individual's biological interest to maximize his or her net biological gains from exchanges with others. When individuals interact with one another, they invoke strategies to maximize their gains. Modern evolutionary theorists have created models of the selection of social strategies by programming computers with a variety of contenders, then playing them off against one another in evolutionary games. The third refinement pertains to the use of evolutionary theory in deciphering the design of mental mechanisms such as those that give rise to moral judgments, moral behaviors, and moral emotions—the domain of evolutionary psychology.

Evolutionary approaches to human behavior have been accused of advocating a strong form of genetic determinism and of neglecting the role played by the environment in the determination of social behaviors. In addition, evolutionary approaches have been accused of assuming that all evolved traits are adaptive and of making up "just so" stories to account for the evolution of traits. None of these accusations is valid.

Evolutionary theorists realize that the environment plays a primary role in the evolution of traits, that genes interact with environmental factors when they design organisms, and that environmental factors play a pivotal role in the development and activation of evolved dispositions. Exactly the same genes may mediate the creation of qualitatively different physical and mental traits when they are activated or silenced by different environmental factors.

Although evolutionary theorists focus on adaptive behaviors, they recognize that evolved mechanisms are far from perfect. The evolved mechanisms that were selected in ancestral environments were simply those that produced the most optimal benefit/cost ratios, compared to other competing mechanisms. Humans and other animals behave in maladaptive ways, especially in environments that differ significantly from those in which they evolved. Although evolutionary psychologists expect evolved mental mechanisms to be designed in ways that helped early humans solve particular adaptive problems, they do not expect them to be designed in unconditional or inflexible ways. To accommodate to changing environments, they expect evolved mechanisms to operate in terms of "if–then" types of decision-making rules of thumb.

Finally, the theories advanced by evolutionary psychologists differ from just so stories because they are derived from a well-established theory; they are consistent with existing evidence, and they are subject to confirmation or disconfirmation through scientific methods.

Although there has not been a great deal of research on Darwin's account of how the moral sense evolved, the basic assumptions of his grand theory of evolution have stood the test of time. Members of sexually-reproducing species vary from one another in numerous ways. Some of these variations are genetically inherited—they are passed from parents to their offspring through the reproductive process. Because some inherited variations help individuals survive and reproduce better than other inherited variations do, they are transported to future generations in greater frequencies. Traits that increase animals' reproductive success, or their fitness, are selected.

The validity of the basic assumptions of Darwin's original theory notwithstanding, during the early 20th century, evolutionary biologists refined his theory of evolution in several significant ways. Three of these refinements, which I discuss in this chapter, have important implications for the evolution of morality. They constitute foundational assumptions of the approach I adopt. First, neo-Darwinian biologists came to understand that genes are the primary unit of inheritance, which enabled them to identify a form of selection that was not fully apparent to Darwin. Second, the dynamics of social selection became better understood. Finally, neo-Darwinian evolutionary theorists—especially evolutionary psychologists—went much further than Darwin did to derive predictions from principles of evolution about how mental mechanisms are designed. Let us consider each of these revisions in turn.

THE ROLE OF GENES

Although Darwin knew that traits can be passed on from parents to offspring, he did not understand how this process occurs. In subsequent years, biologists rediscovered Mendel's research demonstrating that biological inheritance occurs primarily through genes. Understanding that genes are immortal, that they are reshuffled during sexual reproduction, that they come in different forms that exist in different frequencies in the population, and that they play an important role in producing similarities and differences among organisms, improved theorists' understanding of how evolution works.

The human genome consists of somewhere between 20,000 and 25,000 genes, about a third of which exist in different forms, or alleles. Other animals possess exact replicas of many of the genes in the human genome, but most animals possess fewer genes than humans do, as well as some genes that are unique to their species. Chimpanzees and humans share about 95–98% of their DNA. This fact has two implications. First, we are very similar to chimpanzees genetically. Second, a small number of genes can make a huge difference in phenotypes. Theoretically, it would take only one gene to produce animals as different as mice and elephants, because one gene could control the expression of the other genes in the animals' genomes (Ridley, 2003).

As most people know, genes perform two functions: They produce replicas of themselves, and they oversee the construction of the body (including the brain, and therefore the physical and mental mechanisms it houses) by directing the synthesis of proteins. Neo-Darwinian theorists came to understand evolution in terms of the selection of genes, rather than in terms of the survival of the fittest individuals, and this opened the door for an explanation of how traits that dispose individuals to sacrifice their survival and reproductive success for the sake of other individuals who possess copies of the genes that code for biological forms of altruism could evolve.

It is difficult to understand how anyone could dispute that genes play a key role in designing human beings. Compare humans and chimpanzees, or chimpanzees and elephants. Or compare identical twins and fraternal twins. In addition to the obvious physical similarities shared by identical twins—including twins separated and reared apart at a young age—identical twins are much more similar in personality, attitudes, preferences, and intellectual abilities than are fraternal twins.[1]

SOCIAL SELECTION

Darwin's theory of evolution is commonly thought of in terms of survival of the fittest. When we think of the kinds of traits that help animals survive, those that are beneficial to solitary individuals come most easily to mind—traits such as large canine teeth, strong jaws, muscular legs, good sight, and protective shells—which enable animals to prevail over competitors "red in tooth and claw." And when we think of natural selection, we are prone to view nature, or the natural environment, as the agent of selection. However, as Darwin recognized, social traits, including those that induce animals to form groups, to fit in with their fellows, and to behave in cooperative and moral ways also may contribute to their ability to survive and reproduce, and members of groups may play an important role in the selection of these traits.

In view of the millions of years in which humans and their primate and hominin ancestors have lived in groups, we would expect modern humans to possess a set of

---

[1] Studies that have compared identical and fraternal twins reared apart have found systematically stronger correlations between traits such as religious fundamentalism (0.58–0.66 vs. 0.02–0.27), right-wing attitudes (0.62–0.69 vs. 0.00–0.21), and the "Big 5" personality factors (40% of the variance due to direct genetic factors; 10% due to shared environmental factors; 25% due to unique environmental factors; 25% measurement error).

mental mechanisms, or as Darwin called them, social instincts, that dispose them to uphold their groups and that enable them to reap the adaptive benefits of group living. As expressed by Caporael, Dawes, Orbell, and van de Kragt (1989):

> to the extent that exploiting a habitat may be more efficient as a collective rather than an individual process, not only would more successful groups prevail, *but so also would individuals that were better adapted to group living.* Because a group mediates individual contact with the habitat and the number of niches in groups is limited, fitness should be correlated with the evolution of perceptional, affective, and cognitive mechanisms that support the development and maintenance of group membership. . . . Competition within groups should have generated escalating selective pressures for [mental] mechanisms supporting increasingly complex social behavior. (p. 694)

Although Darwin understood that members of groups may contribute to the selection of moral traits, he did not explore as fully as contemporary evolutionary theorists have the role played by social selection in the evolution of morality. Social selection differs from other forms of selection because it tends to be more reciprocal than they are, with two or more individuals selecting traits in each other. The way in which individuals treat others affects not only the survival and reproductive success of recipients (and therefore the traits that evolve through the recipients), it also affects the survival and reproductive success of the actors (and therefore the traits that evolve through them). For example, individuals who are disposed to cooperate with cooperators not only contribute to the welfare of those they help, they also contribute to their own welfare by preserving and interacting with those who end up helping them in return.

The Significance of Conflicts of Interest, Social Dilemmas, and Strategic Interactions in the Evolution of Morality

In addition to cooperating with members of their groups to foster their common biological interests, individuals compete against members of their groups to foster their individual biological interests. In both cases, members of groups constitute an important aspect of individuals' environment. As expressed by the philosopher John Rawls (1999) in the opening pages of his book, *A Theory of Justice*:

> Although a society is a cooperative venture for mutual advantage, it is typically marked by a conflict as well as by an identity of interests. There is an identity of interests since social cooperation makes possible a better life for all than any would have if each were to live solely by his own efforts. There is a conflict of interests since persons are not indifferent as to how the greater benefits produced by their collaboration are distributed, for in order to pursue their ends they each prefer a larger to a lesser share. (p. 4)

The neo-Darwinian evolutionary biologist Alexander (1985) asserted that "agreement seems to be universal . . . that moral (and ethical) questions and problems arise because of conflicts of interest; I have never found an author who disagrees. If there were not conflicts of interest among people and societies it is difficult to see how concepts of right and wrong, ethics and morality, and selfishness and altruism could ever have arisen" (p. 3). Alexander went on to assert that to fully understand such conflicts, we must trace them back to their biological core. When viewed from the perspective of evolution, "the interests of every individual human (i.e., the directions of its striving) are expected to be toward ensuring the indefinite survival of its genes and their copies, whether these are resident in the individual, its descendants, or its collateral relatives." In considering conflicts of interest, it is important to "realize that an evolutionary history of genetic individuality . . . ought to yield individuals evolved to judge partial overlaps of interest with other individuals through, first, proximate mechanisms that correlated with numbers and kinds of genealogical links and, second, opportunities to achieve goals or deflect threats by cooperative efforts with others."

Conflicts of interest give rise to social dilemmas in which "the pursuit of self-interest by individuals in a group leads to less than optimal collective outcomes for everyone in the group" (Caporeal et al., 1989, p. 684). In appropriate conditions, if all members of a group do their share, every one of them can reap more optimal outcomes than he or she could by behaving in selfish ways. However, if other members of the group do their share, individuals may be able to obtain more for themselves by behaving selfishly (giving less than their share and/or taking more) than by behaving fairly or altruistically. But if everyone behaved selfishly, the system of cooperation would disintegrate, producing a tragically ironic outcome: All members of the group would end up with less than they would have gained if they had behaved cooperatively.

In *The Selfish Gene*, Dawkins (1989) offers a good example of a social dilemma in contemporary society—price fixing. If all owners of gas stations agreed to charge the same high price, all of them could get top dollar for their gas. However, if one "cheater" decided to drop the price, customers would flock to this individual's gas station, increasing his or her profit at the expense of the other, more cooperative, owners. In response, the other owners would have no choice but to lower their prices, and a gas price war would ensue. In the end, all owners would end up with less than they could have obtained if they all had adopted the same cooperative strategy, but the cheater would suffer a little less than the other owners would, because his or her losses would be compensated for by the initial gains of cheating.

Contemporary evolutionary theorists (and economists and other theorists) assume that decisions about whether to cooperate or to compete, and when, are guided by social strategies. Attending to the strategic nature of moral decision making enables evolutionary psychologists to account for aspects of morality that are overlooked by other theorists. The ways in which individuals react to the strategies that others invoke determine the extent to which the strategies pay off. It follows that members of groups play a very important role in determining which kinds of strategies evolve.

Game Theory Models of the Evolution of Social Strategies

Whereas Darwin analyzed the evolution of social instincts in terms of their contributions to the survival and reproductive success of members of groups and groups as a whole, neo-Darwinian evolutionary theorists have found it helpful to model the selection of social strategies as games in which players who possess different genes, or more exactly alleles that induce them to adopt different strategies, compete against one another to win fitness-increasing points. As in other games, the strategies that players invoke include offensive and defensive tactics; and as in other games, payoffs are determined by an interaction between the strategies that competing players invoke. Strategies that do well against one strategy may fare poorly against other strategies.

In evolutionary games, winners contribute more copies of the genes that code for their strategies than losers do, and thus more copies of their strategies, to future generations, which affects the distribution of strategies in the population. The distribution of strategies in the population may, under certain conditions (such as when individuals interact with all other members of a population, or when they interact with others randomly) affect the net benefits that the strategies produce.

Strategic interactions among genetically coded strategies may produce three kinds of outcomes: one strategy may defeat all other strategies and saturate the population; two or more strategies may become stable in the population; or strategies may fluctuate in frequency in accordance with changes in the frequency of the other strategies with which they interact. *Evolutionarily stable strategies* are strategies that, when adopted by most members of the population, cannot be beaten by any alternative strategy. Strategies that do well when competing against copies of themselves tend to evolve and become evolutionarily stable.

To illustrate how social strategies evolve, consider two simple hypothetical strategies—hawk and dove—invented by the eminent evolutionary biologist, Maynard Smith (1982). Hawk strategies are based on the decision rule, "always fight as hard as you can for a resource." Dove strategies are based on the decision rule, "Threaten those who compete against you for a resource; if they attack you, run away; if they do not attack you, engage in a posturing contest until one retreats."

It is easy to see that the genetic payoff from the strategy that an animal adopts depends on the strategy invoked by the animals with which it interacts. Individuals adopting hawk strategies do very well against individuals adopting dove strategies, but very poorly against other hawks. The dove strategy is not as vulnerable to big losses as the hawk strategy is, but it is poorly equipped to produce big gains. Although doves lose when they interact with hawks, they avoid the huge costs of engaging in mortal battles; and on average, individuals employing a dove strategy gain a little when they interact with other doves.

The question that Maynard Smith asked was whether either the hawk or dove strategy could become evolutionarily stable, and the answer he derived was "No." Consider, for illustrative purposes a population consisting entirely of doves. Clearly, a mutant hawk would fare very well, causing the proportion of hawks to increase in the population. However, as the proportion of hawks increased, hawks would (under the assumptions of Maynard Smith's model) interact increasingly frequently with other hawks, and therefore suffer greater losses than the remaining doves in the population, which would cause the proportion of hawks to decrease. The interaction between these two strategies could produce an oscillation of hawks and doves in the population or a stable ratio of hawks to doves. If hawk and dove strategies were determined by alleles at a single locus, what evolutionary biologists call a *stable polymorphism* could emerge in the population—a certain number of individuals would adopt one strategy, with an optimally complementary number of other individuals adopting the other strategy. Alternatively, all members of the population could inherit mechanisms that disposed them to behave like both hawks and doves in an optimal, but unpredictable, manner. (Predictable strategies do not fare well, because opponents are able to invoke strategies that exploit them.)

Of course, the model of social evolution illustrated by the hawk and dove strategies is a simple model that is limited in many ways. For example, it models only one type of social problem; it employs only two simple social strategies; it assumes a one-to-one relation between genes and strategies; it fails to account for environmental influences other than the strategies themselves in a population; it assumes that all hawks (and all doves) are equal and that interactions between these strategies always produce the same outcomes. In addition, it assumes that members of groups interact randomly with one another. However, the function of this model is to illustrate the basic principles of social selection, and I think it does this well. In ensuing chapters of this book, I discuss other games, such as the Prisoner's Dilemma, Ultimatum, Dictator, and Public Goods games, and consider the results of research on the evolution of more complex social strategies in conditions that map more exactly those in which we would expect the strategies to have evolved.

Social Evolution and Ideal Moral Systems

There is an important lesson implicit in Maynard Smith's model of the evolution of social strategies. As implied by Darwin when he discussed the role of reason in the evolution of morality, if members of a group were to attempt to reach consensus on what strategy they all should adopt, they should choose a dove-like strategy. If everyone adopted a dove-like strategy and if no one adopted a hawk-like strategy, everyone in the group would be better off than if everyone adopted a hawk-like strategy. In addition, the group would be better off as a whole. Toward the end of this book, I argue that this is equivalent to constructing an ideal moral system.

However, as neo-Darwinian game theorists have demonstrated, Darwin overlooked a very significant implication of this point, namely that there is a huge obstacle to the evolution of rational, morally ideal strategies that if adopted by all, would maximize everyone's gains. In terms of the present example, if everyone in a group adopted a cooperative, dove-like strategy, each member of the group could maximize his or her gains by adopting a selfish hawk-like strategy. In the final parts of this book, I present evidence demonstrating that although humans possess the reasoning abilities necessary to figure out how they should, ideally, behave, these abilities are not usually powerful enough to override more primitive urges that induce people to adopt conditionally selfish social strategies in contexts in which these strategies paid off in ancestral environments. The intellectual ability to understand which social strategies would work best if everyone adopted them coupled with the social ability to induce people to agree to adopt such strategies is one thing; the evolved disposition to invoke these strategies in the face of temptations to behave in ways that pay off better on an individual basis is quite another thing. This difference gives rise to discrepancies between moral reasoning and moral behavior.

EVOLUTIONARY PSYCHOLOGY

Turning to the third revision of Darwin's theory relevant to morality, we enter the domain of evolutionary psychology. I think it is fair to say that as well as being the first evolutionary biologist, Darwin was the first evolutionary psychologist, because he attended to the ways in which mental mechanisms such as those that generate sympathy and impulsive helping are designed at a proximate psychological level. Building on new insights about the process of evolution, contemporary evolutionary psychologists have laid the foundation for the approach to morality that I develop in this book.

At a proximate level of analysis, evolutionary psychologists assume that genes interact with a host of epigenetic and environmental events to guide the construction of the mental mechanisms that (in interaction with a wide array of other factors) produce phenomena such as moral behaviors, moral judgments, and moral emotions. There really is not anything new or controversial in this assumption. It is shared by most, if not all, psychologists. The difference between evolutionary psychologists and other kinds of psychologists is that when evolutionary psychologists attempt to decipher the design of mental mechanisms such as those that induce people to make moral judgments and to behave in moral ways, they attend to an important feature of these mental mechanisms, namely that they are products of evolution. As discussed by Buss (2008), there are several important implications of this focus.

To begin with, in assuming that the mental mechanisms that mediate morality in contemporary humans evolved from mechanisms that were selected thousands or millions of years ago, evolutionary psychologists are attentive to the fact that other animals may possess primitive versions of these mechanisms. Investigating how these mechanisms function in other animals, especially in other primates, helps us understand how early forms of these mechanisms were designed in humans. Frans de Waal's description of precursors of empathy and morality in chimpanzees and other primates, which I review in Chapters 15 and 16, illustrates the value of this aspect of an evolutionary approach. (de Waal, 2009)

It is important to note that even though evolutionary theorists may attend to primitive forms of mental mechanisms in other animals, they do not ignore traits such as sophisticated forms of moral reasoning that are unique to humans, as illustrated in Darwin's account of the evolution of the moral sense. However, viewing such traits from an evolutionary perspective casts light on different aspects of them from those that stand out when they are viewed from other theoretical perspectives. For example, evolutionary theory leads us to expect people to evoke different forms of moral reasoning to solve different types of adaptive problems, and for moral reasoning to be susceptible to self-serving biases.

David Buss and other evolutionary psychologists have likened the mind to a carpenter's tool box, arguing that just as there is no general building tool that can be used to accomplish all the tasks necessary to build a house, there is no general mental tool equipped to accomplish all the tasks necessary to survive and to reproduce. It follows that an evolutionary approach to morality would lead one to expect the mental mechanisms that mediate moral judgments and moral behaviors to be specialized for processing information relevant to the kinds of moral problems they were designed to solve—problems such as relating to authority, resisting temptation, supporting one's friends and relatives, upholding the social order of one's group, exchanging goods and services, catching cheaters, and punishing those who transgress.

This said, evolutionary psychologists are not of one mind about how "domain-specific" and modular we should expect the mind to be. Some evolutionary psychologists, such as Tooby and Cosmides (2005), argue that we should expect the mind to be very modular. Other evolutionary theorists argue that some evolved mechanisms, such as those that regulate learning and reasoning, are designed to solve a wide range of problems in different domains. Some evolutionary theorists have suggested that general purpose mechanisms such as those that endow humans with the capacity to reason were selected in ancestral environments because such environments underwent rapid changes and presented novel adaptive problems. For example, according to Kern Reeve and Paul Sherman (2007):

> hominids spread across the world throughout an incredible diversity of habitats, then proceeded to modify their environments extensively, so there probably has been a consistent premium on our ability to project fitness consequences in novel circumstances. As a result, flexible brain "hardware" and "software" would consistently be favored by selection relative to brains that were locked repositories of adaptive actions in past environments. (p. 91)

Other evolutionary psychologists, such as H. Clark Barrett (2007), have suggested that we should expect decision-making mechanisms to be specialized for processing information in particular domains but for them to be designed in ways that enable individuals to evaluate the information they process and to make flexible decisions within the domains.

The domain-specificity issue raises important questions for accounts of morality. Do people possess a bunch of different mental mechanisms designed to process information about different kinds of moral issues, or do they possess one general-purpose mechanism such as moral reasoning that they use to process information about all moral issues? Do people derive moral judgments pertaining to their obligations to care for others from the same mental mechanisms from which they derive moral judgments about their obligations to treat others fairly, to conform to social conventions, or to punish cheaters? And to complicate matters, might particular kinds of adaptive problems activate more than one mental mechanism? Might, for example, a particular moral problem activate mechanisms that produce empathy, fear, and rational deliberation?

Evolutionary psychologists expect the inputs that activate evolved mental mechanisms to offer information about the types of adaptive problems that the mechanisms evolved to solve (Buss, 2008). It follows that we can figure out the functions of moral judgments and moral behaviors by attending to the events, or inputs, that induce people to make various types of moral judgments and to emit various types of moral behavior, as suggested in Chapter 2.

Evolutionary psychologists also expect people to process the inputs that activate the mechanisms of morality in terms of "if-then" decision rules, which leads to the expectation that the moral decision-making strategies that have evolved through social selection will be designed in conditional, flexible (if–then) ways that are attentive to the adaptive implications of the conditions in which the decisions are made. Note that the "if" in if–then sequences usually pertains to an environmental trigger.

Evolutionary psychologists expect evolved mental mechanisms to produce a variety of outputs, including physiological reactions, the activation of other mental mechanisms, and observable behavior. Most psychological approaches to morality focus on the output from one type of mechanism, such as mechanisms that mediate moral reasoning, or mechanisms that mediate social learning. Evolutionary theory leads us to search for other (often more primitive) sources of morality. Later in this book, I review research indicating that moral thoughts, feelings, and actions are mediated by a variety of hormonal, neurological, emotional, and cognitive processes—some unique to humans and others shared with other animals. In particular, I review research indicating that whereas some moral decisions stem primarily from recently evolved mental mechanisms equipped to process moral information in considered, rational ways, other moral decisions stem primarily from more primitive, automatic, emotional, and intuitive reactions.

Finally, evolutionary psychology leads us to expect the outputs from evolved mechanisms to be directed toward achieving the goals that they evolved to achieve and the purposes for which they originally were designed (which are to solve particular types of adaptive problems). It follows, as I have asserted, that one of the keys to accounting for moral judgments and moral behaviors is to identify the goals that people use these outputs of evolved mechanisms to achieve.

This ends my overview of the revisions of Darwin's theory of morality that guide the neo-Darwinian approach to morality that I develop in the remainder of this book. Neo-Darwinian approaches are commonly misunderstood. Having offered an indication of what these approaches are, it is helpful to clarify what they are not.

MISGUIDED CRITIQUES OF EVOLUTIONARY APPROACHES

Evolutionary approaches to human behavior have been subjected to some quite severe criticisms. Although it is natural to find some theoretical approaches more attractive than others, it does not seem fair to kick aside the approaches that do not appeal to you without taking the time to investigate them. Worse yet, it is destructive and antithetical to the advancement of knowledge to construct straw-men models of the approaches that you do not like and then waste everyone's time knocking these straw-men down, as some critics of evolutionary psychology have done (e.g., Lickliter & Honeycutt, 2003; Turiel, 2006; Saltzstein & Kasachkoff, 2004).

Misguided critiques of evolutionary approaches tend to be based on the following (false) accusations: (1) that evolutionary theorists make incorrect assumptions about the role genes play in the construction of mental mechanisms and the determination of behavior; (2) that evolutionary theorists assume that all evolved traits are adaptive; and (3) that the explanations that evolutionary theorists offer for the origin of phenomena constitute "just so" stories. As a way of clarifying evolutionary approaches to human behavior, let us consider each of these accusations in turn.

Genetic Determinism

In 2003, Robert Lickliter and Hunter Honeycutt published an article in one of the highest impact journals in psychology in which they asserted that evolutionary approaches "represent an unnecessarily reductionistic view of the emergence and maintenance of phenotypic traits by treating genes as causal agents with closed programs" (p. 830) and then went on to argue that to account for the effects of genes, we must attend to interactions among genes, cytoplasm, and enzymes in zygotes and fetuses. The problem is, no self-respecting evolutionary theorist treats genes as causal agents with closed programs. In addition, the types of within-cell interactions of interest to epigenetic theorists are irrelevant to the phenomena that evolutionary theorists attempt to explain. As explained by John Alcock (2001) in a book published before Lickliter and Honeycutt wrote their article:

> The genetic studies immediately relevant to sociobiology are not developmental genetics but population genetics.... Sociobiologists deal directly with the consequences of populational changes in the frequencies of the different variants (alleles) of given genes, not with the physiological means by which particular alleles shape or influence the biochemical pathways of developing individuals. The failure to distinguish between ultimate and proximate research in biology is at the heart of the unfair charge that sociobiologists are trying to establish Genes-R-Us. (pp. 42–43)

Lickliter and Honeycutt (2003) also attributed to evolutionary theorists the assumption that genes "provide the only reliable source of transgenerational inheritance of phenotypic traits and characters" and that genes are the "sole source of developmental information transmitted across generations" (p. 828). Although evolutionary theorists do believe that genes play an important role in transmitting traits and information from generation to generation, evolutionary theorists also recognize that traits and information can be transported to future generations by other processes, such as social learning. As discussed in the previous chapter, Darwin viewed "habit," or learning, as an important factor in the evolution of morality, and as I discuss in ensuing chapters of this volume, many contemporary evolutionary theorists have advanced models that feature the role of social learning in the evolution of traits through gene-cultural co-evolution.

In addition, Lickliter and Honeycutt (2003) saw fit to repeat one of the most popular accusations against evolutionary theory—that it is genetically deterministic (in the strong sense). They accused evolutionary psychologists of assuming that traits are "preformed" in genes, and of believing that these traits "unfold" in their final form at particular stages of development, without any assistance from, or modification by, environmental forces.

In a book that was, again, written before these psychologists published this critique, the eminent evolutionary psychologist David Buss (2004) characterized this accusation as "Misunderstanding 1" about evolutionary psychology, pointing out that "notions of genetic determinism—behaviors caused by genes without input or influence from the environment—are simply false. They are in no way implied by evolutionary theory" (p. 19).[2] As explained by John Alcock (2001), "the proposition that alleles present in human populations have been winnowed by natural selection" (a point that all sociobiologists do accept) differs fundamentally from the idea that "these alleles 'determine' our behavior in some preordained manner," a point that *no* biologist of any sort accepts. "In reality . . . all biologists know that every visible attribute of every organism is the product of a marvelously complex and all-pervasive interaction between genes and environment" (pp. 43–44). Alcock goes on to ask an interesting question, namely why the myth that evolutionary theorists adopt a genetically deterministic approach has prevailed in the face of "the long history of rebuttals to this caricature." His answer is, "because the genetic determinist is too convenient a straw man to be discarded" (p. 44). Other evolutionary theorists who have considered this issue have reached similar conclusions (e.g., Kurzban, 2010).

Finally, Lickliter and Honeycutt (2003) asserted that, in evolutionary theorists' obsession with genes, they pay only lip service to the environment. Nothing could be further from the truth. In an often-cited paper (again written before Lickliter and Honeycutt published their critique of evolutionary psychology), Crawford and Anderson (1989) explain why evolutionary psychology should be considered "an environmentalist discipline."

Evolutionary psychologists attribute an important role to the environment at all levels of the evolutionary process. At an ultimate level, the environment plays a key role in the natural selection of inherited traits. Indeed, the "nature" in natural selection refers to the environment. As explained by Edward Hagen and Donald Symons (2007), "organisms evolved to reproduce in a particular environment; if nothing is known about that environment, almost nothing can be said about what it takes to reproduce in it" (p. 43). Hagen and Symons argue that accounting for the evolution of traits is like deciphering the relation between keys (adaptations) and the locks they were designed to open (environmental problems). You cannot understand one without understanding the other. It follows that one of the most important challenges for understanding the evolution of morality is to identify the environmental problems that the mental mechanisms that give rise to moral judgments and behaviors evolved to solve, which as I have argued, were primarily social in nature.

Evolutionary psychologists also recognize that animals—especially humans—may play a significant role in creating their environments, and that this expands significantly the challenge of accounting for the relation between evolved characteristics and environmental forces. As explained by Kim Stereley (2007), the assumption that the adaptive problems that early humans faced guided the selection of the mental mechanisms they acquired is only half the story. The other half is that the mental mechanisms possessed by early humans induced them to interact with and reshape their environments in ways that enabled them to foster their adaptive interests. For example, it is as valid to say that already-evolved capacities in early humans induced them to hunt and gather as it is to say

---

[2] The second misunderstanding is, "If it is evolutionary, we can't change it." The third is, "Current mechanisms are optimally designed" (pp. 19–20).

that large game and the availability of fruits and nuts were responsible for the selection of hunting and gathering abilities. In a similar vein, as I explain later in this book, evolved capacities to create moral norms interacted with the moral norms that early humans created (an aspect of the social environment) to induce these early humans to behave in moral ways. This point has important implications for social evolution and gene-culture co-evolution.

Although, as discussed, evolutionary psychologists do not study the interactions between genes and other components of cells during development, they recognize that, by itself, a naked gene could not build anything. From the beginning of conception, cells contain the materials that are necessary for the synthesis of proteins. Evolutionary psychologists have likened the building of bodies and the construction of minds to the baking of a cake. Genes are the recipe. Ingredients and the heat in the oven are aspects of the environment. Just as it makes no sense to say that a recipe is more important than ingredients are to the creation of a cake, or vice versa, it makes no sense to say that genes are more important than the environment is to the creation of mental mechanisms in the brain, or vice versa.

With respect to the relation between genes and phenotypes such as observable behaviors, evolutionary theorists do not assume that genes exert direct, automatic, effects on behavior across variations in the environment. Evolutionary theorists recognize that most genes do not operate in this way because genes that design mechanisms that are equipped to accommodate to fitness-relevant variations in environments tend to fare better in the process of natural selection than those that are not able to accommodate.

Most of the traits that are relevant to morality are "facultative," which means that they can assume different forms in different environments. The environment contains triggers that regulate the genes that activate the mental mechanisms that induce people to behave in moral or immoral ways. Environmental triggers, or as social psychologists call them, situational or contextual cues, regulate the ways in which genes are expressed. In addition, humans and other animals develop mechanisms that enable them to assess conditions in their environments and decide how to allocate their time and energy. Such decisions involve trade-offs and compromises that, as I discuss throughout this book, help us account for variations in moral judgments and moral behaviors.

Finally, evolutionary theorists recognize that variations in environmental factors during critical stages of development may produce observable characteristics, or phenotypes, that differ dramatically in form in organisms with exactly the same genes. For example, variations in temperature that affect the expression of a particular gene may determine the sex of turtles and crocodiles, and variations in the social constitution of schools of fish may induce some members to undergo a sex change. In a similar vein, social experiences at various stages of children's lives may switch genes that affect moral dispositions on and off.

Adaptationism

Critics also have accused evolutionary theorists of assuming that all evolved traits are adaptations, perfectly designed to solve recurring adaptive problems, but this is not the case. To begin with, evolutionary psychologists recognize that traits can increase in frequency in a population by random changes in the distribution of genes through "genetic drift." In addition, evolutionary psychologists acknowledge that the process of natural selection can operate only on mutations and variations in structures that have already evolved. In effect, natural selection "jury-rigs" organisms by using the alleles and materials that are available to construct bodies and brains.

Evolutionary theorists also recognize that environments contain constraints that prevent natural selection from producing optimal adaptations. "All adaptations carry costs. Selection favors a mechanism when the benefits outweigh the costs relative to other designs. Thus we have a collection of evolved mechanisms that are reasonably good at solving adaptive problems efficiently but are not designed as optimally as they might be if costs were not a constraint" (Buss, 2004, p. 21). All organisms are full of imperfections, and all behaviors stem from mechanisms and strategies that involve trade-offs between costs and benefits. Natural selection does not create ideal traits, because (among other reasons) the costs of creating and maintaining them outweigh the benefits. Imperfections in the design of evolved mechanisms may induce individuals to behave in genuinely altruistic (that is to say, in biologically and genetically costly) ways.

An important issue that an evolutionary analysis of morality raises is whether the mental mechanisms that produce moral emotions, moral judgments, and moral behaviors evolved because they helped early humans solve moral problems, or whether they evolved because they helped early humans solve other kinds of adaptive problems, then were co-opted or exapted to solve problems in the moral domain. We know, for example, that although the original adaptive function of birds' wings was thermoregulation, they subsequently became "exapted" for flight. In addition, it is possible that manifestations of morality are byproducts of mechanisms that evolved for other purposes (sometimes called "spandrels" by evolutionary theorists).

It is important to note that traits that were adaptive in the environments in which they were selected may be maladaptive in current environments. Indeed, because humans can make significant changes in their environments in short periods of time, traits that were adaptive in one generation, or early in individuals' life span, may be maladaptive in the next generation, or later in their life span—a possibility that also has important implications for the evolution of altruism and morality.

Some theorists, most notably Tooby and Cosmides (1992), have asserted that we should view modern humans as "executors" of adaptations that evolved in what they call the environments of evolutionary adaptedness (EEAs), which differed from modern environments in fitness-relevant ways. These theorists argue that it is misguided to expect the strategies that contemporary humans adopt in modern environments to maximize their fitness. Other theorists disagree.

With respect to morality, sensitivity to this issue leads us to attend to the costs and benefits of behaving in moral ways. On the one hand, modern humans could inherit dispositions to behave in moral (or immoral) ways that paid off for early humans but that are maladaptive in contemporary environments. On the other hand, moral behaviors could maximize people's ultimate biological benefits in ways that are not apparent to those who do not have the insight to understand the ultimate consequences of the strategies they adopt but that are apparent to those who are enlightened enough to understand that moral strategies are better equipped than nonmoral or immoral strategies to advance their interests in the end.

Although it is clear that moral dispositions often induce people to behave in costly ways in modern environments, there are two reasons to expect moral strategies that evolved in earlier environments to pay off biologically in contemporary contexts. First, current environments are similar to ancestral environments in many essential ways. For example, as I discuss in Chapter 13, even though many people live in large cities, most people still form long-term relations with mates, create families, and interact predominantly with a relatively small group of friends and relatives. Second, mechanisms that give rise to human behavior are designed in ways that enable people to accommodate to changes in environments. As expressed by Reeve and Sherman (2007), "If genes build computers that can flexibly choose projected fitness-maximizing behavioral options that can be learned, behavioral adaptation is no longer leashed to a bygone EEA" (p. 92).

Just So Stories

Closely related to the accusation that evolutionary theorists assume that all traits are adaptive is the accusation that evolutionary theorists are prone to make up "just so" stories about how traits evolved (Gould, 1978). Accusing a theorist of making up a just so story boils down to accusing him or her of advancing a deficient theory. There are at least three differences between just so stories, or bad theories, and good theories: (1) just so stories are implausible; (2) they are advanced to account for existing phenomena after the fact; and (3) they are not refined when empirical evidence fails to support them. In contrast, good theories offer plausible accounts of existing phenomena that are consistent with the facts; they give rise to predictions that can be confirmed or disconfirmed; and they can be revised to improve their ability to account for the evidence. Inasmuch as the theories advanced by evolutionary psychologists about the functions of evolved mechanisms generate testable predictions about how these mechanisms should be designed (i.e., in ways that fulfill the functions they are hypothesized to have served in the environments in which they evolved), it is inappropriate to characterize them as just so stories.

Evolutionary accounts of social behavior such as the one I advance in this book are analogous to jigsaw puzzles. To account for a phenomenon such as morality, we need to identify the relevant pieces and put them together in a coherent way to form a recognizable picture or to tell a plausible story. Good theories are based in principles that supply guidance about how parts fit together to form a logically consistent whole. Researchers have produced thousands of pieces. Good theories put them together to form a coherent pattern. When pieces are missing, good theories offer guidance about where to look for the missing pieces and what they should look like. If we find a piece that does not fit in an existing space, we need to revise the theory to create an appropriately shaped opening, and this inevitably will entail changing other pieces as well.

CONCLUSIONS

Although the basic assumptions of Darwin's theory of evolution are well established, neo-Darwinian evolutionary theorists have refined his theory in three ways that have important implications for the evolution of morality. First, they have identified genes as the primary units of selection and explained how this enables them to solve a problem that plagued Darwin pertaining to the evolution of altruism. Second, they have refined Darwin's account of social evolution by attending to the fact that when individuals join forces to promote their welfare, they inevitably experience social dilemmas because it is in each individual's biological interest to maximize his or her net fitness gains at the expense of other members of the group. Game theorists have modeled the evolution of social strategies that individuals could invoke to resolve social dilemmas and have found that strategies that we would consider moral may evolve in conjunction with strategies that we consider immoral. Unfortunately for the evolution of morality, even though ideally moral strategies such as the one implicit in the Golden Rule may be equipped to produce the greatest gains for all members of a group and for the group as a whole, more selfish and less beneficial strategies may end up defeating them during the process of natural selection. Finally, evolutionary psychologists have used aspects of neo-Darwinian theories of evolution to generate hypotheses about how psychological mechanisms such as those that give rise to morality are designed.

Evolutionary theorists have been accused of advocating genetic determinism, assuming that all evolved traits are adaptive, and of inventing just so stories to account for the origin of traits; but none of these accusations is valid. In fact, evolutionary theorists understand that the environment plays an important role in the evolution, development, and activation of mental mechanisms and that many evolved traits are maladaptive. The theories that evolutionary psychologists advance to account for the evolution of mechanisms differ from just so stories in several ways.

Having laid the foundation for an account of the evolution of morality, it is now time to begin the process of constructing it. In the next part of this book, I review theory and research on how four forms of prosocial conduct that people usually consider moral evolved, beginning with obedience to authority, turning to self-control, then considering altruism and cooperation. Following this, I consider how the psychological mechanisms that give rise to these forms of conduct are designed, asking in particular, whether they engender psychologically altruistic and moral motives.

PART TWO

The Evolution of Primitive Prosocial Behaviors

6

THE EVOLUTION OF DEFERENCE

I launch my account of the evolution of forms of conduct that Darwin considered moral by considering the virtue he called obedience, which I interpret more broadly as the disposition to defer to authority and to obey the rules of one's group.

If the enemies of morality are selfish urges to foster one's own interests at the expense of others, then forces that constrain these urges should be morality's friends. Prominent among such forces is the desire to avoid negative consequences from others. Developmental psychologists and evolutionary theorists have suggested that a significant source of morality is the natural inclination of children and adults to show deference toward those who are able to punish them when they behave in immoral ways and to reward them when they behave in moral ways.

The evolutionary roots of deference run deep. Members of most social species are naturally disposed to form dominance and status hierarchies and dominance, subordination, and status are regulated by neurological and hormonal processes.

Dominance hierarchies and status hierarchies structure social relations in ways that instill order in groups. Well-organized, harmonious groups are able to produce more resources for their members than poorly organized, disharmonious groups are. However, there is an inevitable tension in hierarchically organized groups because higher-ranking members of groups have access to more resources than lower-ranking members do. For this reason, high-ranking members tend to have a greater investment than lower-ranking members do in preserving their groups and upholding the rules and norms that define the status quo, and lower-ranking members have more incentive to change their status within the system, to skirt the rules, and to change the social order.

Some theorists have suggested that mental mechanisms such as those that regulate perspective taking and moral reasoning evolved in the context of strategic social interactions aimed at increasing status. In support of this idea, researchers have found that status is positively correlated with social cognitive abilities such as those that enable people to solve social problems, to persuade others to adopt their ideas, to assume leadership positions, and to make a good impression on others (through deception, if necessary).

In his pioneering book *The Moral Judgment of the Child*, Jean Piaget (1932) wrote, "all morality consists in a system of rules, and the essence of morality is to be sought in the respect which the individual acquires for these rules" (p. 13). Piaget examined young children in search of the origin of respect for rules. He found that in their early years, children derive a respect for rules from feelings of respect for authority: "These . . . children harbour an almost mystical respect for rules: rules are eternal, due to the authority of parents . . . and even almighty God" (p. 61). "The obligation to speak the truth, not to steal, etc., are all so many duties which the child feels very deeply, although they do not emanate from his own mind. They are commands coming from the adult and accepted by the child. Originally, therefore, the morality of duty is essentially heteronomous. Right is to obey the will of the adult. Wrong is to have a will of one's own" (p. 195).

However, Piaget discovered, this conception of morality does not prevail throughout people's lives. When children get older and begin to interact predominantly with peers, they develop a more autonomous moral orientation based in mutual respect that induces them to define morality in terms of the rules that uphold cooperative relations among equals. Although this more autonomous sense of morality tends to grow as children develop, it does not replace their old orientation entirely: "Traces of unilateral respect and of inter-individual constraint are to be found everywhere. Equality exists in theory only" (p. 385). Piaget found that children do not abandon the idea that it is right to obey authority after they acquire a more cooperative moral orientation; they retain this idea and invoke it in appropriate contexts. As discussed in Chapter 2, respect for authority probably constitutes a universal moral norm. Obedience to authority is one of the cardinal virtues preached in hierarchically organized groups such as military units, and many people believe that respect for the authority of God and the duty to obey "His" commandments constitute the essence of morality.

There is, of course, a tension between the idea that it is right to respect authority and the idea that it is right to make autonomous moral decisions. Although it seems right to respect authority and to obey the rules and laws of one's society, the kind of unthinking, blind obedience to authority shown by Nazi underlings seems malevolent. Authorities could be corrupt, and the rules they impose could be designed to uphold their interests. On the other hand, although it seems right to think for yourself, to make your own moral decisions, to defend your rights, and to have a will of your own, it seems wrong to defy legitimate authority, to disobey the rules of your group, and to behave in nonconforming, "deviant" ways.

There is a close association between the idea that people are selfish and evil by nature and the idea that the essence of morality lies in respect for authority. Many theorists, most notably the philosopher Thomas Hobbes, have suggested that if people were not constrained by authority, they would end up in interminable, self-defeating conflicts—a war of all against all. Hobbes argued that the only way to preserve cooperative social systems that maximize benefits for members of groups is to establish authorities ("Leviathans") with the power to suppress selfish behaviors by punishing those who violate the rules. When such structures are effective, argued Hobbes, they create egoistic incentives that make it in people's interest to behave morally: People obey rules in order to avoid punishment.

There also is a close association between the idea that people are altruistic and cooperative by nature and the idea that the essence of morality lies in internally motivated, autonomous prosocial dispositions. If people are intrinsically good, then it is best to back off and let them be themselves. In this chapter, I trace the origin of respect for authority and explore its role in inducing people to obey the rules that uphold the social orders of their groups. In ensuing chapters, I review theory and research demonstrating that people also are naturally inclined to behave in socially responsible ways.

SOURCES OF DEFERENCE

Piaget (1932) traced the origin of "heteronomous" conceptions of morality to two interacting internal sources—deficiencies in the reasoning abilities of young children (especially as manifest in cognitive egocentricity and poor perspective-taking abilities) and feelings of unilateral respect "felt by the small for the great" (p. 107). "The child in the presence of his parents has the spontaneous feeling of something greater than and superior to himself. This respect has it roots deep down in certain inborn feelings and is due to a sui generic mixture of fear and affection which develops as a function of the child's relation to his adult environment . . . the adult is omniscient, omnipresent, just and good, the source both of uniformities of nature and of the laws of morality" (p. 375). Further,

> Feelings of authority and respect appear during the first two years, before language, as soon as the little creature has discovered in the big person someone like himself and yet infinitely greater than himself. The feelings compounded of sympathy and fear resulting from this situation explain why the child accepts the examples and, as soon as he has mastered language, the commands coming from his parents, and why, to the simple fact of imitation, there comes so early to be added the feeling of rules and obligations. (p. 378)

To expand, refine, and evaluate Piaget's cognitive-developmental account of the origin of respect for authority, we need to reach back further in time than early stages in the development of children and explain how this sense became "inborn." Let us, therefore, delve into the evolutionary past of our species, and of ancestors to our species as well, in search of the origin of the mechanisms that produce the "sui generic mixture of fear and affection" that gives rise to deferential dispositions.

HOW DEFERENTIAL DISPOSITIONS EVOLVE

Social dispositions evolve because they help members of groups solve social problems. Consider two members of a social species facing a prototypic adaptive problem—each wants the same resource. Each animal has three basic choices: (1) to try to take the resource for himself or herself, (2) to permit the other animal to take the resource, or (3) to share it. The outcome for each animal depends on the choice made by the other animal. If one animal chooses to relinquish the resource, the other animal can gain most by taking it for himself or herself. However, if both animals adopt a selfish, hawk-like strategy like the one discussed in the previous chapter, and attempt to obtain the resource for themselves, they will, at best, waste energy competing with one another, and at worst end up in a costly fight.

As expressed by the evolutionary psychologist David Buss (2008):

> all-out fighting in every encounter with another individual is a foolish strategy. The loser risks injury and death and so would have been better off giving in— relinquishing its territory, food, or mate—from the start. Fighting is also costly for the victor. In addition to the risk of injury from battle, victors allocate precious energetic resources, time and opportunities in battle. So both losers and winners would be better off if each could determine who would win in advance and simply declare a winner without suffering the costs of fighting. By submitting, the loser is able to walk away alive and injury free. (p. 356)

Resolving conflicts of interest by fighting is virtually always a second-choice strategy in the animal kingdom, evoked only when the stakes are very high. It is usually more adaptive for animals to resolve their conflicts by estimating the power of potential opponents and invoking such conditional strategies as, "if my opponent seems more powerful or of higher status than I am, let him or her have the resource in question; if my opponent seems less powerful or of lower status than I am, take it for myself" (see Cummins, 2005; Duntley, 2005; Lorenz, 1966). Deferential strategies enable subordinate members of groups to make the best of a bad situation and live to fight another day. Young, small, and weak members of groups may bide their time until they grow big enough and strong enough to assume a dominant position. Subordinate adults adopt strategies such as forming coalitions and sneaking food and sex to overthrow more dominant members.

Dominance Hierarchies in the Animal Kingdom

It is inefficient for animals that live in relatively stable groups to establish dominance every time they experience a conflict of interest. It is more efficient to establish who is dominant over whom and live with the outcome until something significant changes, and this is exactly what many species do. The product of this process is a dominance hierarchy. Everyone is familiar with the dominance hierarchies or "pecking orders" of hens. In addition, dominance hierarchies have been observed in species as diverse as crickets (Alexander, 1961), crayfish (Barinaga, 1996), and primates (Boehm, 2000; Cheney & Seyfarth, 1990; de Waal, 1982). In chimpanzees, "lower-ranked individuals defer, obey, show loyalty and respect, and yield preference" to higher-ranked members of their groups. Dominance and submissiveness are reinforced on an ongoing basis in groups of chimpanzees (Buss, 2008, p. 358).

Status Hierarchies in the Animal Kingdom

Although size and physical power are significant sources of dominance in all primate species, they are not the only source, and dominance hierarchies are not the most significant feature of their social structure; status hierarchies are. Status may stem from traits other than power. For example, baboons, macaques, and vervet monkeys derive status from their mother's rank (Cheney & Seyfarth, 1990). Other primates derive status from alliances. For example, among chimpanzees, "alpha males who form or already possess strong alliances with other males maintain a relatively high, stable position within the group, while those who have no alliances or weak alliances are ostracized" (Cummins, 2005, p. 685). Subordinate members of such alliances seek to ingratiate themselves to higher ranking members and to build credit by doing favors for them and assisting them in a variety of ways. In return, they receive favors, such as access to female members of their troupes. In addition, members of primate species may derive their status from the esteem in which they are held by members of their groups, which may stem from their ability to contribute to the welfare of the group. Members that are intelligent, that possess specialized knowledge, that have leadership abilities, that are socially skilled, that uphold the implicit norms of their groups, and that display a willingness to foster the interests of their groups tend to be held in high regard. In contrast to subordination enforced by power, deference evoked by prestige tends to be freely conferred.

Neurohormonal Correlates of Dominance and Subordination in Animals

Although Piaget and other developmental psychologists have attributed deference and unilateral respect for authority to deficiencies in children's cognitive abilities, there is a great deal of evidence that deferential dispositions stem from more primitive hormonal processes. Researchers have found positive correlations between status and androgen and serotonin levels in primates. For example, one study found that high-ranking members of vervet monkey groups had twice as much serotonin in their blood than their lower-ranking colleagues did, and several studies found that changes in social status produce changes in hormonal levels: "Following contests of rank, defeated males exhibit a drop in androgen [and serotonin] levels while winners' levels rise" (Cummins, 2005, p. 679.) The function of this neurohormonal system is to motivate animals to behave in fitness-increasing ways. Gaining status engenders positive emotional states that induce animals to hold their position or to try to elevate it even more. Losing status engenders negative emotional states that motivate animals to take measures to regain status or ensure their security. The emotional reactions of athletes (and their fans) supply good examples of these processes in humans.

IMPLICATIONS FOR BEHAVIORAL NORMS AND SOCIAL ORDER IN THE ANIMAL KINGDOM

That members of many species form dominance and status hierarchies that are regulated by primitive neurohormonal processes is well established, but of what relevance is this evidence to the evolution of morality? In the opinion of Denise Cummins and other evolutionary theorists, a great deal, because they believe that the essence of morality lies in obeying rules, and that hierarchical social structures are supported by implicit or explicit rules of acceptable behavior that constrain selfishness and aggression.

> In animal societies, . . . social norms are implicit yet reflected in virtually every activity, including who is allowed to sit next to, play with, share food with, groom,

or mate with whom. . . . To avoid punishment (or ostracism, which can mean death due to predation or starvation), individuals must learn what is permitted, what is forbidden, and what is obliged given their place in the hierarchy, and they must comply with these norms. . . . Individual behavior must be monitored with respect to them and violations responded to effectively. (Cummins, 2005, p. 681)

It is obvious how dominant members of groups are able to advance their interests by upholding the social orders of their groups and punishing subordinate members when they fail to conform to the norms. Though less apparent, subordinate members of groups also may benefit from upholding hierarchical social orders. To begin with, "low-ranking individuals are not simply dominated or exploited; they typically benefit from protection, advice, leadership, and intervention in disputes" (Haslam, 1997, p. 300). In addition, hierarchical social orders structure social exchanges that can benefit all members of groups. As so nicely expressed by Rebecca Flack and Frans de Waal (2000):

Inasmuch as every member [of a group] benefits from a unified, cooperative group, one expects them to care about the society they live in, and to make an effort to improve and strengthen it similar to the way the spider repairs her web, and the beaver maintains the integrity of his dam. Each and every individual has a stake in the quality of the social environment on which its survival depends. In trying to improve this quality for their own purposes, they help many of their group mates at the same time. (p. 14)

Finally, we would expect well-organized, cohesive, cooperative groups to fare better than poorly organized uncooperative groups in conflicts with other groups.

This said, it is important to acknowledge that there is an inevitable tension in hierarchical groups, because "the social stability conferred by strict social hierarchies . . . carries a cost in terms of individual freedom" (Cummins, 2005, p. 679), and because it is in the interest of low status members to elevate their status at a cost to higher status members. As a result, members of groups "continually jockey for position in the hierarchy, rendering it a dynamic form of social organization" (Buss, 2008, pp. 358–359).

An important implication of these observations is that lower-ranking members of groups should be more strongly disposed than higher-ranking members are to violate social norms, to cheat, and to engage in deceptive behaviors—in short to behave in ways that humans consider immoral. Because higher-ranking members have a greater investment in upholding the social order of their groups, they should be more strongly disposed than lower-ranking members are to suffer costs to uphold them.

Animal societies often resemble human feudal societies in that high-status individuals typically take on the role of enforcing these implicit social norms, aggressing against those who violate them and breaking up disputes between lower ranking individuals. . . . For example, high-ranking [primates] often punish violations of social norms as benign as grooming or sharing food with forbidden individuals. In fact, perceived violation of the 'social code' has been designated by many researchers as the single most common cause of aggression in primate societies. (Cummins, 2005, p. 681)

THE EVOLUTION OF DEFERENCE IN THE HUMAN SPECIES

As expressed by the primatologist, Haslam (1997), "there appear to be clear continuities between humans and nonhuman primates regarding the realization and representation of dominance" (p. 304), and by implication, deference. Deferential dispositions evolved in humans for the same reasons they evolved in other primates, and through the same evolutionary processes. Like other primates, humans form dominance hierarchies, are sensitive to status, and seek to improve their rank within groups. However, humans define status in more complex ways than other primates do; they belong to many more groups, and their groups are organized in a greater variety of ways. Although some of the groups formed by humans are dramatically hierarchical; others are more egalitarian.

One of the themes of this book is that, to understand human nature, we need to recognize that humans resemble other primates in some basic ways but differ from them in other ways. Like other primates, humans develop primitive brain structures that dispose them to behave in primitively dominant and submissive ways in contexts in which these forms of conduct paid off in ancestral environments. However, in addition, humans develop brain mechanisms that endow them with a unique capacity to engage in abstract and reflective thought and to communicate through symbolic language. The later-developing brain structures are, literally, built on top of and around the more primitive structures. Early-evolved and later-evolved brain structures communicate with each other, affecting the ways in which they function and the types of behaviors to which they give rise.

Revisiting Piaget's Model of Moral Development

Although Piaget was an astute observer of children's behavior and a brilliant theorist, viewing his observations through the lens of evolutionary theory casts them in a more informative light. Viewed through an evolutionary lens, we would expect children to inherit dominant and deferential dispositions similar to those inherited by other primates, and for these dispositions to be regulated in part by neurohormonal processes. When children experience conflicts of interest with adults who are bigger, stronger, and wiser than they are, we would expect them to feel disposed to submit to their will and to respect their authority, as emphasized by Piaget. However, we would expect there to be more to this story. Viewing deference as an adaptive strategy in social exchanges between dominant and subordinate members of groups, we also would expect smaller, weaker, and low-status children to show deference to bigger, stronger, higher-status children, and for the latter to exert dominance over the former. In addition, we would expect adults to possess both dominating and deferential dispositions, and for each type of disposition to be activated in appropriate contexts. We would, therefore, expect dominance and deference to structure social relations at all stages of people's lives, and the evidence supports this expectation.

Early in life, when children leave the family context and enter the social world of peer relations, they form dominance and status hierarchies (Strayer & Trudel, 1984). Ethological researchers have observed such hierarchies in children as young as 2 years old (Cummins, 1998; Strayer & Strayer, 1976). "In fact, social dominance is the earliest stable dimension of peer group social organization. . . . Even toddlers seem to be acutely aware of these differences in that they prefer to associate with and imitate high-status as opposed to low-status individuals" (Cummins, 2005, p. 680). Like other primates, adolescents tend to form coalitions, to rebel against authority, and to try to elevate their status within their groups.

Later in life, adults belong to many groups that contain dominance and status hierarchies (Richerson & Boyd, 2005). As dramatically demonstrated in Milgram's famous experiments, normal adults possess deferential dispositions that, when activated by powerful authorities, induce them to behave in obedient ways. Other examples of deferential and obedient behaviors can be found in military contexts and cults. As documented in the Jonestown disaster, members of cults may even be willing to commit suicide when commanded to by their leaders (Osherow, 1995). Hero worship of movie stars, rock stars, famous athletes, and other celebrities is rampant in the Western world. Religions demand deference to and supplication of powerful gods.

The Role of Primitive Emotional Reactions in the Regulation of Dominance and Deference in Humans

As expressed by Cummins (2005), "the intimate relationship between social status and neuroendocrine responses [observed in other primates] is plainly evident in modern humans. You may believe you don't think much about status, but your endocrine system shows otherwise" (p. 679). Researchers have found that, as with other primates, high ranking members of human groups have more testosterone and higher levels of serotonin in their blood than low ranking members of groups do, and that "changes in status produce large changes in hormone levels" (p. 679).

Strategic Social Interactions and the Pursuit of Status

Because increases in status are accompanied by greater access to resources and mates, it tends to be in individuals' interest to elevate their status. To accomplish this, they engage in strategic social interactions within groups. Although people may adopt uniquely human tactics—for example, working hard, saving money, getting a promotion, gaining admission to a good university, buying an expensive car, rubbing shoulders with the rich, and imitating famous members of their societies—the overriding strategies that people adopt are similar at their core to those adopted by other primates.

Cummins (2005) has argued that one of the most important determinants of status in humans and other primates is the social cognitive abilities that enable them to fare well in strategic interactions: "*Selection favors those who have social and political intelligence*" (p. 681). High status members of groups tend to be skilled at forming and sustaining coalitions, manipulating and outwitting others, exerting social influence, and learning implicit rules and social norms. Cummins presents evidence showing that dominant members of groups are better than submissive members are at decoding nonverbal cues, interpreting others' intentions, persuading others to accept their ideas, and deceiving others. "Apparently, dominant individuals have (by nature or by learning) an arsenal of methods for leading, persuading, deceiving, or otherwise influencing others" (pp. 687–688). Piaget emphasized the role that such higher-order cognitive abilities as the ability to take the perspective of others and the ability to reason play in moral development.

However, as I will discuss more fully later in this book, people also use such cognitive abilities for immoral purposes.

Upholding Status Hierarchies

As with other primates, the higher people's status, the greater their incentive to uphold the status hierarchies in their groups. High-status members of groups tend to deal with ambitious and deviant behavior by lower-status members in two main ways—opposing it by force or permitting lower-status individuals to take a little more than their status warrants. In an intriguing set of studies, investigators found that people consider it less morally reprehensible for low-status members of groups to cheat high-status members than vice versa. "High status carries an expectation of pastoral responsibility; high-status individuals are expected to monitor compliance with laws and contracts, yet show tolerance during enforcement if the miscreant is of lower status than the cheated individual" (Cummins, 2005, pp. 687–688).

DEFERENCE AND THE ORIGIN OF MORALITY

The anthropologist Christopher Boehm (2000) has traced the origin of morality to the adaptive problems created by hierarchical social orders. As I explain more fully in Chapter 14, Boehm has adduced evidence that early humans possessed innate dominance and deferential dispositions that led to the formation of hierarchical social groups, but as the human species evolved, subordinate members of such groups developed means of suppressing the dominating behavior of more powerful members of their groups, which led to the formation of more egalitarian groups governed by shared rules. Whereas Piaget focused on the tendency for children to behave in increasingly egalitarian ways as they develop, and on the effect of this change on their conceptions of morality, Boehm focused on the tendency for the human species to form increasingly egalitarian social groups as it evolved, and the role that the rules and sanctions upholding egalitarianism played in the evolution of morality.

According to Boehm (2000), the adaptive problems that gave rise to human morality stemmed from "competitive dispositions to dominance" and the social conflicts they produced (p. 97). "Morality is the human invention that addresses such problems, and it is based very heavily upon ancestral dispositions. These were the raw materials, out of which moral communities were forged" (p. 97). Boehm argues that "morality is based heavily on social pressure, punishment, and other kinds of direct social manipulation by which the hostilely aroused majority use their power over [domineering] individuals in the band" (p. 82). In Boehm's view, the most significant psychological source of morality is deference.

I think Boehm is correct in assuming that morality evolved to enable people to maximize their gains from group living, and that to accomplish this, individuals must enforce the implicit or explicit rules that uphold the social orders of their groups. I also think that social orders that uphold unequal or unfair distributions of resources engender problems within groups that members who get less than their share attempt to resolve by creating social structures that uphold more equal distributions of power. However, I would view the control of dominance as one of many manifestations of a more general tendency to prevent members of groups from advancing their interests at the expense of others.

There is an ongoing tension in even the most egalitarian groups that, I believe, has been underemphasized by evolutionary theorists such as Boehm and by developmental psychologists such as Piaget: all people are naturally inclined to want to maximize their gains in interactions with others, and to minimize their costs. To advance their interests, individuals are inclined to manipulate and pressure others to obey the rules and to make the sacrifices necessary to uphold their groups, while themselves violating the rules and shirking their duties when they can get away with it. Both Piaget and Boehm recognize that one of the reasons that people obey the rules that uphold the social orders of their groups is because they are naturally inclined to show deference to authorities and to avoid punishment from others. However, evolutionary theory leads us to expect members of groups to be more strongly inclined to catch and to punish those who cheat them and their friends and relatives than they are to catch and to punish cheating in themselves and their friends and relatives, and research has supported this expectation (Lieberman & Linke, 2007). To account fully for the evolution of morality, we must explain how early humans acquired the disposition to obey rules when no one is watching, to punish themselves when they misbehave, and to suppress their urges to dominate and to exploit others. Darwin made a good beginning on this project, which I will build on in later chapters.

CONCLUSIONS

Developmental psychologists have found that young children view morality in terms of obedience to authority. The psychological dispositions that induce children to obey authority have ancient roots. Deference to authority is regulated by essentially the same neurological and hormonal processes in humans as it is in other primates.

Dispositions to obey authority do not disappear as children get older; they play an important role in social relations among adults. Humans and other primates are naturally inclined to form dominance hierarchies and status hierarchies in which those who are relatively high in the hierarchy suppress selfish behaviors in those who are lower. Dominance and status hierarchies structure social relations among members of groups, creating social order.

Although hierarchical social orders tend to foster group-members' interests better than no social order does, there is an inevitable tension in dominance and status hier-archies, due to the costs of subordination and the benefits of domination and status. As a result, members of hierarchically organized groups engage in strategic social interac-tions aimed at increasing their social status and access to resources. Theorists have suggested that this process played an important role in the evolution of social intelli-gence and morality.

In large part, morality involves the suppression of selfishness. Throughout the ages, philosophers and social scientists have been attentive to the limitations of suppressing selfishness through external means. Developmental and evolutionary theorists have argued that externally imposed morality, reinforced by punishment, is inferior to internally directed morality based on cooperation among equals, because the latter is more balanced and stable. Although some theorists have argued that there is a natural tendency for the morality of cooperation to replace the morality of constraint, both developmentally and phylogenetically, the evidence indicates that deferential dispositions play an important role in regulating people's social behavior and influencing their conceptions of morality throughout their lives.

7

THE EVOLUTION OF SELF-CONTROL

Like other animals, humans inherit urges and desires that tempt them to do things that they believe are wrong. To behave in moral ways, people must resist these temptations. As discussed by Darwin, "self-command," referred to nowadays as self-control or self-regulation, is an important aspect of morality.

Psychological research has focused on the development of self-control in children and the cognitive processes people invoke to delay gratification and to sustain their commitments. The capacity for self-control tends to increase as people grow older. Individual differences in self-control have been found to be remarkably stable over time and to be correlated with measures of success and social adjustment. Young children who are poor at delaying gratification are more likely than those who are good at delaying gratification to develop social problems as adults.

The types of goals that people set, the ways in which they frame them, their expectations about achieving them, and the strategies they invoke to sustain effort affect their success. Studies have found that optimistic people who harbor "positive illusions" about the future and who believe in their ability to achieve goals are more likely to succeed than pessimistic people are. Although most people are able to exert internal control over their behavior, people may lose touch with their moral standards and values in strong situations, especially when they are members of an emotional crowd.

To fully understand self-control, we must attend to the adaptive functions it evolved to serve. The reason that humans and other animals are able to suppress their immediate desires in order to achieve such long-term goals as having enough food to see them through the winter and having enough friends to help them when they are in need is because these strategies are optimal in appropriate conditions. The reason that people sometimes invoke strategies that induce them to maximize their pleasure and indulge themselves at the expense of others is because these strategies paid off better in certain conditions in ancestral environments than strategies that induced them to delay gratification, to forgo immediate pleasures, and to behave in temperate ways. Contemporary evolutionary theorists view the conflicts between selfish and social instincts discussed by Darwin in terms of conflicts between adaptive strategies. The decisions that animals make about delaying gratification involve tradeoffs between the certainty of immediate rewards and the greater value of delayed rewards.

The Seven Deadly Sins stem from behavioral strategies that pay off in some contexts but not in others. The biological benefits of gluttony, wrath, lust, avarice, and sloth were probably greater in the environments in which humans evolved than they are in contemporary environments. Hunters and gatherers who conserved their energy, stored fat on their bodies, and hoarded excess resources tended to fare better than those who did not. However, these strategies may be maladaptive in modern environments in which fattening foods are easily available and in which people must work hard and persevere over long periods of time to elevate their status and achieve success.

The story of self-control in humans is a variation on the good-news, bad-news theme of this book. On the dark side, modern humans are shackled with self-indulgent, original-sin-like dispositions that paid off better in early environments than they do in modern environments. Modern humans who fail to exert self-control often pay a terrible price. On the bright side, however, the large brains inherited by modern humans endow them with means unavailable to any other animal to cope with their primitive urges in constructive, effective, and socially acceptable ways.

We all have faced temptations of the flesh and other desires that induce us to behave in ways we consider immoral. Everyone has struggled to resist the seductive enticements of gluttony, lust, envy, greed, wrath, sloth, and pride. We all have struggled to keep our commitments and to muster the willpower to do what we believe we should in the face of temptations to give up and compromise our values.

As discussed in Chapter 4, Darwin included such aspects of "self-command" as temperance and chastity among the virtues he considered moral. Aristotle considered temperance a cardinal virtue. Some philosophers of ethics view self-regulation or self-governance as the essence of morality. In their view, humans are the only animals capable of behaving in moral ways because humans are the only animals capable of evaluating their urges, inclinations, and options in terms of moral standards, figuring out which courses of action are right, carrying them out because they consider them moral, and experiencing guilt when they fail to live up to their principles of morality. However, some—perhaps even most—forms of self-control seem more appropriately characterized as prudential than as virtuous because people often are motivated to control their urges and desires in order to improve their ability to maximize morally questionable long-term gains, such as succeeding at the expense of others. To qualify as moral, the purposes that self-control serves and the goals that people use it to achieve must be moral.

Although most of the forms of conduct and character traits that people consider moral require forgoing immediate, direct, short-term rewards in order to obtain delayed, indirect, long-term rewards, I find it interesting that some people view extreme forms of self-control such as the ascetic behaviors displayed by monks, nuns, and priests as highly moral. I suspect that such attributions are products of cognitive overgeneralizations. People unconsciously infer that, because resisting the temptation to behave in greedy, gluttonous, and lustful ways are good, completely suppressing the urge to behave in these ways must be very good. Although people who exert extreme self-control seem more moral than those who fail to exert any self-control, I would side with Aristotle, who argued that to qualify as a virtue, self-control must come in moderation.

Psychologists have conducted a great deal of research on self-control. Most studies have investigated the development of self-control in children. Some have followed up children who scored high and low on such aspects of self-control as the ability to delay gratification to see how they turned out as adults. Other studies have examined individual differences in self-control, and still others have attempted to determine which cognitive and emotional processes contribute most to self-regulation. I review psychological research on self-control on its own terms and then explain how evolutionary theory can deepen our understanding of it by attending to the adaptive functions it served in ancestral environments.

THE DEVELOPMENT OF SELF-CONTROL IN CHILDREN

Children are infamous for demanding that their needs be satisfied NOW. Many studies have found that younger children have less self-control than older children do. The older and the more cognitively developed children become, the better able they are to delay gratification by, for example, resisting the temptation to take an immediately available small reward in order to obtain a larger delayed reward (Mischel, Cantor, & Feldman, 1996, p. 338).

Two of the most interesting findings that have come out of research on self-control in children pertain to the stability of individual differences across the life span and the correlation between measures of self-control in children and measures of cognitive and social competence in adults: "Seconds of preschool delay [of gratification] time [have been] found to significantly predict verbal and quantitative scores on the . . . SAT and parental ratings of competencies including ability to use and respond to reason, planful-ness, ability to handle stress, ability to delay gratification, self-control in frustrating situa-tions, and ability to concentrate without becoming distracted" (Mischel et al., 1996, p. 351). Individual differences in impulsiveness in young children have been found to relate to a variety of measures of maladjustment and antisocial behavior in adolescents and adults.

With respect to the kinds of mental mechanisms that mediate self-control, a great deal of evidence suggests that self-control is related to the development of executive functions in the brain that enable people to anticipate consequences, to construct detailed plans, to invoke effective need-fulfilling tactics, and to reflect on, and learn from, experience.

SELF-CONTROL IN ADULTS

Adults are somewhat paradoxical with respect to self-control. They usually are able to control their sexual desires, to resist the temptation to overeat, to refrain from assaulting others when they are angry, to work for long periods of time to achieve their goals, to satisfy their needs in ways that contribute to the welfare of others. However, on occasion, seemingly well-adjusted people eat and drink to excess, succumb to their sexual urges, lose their tempers, and cheat their friends and relatives, even when they end up paying dearly for it. We all make resolutions that we fail to keep. Scandals involving prominent government leaders, popular religious figures, athletes, and other celebrities frequently make the news. Studies have supported the old aphorism that the road to hell is paved with good intentions: "Experimental research on delay of gratification has demonstrated that there is only a modest correlation between choice to delay (i.e., forming the intention) to wait for the more valuable reward and effective waiting (i.e., actualizing this intention" (Mischel et al. Feldman, 1996, p. 342).

INDIVIDUAL DIFFERENCES IN SELF-CONTROL

When I think about self-control, positive and negative extremes come most easily to mind. On the one hand, I think of people who put their noses to the grindstone day after day, denying themselves immediate pleasures, showing self-discipline, and working hard to achieve success. On the other hand, I think of people who live for the moment, eat to excess, drink themselves silly, lose their tempers, and suffer from a variety of addictions. What is the source of such differences?

A great deal of research has addressed this question. In a review of research on the ability to delay gratification, Mischel et al. (1996) identify five main correlates: (1) intelligence, (2) "ego control" (3) orientation toward the future, (4) achievement motivation and aspiration, and (5) social responsibility. In contrast, "the tendency to choose to take [an] immediately available reward [has been found to be] associated with lower social and cognitive competence, impulsivity, orientation toward the present, and lower achievement orientation" (p. 338).

In large part, self-control involves setting standards for one's conduct and sustaining the commitment to live up to them. Some of the standards people set for themselves pertain to what, ideally, they aspire to accomplish (their "ideal selves"). Other standards pertain to the sense that they are morally obliged to behave in certain ways (their "ought selves"). Although people may construct their own standards, a great deal of research demonstrates that the standards most people adopt for their conduct are influenced by the social norms of their groups, the models to whom they are exposed, and the standards invoked by other people present when they make decisions. If the crowd is eating and drinking to excess, as people often do at parties, then people tend to believe that it is okay to indulge themselves also.

Studies also have found that people's awareness of their internal standards (their "self-awareness") may vary considerably across situations. In some "strong" situations, people become "deindividuated," lose awareness of their personal standards, adopt a mob or pack mentality, are susceptible to behavioral contagion, and behave in immoral ways. Although "some individuals may be characteristically prone to regulate their behavior in line with personal (or situational) standards . . . some contexts, involving particularly salient social identities and strong social norms powerfully evoke individuals' conformity to social standards, even when these are in conflict with personal attitudes, values and standards" (Mischel et al., 1996, p. 339).

Of course, there are significant differences among people in their tendency to invoke internal standards or to adopt the standards that are most salient in the situations they encounter. Some people are internally oriented and consistent; others are externally oriented and easily influenced by the demands of the contexts they encounter.

Some people stay more or less the same across situations; others change like chameleons from one social setting to another.

Examining the ways in which people who show a lot of self-control differ from people who suffer from deficits in self-control supplies a basis for understanding how people can improve their self-control. Most of the studies conducted by psychologists on these issues implicate high-order cognitive processes. Of special relevance to morality, some studies have found that self-control can be improved when people define the goals they set for themselves in ways that are relevant to their sense of self. As I discuss more fully in Chapter 19, one of the distinguishing features of moral exemplars is the importance they attach to being a moral person. In addition, people's expectations about the outcomes available through sustained effort, and their beliefs about their ability to influence their fates, especially with respect to their ability to achieve the goals they set for themselves (which has been called "self-efficacy" by Bandura, 1991), play important roles in their ability to sustain the effort necessary to achieve their goals.

Many studies have found that believing in oneself and one's ability to overcome obstacles and to achieve goals—optimism and constructive thinking—may engender an "illusion of control" that creates a self-fulfilling prophesy (see Krebs, Denton, & Higgins, 1988 for a review of the literature). "When a person encounters serious obstacles to goal attainment, positive construals of the self and a belief that one has many possibilities and options may make cognitively available alternative action plans for self-improvement and goal pursuit. . . . In turn, this creates a positive outcome focus . . . that increases task commitment even in the face of difficulties and threats to self-esteem" (Mischel et al., 1996, p. 337).

Studies also have found that people are better able to sustain their commitment to goals when they define their goals in positive, approach-oriented terms (e.g., you will be rewarded in the end if you behave morally) than when they define them in negative, avoidance-oriented terms (e.g., you will rot in hell if you succumb to temptation). In addition, studies have found that self-control is improved when people perform mental simulations of strategies designed to enable them to achieve long-term goals, when they engage in self-instruction, and when they make public commitments to achieve the goals, and when they negotiate contracts with others to achieve their goals through a "buddy system."

In summary, psychological research on self-control has focused mainly on the role of high-order cognitive abilities in the regulation of behavior. Children whose brains have not fully developed are seen as relatively weak-willed agents. As they acquire increasingly sophisticated mental abilities, they become better able to delay gratification and control their impulses. The differences in self-control among adults that researchers have identified are related to differences in cognitive abilities. None of this is inconsistent with evolutionary theory. However, when viewed from an evolutionary perspective, it becomes clear that to account fully for the development of self-control, we also must attend to the fact that many animals with very small brains are able to delay gratification for long periods of time, and to exert other forms of self-control. To understand self-control, we need to understand the biological functions that the mental mechanisms that regulate it evolved to serve and why they do not always operate effectively.

AN EVOLUTIONARY ACCOUNT OF SELF-CONTROL

Traits that relate to willpower, such as conscientiousness and ego strength, as well as traits that relate to a lack of self-control, such as impulsiveness, are highly heritable (Mischel et al., 1996). Viewed in evolutionary terms, humans and other animals inherit genes that regulate the creation of motivational systems, urges, desires, wants, and needs that dispose them to behave in ways that help them to survive and reproduce. We know that Darwin viewed these motivational systems as instincts and drew a distinction between selfish instincts such as hunger and avariciousness and social instincts such as the maternal instinct, the need for affiliation, and the need for approval. Darwin emphasized the moral implications of conflicts between selfish instincts and social instincts. Humans (and other animals) inevitably must decide whether to indulge their own needs at the expense of others or whether to suppress them or meet them in socially acceptable ways. Should I maximize my immediate pleasure by eating, drinking, or having sex to excess, by venting my spleen, or by procrastinating; or should I practice self-restraint and fulfill my needs in moderation? Humans and other animals inevitably are called on to decide whether to take a relatively small benefit immediately or whether to delay gratification in order to obtain a larger benefit. In some cases, which are well illustrated in game shows, people must decide whether to take a bird in the hand, or try for two in the bush.

In Chapter 3, I mentioned that selfish survival and reproductive strategies that induce animals to meet their immediate needs without constraint may have certain adaptive advantages. For example, eating to excess may maximize the calories available to an animal. Mating with as many animals as possible may maximize an animal's reproductive success. Carpe diem. However, I also pointed out that selfish and self-indulgent strategies are limited adaptively in a variety of ways. For example, selfish consumption strategies such as, "eat and drink as much as you can without concern for others" may end up jeopardizing the health of the animals that invoke them, because they may deplete resources that animals need in the future—including members of their groups—and because they may evoke punitive reactions from others. Both Aristotle and Darwin suggested that one of the most significant incentives to self-control is the value people attach to the approval of others, which often reaps long-term benefits. Selfish reproductive strategies such as "mate as often as possible" may not be optimal because they produce more offspring than animals are able to rear to maturity. In some conditions, individuals can improve their chances of surviving, reproducing, and propagating their genes by satisfying their needs in moderation, delaying gratification, resisting the temptation to indulge themselves, and saving for a rainy day.

Self-Control in the Animal Kingdom

Strategies that involve delaying gratification are pervasive in the animal kingdom. All animals must invest some effort to obtain resources, and many animals forgo immediate pleasures to foster their long-term personal and adaptive interests. Everyone is familiar with the hoarding behavior of squirrels. In a couple of months at the end of the summer, industrious squirrels may store more than 3000 items of food, such as acorns and pinecones, which they consume in the winter. One could say that these squirrels are poster-children for perseverance and delay of gratification. Their behavior is no evolutionary mystery: In ancestral environments, squirrels that inherited mental mechanisms that gave rise to hoarding strategies were more likely to survive and to reproduce than squirrels that did not.

Some evolved mechanisms are designed to optimize tradeoffs between the certainty of immediate rewards and the uncertainty of delayed, but potentially more fitness-increasing, rewards. Research on humans indicates that people's decisions about delaying gratification depend on the relative value they attach to immediate rewards, compared to the value they attach to delayed rewards, minus the psychological costs of waiting for the delayed rewards (Rachlin, 2002). Interestingly, people who choose to take a relatively small reward today rather than waiting for a larger reward tomorrow will choose to wait until January 31 to obtain a larger reward than they could obtain on January 30 (Ainslie, 1975; Siegel & Rachlin, 1995; Thaler & Shefrin, 2005).

What counts in evolution are the long-term consequences of choices. Most of the prosocial strategies discussed so far in this book constitute investments that necessitate delaying gratification and suffering short-term costs. For example, subordinate members of primate groups may constrain their selfish urges for years, until they gain the strength, coalitional power, or status to prevail in competitions with stronger members; and as I discuss in later chapters, people may make long-term investments in those on whom their ultimate fitness is dependent.

AN EVOLUTIONARY ACCOUNT OF THE SEVEN DEADLY SINS

The Seven Deadly Sins stem from strategies and dispositions that were adaptive to humans and other animals in the environments in which they evolved. Gluttony and sloth induce animals to optimize the balance between calories in and calories out. It is in animals' interest to reduce the amount of food they need by conserving their energy. This is why, if you observe animals in the wild—not just sloths but other animals as well—you will find them lying around, sleeping most of the time. The harder an animal must work to survive, the more food it must consume to create the fuel. Most animals are thin because the biological costs of producing excess fat outweighed the biological benefits in their ancestors. Natural selection designed humans in the same way. It is safe to assume that, like other animals, our hunter and gatherer ancestors were thin, as are contemporary hunter and gatherers and people from most third-world countries who have to work hard to make a living.

Gluttony—consuming as much food as one is able to devour in a sitting—and sloth—conserving one's energy—are good strategies for animals that must burn a large number of calories to survive and for whom food is a scare and undependable resource. In an important sense, gluttony is akin to putting money in the bank, and sloth is akin to frugality. Animals save the resources they need to survive as fat on their bodies, and they expend these resources as sparingly as possible. Many animals fatten themselves up for the winter, then hibernate ("slothfully") until resources become available in the spring. Elephant seals are a notable example of a species that stores resources as fat.

In a book titled *Mean Genes*, Burnham and Phelan (2000) sum up the points I have been making nicely in this way:

> For our ancestors . . . saving through markets and money was not an option. Successful people would ram as much as possible into their own stomachs and those of their genetic relatives. . . . In such an environment, the best way to save is, paradoxically, to consume. Rather than leave some precious energy lying around to mold or be stolen, put it in your stomach and have your body convert the food into an energy savings account. . . . As we struggle to save money, our mammalian heritage lurks in the background. We *know* we ought to put some money in the bank, but consuming just *feels* so good. (p. 19)

Avarice fits well in this pattern. In addition to storing calorie-producing fuel in their bodies as fat, animals such as squirrels may bury and hide food for a rainy day. There is a great deal of adaptive value in miserly, hoarding strategies in species that face famines as a part of their lives. As expressed by Burnham and Phelan (2000), "for our ancestors in a harsh world, greed paid off in the only currencies that matter to genes—survival and the ability to have offspring. From them, we have inherited a greediness that manifests itself today as a desire to accumulate money and possessions. So even though wealth may not relate to babies in the industrialized world, our instincts come from a time when concerns over material possessions were crucial" (p. 120).

Wrath and the aggressive behaviors to which it gives rise are adaptive strategies for animals that are relatively powerful in dominance hierarchies. The function of envy is to motivate animals to work hard to elevate their position in status hierarchies. Sexual desire, or lust, evolved to induce animals to replicate their genes through sexual reproduction.

Pride is a complex emotion that may assume at least two forms, which have been called "hubristic pride" and "authentic pride" by Tracy, Cheng, Robins, and Trzesniewski (2009). Tracy and her colleagues suggest that the general function of pride is to reinforce behaviors that evoke respect and elevate status. Hubristic pride motivates people to elevate their status by behaving in overbearing, aggressive, and dominant ways. Authentic pride motivates people to elevate their status by working hard, doing well, and contributing to their groups.

The medieval theologians who prepared the list of the Seven Deadly Sins did not consult me, but if they had, I would have suggested that they add cowardice to their list. Cowardice stems from fear, which evolved because it helped animals to survive. Members of species low on the food chain that were cautious, fearful, and quick to take flight fared better than those that were less "cowardly."

Viewing the Seven Deadly Sins from the perspective of evolution as adaptive behavioral strategies raises the question, why do we consider them immoral in humans? The most obvious answer to this question is because they dispose people to behave in ways that harm other members of their groups. In Darwin's terms, these urges induce people to violate their social instincts. It is fine to save resources, to eat, to have sex, to rest, to avoid danger, to stick up for yourself, and to feel good about your accomplishments, but it is not okay to do so in ways that jeopardize the welfare of others, especially members of your group with whom you have formed cooperative alliances. In addition, I think people consider the Seven Deadly Sins immoral for a less obvious reason. As I discuss toward the end of this chapter, in modern environments, people who indulge themselves may jeopardize their own welfare, which reduces their ability to help others and to contribute their share to their groups.

WHY HUMANS AND OTHER ANIMALS DO NOT EXHIBIT OPTIMAL LEVELS OF SELF-CONTROL

Perhaps the most important question about self-control is, why people do not possess more of it, especially when it helps them foster their long-term interests. Why do people so often fail to forgo short-term pleasures in order to obtain long-term rewards? In *Mean Genes*, Burnham and Phelan (2000) offer the following guidance: "Our brains have been designed by genetic evolution. Once we understand that design, it is no longer surprising that we experience tensions in our marriages, that our waistlines are bigger than we'd like, and that Big Macs are tastier than brown rice. To understand ourselves and our world, we need to look not to Sigmund Freud, but rather to Charles Darwin" (p. 4).

Burnham and Phelan attribute deficiencies in self-control to the mismatch between mechanisms that evolved in ancestral environments and the demands and opportunities in modern environments:

> Our world is changing at dizzying speed. A new computer is outdated by the time it is installed, and a week seems like an eternity in the Internet world. In contrast, evolution is ploddingly slow, and human genes have not changed very much in thousands of years. . . . [The] mismatch between our genes' natural world and the modern world causes many problems. . . . For example, even though wealth may not relate to babies in the industrialized world, our instincts come from a time when concerns over material possessions were crucial. (p. 120).

These writers go on to make a very important point, namely that modern environments do not just happen to contain more temptations; people intentionally or unintentionally structure modern environments in ways that enable them to exploit others' "outdated instincts" through advertising and other inducements. The carefully crafted, sinister campaigns of the tobacco industry, which engender the desire to smoke in young people by portraying smoking as an activity engaged in by high-status, popular, and "cool" people is a case in point.

IMPROVING SELF-CONTROL

In closing, let me illustrate a point I made in Chapter 5 pertaining to the false accusations that evolutionary approaches to human behavior are genetically deterministic and that evolutionary approaches are inattentive to the role that the environment plays in selecting, shaping, and activating evolved mechanisms. To understand why people sometimes succumb to temptation and sometimes exert self-control, we need to attend to the "if–then" nature of evolved mental mechanisms and the ways in which they are calibrated during development.

Burnham and Phelan (2000) offer several suggestions for "reining in our passions" and improving self-control. They begin by questioning the effectiveness of pure self-discipline approaches in which people set goals and doggedly pursue them. Burnham and Phelan argue that "some temptations are better avoided than resisted." Second, they promote the idea of using modern technology to create products that satisfy primitive desires, such as our desire for sweets, without producing the negative effects. Third, they recommend that, like Odysseus who tied himself to the mast of his ship to resist the songs of the Sirens, people should make "preemptive strikes" that reduce the probability of succumbing to temptation. For example, people could eat healthy foods before going to a banquet.

CONCLUSIONS

Self-control is an important aspect of morality. It is necessary for most moral virtues. The mental mechanisms that mediate decisions about how people satisfy their needs evolved in environments in which some short-term strategies paid off better than they do in modern environments. Therefore, in some contexts, people are naturally inclined to show less self-control than they should in order to maximize their long-term gains. Although individual differences in self-control are heritable, and although they manifest themselves in infancy and extend throughout the life span, the capacity for self-control tends to increase as people develop and can be improved by adopting a variety of cognitive strategies.

8

THE EVOLUTION OF ALTRUISM THROUGH
SEXUAL SELECTION

To account for the evolution of morality, we must solve the problem that plagued Darwin. How can dispositions to behave in ways that improve the chances of others surviving and reproducing evolve if individuals who sacrifice their interests for the sake of others fare worse biologically than individuals who promote their interests at the expense of others? Accounting for evidence of altruism has played a significant role in refinements of evolutionary theory.

Evolutionary theorists have identified four main ways in which altruism can evolve. This is good news for those who are inclined to look for the best in human nature. Not only may people be altruistic by nature, they may be naturally disposed to emit four types of altruism. In this chapter, I explain how altruistic dispositions could evolve through sexual selection. In the next chapter, I review theory and research on the evolution of altruism through kin selection, and in the ensuing chapter, I discuss group-selected forms of altruism and altruism that stems from mental mechanisms that are imperfectly designed.

Darwin paved the way for our understanding of sexually selected forms of altruism by recognizing that adaptations that affect reproduction are as, or more, important than adaptations that affect survival. Although animals may compete aggressively against members of the same sex for access to mates, they also may attempt to woo mates in more beneficent ways by demonstrating that they are willing and able to invest in these mates and their offspring. When individuals choose mates, they serve as agents of natural selection—or more precisely, agents of sexual selection.

The basic idea underlying the evolution of altruism through sexual selection is that altruistic traits that diminish animals' chances of surviving can evolve if they increase animals' reproductive success. In many species, such as our own, animals are selective when they choose mates. Although females tend to be more selective than males are, males also may discriminate among potential mates. In humans, mate selection is complicated by mutual choice.

A great deal of evidence supports the idea that humans are attracted to mates who possess altruistic traits. It is in the reproductive interest of members of both sexes to mate with individuals who are disposed to sacrifice their interests to help them and their offspring, In addition, altruistic traits signal "good genes"; they constitute costly signals that indicate that those who posses them have been strong and vital enough to survive in spite of them.

Although issues pertaining to sex are closely associated with morality in the minds of most people, psychological accounts of morality tend to skirt such issues.

Everyone has pondered the "altruism question." Are people capable of behaving in genuinely altruistic ways, or are apparent acts of altruism really selfishness in disguise? Scholars have debated this question for centuries, and I have spent a large portion of my career attempting to answer it. If I have learned anything important, it is that, like questions about morality, the altruism question has been confounded by differences in conceptions of what altruism is and how it should be defined. Just as the conclusions that laypeople and scholars draw about people's capacity for morality depend on how they define morality, the conclusions they draw about people's capacity for altruism depend on how they define altruism.

In Chapter 3, I distinguished between biological definitions of altruism based on the biological consequences of social behaviors and psychological definitions of altruism based on motives and intentions. It is now time to make some finer distinctions and acknowledge that there are several types of biological altruism.

TYPES OF BIOLOGICAL ALTRUISM

Although evolutionary theorists agree that to meet the criteria for biological altruism, animals must behave in ways that are costly to them and beneficial to recipients, theorists have reckoned costs and benefits in different ways. Some theorists have reckoned costs and benefits in terms of the probability of surviving; others have reckoned them in terms of reproductive success, and still others have reckoned them in terms of the propagation of genes. When costs and benefits are reckoned in terms of survival, behaviors that increase recipients' prospects of surviving and reduce donors' prospects of surviving qualify as altruistic. However, when costs and benefits are defined in terms of reproductive success, behaviors that reduce one's chances of surviving in order to increase one's chances of reproducing do not qualify as altruistic. And when the bar is set at an even more ultimate level, sacrificing one's reproductive success in order to help those who possess copies of one's genes fails to meet the criterion for altruism.

Faced with different criteria for biological forms of altruism, what should we do? It seems misguided to select one, reject the others, and say that behaviors that meet one's preferred criterion qualify as altruistic, whereas behaviors that meet the other criteria do not. It is less useful to decide which type of behavior should be blessed with the label than to distinguish among the behaviors that have been endowed with it. For the present purpose, it is particularly important to distinguish between the types of altruism that are relevant to morality and those that are not.

It is helpful to identify four types of biological altruism. In all four types, donors behave in ways that benefit recipients at a cost to themselves. In the first type—sexually selected altruism—donors suffer costs to their prospects of surviving that are compensated for by gains in their reproductive success. In the second type—kin-selected altruism—donors suffer direct costs to their chances of surviving and/or reproducing that are compensated for by indirect gains to the genetic success of their relatives. In the third type—group-selected altruism—individuals suffer costs to their survival and/or reproductive success that increase the success of their groups, which contain members who possess copies of the genes that dispose them to behave in altruistic ways. In the final type, which I call maladaptive altruism, individuals behave in ways that increase the probability that recipients' genes will be propagated at a cost to the propagation of the alleles that dispose them to behave in altruistic ways. For some evolutionary theorists, this is the only form of altruism that qualifies as altruistic, because it is the only form in which the genetic costs of helping others outweigh the genetic benefits—or, put another way, the only form in which animals increase the inclusive fitness of other animals at a cost to their own inclusive fitness. Maladaptive altruism can evolve in two ways: (1) when the net gains of the social strategies that sometimes induce individuals to make altruistic "mistakes" outweigh the costs of the altruistic "mistakes"; and (2) when mental mechanisms that induced individuals to behave in adaptive, genetically selfish, ways in the environments in which they evolved induce them to behave in maladaptive, genetically altruistic, ways in contemporary environments.[1] In the remainder of this chapter, I discuss sexually selected forms of altruism. In Chapter 9, I discuss kin-selected forms of altruism, and in Chapter 10 I discuss group-selected and maladaptive forms of altruism.

SEXUAL SELECTION

To understand how altruism can evolve through sexual selection, we must understand how sexual selection works. The most common way for members of sexually reproducing species to get replicas of their genes into the next generation is to mate and produce off-spring, which is the method that Darwin featured in his theory. In most species, mating is a cooperative social act in which two animals coordinate their efforts to create a vehicle that carries replicas of half of their genes and replicas of half of their mate's genes into future generations.

It is in each individual's genetic interest to mate with partners who possess the most viable complement of genes to accompany his or her own complement in the journey to the next generation. As explained by Geoffrey Miller (1998), "Random mating is stupid mating. It pays to be choosy because in a sexually reproducing species, the genetic quality of your mate will determine half the genetic quality of your offspring. Ugly, unhealthy mates yield ugly, unhealthy offspring. By forming a joint genetic venture with an attractive, high-quality mate, one's genes are much more likely to be passed on" (p. 93). And as explained by Moller (2008), "genetic benefits of . . . mate preferences may arise from the effects of 'good' genes, such as parasite resistance genes . . . or general viability genes . . .

---

[1] In Chapter 11, I discuss another type of behavior, which has been called "reciprocal altruism," that occurs when donors who suffer small costs to help others are compensated for by return benefits from those they help or from other members of their groups. As explained in a footnote in Chapter 1, I do not believe that reciprocal altruism meets the criteria for biological altruism.

genes for attractiveness of sons . . . or compatible genes that result in offspring with an optimal mix of maternal and paternal genes" (p. 20).

When individuals discriminate among potential mates, they serve as agents of selection. After Darwin published *On the Origin of Species*, in which he emphasized the role that nature plays in selecting traits that favor survival, he became increasingly attentive to the role that members of the opposite sex play in selecting traits that favor reproductive success. He labeled this form of selection sexual selection. Sexual selection is an important type of social selection.

Reproductive Strategies and Forms of Sexual Selection

Members of different species employ different kinds of strategies to propagate their genes through sexual reproduction. Members of some species—fish and insects for example— produce large numbers of offspring in which they invest very little. Members of other species, such as our own, produce a relatively small number of offspring that require a great deal of parental investment. In these species, it is especially important to select mates that possess a good complement of genes, defined as a complement that designs mechanisms that maximize the probability that the offspring who inherit them will survive and reproduce.

Darwin identified two forms of sexual selection: same-sex competition for mates (especially male–male competition for females), and opposite-sex choice (especially female choice, which is much more prevalent in the animal kingdom than male choice is). Darwin recognized that these two forms of sexual selection usually go together: When one sex is selective, it encourages competition by the other sex, either directly (e.g., by fighting for a mate) or indirectly (e.g., by locating or seducing more mates than rivals do). As pointed out by R. A. Fischer (1930), (female) choice can lead to runaway sexual selection of extreme forms of traits (such as peacocks' feathers). For example, females inherit a preference for gaudy-colored males and mate with them, producing gaudy-colored sons and daughters with a preference for gaudy colors. The preferences and gaudy signals co-evolve.

When members of the same sex compete against one another for sexual access to the opposite sex, those that possess mechanisms that enable them to win such competitions contribute more copies of their genes to succeeding generations than those that do not. Traits that we generally consider selfish, such as those associated with strength, fighting ability, and aggressiveness; traits that constitute "weapons" such as horns, claws, and large teeth; and traits that constitute "armor," such as turtles' shells, have evolved through sexual selection in species that engage in physical contests with members of their own sex for access to mates.

Mutual Choice

If there were no restrictions on animals' choice of partners, the most attractive members of groups would be very busy indeed. However, this is usually not the case, especially among humans. It accomplishes little to select the most attractive individual in your group as a mate if he or she is not interested in you. In species in which both sexes exert some choice over those with whom they mate, the challenge (i.e., the adaptive problem) is to negotiate an optimal match. In crass economic terms, each animal has a package of goods to trade, and each is motivated to get the best package in return. The value of each package is determined by the extent to which it signals that those who possess it are willing and able to improve the welfare of their mates and offspring (and, perhaps, their mates' relatives) directly or indirectly.

Mutual choice tends to produce unions of animals that possess packages worth roughly the same amount to each partner, or more exactly, packages that each partner perceives to be equal to, or of greater value than, his or her own. An interesting implication of this trend is that we would expect animals that believe that their partner's package is worth more than their own to be inclined to compensate in appropriate ways. Consistent with this expectation, researchers have found that in many bird species, the more attractive partner does less work (and tends to be more promiscuous) than the less attractive partner (Miller, 1998).

Sex Differences in Reproductive Strategies

Between the two sexes, we would expect the one that has the slower reproductive rate and the one that makes the greater investment in his or her offspring to be more choosy about the quality of his or her mates. In most mammalian species, females are more choosy than males are. Three factors may contribute to this sex difference. First, because female mammals produce significantly fewer (and larger) gametes than males do, they are able, in their lifetimes, to produce far fewer offspring than males are able to produce. For example, human males possess the ability to sire thousands and thousands of offspring (from different mates), compared to one every year or so for females (in the absence of multiple births). Second, there tend to be fewer available sexually receptive females than males in mammalian groups, because females are sexually unreceptive for some period of time after they get pregnant and give birth. And finally, females are required to invest more of their resources than males are in their offspring during and after pregnancy.

Costly Signaling

To select an ideal mate, individuals must rely on some observable characteristic, indicator, or signal. We would expect traits that signal the ability to survive and to reproduce to be high on most animals' list of preferences. After one sex develops a preference for a particular trait, it is in the interest of the other sex to display it in the least costly way—even if this entails faking it. However, it is in the interest of the choosing sex to detect false advertisements. According to costly signaling theorists, this eventually leads to the selection of costly indicators, because such indicators validly signal an animal's ability to survive and to reproduce (Zahavi & Zahavi, 1997). A paradoxical consequence of this process is that animals may end up demonstrating that they have good genes by displaying traits that constitute a burden to survival. In effect, such animals are saying, "Look at me, I am strong enough and healthy enough to survive in spite of this handicap." Individuals who can afford a large handicap must be more viable than individuals who have smaller handicapping traits. Big signalers can afford to "waste" some of their viability and still have residual viability greater than that of small signalers, and this fact renders the handicapping trait an "honest" signal of viability" (Scheyd et al., 2008, p. 5).

The most often-cited example of a costly signal is the peacock's tail. Male peacocks display their feathers to peahens, who select as mates the ones with the most attractive displays (for example, feathers with the largest number of "eyespots"). As explained by Matt Ridley (1996), "A peacock's tail is, simultaneously, a testament to naturally selected female preferences for eye-like objects, a runaway product of despotic fashion among peahens, and a handicap that reveals its possessor's condition" (pp. 161–162).

An intriguing aspect of sexual selection, which has important implications for the evolution of altruism, is that the preferences that animals inherit may be arbitrary or even maladaptive byproducts of other mechanisms, such as those that produce sensory biases. Assume, for example, that for whatever reason a species of birds inherits a preference for a particular color, maybe the color of its eggs. Then assume that some members of the species develop feathers of this color, which are attractive to the opposite sex. Through runaway sexual selection, members of this species could develop increasingly large proportions of feathers of this color: "Runaway can happen in any sensory modality. Animals' eyes respond to color and form on tails and face; ears respond to loud, complex songs by birds and whales; noses respond to intense pheromones such as musk deer scent; skin responds to grooming, foreplay and genital stimulation" (Miller, 1998, p. 98).

SEXUALLY SELECTED ALTRUISM

In species that form pair-bonds and sire offspring that need a great deal of assistance after they are born, we would expect individuals to prefer mates that possessed two kinds of traits—altruistic traits that indicate that they are *willing* to offer the kind of assistance their mates and offspring need and competence-related traits that indicate that they are *able* to provide the assistance. Thus, we would expect members of both sexes to prefer healthy, strong, vigorous, powerful, intelligent, and dominant partners that are disposed to sacrifice their personal (survival) interests over relatively long periods of time for the sake of their mates and their offspring. In animals that live in groups, we also would expect those that possessed these qualities to enjoy relatively high status, further elevating their value as mates.

There is a tension between altruistic traits that render animals willing to suffer survival costs for the sake of their mates and offspring, and traits that signal good genes that increase their offspring's chances of dominating other members of their groups. Although individuals may benefit from choosing altruistic mates, they may suffer genetically from producing altruistic offspring that are disposed to sacrifice their survival interests for the sake of others. And although individuals may benefit genetically from producing powerful and competitive offspring, they may suffer personally from choosing mates that dominate and exploit them and their offspring.

There are several ways in which animals may resolve this tension. First, as long as the mechanisms that give rise to power are designed by different sets of genes from the mechanisms that give rise to care, animals could have their cake and eat it too by selecting mates with both sets of genes—mates that are both powerful and caring. Second, females could form pair-bonds with altruistic males disposed to help them and their offspring, then engage in "extramarital" affairs with dominant males that display qualities that signal that they possess good genes. Finally, as such cost-signaling theorists as Zahavi (1995) have explained, animals may behave in altruistic ways in order to signal that they possess the kinds of good genes that make individuals powerful.

Costly helping behaviors are particularly prevalent in the animal kingdom during courtship. As explained by Miller (2007), courtship generosity in humans has:

> clear parallels to courtship feeding by animals, in which nuptial gifts are given by males to females as good-genes indicators and good-parent investments. . . . Human courtship generosity would include altruism, kindness, and sympathy to the sexual partner, to his or her children from previous relationships (step-children), and to his or her family members (in-laws). Since this sort of courtship generosity is directed at nonrelatives and is not expected to be reciprocated, it is hard to explain through kin selection or reciprocal altruism, and it qualifies as evolutionary altruism by traditional definitions. (p. 105)

Heroism also may constitute a behavioral example of costly signaling. Heroic animals that risk their lives to save members of their groups display their ability to survive in the face of threats that others are unwilling or unable to endure. In addition, because it is in the adaptive interest of members of groups to promote heroism (for example, during war in the human species), they may reward heroes in a variety of ways, especially by elevating their status, which may increase their desirability as mates. Even when humans die while performing heroic deeds, their mates and offspring may benefit, as is the case for "martyrs" in the Middle East.

False Displays

In species that seek altruistic mates, it is in the interest of suitors to put on displays that exaggerate their capacity for altruism (Alcock, 1998). However, as discussed, it also is in the interest of those doing the choosing to see through such ruses and to make accurate judgments. Although we would expect these interacting processes to lead to arms races in which actors became better and better at creating false impressions, and observers became better and better at detecting them, there is a natural constraint on the refinement of false impressions, namely that, in the end, the animals putting on the display either behave altruistically—that is to say, emit a *costly* signal—or they do not.

Sexually Selected Altruism in the Human Species

There are good reasons to believe that sexual selection exerted a strong effect on the evolution of altruism in the human species. Compared to other animals, humans produce a small number of offspring that require a great deal of assistance over a long period of time. Therefore, it is in the interest of members of both sexes to select partners with good genes who are willing and able to make the sacrifices necessary to ensure that their offspring survive and thrive. As would be expected from these constraints, humans stand out in the animal kingdom in terms of the magnitude of mutual choice in mate selection and the length of the pair bonds that they form (Geary, 2000).

Some years ago, the evolutionary theorist, Owen Lovejoy, argued that in the harsh ecological conditions in which early humans evolved, the probability of surviving was increased by forming monogamous partnerships and adopting a division of labor in which females maintained a home base and tended dependent offspring while their partners hunted and obtained provisions for their families (Lovejoy, 1981). According to Lovejoy, males selected females who were disposed to be faithful to them, and females selected males who were disposed to care for and provision them and their families. The value of altruism in males was further increased by the social status of their families. Studies have found that groups of hunter–gatherers favor the families of proficient hunters who share their bounty with others (Alvard & Nolin, 2002; Hawkes, Beliege, & Bird, 2002). In effect, partners and families of generous individuals bask in their reflected glory.

However, critics have identified several problems with Lovejoy's model (Hawkes et al., 2002; Kaplan, Gurven, & Lancaster, 2007). First, it is not clear that early humans resided in groups formed by nuclear families. Second, if early humans were monogamous, we would expect men and women to be roughly similar in size, as other species that practice monogamy are; however, as explained by Miller (1998), "our moderate size dimorphism is consistent with our species having evolved under a moderately polygynous mating system, with more intense sexual competition between males than between females" (p. 110).

Like contemporary humans, I suspect that early humans were a mixed bag. On the one hand, modern humans form pair bonds and nuclear families, and monogamy is the most prevalent type of mating system in the world. On the other hand, various forms of polygamy also are practiced in most cultures. People from virtually all cultures change partners, have extramarital affairs, and share parenting responsibilities with relatives. Miller (1998) summarizes the findings from cross-cultural research on human mating systems as follows: "Each sex probably evolved a multitude of flexible [i.e., facultative] strategies . . . [that] might depend on . . . personal attributes (e.g., age, health, attractiveness, parenting skills, social skills, and seduction skills), the state of his or her kin network and social network (e.g., number of dependable child-care helpers), and various ecological conditions (e.g., reliability and patchiness of resources, foraging costs, and dangers) and demographic conditions (e.g., operational sex ratio)" (p. 109).

Flexibility in mating strategies implies flexibility in altruistic dispositions. Humans possess the capacity to make commitments to, and show devotion toward, their mates and offspring, but they also possess the capacity to behave in more selfish ways. The decisions they end up making are affected by a variety of conditional factors.

Sex Differences in Mating Strategies

Research on mate selection in humans has tended to focus on sex differences in mating strategies that stem from the large difference in the reproductive potential of males and females and from the greater investment that females are usually required to make in their offspring. Studies have found that men are more promiscuous than women are, and men place a higher value than women do on fidelity and traits such as physical attractiveness and youth that are associated with fertility, whereas women are more choosy than men are, and women place a higher value than men do on signs of status, power, wealth, and the ability to accumulate resources (Buss, 2008). In a particularly interesting study, Graziano, Jensen-Campbell, Todd, and Finch (1997) found that women tend to be attracted to two types of men—those who are dominant and those who are caring. These investigators suggested that ecological ("if") conditions determine the relative prominence of each quality: "In harsh, hostile environments, women's usually strong preference for an agreeable partner may be overcome by the need for a dominant partner. In more hospitable ecologies, the pattern may be reversed" (p. 163). Interestingly, these investigators also found that women are less conscious of their preference for dominant men than they are for their preference for caring men.

Although sex differences in mating strategies have captured a great deal of attention, I believe that another set of findings from research on mate preferences is as, or more, important than the findings on sex differences—especially for accounts of the evolution of morality—namely that members of both sexes place a very high value on altruistic and moral traits in long-term partners (Buss, 2008). Men and women display strong preferences for mates who are kind, empathic, loving, forgiving, trustworthy, nice, agreeable, honest, and heroic (Miller, 2007); and members of both sexes are repelled by selfish, unloving, untrustworthy, disagreeable, dishonest, and cowardly partners. Moral traits signal good mental health, which in turn signals good genes; and immoral traits signal poor mental health and bad genes (i.e., genotypes with a high mutation load).

In summary, there are compelling reasons to believe that altruistic traits evolved through sexual selection in the human species. Whom would you prefer as a mate: a selfish partner disposed to foster his or her survival at your expense, or an altruistic partner willing to sacrifice his or her interests to help you and your offspring? Inasmuch as early humans discriminated in favor of mates who displayed biologically altruistic traits and against mates who displayed biologically selfish traits, they would have contributed to the selection of the former. Although dispositions to invest in one's mate and offspring are particularly attractive to members of the opposite sex, more broadly based altruistic dispositions also could have evolved through sexual selection because such dispositions signal good genes and increase individuals' status within groups, which in turn increases their access to resources and mates. This said, we also would expect mechanisms designed through sexual selection to dispose individuals to behave in biologically altruistic ways only in conditions in which such behaviors were necessary to foster early humans' reproductive success. For example, we would expect individuals to be more strongly inclined to sacrifice their personal interests for the sake of potential mates during courtship than after they have mated.

Sex and Morality

Before closing this discussion of sexual selection, it is worth noting that mating—or "having sex"—gives rise to a suite of moral issues in the human species that are ignored in most psychological and philosophical accounts of morality. To begin with, sexual behavior is guided by customs that prescribe when people may have sex (for example, when they are of age, when they are in private, when they are married), how they may have sex (for example, by engaging in sexual intercourse, not masturbation or sodomy), and with whom (for example, with their spouses, but not with other animals, children, other people's spouses, or those who do not consent). Although the specifics of such customs may vary considerably across and within cultures, mating behavior is governed by implicit or explicit standards in all groups. Accounts of morality that focus on rules and norms regulating the acquisition of resources relevant to survival are incomplete. Morality also pertains to rules and norms relevant to reproduction.

Second, as discussed, it is in individuals' interest to exaggerate and fake the traits that members of the opposite sex find attractive. Therefore, we would expect people to be disposed to behave in deceptive ways in the mating game. Finally, mating and rearing offspring give rise to social dilemmas. Two partners who coordinate their efforts cooperatively can increase their inclusive fitness more than two partners who selfishly seek to maximize their gains at each other's expense. However, if one partner behaves fairly or altruistically and fulfills her or his commitments to the other partner and their offspring, the other partner may be able to maximize his or her gains by cheating.

CONCLUSIONS

Biological forms of altruism can evolve in several ways, one of which is through sexual selection. It is in the genetic interest of members of sexually reproducing species that need assistance to survive and to rear their offspring to select mates that not only possess "good genes" but also that signal that they are willing and able to suffer personal costs in order to support their family. One way of displaying good genes is to demonstrate that one is able to survive even though one possesses a biologically altruistic "handicap" because one is disposed to sacrifice one's welfare for the sake of others.

Although we might expect individuals to favor discriminating mates who are disposed to help them and their offspring but not other members of their groups, individuals who possess general altruistic dispositions may be attractive because these dispositions elevate their status and signal that they possess good genes.

Although it is in animals' interest to misrepresent their willingness and ability to treat potential mates and offspring in biologically altruistic ways by sending false signals, it is in the interest of those who are selecting mates to detect such misrepresentations. Arms races may ensue in which dispositions to behave in genuinely altruistic ways (defined as a willingness to behave in ways that are costly to one's own biological welfare in order to improve the biological welfare of one's mates and offspring) evolve.

The sexual selection of altruistic dispositions is complicated in the human species because members of both sexes serve as agents of selection. Although studies on mate choice have featured sex differences, the data indicate that members of both sexes prefer mates who possess altruistic qualities.

Prohibitions and permissions pertaining to sexual behavior are neglected by most theories of morality, even though they are prominent among the moral norms of all cultures. Evolutionary theory offers an account of such norms.

9

THE EVOLUTION OF ALTRUISM
THROUGH KIN SELECTION

We know that when Darwin was grappling with the problem that evidence of altruism presented to his theory of evolution, it occurred to him that even if altruistic and moral individuals were less likely to survive and to reproduce than their selfish compatriots were, their "tribe would still include their blood-relations" who could pass their biologically altruistic traits on to future generations. However, because Darwin did not understand that genes were the unit of inheritance, he did not fully appreciate the significance of this insight.

Our understanding of the evolution of biological forms of altruism was advanced significantly when William Hamilton attended to the implications of the idea that individuals can contribute to the evolution of traits by helping blood relatives who possess copies of the genes that code for the traits. In particular, Hamilton explained how mechanisms could evolve that were designed in terms of the decision rule, "help others when the genetic costs to you are less than the genetic benefits to recipients, discounted inversely by their degree of relatedness" (1964). Hamilton's essential insight was that there is more than one way to propagate genes. Individuals can propagate their genes directly by helping themselves, and in addition they can propagate them indirectly by helping relatives who possess copies of their genes.

Kin selection is a complex process that is widely misunderstood. Hamilton's rule does not imply that individuals will distribute their helping to others in accordance with how closely related they are; rather, it implies that individuals will favor themselves and the relatives that are most likely to share the genes that code for altruism and transmit them to future generations. Hamilton's rule also implies that individuals will be most likely to help their relatives when the costs of helping them are low and the benefits bestowed on them are high.

The proximate mechanisms that dispose animals to help their kin may be designed in different ways in different species. The evidence suggests that humans (and many other animals) rely on three cues to distinguish their kin from others—how much they look (and smell) like them, how familiar they are, and close to them they reside. Because kin recognition mechanisms are designed in imperfect ways, people may end up helping others who look and act like their kin, even though it contributes little or nothing to the propagation of their genes.

There is a great deal of evidence that humans and other animals are disposed to allocate their altruism in accordance with Hamilton's rule by, for example, sacrificing their interests for the sake of their kin, and favoring those who are most closely related to them and those with the highest reproductive potential.

The prolonged dependency of infants looms large among the adaptive problems that favored the evolution of biological and psychological forms of altruism in the human species. Not only did it increase the value of mates who possessed caring dispositions, it increased the genetic benefits of dispositions to nurture offspring (Flinn & Low, 1986; Lancaster & Lancaster, 1987; MacDonald, 1997). The theoretical significance of parental care is easy to overlook. The investments that parents make in their offspring provide clear and pervasive evidence that mental mechanisms that induce individuals to sacrifice their own chances of surviving and reproducing to increase the chances that other individuals will survive and reproduce have evolved in humans and in other species. Inasmuch as parental care qualifies as biologically altruistic, it transforms the central question about altruism from whether a capacity for biological altruism can evolve to how broadly based this capacity is. We know that mental mechanisms that dispose individuals to sacrifice their personal interests for the sake of their offspring can evolve; the question is what activates these mechanisms? Are they activated only by offspring, or can they be activated by other individuals as well? This question boils down to asking how the mental mechanisms that dispose animals to invest in their offspring are designed.

When discussing Darwin's account of the evolution of morality, I mentioned that he flirted with the idea that moral traits could evolve through a form of selection that came to be called kin selection. After asserting that tribes containing members with superior mental abilities would supplant less intelligent tribes, and that members of these tribes would produce mentally superior children, Darwin (1874) wrote: "Even if [altruistic members of mentally superior tribes] left no children, the tribe would still include their blood relations; and it has been ascertained by agriculturists that by preserving and breeding from the family of an animal, which then slaughtered was found to be valuable, the desired character has been obtained" (p. 126). However, Darwin did not understand how this occurred and therefore did not appreciate the significance of the idea.

Almost a century after Darwin published *The Descent of Man*, armed with the understanding that genes are the primary unit of selection, William Hamilton (1964) explored the implications of Darwin's idea. Hamilton's basic insight was that parental investment is most appropriately viewed as the most common form of a more general gene-propagation strategy—assisting (and suppressing selfishness toward) those with whom one shares genes by immediate common descent. Imagine a population of animals that possess a set of genes that guide the construction of mechanisms that regulate decisions about whether or not to help others. Some animals possess alleles that dispose them to help only themselves; other animals possess alleles that dispose them to help other members of their groups. The former are able to propagate their genes in only one way—by helping themselves. The latter are able to propagate their genes in two ways, by helping themselves survive and reproduce, and by helping animals that possess copies of their alleles survive and reproduce. Although the behaviors to which the latter set of genes give rise may be individually and biologically altruistic, they are genetically selfish (and therefore do not constitute any challenge to neo-Darwinian theories of evolution).

Hamilton asserted that altruism can evolve (that is to say, can pay off genetically) when the fitness costs to animals of behaving altruistically (C) are lower than the fitness benefits (B) they bestow on blood relatives, devalued inversely by their degree of relatedness (r). Degree of relatedness reflects the probability that the donor and recipient inherited the genes that code for altruism from an immediate common ancestor such as a parent or grandparent. Hamilton's rule implies that genes that code for selfish behaviors will be eliminated when the fitness costs to the relatives of the individuals possessing the genes augmented by their degree of relatedness are greater than the fitness benefits to the individuals emitting the selfish behaviors.

It is important to remember that if the conditions stipulated in Hamilton's rule are not met, mechanisms giving rise to kin-selected altruism will not evolve. In most situations the most effective way for animals to propagate their genes is to help themselves and their offspring survive and reproduce. When animals help themselves, they are 100% sure that the recipient (themselves) possesses copies of the genes that guided the development of the mental mechanisms that mediate the decision, and the benefits of the act are not devalued by degree of relatedness. When individuals help their offspring, they are directly fostering their reproductive success.

In Hamilton's formula, degree of relatedness is a discounting factor. It discounts the value of benefits in inverse proportion to degree of relatedness. The more distantly related a donor and recipient are, the greater the extent to which the benefits to the recipient are discounted, so the larger the benefits must be to outweigh the costs. Holding the costs of helping constant, animals can propagate their genes by helping a relative only if the fitness benefits they bestow on the relative supersede the amount to which the benefits are discounted by degree of relatedness. So, for example, in order for a disposition to evolve that induces animals to help their brothers rather than to help themselves, the fitness benefits to their brothers (for example in reproductive success) would have to be more than twice as great as the fitness benefits the animals would obtain by helping themselves.

Hamilton's rule pertains to the *process of evolution* or, more exactly, the process through which genes increase in frequency in the population. It prescribes the conditions under which mental mechanisms and dispositions could evolve that induce animals to behave in ways that are biologically costly to themselves (i.e., that reduce their direct fitness) but beneficial to their relatives (i.e., that increase the animals' indirect, or "inclusive" fitness). Explaining how mental mechanisms that produce these results evolved takes us a long way toward solving the problem that Darwin considered potentially "fatal" to his theory.

SOME SUBTLETIES OF KIN SELECTION

Although Hamilton's rule seems simple, the mathematics through which Hamilton derived it is complex, and it is widely misinterpreted, as is his concept of inclusive fitness.

As Kurland and Gaulin (2005) explain in an excellent review of theory and research on kin selection, some misunderstandings stem from failing to distinguish between the probability of sharing a gene with relatives and the probability of sharing it with nonrelatives in the population. Other misunderstandings stem from the failure to recognize that the only increases in indirect fitness that count in measures of inclusive fitness are those that stem directly from the added benefits that individuals bestow on their relatives through their efforts and that these benefits need to be excluded from measures of their relatives' direct fitness. Still other misunderstandings of Hamilton's rule stem from confusing kin selection theory and genetic similarity theory (Rushton, Russell, & Wells, 1984). Kin selection theory gives rise to the prediction that animals will behave in biologically altruistic ways toward their kin because kin are more likely than non-kin to share *genes that code for altruism*. In contrast, genetic similarity theory gives rise to the prediction that animals will favor those with whom they share the most genes (of all types). The two theories converge only inasmuch as phenotypic signs of genetic similarity signal degree of genealogical relatedness (the r in Hamilton's formula).

It is important to note that, at best, closeness of kinship supplies only a rough indication of whether a recipient possesses a copy of a particular gene or set of genes. For example, even if animals were perfectly able to detect how closely related they were to their brothers, sisters, nephews, nieces and so on (which they are not), they could improve their hit rates by, at best, only 50%, 25%, and so on. Clearly, it would be much more efficient to be able to detect whether or not other individuals possess copies of your altruism-coding genes than to be able to detect how closely related they are to you. The most direct and efficient way of accomplishing this would be for an altruism-coding gene to generate a phenotypic quality (such as a green beard) that signaled that an individual possessed the gene. Richard Dawkins (1989) dubbed this the "Green Beard Effect." Although such genes could, theoretically, evolve, most—but not all (Rushton, 1999)—evolutionary theorists consider it highly improbable that they have evolved.[1] It might seem that altruistic individuals could distinguish between those who do and do not possess copies of their altruism-coding genes by determining whether or not they behave altruistically. However, inasmuch as the mechanisms that produce the altruism would have had to be discriminating to evolve (that is to say, directed toward recipients who possess replicas of the genes that designed the mechanisms), we end up in a "Green Beard" problem.

What Hamilton's Rule Does and Does Not Imply

In view of the theoretical significance of Hamilton's rule, it is important to understand clearly what it does and does not imply about the evolution of altruism. Hamilton's rule outlines the conditions under which helping relatives pays off better genetically than helping oneself. For example, on Hamilton's rule, genes that code for altruism could

---

[1] One reason is because if one allele is able to achieve this effect, then other alleles also should be able to, which would result in a tug of war among genes. See Kurland and Gaulin (2005) and Rushton (1999).

evolve if the indirect genetic benefits that animals reap by helping a full sibling are more than twice as great as the (direct) genetic costs to themselves of helping the sibling, or if the indirect benefits of helping a cousin are more than four times as great as the direct genetic costs, and so on. This rule also implies that genes that code for altruism could evolve if the net benefits of altruistic acts to more than one relative outweigh the costs to the altruist: "If an individual dies in order to save ten close relatives, one copy of the kin-altruism gene may be lost, but a larger number of copies of the same gene is saved" (Dawkins, 1989, p. 90).

Although Hamilton's rule prescribes that, all else equal, the more highly related animals are to the recipients of their assistance, the more likely it will be that genes that code for altruism will be selected, it does not lead us to expect animals to distribute their altruism in proportion to the degree of relatedness of recipients—for example, helping sisters 50% of the time, cousins 25% of the time, and so on. It implies that if animals were repeatedly faced with decisions about whether, for example, to help their sisters or their cousins, (all else equal), they would always help their sisters.

But all else is often not equal, and on Hamilton's rule, animals should be evolved to favor relatives that are best equipped to propagate replicas of their genes. Animals that sacrificed their own interests to help a relative that was on the verge of death would contribute little or nothing to the propagation of copies of the genes coding for the helping behaviors no matter how high their degree of relatedness. It follows that on Hamilton's rule we could expect animals to be more strongly inclined to help distant blood relatives with high reproductive potential than to help closer relatives with low reproductive potential, because the genetic benefits would be greater for the former than for the latter. In addition, we would not expect animals to be equally inclined to help all their brothers and sisters (or offspring), or for grandchildren to be as likely to help their grandparents as vice versa. An unfortunate implication of this process, which exerts significant constraints on the evolution of morality, is that animals may be disposed to favor relatives who possess qualities such as high status, dominance, and interpersonal attractiveness that correlate with reproductive success.

With respect to costs and benefits, Hamilton's rule implies that altruistic dispositions should be activated when animals are able to bestow relatively large benefits on their relatives at relatively low costs to themselves (with costs and benefits defined in terms of the probability of surviving and reproducing). Animals might, for example, be able to save the life of a relative or group of relatives (a huge benefit to the relatives) by warning them of danger, at virtually no cost to themselves. Old and infirm animals that are not able to benefit themselves reproductively can maximize their chances of propagating their genes by helping younger and healthier relatives. Indeed, the only gene-propagating strategy available to animals that are unable to bear additional offspring is to help others who possess copies of their genes.

Theoretical Possibilities versus Empirical Realities

Explaining how mechanisms that induce animals to behave altruistically could evolve does not equate to establishing that such mechanisms have evolved in any given species. For such mechanisms to evolve, the necessary mutations would have had to have occurred, and the species would have had to have lived in environments that enabled them to meet the conditions of Hamilton's rule. We would expect altruistic dispositions to evolve in animals that form groups of closely related individuals and live in conditions that enable them to bestow large fitness benefits on their relatives at little cost to themselves, but we would not expect such dispositions to evolve in animals that do not meet these conditions.

THE DESIGN OF MECHANISMS THAT DISPOSE ANIMALS TO HELP KIN

Hamilton's rule pertains to the ultimate effects of helping behaviors, not to the proximate means of achieving these effects. It offers an account of the genetic consequences of decisions about whether or not to help others; it does not specify how animals derive such decisions. Members of different species could, and undoubtedly do, make these decisions in different ways. To determine how animals derive decisions about helping kin, we must decipher the ways in which these mechanisms are designed.

The most obvious way for the mental mechanisms that dispose animals to behave in ways that meet the conditions in Hamilton's rule to be designed would be in terms of an algorithm corresponding to Hamilton's formula. Faced with someone in need of help, animals could calculate the fitness costs to them and the fitness benefits to the recipient, determine how closely related they were to the recipient, devalue the benefits accordingly, weigh the costs against the devalued benefits, and derive a decision. Although animals might behave as though they perform such calculations, and although their decisions might correspond to the products of such calculations, it is highly improbable that the mental mechanisms that mediated the evolution of kin-selected altruism were designed in this way in any species. Most animals do not possess the mental abilities necessary to perform such calculations, and even if they did, they do not have access to the information necessary to make a decision. Consider for example animals' ability to determine how highly related they are to others (the r factor in Hamilton's formula).

Reckoning Relatedness

If the most morally significant question about the evolution of altruism through kin selection pertains to the breadth of others able to activate kin-selected altruistic dispositions, it becomes critically important to understand how humans and other animals determine how closely related they are to those in need of help and how precisely kin recognition mechanisms are designed. The evidence does not indicate that animals are able to determine degree of relatedness directly or accurately. Rather, the evidence indicates that animals base their decisions about whom to help on phenotypic cues that are roughly associated with kinship—attributes that tend to be more characteristic of kin than they are of non-kin, and attributes that close relatives tend to possess in greater degree than distant relatives do. Animal researchers have found that the three most prominent "kin recognition" cues are proximity, familiarity, and phenotypic similarity (Burnstein, 2005).

Proximity. Animals that are born in litters and remain in family groups for relatively long periods of time end up living in close proximity to their relatives. In some species, animals that leave their families to form families of their own also reside close to their relatives. In species such as these—probablly including early humans—individuals could end up meeting the conditions in Hamilton's formula by directing their altruism toward those who live close to them. This could occur naturally without any ability to detect degree of relatedness if, for example, the probability of interacting with particular members of one's group were highly correlated with their degree of relatedness.

Familiarity. Proximity is highly correlated with familiarity. Animals that live in close proximity become familiar with one another. Familiarity seems to play an important role in kin recognition among humans. Studies have found that infants quickly acquire the ability to distinguish their mothers from other mothers shortly after birth on the basis of familiarity with their voices, odors, and physical appearance. Mothers also make similar discriminations with respect to their infants (Bjorklund & Pellegrini, 2002). There is a great deal of evidence that familiarity increases interpersonal attraction (Zajonc, 1968), which in turn is associated with altruism. (The evidence also indicates that when it comes to choosing sexual partners, humans discriminate against those with whom they were reared—a phenomenon called the Westermarck effect. Divorce rates and infertility rates are anomalously high among partners who were reared together in the same family.) Note that familiarity is acquired through experience. Humans and other animals seem to be exceptionally good at remembering those which whom they have interacted (Burnstein, 2005).

Phenotype matching. Humans and other animals also appear to distinguish between kin and non-kin on the basis of a process called "phenotype matching." They compare qualities possessed by others with cognitive representations or memory codes of qualities they (or their parents) possess, and favor the people who are most like them. Some studies have found that humans and other animals base such comparisons on odor. Other studies have found that humans base such comparisons on facial similarity. Studies that have employed a technique called digital morphing have produced particularly intriguing results. In such studies, investigators create two types of virtual faces—faces of strangers (called "non-self morphs"), and faces that blend the faces of strangers with the features of the people charged with making decisions ("self-morphs")—and assess individuals' reactions to each type of morph. Investigators employing this method have found that people report feeling more strongly inclined to trust, to like, and to assist those whose faces are similar to theirs than those whose faces are different (DeBruine, 2002). Interestingly, the preferences of men for infants who resemble them appear to be more strongly affected by facial similarity than the comparable preferences of women, which may reflect sex differences in certainty about paternity and maternity (Platek, Burch, Panyavin, Wasserman, & Gallup, 2003).

DECISION-MAKING PROCESSES

In accounting for the evolution of altruism and other aspects of morality, it is important to recognize that humans and other mammals are not cold-blooded machines that derive decisions about whether or not help others on the basis of computer-like cost–benefit calculations like the one in Hamilton's formula. In humans and other primate species, the mental mechanisms that produce such decisions seem to run hot, or at least warm, in most contexts. When people perceive that their relatives need help, they do not perform rational cost–benefit analyses; they experience emotions such as empathy and sympathy that engender altruistic motives.

This raises an interesting possibility, namely that with respect to proximate mechanisms, degree of relatedness is important in altruistic decisions only inasmuch as it is associated with positive emotional connections between people. On this line of thought, the reason that we are strongly disposed to help our relatives is because we feel close to them and like them, perhaps because they are familiar, similar to us, and so on. Even if the evolutionary action in Hamilton's formula is in degree of relatedness, the proximate psychological action could be in the positive emotions people feel toward others.

Not surprisingly, many studies have found that people are more inclined to help those they like and love than those they do not like and love (Korchmaros & Kenny, 2001). However, there seems to be something more than positive feelings involved in the disposition to help kin. If dispositions to help one's kin stemmed only from close emotional bonds, we would not expect there to be any effect for kinship after we control for emotional closeness. Put another way, if all that mattered were feelings of closeness, or love, or empathy, then we would not expect people to behave differently toward friends they love than they do toward relatives they love, or toward close and distant relatives to whom they feel equally close. However, there is evidence that they do. For example, in one study, neither the amount of affection people felt for those for whom they were willing to suffer pain (in order to make money for them) nor the amount of contact they had with the recipients modified the preferences they showed for their kin (Fieldman, Plotkin, Dunbar, Robertson, & McFarland: described in Barrett, Dunbar, & Lycett, 2002). Other studies have found that even after holding factors such as emotional closeness, empathic concern, and perceptions of similarity constant, people are prone to allocate their altruism in relation to degree of relatedness (Kruger, 2003). Findings such as these do not imply that feelings toward others do not matter; they imply that they are not the whole story. As expressed by Burnstein (2005), "One obvious implication is that genetic relatedness may spontaneously prime an impulse to behave altruistically. To the extent emergencies were common in the ancestral environment . . . not bothering to check for liking or disliking might well contribute to fitness" (p. 539).

Design Precision

Returning again to the range of recipients issue, if kin-recognition mechanisms were precisely designed and if current environments were similar to ancestral environments, we would expect humans and other animals to allocate their altruism in discriminating ways, rendering it nepotistic. On the other hand, if the mechanisms were imprecisely designed and if the current environment differed in relevant ways from ancestral environments, we would expect animals to make genetically costly mistakes and for the mechanisms to "misfire," causing the animals to allocate their altruism more broadly. These issues have two significant implications for the evolution of morality. First, inasmuch as such mistakes entail behaving in ways that foster the genetic success of recipients who do not share copies of one's genes at a cost to one's own genetic success, they would qualify as genetically altruistic. Second, inasmuch as high standards of morality require individuals to allocate their altruism impartially and fairly, the less precise that kin-recognition mechanisms are (the more they "misfire"), the less discriminating they would be, disposing individuals to help broader ranges of people.

Evolutionary theorists disagree about the extent to which kin selection supplies a plausible account of the tendency for modern humans to help people other than their kin. Some theorists argue that kin recognition mechanisms that reliably signaled kinship in ancestral environments misfire in modern environments, inducing people to help those who are familiar to them, similar to them, members of their in-groups, and so on (Johnson, Stopka, & Knights, 2003; van den Berghe, 1983). Other theorists argue that contemporary humans are quite good at distinguishing between kin and non-kin and that it is implausible that the mechanisms that dispose people to help non-kin (especially strangers whom they never expect to see again) evolved through kin selection (Fehr & Gächter, 2003). Given the difficulties of reconstructing ancestral environments, the best way to settle this issue is to find out how good modern humans are at discerning how closely related they are to those they are inclined to help and whether they are more strongly inclined to help close relatives than they are to help distant relatives. Let us, therefore, consider the relevant research.

Research on Altruism Among Kin

Jeffrey Kurland, Steven Gaulin, and Eugene Burnstein have published excellent reviews of research indicating that people are strongly disposed to help their kin and that they tend to favor close kin over distant kin (see Buss, 2005). Field studies have found that members of bands and tribes favor their kin in a variety of ways, for example by extending greater amounts of assistance to them, and by sharing more resources with them than they share with other members of their groups (Hawkes, 1983; Kaplan & Hill, 1985). Studies on people from the Western world have revealed that the assets people bequeath to recipients in their wills are highly correlated with their degree of relatedness (Smith, Kish, & Crawford, 1987). Other studies have found that when individuals are asked how they would distribute money they won from a lottery, they say that they would favor recipients in terms of how closely related they are to them (Webster, 2003).

Several studies have found that people say that they would be more willing to help those to whom they are closely related than those to whom they are distantly related, especially when the costs of helping are high (e.g., in life-threatening situations) (Burnstein, Crandall, & Kitayama, 1994). And this may not be all talk. Investigators found that the amount of pain individuals are willing to suffer in order to earn money for others increases systematically with how closely related they are to them (Burnstein, 2005). In a real-life study of people trapped in burning buildings in a vacation complex in England, Sime (1983) found that vacationers were significantly more likely to stick with their relatives, risk their lives to locate them, and assist them than they were to help their friends.

In an interesting study on polygynous Mormons, Jankowiak, and Diderich (2000) found that members of the same family favored their full siblings over their half siblings in a variety of ways. Segal (1984) found that identical twins feel closer to one another and are more strongly disposed to help one another than fraternal twins are. In addition, a great deal of research has found that people are significantly less likely to abuse and to kill their blood relatives in family contexts than they are to abuse and to kill those with whom they do not share a blood relationship. "It now appears that living with a stepparent is the single greatest risk factor for child abuse" (Kurland & Gaulin, 2005, p. 464).

Studies also have found that people discriminate among their relatives in terms of their reproductive potential and certainty of relatedness. People with low reproductive potential are more likely to help kin with high reproductive potential than vice versa, and relatives are more likely to help kin from their mothers' side of the family than from their fathers' side of the family (Essock-Vitale & McGuire, 1985). Parents tend to grieve more after the death of offspring with high reproductive potential than after the death of offspring with low reproductive potential. Mothers, maternal aunts, and grandmothers grieve more than fathers and relatives from the fathers' side (Littlefield & Rushton, 1986).

Hamilton's rule leads us to expect the probability that an individual will help a group of people to increase in proportion to the number of relatives in the group and for individuals to be more likely to help groups containing close relatives than to help groups containing distant relatives (and to be more willing to suffer high costs). In a series of studies, Wang (2002) found that when individuals are faced with decisions about helping groups of relatives in perilous situations, they tend to identify with the group as a whole and adopt a "live or die together" type of decision rule similar to the one that the people in England seemed to have adopted during the vacation complex fire. Interestingly, in addition, participants in Wang's studies were significantly more likely to advocate guaranteeing the survival of two close relatives (but not two distant relatives) than to advocate increasing the probability that all members of six person groups containing both close and distant relatives would survive.

CONCLUSIONS

Humans are inclined to help their kin—no question about it—and, in general, they are more strongly inclined to help close kin than they are to help distant kin. It is not entirely clear, however, how broadly based these dispositions are and what activates them. People also are more strongly disposed to help those who are familiar to them and similar to them than they are to help strangers. People are more strongly disposed to help in-group members than to help out-group members. And people also are strongly disposed to help their friends and those with whom they empathize. However, as I discuss in Chapters 13 and 14, many people also are inclined to help strangers whom they never expect to see again. It is very difficult to determine whether these dispositions evolved through kin selection or whether they evolved through some other process.

10

THE EVOLUTION OF ALTRUISM THROUGH
GROUP SELECTION AND IMPERFECT DESIGN

In this chapter, I discuss the last two ways in which biological forms of altruism can evolve. I begin by revisiting Darwin's consideration of the possibility that altruism can evolve through group selection. The basic idea underlying the group selection of altruism is simple: Groups containing individuals who inherit dispositions to sacrifice their survival and reproductive interests for the sake of their groups will outcompete more selfish groups, and through this process the altruistic dispositions possessed by the good guys in the altruistic groups will be preserved and passed on to future generations. However, Darwin was aware that there is a significant problem with this idea, namely that we would expect selfish individuals within altruistic groups to fare better than their altruistic compatriots, increasing in number until they eventually replaced them all.

During the past half century, relatively few evolutionary theorists have accepted the idea that biological forms of altruism have evolved through group selection, because it is difficult to meet the conditions that would enable the selection of altruism between groups to outpace the selection of selfishness within groups. However, in recent years some prominent evolutionary theorists have advanced theoretical arguments in support of the idea that altruism can evolve through group selection, and they have adduced evidence that altruistic dispositions have evolved through this process in the human species.

Using altruistic behaviors that stem from social learning and reasoning mechanisms as examples, I close my account of the evolution of altruism by explaining how "pure" forms of evolutionary altruism—that is to say, dispositions to behave in ways that foster the biological and genetic welfare of recipients at a cost to the biological and genetic welfare of donors— can evolve through imperfections in the design of evolved mechanisms. I discuss the significance of manipulation in the evolution of altruism and point out that mental mechanisms that disposed early humans to behave in genetically selfish fitness-increasing ways in the environments in which they lived may dispose modern humans to behave in genetically altruistic fitness-reducing ways in modern environments.

As mentioned in the earlier discussion of Darwin's theory of the evolution of the moral sense, Darwin (1874) entertained the idea that moral traits could evolve through group selection. Here, in more detail, is what he wrote:

> It must not be forgotten that although a high standard of morality gives but a slight or no advantage to each individual man and his children over the other men of the same tribe, yet that an increase in the number of well-endowed men and an advancement in the standard of morality will certainly give an immense advantage to one tribe over another. A tribe including many members who, from possessing in a high degree the spirit of patriotism, fidelity, obedience, courage, and sympathy, were always ready to aid one another, and to sacrifice themselves for the common good, would be victorious over most other tribes; and this would be natural selection. At all times throughout the world, tribes have supplanted other tribes; and as morality is one important element in their success, the standard of morality and the number of well-endowed men will thus everywhere tend to rise and increase. (p. 129)

Note that Darwin did not set up the contrast between individual selection and group selection exclusively in terms of selfishness versus altruism—he set it up in terms of a high versus a low standard of morality, with the standard defined in terms of promotion of the common good. In addition, Darwin did not argue that a high standard of morality would inevitably prove biologically costly to members of groups; indeed, he allowed that it might even give them a "slight" advantage.

The idea that altruism has evolved through group selection has popular appeal because it seems plausible that groups that contain individuals who are disposed to support each other, to cooperate, and to sacrifice their individual interests to advance the interests of their groups would prevail over groups of selfish individuals in intergroup competitions. If groups containing individuals with biologically altruistic dispositions prevailed over groups containing individuals with biologically selfish dispositions, the altruistic dispositions could be selected and the selfish dispositions could become extinct.

The problem is that to evolve through group selection biologically altruistic strategies must contain a means of resolving the kinds of social dilemmas discussed in Chapter 5. Although groups containing biologically altruistic members may fare better than groups containing biologically selfish individuals, we need to consider the reproductive success of the good guys and the bad guys within the altruistic groups. Darwin (1874) recognized this problem, acknowledging that "it is extremely doubtful whether the offspring of the most sympathetic and benevolent parents, or of those which were the most faithful to their comrades, would be reared in greater number than the children of selfish and treacherous parents of the same tribe. He who was ready to sacrifice his life, as many a savage has been, rather than betray his comrades, would often leave no offspring to inherit his noble nature" (p. 103).

If selfish individuals who were genetically disposed to foster their own survival and reproductive success at the expense of more altruistic members of their groups ended up producing more offspring than the altruistic members did (i.e., if their selfish strategies were successful), the proportion of selfish individuals would increase within groups and eventually saturate them. The question is, when within-group selection for selfishness competes against between-group selection for altruism, which process ends up prevailing? Most contemporary evolutionary theorists believe that the answer is within-group selection of selfishness because they believe that selection at the level of individuals is more powerful than selection at the level of groups. However, in a book entitled "*Unto Others: The Evolution and Psychology of Unselfish Behavior*" and a series of articles, Elliott Sober and David Sloan Wilson (2000) have attempted to explain how altruistic dispositions could evolve through group selection.

Consider an example of the evolution of altruism through group selection given by D. S. Wilson, based on a study on lions. Heinsohn and Packer (1995) observed prides of lions in the wild and found that certain members consistently risked their welfare by being the first to respond to signs that another lion had invaded their territory. These researchers searched for compensatory benefits of this apparently altruistic behavior, such as greater access to resources, high rank in the dominance hierarchy, a disproportionately high reproductive rate, and so on, but could not find any. After analyzing all their data, Heinsohn and Packer reached the following conclusion: "Female lions share a common resource, the territory; but only a proportion of females pay the full costs of territorial defense. If too few females accept the responsibilities of leadership, the territory will be lost. If enough females cooperate to defend the range, their territory is maintained, but their collective effort is vulnerable to abuse by their companions. Leaders do not gain 'additional benefits' from leading, but they do provide an opportunity for laggards to gain a free ride" (p. 1262).

The question raised by this study is, how did the seemingly altruistic willingness of some lions to sacrifice their welfare for the sake of their groups evolve? One possibility is that the selfish lions that failed to step up and do their share were punished, but Heinsohn and Packer could not find any evidence that the selfish lions suffered any costs from their selfish behavior. Certainly, they were not punished by the other members of their prides, as humans who behave selfishly often are by other members of their groups.

According to D. S. Wilson (Wilson & Wilson, 2008) the most obvious interpretation of Heinsohn and Packer's findings is that the disposition to risk one's welfare to defend a territory evolved because altruistic groups (i.e., prides of lions) outcompeted selfish groups. The groups that formed during each generation contained different proportions of altruists, and those that contained a disproportionately high number of altruists fared better than those that contained a disproportionately low number, mediating the evolution of altruism.

But what kind of altruism? If the "altruistic" behaviors in question (stepping up to defend one's territory) were not biologically altruistic, there is really nothing (from an evolutionary perspective) to explain, and it is unclear that they were. To establish that the territorially defensive behaviors were biologically altruistic, one would have to establish that they lowered the probability that the "altruistic" lions would survive and reproduce, compared to the "selfish" lions. It is not enough to establish that the "altruistic" lions failed to gain particular proximate benefits or that they were more likely than the "selfish" lions to suffer particular proximate costs. One of the classic problems with attributions of altruism is that seemingly altruistic individuals could be reaping subtle benefits that are not apparent to observers such as Heinsohn and Packer. Put another way, to establish that the lions that failed to step up to defend their territories were more biologically selfish than the lions that stepped up, one would have to establish that the selfish laggards survived and reproduced in greater numbers than the more "altruistic" members of their groups did.

Although virtually all evolutionary theorists agree that group selection is a theoretical possibility, skeptical evolutionary theorists have raised two main arguments against invoking it as an explanation for the evolution of altruism. First, they have argued that when you boil group selection down to its mathematical essence, it reduces to kin selection. The idea underlying this argument is that the action in group selection stems from individuals who possess genes that dispose them to behave in biologically altruistic ways contributing to the propagation of these genes by helping other members of their groups who possess replicas of them. Although the recipients may not qualify as kin, kinship is not really where the action is in kin selection. The action stems from the same source as it does in group selection—in individuals fostering the survival and reproductive success of others who share the genes that dispose them to behave in bio-logically altruistic ways.

Second, skeptical evolutionary theorists have argued that the conditions necessary for group selection are so demanding that it is unlikely that they have been met in any but a few species. To overpower within-group selection for selfishness, groups of altruists would have to be relatively large and self-contained, and the probability of stably selfish individuals infiltrating altruistic groups would have to be low. The between-group variance in altruism would have to be relatively large, compared to the within-group variance (because the rate of natural selection is dependent on the amount of variation in populations). Although migration from one group to another, or dispersal, usually decreases between-group variation, D. S. Wilson (Wilson & Wilson, 2008) has pointed out that there are some conditions under which dispersal could increase between-group variation, such as for example, if altruistic individuals left selfish groups to join more altruistic groups. In the end, for altruism to evolve through group selection, altruistic groups would have to produce more offspring than selfish groups did, and the benefits of selfishness within altruistic groups would have to be prevented from escalating in an exponential manner. One way in which this could occur is for groups to break up and reform at some optimal point in time.

Although many, if not most, evolutionary theorists consider it unlikely that these conditions were met in groups of early humans, especially in view of the consistent trend among other primates to change groups in a "fission and fusion" manner (de Waal, 2006), some theorists, whose ideas I discuss in Chapters 13 and 14, have argued that, with the aid of cultural evolution, the conditions necessary for the group selection of altruism were, indeed, met in the human species (Boehm, 1999; Richerson & Boyd, 2005; Sober & Wilson, 1998). Alexander (1990) has suggested that tribal warfare would have favored group selection of altruism, and contemporary researchers have found that members of groups become increasingly altruistic when their groups compete against other groups (Bornstein & Ben-Yossef, 1994). Robert Kurzban and C. Athena Aktipis (2007) have proposed that one should look for evidence of group-level selection in the design of the adaptations that we would expect it to have forged, and as I discuss later in this book, there is compelling evidence that humans are strongly disposed to uphold their groups in certain conditions.

THE EVOLUTION OF ALTRUISM THROUGH IMPRECISELY DESIGNED MECHANISMS

In Chapter 5, I explained that evolutionary theorists do not expect evolved mechanisms to be designed in perfect ways because natural selection operates on randomly occurring mutations that produce changes in previously evolved structures and traits. I asserted that natural selection jury-rigs mental mechanisms by altering previously evolved adaptations to produce "exaptations," and I acknowledged that this process may produce by-products, incidental effects, and "spandrels" that either do not serve any adaptive function, or that produce maladaptive "mistakes" (by mistakes, I mean behaviors that decrease animals' inclusive fitness). I also pointed out that all adaptations carry costs and that the mechanisms that evolve are those with the most favorable benefit–cost ratios. All organisms end up with a set of evolved mechanisms that are "reasonably good at solving adaptive problems efficiently but are not designed as optimally as they might be if costs were not a constraint" (Buss, 2004, p. 21). Finally, I pointed out that the adaptive value of evolved mechanisms is determined by the environments in which they evolve, and when environments change, previously adaptive mechanisms may induce animals to behave in maladaptive ways.

I discussed an important implication of these considerations in the previous chapter with respect to kin selection: Due to imperfections in the design of evolved kin recognition mechanisms, animals may help nonrelatives who resemble relatives. If these helping behaviors are sufficiently costly, they would qualify as biologically and genetically altruistic. In such cases, costly altruistic behaviors are by-products or mistakes of mechanisms and strategies that, on balance, produce biologically and/or genetically beneficial outcomes. For example, although the strategy, "help those who live close to you or those who resemble you physically" might occasionally induce people to help nonrelatives, it could evolve if the ultimate biological and genetic benefits of the "hits" outweighed the ultimate costs of the "misses" (especially if there were "kicker" benefits from helping nonrelatives, such as an enhanced reputation or an increase in one's attractiveness as an exchange partner or mate). The greater the fitness benefits an adaptation produces, the greater its capacity to tolerate maladaptive mistakes.

In addition to the maladaptive biologically and genetically altruistic mistakes produced by kin-recognition mechanisms, the maladaptive mistakes produced by two other types of adaptations—social learning mechanisms and reasoning mechanisms—deserve special mention.

Altruism as a By-product of "Docility"

Many theorists have pointed out that, due to people's "bounded rationality," it is impossible for them to acquire by themselves all the adaptive knowledge accumulated by members of their cultures. Think of how little we would know and how many mistakes we would make if we had to learn everything on our own without any help from others. The cognitive scientist, Herbert Simon (1990), has suggested that, because it is impossible for people to learn on their own all the knowledge accumulated by members of their cultures and passed down through the generations, it is adaptive to copy others and to comply with their injunctions in relatively undiscriminating ways. Simon (1990) argues that simple social learning heuristics such as "believe what others say," "copy behaviors that pay off for others," and "go along with the crowd" were so adaptive to early humans that these heuristics evolved even though they occasionally induced early humans to behave in biologically altruistic ways.

I see two related problems with Simon's account of the evolution of altruism. First, people are exposed to all kinds of contradictory ideas and could not possibly accept them all. To quote David Buss (1999):

> ... because 'information' emanating from other individuals in one's social group is limitless, a potentially infinite array of ideas compete for the limited attention span of humans. Evolved psychological mechanisms in the receivers must sift through this barrage of ideas, selecting only a small subset for psychological reconstruc-tion. The subset that is selectively adopted and internally reconstructed in indi-viduals depends on a foundation of evolved psychological mechanisms. (p. 406)

Second, as I have mentioned, the mechanisms that mediate social learning and conformity are selective. We would not expect people to be inclined to accept ideas and to copy behaviors that consistently jeopardized their biological welfare, including ideas and behaviors that are biologically and genetically altruistic in nature. Although evolved mechanisms may not be perfect, we would expect variations that disposed individuals to make decisions that increased their inclusive fitness to have fared better in the process of natural selection than those that disposed individuals to make fitness-reducing decisions. Therefore, we would expect evolved social learning mechanisms to be discriminating in biologically beneficial ways.

A great deal of evidence supports this expectation. Studies have found that people are particularly receptive to moral judgments made by those who have a vested interest in their welfare, those they like and respect, those who are similar to them, those who are nurturing, and those who have control over their fates (Burton & Kunce, 1995, pp. 151–152). As expressed by Flinn and Alexander (1982), the mental mechanisms that regulate people's responses to inputs from others are designed in terms of decision rules such as "accept advice and instruction from those with an interest in one's suc-cess" and "view skeptically advice and instruction from those with conflicting interests with regard to the topic being instructed." People also are more strongly disposed to copy moral judgments made by the most fit, admired, respected, successful, powerful, and wise members of their groups than they are to copy the moral judgments of those who do not possess these qualities (Chaiken, 1987; Flinn & Alexander, 1982). Finally, people are inclined to conform to "tried and true" normative judgments that are preva-lent in their groups.

Altruism as a By-product of Reason

As discussed, Darwin (1874) believed that the ability to reason disposes people to behave in moral ways because it enables them to perceive the long-term benefits of moral strategies. In particular, Darwin believed that humans' capacity to reason enables them to understand that it is in their long-term interest to uphold the interests of their communities and to figure out which customs are best equipped to help them achieve this effect. For example, he suggested that "as the reasoning powers and foresight of the members [of early human groups] became improved, each man would soon learn from experience that if he aided his fellow-men, he would commonly receive aid in return" (p. 127). On this line of thought, the capacity to reason induces people to help others and to uphold their groups because it enables them to see that these social investments pay off better than more selfish alternatives in the end—a form of enlightened self-interest. When writers talk about rational self-interest and economic man, they are referring to this function. However, as praiseworthy as such behaviors may be, they do not meet the criteria for biological forms of altruism because they do not reduce the probability that those who emit them will survive and reproduce.

In order for reasoning abilities to give rise to biologically altruistic behaviors, they would have to dispose people to sacrifice or jeopardize their survival and reproductive success for the sake of others. The contemporary evolutionary biologist, George Williams, has described one way in which this could occur. Williams (1989) suggests that although reasoning abilities evolved because they enabled early humans to maximize their biological gains in the social arena by, for example, enabling them to see through others' attempts to manipulate through persuasive messages, "in its boundless stupidity [the] evolutionary process incidentally designed machinery [i.e., reasoning abilities] capable of answering other sorts of questions, such as, is this message one of help or harm for what I really want in the world?" (p. 212). On this line of thought, altruism could be an incidental by-product of reasoning abilities that evolved to serve other adaptive functions.

The Role of Manipulation in the Evolution of Altruism

Inasmuch as it is in people's interest to manipulate others into treating them in biologically altruistic ways, we would expect people to be disposed to prey on the imperfections in the evolved mental mechanisms of others, such as those that regulate kin recognition, social learning, and reasoning. Like cuckoo birds that trick neighboring members of their species into sitting on their eggs, and like big fish that dangle wormlike enticements in front of smaller fish, humans manipulate others into behaving in biologically altruistic ways by acting as though they are their kin, by exaggerating the value of the assistance they have proffered to them, by misrepresenting their value as mates, by praising altruistic martyrs, by persuading others that altruism pays off, and so on. Inasmuch as these tactics are successful, they constitute important sources of altruism. Later, I argue that mutual manipulation in the social arena played a key role in the evolution of moral judgments, moral beliefs, and moral norms.

Anachronistic Altruism

As discussed, evolved mechanisms may induce individuals to behave in maladaptive ways because they were designed in ancestral environments that differ in significant ways from the current environments in which they are activated. Popular examples include humans' attraction to sweets, and moths' attraction to flames. Anachronisms—mechanisms, dispositions, strategies, and decision rules that were adaptive in earlier environments but are maladaptive in current environments—could have evolved through all forms of selection. For example, individuals could be disposed to help their relatives even though, in current environments, their relatives could survive and reproduce without their assistance, and people could be disposed to help members of their in-groups even though their groups no longer contain relatives. Anachronisms are significant in the evolution of altruism because they can dispose people to behave in genuinely biologically and genetically altruistic ways that increase the inclusive fitness of recipients at a cost to their own inclusive fitness.

CONCLUSIONS

Contemporary evolutionary theorists have offered several solutions to the problem that evidence of biological forms of altruism created for Darwin's theory of evolution. In Chapters 8 and 9, I explained how altruistic dispositions could evolve through sexual selection and kin selection, and I reviewed evidence demonstrating that such dispositions have, in fact, evolved in the human species and in other species. In this chapter, I updated and evaluated Darwin's idea that biological forms of altruism can evolve through group selection, and I discussed several ways in which altruistic behaviors can stem from imperfections in the design of mental mechanisms that dispose people to behave in otherwise adaptive ways.

A challenging question raised by the multiple paths to altruism available in the process of evolution is whether each path has led to different altruism-producing mental mechanisms, or whether the different forms of selection have operated on the same mental mechanisms. Clearly, biologically altruistic behaviors that stem from social learning and reasoning are mediated by different mental mechanisms from those that give rise to kin-selected and sexually selected forms of altruism. However, it seems plausible that some of the proximate mental mechanisms that dispose individuals to help their offspring, mates, more distant kin, and other members of their groups share certain properties. For example, as I will discuss, they seem to be regulated by the same hormones and to generate similar psychological states, such as those that people experience as feelings of attachment, commitment, and love. One plausible possibility is that the first mental mechanism to originate disposed mammals to care for and to assist their offspring, and this mechanism evolved in ways that enabled it to be activated by mates, other kin, and other members of one's group. Whatever the case, the theory and research reviewed in this chapter enable us to conclude with great assurance that a capacity to behave in biologically altruistic ways has evolved in humans and other animals. How good, or moral, this renders people is another question, which I will address in the penultimate chapter of this book.

11

THE EVOLUTION OF COOPERATION

I have suggested that one of the most significant shortcomings of Darwin's model of the evolution of morality was his failure to appreciate the implications of the evolution of cooperation. At first glance, it might seem like an easy task to account for the evolution of mechanisms that dispose animals to behave in cooperative ways because it is easy to identify situations in which two or more animals that coordinate their efforts and exchange goods and services fare better than animals that attempt to advance their interests at others' expense. Darwin offered many examples of such cooperative behaviors. However, as discussed in Chapter 5, Darwin did not seem to recognize a significant obstacle to the evolution of cooperation, namely that members of cooperative groups may be able to maximize their benefits by doing less and taking more than their share. For cooperative strategies to evolve, they must contain defenses against exploitation by cheaters and free-riders.

Scientists have observed several forms of cooperation in the animal kingdom. In some cases, animals help one another incidentally in the process of pursuing their own interests. In other cases, animals coordinate their efforts to solve problems that would be more costly to solve on their own. And in still other cases, animals take turns and share resources that they do not need, rather than suffering the costs of competing with others. It is relatively easy to explain how these forms of cooperation evolved because the benefits of cooperation and costs of cheating are obvious.

As mentioned in the introductory chapter, the renowned evolutionary biologist Robert Trivers explained how concrete reciprocity could evolve. Game theorists who have modeled the evolution of cooperation have found that "Tit for Tat" is a winning strategy in conducive contexts. However, evidence of reciprocity among social species other than humans is sparser than most evolutionary theorists expected.

Although Tit for Tat is a potentially powerful strategy, because it is enables those who invoke it to reap the benefits of cooperating with cooperators and cut their losses against cheaters, it is limited in at least one important respect: One selfish mistake can launch a mutually destructive even-the-score blood feud. For this reason, game theorists have found that kinder, gentler forms of reciprocity that enable players to correct their mistakes, or that induce them to forgive those who have cheated them once, produce greater gains than inflexible Tit-for-Tat strategies do.

One of the keys to understanding how cooperative strategies have evolved is to recognize the significance of selective interaction. As long as cooperators are able to identify other cooperators and to interact exclusively with them, they can fare better than more selfish individuals do. As a result, mechanisms that enable humans and other animals to identify cooperators have evolved. However, the battle between selfishness and cooperation does not end there because individuals who deceive others into viewing them as cooperators without suffering the costs of cooperating can fare better than genuine cooperators do. When we look at the human species, we can see the products of an arms race process in which better deception mechanisms have increased the adaptive value of better deception-detection mechanisms, and so on.

There is a great deal of evidence that humans do not invoke Tit-for-Tat strategies when they interact with their friends and members of their in-groups. People may help their friends over long periods of time without any expectation of immediate return. Evolutionary theorists have accounted for such behaviors in terms of the value of upholding beneficial relationships, cultivating credit, and fostering long-term security. Although you probably do not expect your friends to repay every favor you do for them, you do expect them to be there for you in times of need, when you are least able to pay them back.

Defined biologically, two or more animals cooperate when their actions have the effect of contributing to each other's fitness, whatever the animals' intentions. On this definition, members of all social species behave in cooperative ways, because the ways in which they behave end up contributing to the fitness of those with whom they associate, and the ways in which those who benefit from their behaviors behave end up contributing to their fitness. However, this definition of cooperation does not capture the psychological meaning it has for most people. For most people, the idea of cooperation implies a more direct and intentional coordination of behaviors for mutual benefit.

All forms of cooperation involve giving and receiving—whether intentionally or unintentionally. Members of cooperative teams help one another acquire benefits that they could not acquire on their own, or at least benefits that it would be more costly for them to acquire on their own. What goes around, comes around, in spades. However, as discussed, in order for such dispositions to evolve, they must overcome a significant obstacle, namely the adaptive potential in cheating and free-riding, defined as reaping the benefits of others' contributions without suffering the costs of contributing one's share in return. To reap the benefits of cooperation, cooperators must somehow protect themselves against exploitation by selfish cheaters.

Biologists have identified several forms of cooperation, ranging from those in which animals help others as an unintentional byproduct of helping themselves to those in which animals accrue unintended benefits from acts that are aimed at improving the welfare of others. The main ways in which forms of cooperation differ from each other pertain to the extent to which individuals intend to help one another and how directly the benefits they receive follow from the assistance they proffer. I begin by discussing simple forms that are relatively easy to explain—those that involve animals incidentally helping others while pursuing self-serving goals—then turn by degrees to more complex forms that are more difficult to explain—forms of cooperation that appear to involve more altruism, and therefore that seem more moral.

INCIDENTAL HELPING

Nature is a delicately balanced ecosystem. Animals that live in the same environment may help one another incidentally as they go about their business without engaging in any direct interaction. For example, in obtaining food for itself, an animal might kill a predator of another species. One animal's feces may be another animal's food. The mere presence of other animals may discourage a predator from attacking individuals in a group. In such cases, animals do not intend to help those who benefit from their behaviors; they are simply doing what they need to do to survive, and the benefits to others are incidental.

In addition to bestowing incidental benefits on other animals indirectly, animals may behave in ways that bestow more direct and obvious benefits on others while fostering their own fitness. For example, one fish may clean another to obtain nutrition. Because such behaviors end up fostering the welfare of the animals who emit them, it is easy to explain how the mechanisms that produce them evolved, and these do not seem to have much to do with morality.

MUTUALISM

As discussed in Chapter 5, members of social species may join forces with others to kill prey, to fend off predators, to defend territory, to mate, and to care for offspring (Dugatkin, 1997; Sachs, Mueller, Wilcox, & Bull, 2004). For example, lions may coordinate their efforts to kill animals such as antelopes that are bigger than they are, and musk oxen may form circles to defend themselves against predators. The adaptive logic underlying mutualism is that animals that work together to obtain a resource, then share it, end up with more than they would if they had tried to obtain the resource on their own. Several theorists have suggested that the prevalence and significance of mutualism have been underestimated in the literature on cooperation (e.g., Nesse, 2001). "Mutualism may be the most prevalent form of cooperation; it occurs frequently across a wide variety of taxa" (Stevens, Cushman, & Hauser, 2005). As explained by Scheel and Packer (1991), mutualism tends to evolve in species that live in relatively hostile environments because individuals need assistance from members of their groups to survive.

When animals join forces to solve adaptive problems, it might seem *as though* they are going about the business of advancing their adaptive interests in essentially the same ways in which they would on their own. However, this is often not the case because they must coordinate their efforts to produce the benefits. We can see such coordination in the kinds of "behavioral synchrony" necessary to shake hands, to dance, and to mate, and in a different form, when animals adopt divisions of labor. For example, Conner, Smolker, and Richards (1992) found that when dolphins engage in group hunting, one member of the group chases a prey toward other members, who lie in wait. To coordinate their behavior in these ways, animals need mental mechanisms that enable them to assume complementary roles.

Within groups, animals may differ in traits that enable them to help solve group problems. For example, some members of a group may be able to run fast; other members may have strong jaws, and so on. This has two important implications. First, in contexts in which individuals are able to choose collaborative partners from within their groups, they should select those whose abilities best complement their own. If they are well equipped to do one part, they should select partners that are well equipped to do the other parts necessary to achieve the goal (Hill, 2002; Simpson & Campbell, 2005; Tooby & Cosmides, 1996). As I discuss more fully later in this chapter, such personnel selection could occur independently across tasks, or it could give rise to ongoing, long-term associations and pair bonds. Second, members of groups may specialize at one component of a task, giving rise to enduring divisions of labor within groups. Animals that are good at one task perform one service, whereas animals that are good at other tasks perform other services. Such specialization could give rise to sex differences and to other stable individual differences within groups—for example, the chasers, the attackers, the sentinels, and so on.

Animals also may be able to maximize their gains by pooling their resources to produce public goods that they share. For example, members of a group (e.g., beavers) may coordinate their efforts to build a group shelter. Or members of a group may contribute to a store of food for the winter. In addition, group members may foster their interests by showing constraint with respect to the depletion of shared resources.

Many experts on human evolution have concluded that mutualism and other forms of cooperation were instrumental in the evolution of the human species. For example, Leakey and Lewin (1977) concluded that:

> throughout our evolutionary history, particularly since the rise of a hunting way of life, there must have been extreme selective pressure in favor of our ability to cooperate as a group: organized food gathering and hunts are successful only if each member of the band knows his task and joins in with the activity of his fellows. The degree of selective pressure toward cooperation, group awareness and identification was so strong, and the period over which it operated was so extended, that it can hardly have failed to have become embedded to some degree in our genetic makeup. (p. 45)

Tooby and Devore (1987) identified 15 "zoologically unique" features of early humans that distinguished them from other primates. Two of these features—large and structurally complex coalitions, and group-against-group aggression (i.e., primitive wars)—are based in mutualism. It is difficult to exaggerate the magnitude of mutualism in contemporary human society.

SHARING AND TURN-TAKING

Members of groups inevitably need and want resources that others possess. As discussed in Chapter 6, the selfish strategy of trying to obtain goods and services by force may be costly in terms of energy and risk, especially when those who possess the resources are relatively powerful. Animals that adopt more cooperative strategies such as sharing the resources or taking turns consuming them may fare better than animals that try to take them for themselves. We would expect mechanisms that give rise to turn-taking and sharing to evolve when the net benefits from settling for part of a resource are greater than the benefits animals would receive if they competed for the whole thing. In some cases, it costs little or nothing to share. Revisiting an earlier example, animals that possess more meat or fruit than they could consume before the food goes rotten would lose little or nothing by sharing it. Indeed, by sharing, they could avoid the costs of being harassed by others.

CONCRETE RECIPROCITY

Although sharing things that you do not need may not cost you much, it also does not contribute much to your welfare. When one individual possesses a resource that is valuable to another individual, but worth relatively little to him or her, a potentially profitable strategy is to trade it for something he or she needs. Such trading may have originated from dispositions to permit others to take things that individuals do not really need (called "tolerated theft" in the primate literature).

Some situations lend themselves to simultaneous trading—in effect giving with one hand and taking with another—because two individuals possess goods or services that the other wants. In other situations, this is not possible. Consider grooming, for example. Although two animals could engage in simultaneous, face to face grooming, it would be difficult for them to groom each others' backs simultaneously. The animals could solve this problem by taking turns grooming each other: You scratch my back, then I'll scratch yours. The benefits of exchanging goods and services could be greatly increased if individuals could, in effect, make deals with others: "I will help you when you need help in return for you helping me when I need help"; or "I will give you resources that you need now in return for a commitment to give me resources that I need when you are able to provide them."

Reciprocity is a paradoxical phenomenon that I believe played an important role in the evolution of morality in the human species. Because reciprocity involves giving and receiving, it has both altruistic and selfish components at a proximate level of analysis. The initial act of giving seems altruistic, because it entails helping a recipient at a cost to oneself. The act of reciprocating also seems altruistic, because it too involves helping a recipient at a cost to oneself. However, viewed in terms of the net benefits of the exchange, reciprocity is at best cooperative, and at worst selfish. When individuals reciprocate, they trade items of relatively little value to them for items of greater value to them, with both trading partners coming out ahead through gains in trade. "Reciprocal altruism is the exchange of [altruistic] acts between individuals so as to produce a net benefit on both sides. Reciprocal altruism is one kind of return-benefit altruism" (Trivers, 2006, p. 68). As I have explained, because "reciprocal altruism" produces ultimate biological benefits to those who practice it, it does not qualify as biologically altruistic.

To evolve, delayed forms of reciprocity must overcome two types of obstacles—one dis-positional; the other intellectual. Unconditional dispositions to make proximately altruistic overtures and unconditional dispositions to pay others back stand little chance of reaping greater immediate benefits than dispositions to take the money and run. Even if a substantial portion of a group inherited the disposition to make cooperative overtures, they could end up getting exploited by those who were not disposed to reciprocate. And as I discuss in Chapter 15, some delayed forms of reciprocity require sophisticated mental abilities.

Game Theory Research on the Evolution of Reciprocity

I introduced game theory models of evolution in Chapter 5. It is now appropriate to consider the game that has been used most pervasively, the Prisoner's Dilemma, and the role it has played in accounting for the evolution of cooperation. There are two players in Prisoner's Dilemmas. Each player must select one of two options—either to cooperate or to behave selfishly (to "defect"). In some games, players must make this choice simultaneously, and in other games, they must make it sequentially. Some games are one-off; others are iterated. Players may or may not know how many iterations there will be in the game.

Prisoner's Dilemmas are significant because they model decisions in which individuals must decide whether to pursue their selfish interests at the expense of others or whether to foster the common good. These dilemmas are complex, because the outcomes for both players depend on the interaction between the choices they make. If both players make a cooperative choice, each wins a middling number of points (e.g., three). If both players make a selfish choice, each ends up with fewer points (e.g., one). If one player makes a cooperative choice and the other player makes a selfish choice, the cooperative player— now "the sucker"—fails to gain any points, and the selfish player—now the cheater—wins a relatively large number of points (e.g., five). The exact number of points does not really matter in Prisoner's Dilemmas. To qualify as a Prisoner's Dilemma, the payoffs in exchanges must be ordered as follows: (1) cheaters who exploit cooperators earn the most (2) two cooperators earn the next most, (3) two cheaters earn the third most, and (4) cooperators who are exploited by cheaters earn the least.

Prisoner's Dilemmas abound in our lives, because people frequently encounter situations in which they are able to advance their interests in ways that, if adopted by others, would produce undesirable results. In Chapter 5, I discussed price-fixing as an example. Other examples include deciding whether or not to do one's share in such group projects as school assignments, household chores, and committee work. In addition, people face Prisoner's Dilemmas when they decide whether or not to pay their taxes, whether or not to contribute to public broadcasting, and whether or not to exploit resources such as fish, game, minerals, and trees.

In an award-winning study using Prisoner's Dilemmas, Axelrod and Hamilton (1981) solicited a variety of strategies from game theory experts and played them off against each other in computerized round-robin simulations of natural selection. These researchers made the simplifying assumption that each strategy was determined by an allele, or set of alleles, and that each point in the game represented an offspring, or replication of the strategy. Thus, in contrast to relatively small increments to the fitness of individuals that accrue from specific behavioral acts such as being groomed and receiving food, the points in Axelrod and Hamilton's games corresponded to the ultimate effects of strategies on the number of replicas of genes or offspring that individuals contribute to the population. Axelrod and Hamilton assumed that the environment has a limited carrying capacity, and therefore that an increase in the frequency of one strategy entails a decrease in the frequency of other strategies.

After Axelrod and Hamilton played the strategies off against each other in one game, which represented one generation, they played the winners, or survivors, off against one another in another game, representing the next generation, and so on, in an iterated manner. Note that the "climate," or set of strategies in the competition changes from generation to generation, with the most successful strategies increasing in number, and therefore interacting more frequently with replicas of themselves.

Axelrod and Hamilton wanted to know which inherited strategies (i.e., alleles) would be selected (i.e., win and contribute the most replicas of themselves, or offspring, to future generations) in competitions against other inherited strategies, and whether the process of selection would produce an evolutionarily stable result similar to the Nash equilibrium of economic games: "Is there a strategy (or mixture of strategies) such that if most members of the population adopt it, no mutant strategy can invade the population by natural selection?" Are there strategies that, if adopted by the individuals who are competing against one another, guarantee that they will not end up worse off than individuals playing other strategies? Axelrod and Hamilton were particularly interested in whether any cooperative strategy could invade a population of selfish strategies, and become evolutionarily stable.

Axelrod and Hamilton's games modeled several basic principles of social evolution. Pairs (i.e., groups) of cooperators produce more offspring than pairs (groups) of selfish individualists. In addition, each member of a pair or group of cooperating individuals produces more offspring than each member of a selfish dyad or group. However, within pairs or groups containing a mixture of cooperators and selfish individuals, selfish individuals produce more offspring than cooperative individuals do. Prisoner's Dilemmas model individual level selection within groups containing cooperative and selfish members (favoring selfish strategies) and group-level selection between groups of cooperators *versus* groups of selfish individualists (favoring cooperative and altruistic strategies) (Dugatkin & Reeve, 1994; Sober & Wilson, 1998).

Unconditional Selfishness versus Unconditional Cooperation

Consider first a contest between players invoking unconditionally selfish strategies and players invoking unconditionally cooperative or altruistic strategies. It is easy to see that the unconditionally selfish players will defeat the unconditionally cooperative and altruistic players, hands down. For this reason, selfish strategies are widely considered to be based on rational choices. In Axelrod and Hamilton's games, when selfish players compete against unconditionally cooperative partners, they contribute five replicas of their selfish strategies to future generations compared to none for their opponents. Against other unconditionally selfish partners, selfish players contribute one replica of their strategy to future generations, matched by one from their opponents. Because unconditional selfishness is always a potential player in evolutionary games, we must conclude that no species will ever be evolved to behave in unconditionally altruistic or unconditionally cooperative ways. If this were required for morality (I will argue it is not), no species would qualify as moral by nature.

Tragic Ironies

As I discuss more fully in Chapter 19, if everyone adopted unconditionally cooperative strategies, the world would be a utopia. If everyone did his or her share, we could produce significantly more resources than we are currently able to produce. We could save all the time and money we invest in institutions created to catch and punish cheaters, and improve the quality of life for all. However, this will never occur as long as selfish individuals are able to exploit unconditional cooperators. In a population containing only unconditionally cooperative and unconditionally selfish strategies, unconditional selfishness will evolve and become evolutionarily stable.

It is important to note, however, that even though unconditionally selfish strategies are stable (thus capable of defining the nature of species), as they increase in number and interact more and more with other unconditionally selfish strategies, they pay off more and more poorly. Achieving an evolutionary equilibrium is not the same as achieving an optimal outcome. In the conditions modeled in Prisoner's Dilemma games, two selfish players end up in low-paying (one point) draws. The social psychologist, Roger Brown (1984), eloquently described the paradoxically self-defeating consequences of the evolution of unconditional selfishness. Imagining a group of good-hearted Christian birds dependent for their survival on being groomed, Roger Brown considered the ultimate effect of a mutant cheater that reaped the benefits of being groomed without suffering the costs of grooming others. Because this cheater would fare better than his more altruistic fellows, he would leave more offspring, who would inherit his selfish nature. These selfish offspring would leave more selfish offspring, and so on, exponentially increasing the number of selfish individuals in the population. In the end, "Christians would altruize themselves into extinction. And once grooming birds had become extinct, so eventually would cheaters; one imagines a pathetic final act in which all birds on the stage present to one another heads that none will groom."

Tit for Tat

That unconditional selfishness always defeats unconditional cooperation does not mean that all forms of cooperation are doomed to lose evolutionary contests. If we deconstruct the problem, it would seem that a conditionally cooperative disposition that enabled a player to reap the benefits of cooperating with cooperators while avoiding the costs of exploitation by selfish exploiters should be equipped to defeat unconditionally selfish strategies. The Canadian game theorist, Antol Rappaport submitted a simple strategy called Tit for Tat to Axelrod's contest that proved to fill this bill. Tit for Tat is based in the decision rule, "be nice, then get even," or, put in other ways, "help others, then do to them as they did to you"; "invite mutually beneficial cooperative exchanges by making low-cost giving overtures to others, then copy their response." After the first exchange, Tit for Tat produces iterations of reciprocal exchanges between both cooperative and selfish players. In effect, cooperative strategies induce Tit for Tat to behave cooperatively, and selfish strategies induce Tit for Tat to behave selfishly.

As Axelrod explained, it is appropriate to characterize Tit for Tat as "nice," because it opens with an altruistic overture and pays back good deeds. It also is appropriate to characterize it as retaliatory and somewhat forgiving, because it punishes cheaters and rewards repentant cheaters who decide to cooperate. However, Tit for Tat is no sucker (at least after the first move), because it repays selfishness with selfishness.

The Evolution of Tit-for-Tat Strategies

At first glance, it might seem that Tit for Tat is destined to lose evolutionary games. For openers, it never wins on any given exchange; the best it does is tie. If the other player makes a cooperative choice and Tit for Tat makes a cooperative choice, both players get 3 points. If the other player makes a selfish choice and Tit for Tat makes a selfish choice, both players get 1 point. Tit for Tat never gains 5 points because it never behaves selfishly toward a cooperator, and Tit for Tat loses 0–5 on the first exchange with players making selfish choices.

If the game involved only Tit-for-Tat strategists interacting with selfish strategists, Tit for Tat would lose by a hair. However, the game also involves Tit-for-Tat strategists interacting with other Tit-for-Tat strategists and other cooperative strategists. *Although selfish strategies suffer from low payoffs when they interact with one another and with Tit-for-Tat strategists after the first exchange, Tit-for-Tat strategies enjoy moderately high payoffs from exchanges with cooperative players.*

Axelrod and Hamilton found that in a population containing a sufficient number of Tit-for-Tat strategies (and other cooperative strategies), Tit for Tat could defeat unconditionally selfish strategies because it could reap as many benefits as selfish strategists after the first exchange with them, plus all the benefits of exchanges with other Tit-for-Tat strategists, without suffering the costs of unprotected cooperation. "TIT FOR TAT won the tournaments not by beating the other players, but by eliciting behavior from the other player that allowed both to do well. . . . So in a non-zero sum world, you do not have to do better than the other player to do well for yourself. . . . when interacting with many other players . . . the other's success is virtually a prerequisite for doing well yourself" (Axelrod & Hamilton, 1981). The principle underlying this outcome pertains to the benefits of cooperating with cooperators, which I believe was critically important in the evolution of morality.

Note that there is a fringe benefit from the evolution of Tit-for-Tat strategies, namely that it opens the door for the evolution of more unconditionally cooperative and altruistic strategies. Indeed, in an environment replete with Tit-for-Tat strategists, one could not tell the difference between conditionally and unconditionally cooperative strategies because the individuals employing them would make the same cooperative choices. However, ironically, opening the door for unconditionally cooperative or altruistic strategies also opens the door for the reemergence of selfish strategies, which benefit by exploiting the unconditional generosity of the do-gooders.

Game theory simulations of evolution are designed to determine which kinds of strategy could evolve and become evolutionarily stable. "Could" evolve is quite different from "has" evolved. Lots of things are possible, but most never occur. What we really want to know is whether dispositions to reciprocate have evolved in humans or any other species.

Concrete Reciprocity in Other Animals

Although we might expect Tit-for-Tat–like reciprocity to be prevalent in the animal kingdom, this does not seem to be the case. Only a few biologists have reported observing delayed reciprocal exchanges in species they have observed (see Trivers, 1985 and Dugatkin, 1997, for reviews of research), and some of the claims have been challenged. In one study, Hart and Hart (1992) found that impalas engage in short bouts of alternative grooming; however, the delay between giving and receiving is very short. As I will discuss more fully later, theorists such as Stevens et al. (2005) have argued that the reason that delayed forms of reciprocity (and delayed forms of punishment) are so rare in the animal kingdom is because relatively few animals possess the intellectual abilities necessary to sustain them.

The most widely discussed research on delayed reciprocity in animals pertains to the fascinating behavior of vampire bats (Wilkinson, 1990). Vampire bats live in relatively stable social groups of about 8–12 roostmates, which consist mainly of kin, but usually include some non-kin as well. These animals fly out of their roosts each evening to forage for blood from cows, horses, and other animals. If a bat fails to obtain blood within a period of 60 hours, it may starve to death. Female vampire bats possess the ability to regurgitate blood to feed their young. The biologist, Gerry Wilkinson observed a group of vampire bats and recorded incidents of regurgitation. As expected, he found that most incidents involved mothers regurgitating blood for their infant offspring, and most of the remaining incidents involved grandmothers regurgitating for their grandchildren. However, Wilkinson also found that some bats regurgitated blood for nonrelated members of their groups.

To test the hypothesis that these incidents were products of a Tit-for-Tat kind of strategy, Wilkinson performed an experiment on eight nonrelated bats. He alternatively starved one of them while the others became sated with blood. He then returned the starving bat to the group, determined which other bats regurgitated blood for the hungry bat, then recorded whether helping a fellow bat increased the probability of receiving help from the recipient in the future. Wilkinson found that the bats did in fact reciprocate, and he concluded that vampire bats possess the ability to engage in a delayed form of concrete reciprocity.

Note the conditions for the evolution of reciprocity met by vampire bats. They live in relatively stable groups. They have relatively large brains for animals of their size, and they are able to recognize members of their groups and remember who has helped them and repaid them. They experience situations in which they suffer from life-threatening needs that other bats can help them satisfy at a relatively small cost to themselves. They are able to "exapt" an adaptation designed to feed their infants. And, finally, they are able to detect whether their roostmates are cheating (refusing to reciprocate blood when they are able to) by examining how distended their stomachs are after foraging.

The most appropriate place to look for precursors of the forms of cooperation practiced by humans is in other primates. In one study, Packer (1977) found that baboons formed coalitions to gain access to reproductively receptive females, then took turns mating; however, Bercovitch (1988) failed to replicate this finding. Hauser and his colleagues (2003) reported that cotton-top tamarins were willing to pull a tool that supplied food to other tamarins who returned the favor after a short delay, but questions have been raised about Hauser's research. Studies by de Waal and others have established that chimpanzees engage in calculated forms of delayed reciprocity in which they remember who has helped them, track credits and debts to particular partners, and repay them either in kind or in some other currency (see Kappeler & van Schaik, 2006, for a review). For example, chimpanzees are more likely to assist those who have assisted them in agonistic exchanges with others ("one good turn deserves another") and to aggress against those who have sided with others against them ("an eye for an eye") (de Waal & Luttrell, 1988). In addition, chimpanzees are more likely to share food with those who have groomed them earlier in the day. If we accept the idea that chimpanzees inherit mechanisms that dispose them to engage in delayed forms of reciprocity (and other forms of cooperation), we can conclude that they possess mental mechanisms that enable them to solve fundamental social dilemmas in primitively fair ways.

Concrete Reciprocity in Humans

Among the 15 unique hominid characteristics attributed to early humans by Tooby and Devore (1987), one pertains directly to reciprocity ("unprecedented development in the frequency and degree of reciprocity and the variety of its manifestations") and three are closely linked ("unparalleled degree of negotiation, intercontingent behavior, and social exchange"; "an increased division of labor between the sexes"; and "mating negotiation and exchange, probably consisting of wife exchange among groups").

Among the strategies invoked by modern humans who play Prisoner's Dilemma games, Tit-for-Tat–like strategies are the most popular (Rapoport, 1965), and in the real world, people engage in concrete forms of reciprocity on an ongoing basis. Children trade cards, stickers, and trinkets. Adults lend tools to their friends, exchange dinner invitations, and alternate picking up the check at restaurants. One partner cooks the meal; the other partner does the dishes. Those who help others when they are in need expect to be helped in return when they are in need. And, on the negative side, blood feuds abound. Following an examination of social practices in a selection of cultures, the sociologist, Gouldner (1960), concluded: "A norm of reciprocity is, I suspect, no less universal and important . . . than the incest taboo" (p. 178). When people say things such as "you scratch my back and I'll scratch yours"; "quid pro quo"; and "don't get mad, get even," they are expressing Tit-for-Tat strategies.

Why did dispositions to reciprocate evolve in the humans species but not in other species that could profit from them? Trivers (1985) suggested that, "during the Pleistocene, and probably before, a hominid species would have met the preconditions for the evolution of reciprocal altruism; for example, long life span, low dispersal rate, life in small, mutually dependent and stable social groups, and a long period of parental care leading to extensive contacts with close relatives over many years" (p. 386). Early humans accumulated resources that could be traded. The creation of weapons would have equalized power among members of groups. The invention of tools would have rendered specialization and divisions of labor increasingly adaptive. In addition, as emphasized by Stevens et al. (1995), humans possess the mental abilities necessary to create and to sustain delayed forms of reciprocity.

The Adaptive Limitations of Concrete Reciprocity

It is important to note that strategies that evolve in one environment (e.g., an environment in which the probability of interacting with cooperative strategies is high) may not evolve in other environments (e.g., environments in which the probability of interacting with selfish strategies is high). The outcome of Axelrod and Hamilton's games depended on which strategies were entered in the contests: "It [is] apparent that Tit-for-tat's success in the Axelrod tournaments was largely a function of their [the tournaments'] form. The tournaments just happened not to show up [the] weaknesses [of the Tit-for-Tat strategy]. In a world where mistakes are made, Tit-for-tat is a second-rate strategy, and all sorts of other strategies prove better" (Ridley, 1996, p. 75).

Tit-for-Tat strategies are limited in three respects. First, they are not equipped to invade a population of selfish strategies unless they invade in clusters that enable them to interact predominantly with replicas of themselves. This raises the question, how could such clusters have originated in the first place, especially if we assume an original state of unconditional selfishness? Second, Tit-for-Tat strategies do not become evolutionarily stable, because they open the door for more unconditionally cooperative and altruistic strategies, which in turn open the door for more selfish strategies. Finally, one selfish defection in an exchange between two Tit-for-Tat strategists locks them into a mutually recriminating and self-defeating series of selfish exchanges or blood feuds. Although Axelrod and Hamilton characterized Tit for Tat as "forgiving," Tit-for-Tat strategists stop responding to selfishness with selfishness only after their selfish partners change their ways.

The Evolution of Kinder, Gentler Forms of Concrete Reciprocity

As expressed by Trivers (2006), "TfT and Axelrod and Hamilton (1981) spread like wildfire through the literature, so that soon all reciprocal interactions seemed to be formulated in terms of the PD [Prisoner's Dilemma]. . . . It soon seemed that theorists and empiricists alike were forgetting that iterated games of PD amount to a highly artificial model of social interactions; each successive interaction simultaneous, costs and benefits never varying, options limited to only two moves, no errors, no escalated punishment, no population variability within traits, and so on" (p. 70). Following the publication of Axelrod and Hamilton's findings, game theorists changed the parameters of Prisoner's Dilemma games to render them truer to the process of evolution, and pitted social strategies against one another in different types of games (Dugatkin, 1997; Axelrod, 1988; Gintis, 2000). To quote Dugatkin (1997), "Modifications to the IPD [iterated Prisoner's Dilemma] include variations in population structure, number of players, number of strategies, relatedness of players, stochasticity of strategies, stochasticity of environment, amount of memory, possibility of individual recognition, norms, ostracism, mobility of players, and mistakes by players" (p. 24).

Game theory simulations of the evolution of social strategies that followed Axelrod and Hamilton's studies produced findings of special relevance to the evolution of morality. Although some research revealed that it is more difficult for cooperative strategies to evolve in large groups than it is for them to evolve in small groups (Boyd & Richerson,

1992), other research demonstrated that changing the parameters of Prisoner's Dilemma games enabled strategies that were "nicer" or more altruistic than Tit for Tat to evolve in small groups (Ridley, 1996).

Strategies in the original Axelrod and Hamilton simulations operated with mathematical precision and always produced exactly the same payoffs against other strategies, but individuals do not behave in such strictly determined ways in the real world, and natural selection operates probabilistically (stochastically). A significant limitation of Tit for Tat stems from its inflexible intolerance of negative mistakes. Theorists have pointed out that errors, accidents, and random events may play a very important role in the evolution of social strategies (Dugatkin, 1997). Consider two Tit-for-Tat strategists interacting in a mutually beneficial way. One makes a mistake or has a selfish moment. The other reciprocates the selfishness, precipitating a mutually self-defeating blood feud. Clearly, it is in the interest of both players to reestablish the string of mutually beneficial cooperative exchanges, which can be accomplished either by the selfish player making up for his or her mistake or by the Tit-for-Tat strategist giving the selfish player a second chance. Game theorists have found that such strategies as "Tit for Two Tats," "Generous Tit for Tat" (which overlooks defections about one-third of the time), "Contrite Tit for Tat," "Pavlov" (win-stay, lose-switch), and "Firm but Fair" (which is like Pavlov, except players continue cooperating after being suckered in the last round) that were equipped to break self-defeating iterations of selfishness, avoid exploitation by unrepentantly selfish strategies, and exploit unconditional do-gooders prevailed over strict Tit for Tat strategies in some conditions (Ridley, 1996). This research demonstrated that in order for cooperation to pay off better than selfishness, it must be conditional, discriminating, and structured in ways that prevent it from being exploited by cheaters. As discussed, unconditional cooperation opens the door for selfishness.

Repairing Damaged Relations

Game theory research following Axelrod and Hamilton's studies offered an account of the evolution of generosity, reparation, and forgiveness. As documented by de Waal and his colleagues, other primates take measures to repair damaged social relations. They often seem to forgive those who have trespassed against them, and they engage in reconciliation behaviors (Flack & de Waal, 2000). There is a substantial literature on forgiveness in humans, which I review in Chapter 12. As implied by sayings such as "two wrongs don't make a right," "everyone makes mistakes," "forgive and forget," and "forgive those who transgress against you for they know not what they do," humans recognize the value of repairing broken relations and reestablishing cooperative exchanges.

THE SIGNIFICANCE OF SELECTIVE INTERACTION

In Axelrod and Hamilton's simulations of evolution, each player was programmed to interact with all other players on an equally probable basis. However, in all social species, individuals interact with members of their groups in more discriminating ways. This has important implications for the evolution of cooperation because any factor that increases the probability of individuals interacting with others like them—called autocorrelation in the literature—will favor the evolution of cooperation (Skyrms, 2000). The key condition necessary for the evolution of cooperation is that good guys interact with good guys and/or that bad guys interact with bad guys.

One source of selective interaction is spatial segregation. Members of some social species stick relatively close to home "patches," mating with those in their patches. This is theoretically important, because it increases genetic similarity within groups, which favors group selection and the evolution of cooperation (Harms, 2000). However, I believe another source of selective interaction played a more significant role in the evolution of cooperation and morality in the human species.

It makes little sense to interact with all members of one's group in an equally probable or random way, as players were programmed to do in Axelrod and Hamilton's computer contests. Why would anyone want to continue to engage in exchanges with those who exploit them? Although Tit-for-Tat strategists reacted to exploitation by reverting to selfishness, they nonetheless continued to engage in low-payoff exchanges with selfish players. This is not usually what happens in social species, for good reason because there is a much more effective way to deal with those who exploit us. We can write them off and refuse to interact with them at all. Even more effectively, we can observe members of our groups, determine whether they are disposed to behave in selfish or cooperative ways, and interact selectively with those who are disposed to cooperate. Game theorists have demonstrated that strategies that induce individuals to behave cooperatively toward those whom they observe behaving cooperatively can evolve in small groups (Nowak & Sigmund, 1998; Skyrms, 2000; Wedekind & Milinski, 2000).

Being rejected by those who are disposed to cooperate may prove costly, forcing selfish players to engage in low-payoff exchanges with other selfish players, or worse yet, depriving them of the opportunity to interact with anyone at all. Shunned individuals may, in effect, be kicked out of the game—indeed, out of all games. The wages of selfishness may be ostracism, which in many species equates to death. Recent studies have found that social exclusion evokes affective and neurological responses similar to those evoked by physically painful stimuli (Eisenberger, Lieberman, & Williams, 2003).

To reap the benefits of the strategy, "cooperate with cooperators," animals must be willing to cooperate, be able to detect other cooperators, and be disposed to interact with them, and avoid exchanges with noncooperators. More generally, we would expect animals to be disposed to engage in social exchanges with those from whom they stand to gain the most in trade, which can be fostered by selecting exchange partners who possess the greatest promise of bestowing valuable benefits on them and whom they can help the most at the least cost to themselves. It follows that animals should be attentive to the extent to which the resources they have to offer complement the resources others have to offer.

Tooby and Cosmides (1996) have published an insightful analysis of the dynamics of selective interaction. They point out that members of groups have a finite amount of time and energy to allocate to interactions with others and that it is their interest to fill their "association niches" with partners who possess the greatest potential to help them at the least cost. Tooby and Cosmides list several factors that they expect individuals to consider when deciding how to fill their association niches—factors such as how many partners they already have, what a potential partner has to offer, how well the things that others have to offer fit with what they have to offer, whether potential partners can obtain benefits from others (how "irreplaceable" they are), and so on. Tooby and Cosmides suggest that individuals should be adapted to monitor the level of commitment others have toward them by attending to "the magnitude of the cost they are willing to incur per unit of benefit they are willing to deliver" (p. 136).

Animals may gauge the potential value of exchange partners from information about the resources they possess and how potential partners have treated them and others in the past. In addition, humans may base such judgments on what potential exchange partners say to them—for example the commitments they make—and on what third parties say about potential exchange partners (which is probably why gossip is so prevalent in the human species).

Mutual Choice and the Paradox of Popularity

Resolving to restrict your interactions to exchanges with good guys will not do you any good unless the good guys also select you, and this creates a second challenge similar to the challenge faced by individuals when they select mates. After you have selected an exchange partner, you must induce him or her to select you. To accomplish this, Tooby and Cosmides (1996) have argued, members of groups attempt to elevate their "association value" and make themselves irreplaceable. One way of attracting cooperative and altruistic exchange partners is to be willing and able to give them the goods and services they need.

An important byproduct of the strategy of cooperating with cooperators is that it increases the value of cooperating (because being selected as an exchange partner, or being popular, produces long-term gains in trade). The adaptive value of selecting good guys as exchange partners and being selected by good guys in return gives rise to a pleasant paradox. Individuals can maximize their gains by sacrificing their interests for others, as long as the benefits they receive from being viewed as an attractive exchange partner outweigh the costs of the sacrifices they incur to make a good impression. It may well pay off to enhance your social image by treating members of your group altruistically in public, even if they fail to reciprocate, because it induces third parties to select you as an exchange partner.

Impression Management

There is, however, a little glitch in this lovely logic. Strictly speaking, individuals do not base their decisions about social exchange on how others behave; they base them on their *beliefs* about how others have behaved, and perhaps more importantly, on their beliefs about how they will behave in future. What pays off in the social world is not what you do or who you are, but rather what others think about you—the impressions others form of you, that is, your reputation (Goffman, 1959). It is in individuals' interest to put on displays designed to induce members of their groups to overestimate their generosity and underestimate their selfishness. This is why people invoke more generous principles of resource allocation in front of audiences than they do in private, especially when the audiences contain members whose opinions they value and with whom they anticipate interacting in the future (Austin, 1980). Evolutionary theorists such as Nesse (2001) have suggested that, endowed with language, humans induce others to believe they are willing to help them by making promises and other kinds of commitments.

Fortunately, though, the selection of strategies designed to induce others to view us as more altruistic than we actually are is constrained by at least two factors. First, inasmuch as it is biologically costly to be deceived and manipulated, we would expect mechanisms designed to detect deception and to guard against manipulation to evolve. Cosmides (1989) and Cosmides and Tooby (2005) have advanced a great deal of evidence showing that our reasoning abilities are designed in ways that render us proficient at detecting cheating in the social arena. Second, false impressions are constrained by reality. To be perceived as altruistic, one must put on displays of altruism, which inevitably entails helping others. Through the medium of language—in particular gossip—members of groups can share information about the selfishness of others, reducing the opportunity to create false impressions and exploit others with impunity. Research on humans has found that people are surprisingly good at identifying those who are disposed to cooperate, even after very brief encounters (Frank, 1988). The better people are at detecting false advertisements of altruism, the more genuinely altruistic—that is to say, costly—displays of altruism would have to be to reap the rewards of making a good impression. This process is a variation on the costly signaling theme introduced in Chapter 8.

Impression-management and deception-detection and prevention mechanisms must have evolved through an arms-race type of process, with deception-detection and prevention mechanisms selecting for improved impression-management mechanisms, and improved impression-management mechanisms selecting for improved deception-detection and prevention mechanisms (Trivers, 1985). To complicate matters, each individual is both an actor and an audience, a deceiver and a detector. Social exchanges are akin to sports games. Each player makes offensive moves (attempts to deceive and manipulate the other) and defensive moves (guards against being deceived and manipulated).

It is important, however, to recognize that it is not always in an observer's interest to detect deception in others. We would expect deception-detection mechanisms to be calibrated in accordance with the costs and benefits of detecting deception. In general, it is more beneficial to detect deception in those whose interests conflict with ours—members of out-groups and enemies—than in those with whom we share interests (see Krebs & Denton, 1997; 2005 for reviews of relevant research). Indeed, when we benefit from the gains of others, it may be in our interest to support their deception and self-deception (Denton & Zarbatany, 1996). Kathy Denton and I have argued that partners and other individuals who share common fates often engage in a process of mutual self-deception, or "benign folie a deux," in which each supports the other's social illusions (Krebs & Denton, 2009).

Impression Management, Deception Detection, and Morality

Deceiving others about how good we are does not seem right, but people may need to behave in fair and generous ways in order to cultivate the appearance of goodness. Structures designed to detect and to prevent deception may constrain people from engaging in immoral behaviors. Weak detection and prevention mechanisms–gullibility, tolerance of deviance, and susceptibility to exploitation—may encourage others to behave immorally.

LONG-TERM SOCIAL INVESTMENTS

Earlier, I made the point that members of groups may help one another incidentally as they go about their business. I now want to emphasize an important implication of this point, which I discussed in Chapter 6 with respect to hierarchical social orders, namely that inasmuch as the mere existence of a group is biologically beneficial to each member (and to members of others groups, or even to other species), each member has a vested, long-term interest in the welfare of the group. In some contexts—for example, in wars—it may be possible for individuals to help their groups as a whole—that is to say, all members of the group. In other contexts, individuals must decide which members of their groups to help. Earlier I made the point that it is in individuals' interest to select partners with whom they can most profitably coordinate their efforts in mutual endeavors and with whom they can gain the most in trade. I now want to extend this principle to long-term social investments.

Animals that form enduring pair bonds may operate as a unit, helping one another build shelters, produce and rear offspring, fend off predators, and defend territory (Ellis, 1998). In such cases, it is in each individual's interest to uphold the welfare of his or her partner because this upholds the welfare of the unit of which he or she is a part. Not only do partners coordinate their efforts to achieve mutually beneficial goals, they also engage in ongoing social exchanges across many domains. However, as expressed by Geoffrey Miller (2007):

> In game theory terms, [marriages] are iterated, mixed-motive games with very complex conflicts and confluences of interest, many possible equilibria, and incomplete information about the other player's possible tactics and preferences. Some of a potential mate's moral virtues could function as signals that maximize one's payoffs and minimize one's risks in such relationship games. For example, moral capacities for conscientiousness and patience may signal a partner's likelihood of playing mutually beneficial strategies given the repeated interaction nature of long-term relationships. . . . A moral preference for romantic commitment over violent aggression may signal that a partner will seek to sustain a cooperative relationship through promises rather than threats. In each case, the moral trait as a good partner indicator may seem intuitively attractive for its own sake. (p. 101)

In addition to forming pair bonds, members of groups may form enduring "friendships" or coalitions, supporting their friends against other members of their group, and showing preference for their friends as exchange partners. Coalitions are prevalent in primates such as chimpanzees and baboons (de Waal, 1996; Packer, 1977; Trivers, 1985). Research on several social species, including horses, baboons, and humans has found that quantity and quality of friendships that animals form are quite highly related to their survival and reproductive success. Animals with strong social networks suffer less than their less connected peers from high levels of stress. Among humans, socially isolated people have higher blood pressure and more sleep disorders than people who have friends, and their wounds take longer to heal. Having friends is good for your health.[1]

Long-Term Social Investments in Humans

Humans are disposed to form stable, more or less monogamous pair bonds (marriages), friendships, and cliques. Several investigators have pointed out that people rarely engage in concrete, Tit-for-Tat–like forms of reciprocity when interacting with their spouses and friends (Clark & Mills, 1993; Shackelford & Buss, 1996; Tooby & Cosmides, 1996). People often make significant sacrifices for their friends with no expectation of compensation and support them over long periods of time without any expectation of immediate returns (Simpson & Campbell, 2005). Indeed, people may feel offended when their friends adopt an "exchange orientation" and offer to pay them back (Clark & Mills, 1993).

In accounting for the evolution of the types of social strategies adopted by friends, Tooby and Cosmides (1996) alluded to a phenomenon called The Banker's Paradox—the tendency of banks to be least likely to lend money to people when they are most in need. Tooby and Cosmides suggested that it would be in individuals' adaptive interest to suffer the relatively small costs of helping friends over long periods of time if such acts increased the probability that their friends (i.e., "bankers") would be there for them when their fitness was in serious jeopardy. In effect, it pays off for people to invest in their friends as insurance policies to foster their long-term security and fitness. A friend in need is a friend indeed. As conveyed by Lotto 649 advertisements, you never know when one of your friends will strike it rich.

Revisiting Axelrod and Hamilton's games, we recall that the costs and benefits of all exchanges were reckoned in terms of ultimate benefits, namely the number of offspring contributed to future generations. However, most of the resources people exchange in the real world make relatively minor contributions to their reproductive success. It could pay off biologically for an individual to do many small favors for a partner or friend in return for one big favor—100 tits for one big TAT.

CONCLUSIONS

In Chapter 2, I asserted that cooperation constitutes a central aspect of morality, especially as it pertains to justice. To account for the evolution of mechanisms that dispose animals to behave in cooperative ways, we must explain how the strategies that cooperating animals employ protect them from being exploited by selfish cheaters. This is relatively easy to do with respect to primitive forms of cooperation such as mutualism because the costs of cheating are immediate and obvious: If two or more animals fail to do their share,

---

[1] Source: *Science:* http://news.sciencemag.org/sciencenow/2010/07/friendly-baboons-live-longer.html?etoc

they fail to produce anything to share. It is more difficult to explain how more complex forms of cooperation such as those that involve delayed forms of reciprocity and long-term investments in friends and in-group members have evolved because they are more susceptible to cheating. Individuals who help friends in need over long periods of time render themselves vulnerable to exploitation. Individuals who cultivate cooperative public images but cheat in private may fare better than those who suffer the costs of genuine cooperation. The evidence suggests that mechanisms designed to deceive others and mechanisms designed to catch and punish cheaters have evolved in an arms-race manner. Humans are disposed to engage in complex forms of cooperation—no doubt about it—but they also may well be more strongly disposed than they would like to admit to give less than their share and to take more when they can get away with it.

12

PSYCHOLOGICAL AND NEUROLOGICAL SOURCES OF PRIMITIVE PROSOCIAL BEHAVIORS

Having considered how dispositions to behave in prosocial ways have evolved in humans and other animals, it is now time to take a closer look at the mental mechanisms that mediate these forms of conduct, and ask how they are designed.[1] Mapping the design of the mental mechanisms that dispose people to behave in prosocial ways can pay two kinds of dividends. First, determining what kinds of motivational states dispose people to emit various forms of prosocial conduct can supply a basis for drawing conclusions about human nature. When people defer to authority, help others, and cooperate, are they attempting to advance their own interests, or are they motivated to achieve unselfish goals? Second, discovering what activates the mental mechanisms that induce people to behave in prosocial ways can offer guidance for those who seek to promote these forms of conduct.

Psychologists and neurologists have found that prosocial behaviors may stem from a variety of mental mechanisms. Attending to the order in which they evolved is helpful in organizing them and deciphering how they are designed. Some mechanisms, which humans share with other animals, originated millions of years ago. They are located in the inner recesses of the brain. Other mechanisms originated more recently. They are unique to the human species, and have circuits in the outer, frontal parts of the brain.

One of the most primitive forms of prosocial behavior that has been studied by psychologists is impulsive helping in emergencies. Consistent with Darwin's early ideas, but against the intuitions of those who assume that all forms of human altruism stem from higher cognitive processes (and also against the intuitions of those who assume that people are selfish by nature), psychologists have found that, in certain conditions, people who encounter others in life-threatening emergencies experience a "fight or flight" reaction that stems from primitive brain processes and induces them to help victims in an impulsive manner, without

---

[1] In Chapter 7, I discussed the ways in which the proximate mechanisms that mediate self-control are designed.

concern for their own welfare. People who have performed heroic acts such as running into burning buildings to save children are probably telling the truth when they say that they did so without thinking.

Primitive learning mechanisms are another proximate source of prosocial behavior. The operating principles of mental mechanisms that guide learning are designed in ways that parallel the operating principles that guide evolution. Both are regulated by the selection and retention of behaviors that produce beneficial outcome, and by the extinction of behaviors that produce costly outcomes. In the same ways that natural selection can design mechanisms that dispose people to behave in biologically altruistic ways, parents and other socializing agents can teach children to sacrifice their needs for the sake of others.

A variety of emotional reactions, which are associated with particular brain circuits and hormonal processes, have been found to dispose people to behave in prosocial ways. Deferential behaviors have been found to stem from mixtures of fear and admiration. Altruistic behaviors have been found to stem from empathic, sympathetic, affectionate, reactions evoked when people care for and identify with others. Emotions such as gratitude, pride, guilt, shame, indignation, vindictiveness, and forgiveness uphold systems of cooperative exchange.

Although cynics have argued that the motives engendered by empathy and sympathy are selfish in nature, several studies have supported Darwin's contention that these psychological states dispose people to want to help others as an end in itself.

Theorists have suggested that the emotions that induce people to uphold systems of cooperation evolved because they rendered people willing to forgo immediate benefits and to suffer immediate costs in order to maximize long-term gains. Emotion-producing mechanisms that induce people to make costly investments in members of their groups evolved because the fitness of those making the investments was linked to the fitness of those in whom they invested. Emotion-producing mechanisms that induce people to make and to uphold commitments evolved because the long-term benefits of credibility and a reputation for trustworthiness outweighed the short-term costs of keeping promises and carrying out threats.

In earlier chapters, I offered accounts of how the mental mechanisms that give rise to the forms of prosocial conduct that people usually consider moral evolved. It is now time to take a look at how these proximate mechanisms are designed. There has been a great deal of research on proximate sources of prosocial behaviors. Developmental psychologists have attempted to determine how the mental mechanisms that induce people to behave in prosocial ways originate in infants and how these mechanisms change as children develop. Social psychologists have attempted to determine how these mechanisms are activated in adults and the kinds of motivational states they engender. Neuroscientists have attempted to determine where these mechanisms are located in people's brains and how they affect people's physiological states, especially the balance of their hormones.

Guided by evolutionary theory, I organize the mental mechanisms that give rise to prosocial behaviors in terms of the order in which I think they emerged phylogenetically, beginning with primitive mechanisms that humans share with other animals and ending with complex mechanisms unique to the human species. In this chapter, I consider the primitive mechanisms, beginning with those that give rise to reflexive and impulsive helping behaviors, followed by those that regulate learning, and ending with those that produce emotional experiences. In Chapter 15, I consider more uniquely human mechanisms, such as those that endow humans with the abstract perspective-taking abilities and the ability to reason.

MECHANISMS THAT PRODUCE PRIMITIVE IMPULSES

Like other animals, humans sometimes react in reflexive, impulsive ways to stimuli such as loud noises and social threats, with little apparent thought or deliberation. It is easy to think of examples of people reacting in impulsively selfish and aggressive ways. However, as Darwin pointed out, animals also may react in impulsively helpful ways.

Research on impulsive helping has an interesting history in social psychology. Inspired by the famous Kitty Genovese case, in which a large number of observers stood by and watched while a woman was slowly murdered, social psychologists conducted a number of studies designed to determine why people fail to help others in emergencies. The main finding from this research came to be called "the bystander effect:" People are less likely to intervene when there are other bystanders present than when they are the only one available to help. Social psychologists attributed this effect to a diffusion of responsibility.

As research on bystander intervention progressed, some studies failed to find the bystander effect, finding instead that virtually all bystanders intervened to help victims, even when they were in a crowd. At first, these failures to replicate the bystander effect were treated as anomalies, but as they grew in number, it occurred to some social psychologists to compare the studies that failed to find a bystander effect with those that found one, in an attempt to identify the source of the difference (Latané, Nida, & Wilson, 1981).

This comparison produced an unexpected finding. Although we would expect people to be less likely to intervene in severe emergencies in which the costs of helping are high than they are to intervene in less dangerous emergencies in which the costs of helping are low, the opposite proved to be the case. Researchers found that, in some conditions, bystanders were significantly more likely to intervene in clear, realistic, extreme emergencies than they were to intervene in less potentially costly cases, regardless of whether other bystanders were present or not. More surprisingly, participants intervened immediately, without much apparent thought, seemingly oblivious to their own welfare. For example, in one study in which a victim appeared to have been electrocuted, bystanders grabbed the victim, even though, had the emergency been real, they would have endangered their own lives (Clark & Word, 1974). In another study, participants jeopardized their own welfare to stop an "attempted rape" perpetrated by a threatening attacker (Anderson, 1974).

The social psychologists who were attempting to explain these findings noted that, "not coincidentally, the same factors that facilitate impulsive helping—clarity, reality, involvement with the victim—have also been demonstrated to be related to greater levels of bystander arousal" (Piliavin et al., 1981). These psychologists concluded that impulsive helping is mediated by different mental mechanisms from nonimpulsive forms of helping. They suggested that when people encounter a person in need, they process the information in the situation at a preconscious level and categorize it in one of two ways—as something interesting that they should attend to and interpret, or as an emergency. If they categorize the event as "something interesting," they experience a "wait and see" orienting response that induces them to attend to the costs and benefits of various courses of action, which tends to diminish the probability that they will intervene, especially if others are available to help (thus producing the bystander effect). However, if they categorize the event as an emergency, they experience a "fight or flight" reaction that induces them to narrow their attention, focus on the plight of the victim, truncate the processing of further information, and react impulsively, without any further thought. "Cost considerations become peripheral and not attended to" (p. 239). These researchers speculated that "there may be an evolutionary basis for . . . impulsive helping" (p. 180).

Well, there has to be an evolutionary basis for impulsive helping; the question is, what kind of basis? The mechanisms that induce people to engage in impulsive helping could have evolved because they increased the inclusive fitness of early humans by, for example, inducing them to help their offspring and other relatives, or they could have evolved as a maladaptive byproduct of other mechanisms, such as those that give rise to fight or flight responses. Whatever the biological benefits of impulsive helping, it does not seem plausible that those who engage in it are motivated to increase their own welfare. The terminal goal of impulsive helping seems to be to help a victim, as an end in itself, without any thought of increasing one's own pleasure, reducing vicariously experienced pain, gaining social approval, or feeling good about oneself.

PRIMITIVE LEARNING MECHANISMS

During the middle of the 20th century, theorists such as B. F. Skinner argued that humans inherit learning mechanisms that are designed in essentially the same ways as the learning mechanisms of other animals and that these mechanisms regulate virtually all their behavior. As demonstrated by learning theorists such as Justin Aronfreed (1968), humans and other animals can be taught to behave in prosocial ways by rewarding them when they do good (and intend to do good) and punishing them when they are bad (and intend to be bad). Learning theorists have demonstrated that social approval and disapproval can acquire reinforcing qualities through their association with physically rewarding and punishing experiences. As I will explain, this research has important implications for the development of conscience.

The proximate mechanisms that regulate learning (or, more exactly, that regulate operant conditioning) are designed in ways that correspond to the ultimate mechanisms that regulate natural selection. Both involve the shaping of mental mechanisms through the consequences of the behaviors they produce; and both are regulated by processes of selection, retention, and extinction. Individuals emit all kinds of behaviors. Some behaviors increase their welfare; others diminish it. The behaviors that increase individuals' welfare are selected and repeated; the behaviors that diminish it are rendered extinct, or extinguished.

In Chapter 3, I explained that biologically and genetically altruistic behaviors need not violate the laws of natural selection because mechanisms that disposed early humans to behave in fitness-increasing ways may induce modern humans to behave in fitness-reducing ways. A similar point can be made with respect to the laws of learning. Once a behavior is learned, it may persist for a long time even though it fails to produce, or to be followed by, beneficial effects. Some costly habits (which originally were acquired because they reaped immediate rewards) are hard to break. For example, a person might continue supporting a friend in need far after the initial rewards came to an end. In addition, as the learning theorist Rachlin (2002) has demonstrated, learning mechanisms may be designed in ways that induce people to engage in behaviors that are costly immediately after they are emitted (and, therefore, on his definition, that qualify as altruistic) but that pay off in the long run because they constitute aspects of behavioral strategies that optimize people's long-term benefits.

Finally, it is important to keep in mind that the definitions of altruism employed by evolutionary and learning theorists are based on the consequences of actions, not on the motivational state of actors. When people repeat behaviors that have paid off, especially those that have produced pleasure, it might seem that they are driven by psychologically selfish motives, and that they are trying to obtain benefits for themselves, but this is not necessarily the case. They could be motivated to achieve goals such as helping others, and the rewards that reinforce the behaviors could be incidental byproducts of their altruistic behaviors. If, for example, a person who rushed into a burning building to save a child's life later received a hero's medal, it would not be appropriate to conclude without supporting evidence that the altruistic behavior was motivated by the desire to receive this reward.

MECHANISMS THAT PRODUCE PRIMITIVE EMOTIONAL REACTIONS

People often account for prosocial behaviors by attributing them to emotional states. "She comforted him because she felt sorry for him." "He returned the favor because he felt gratitude." "She did it out of love." "He donated to charity in order to allay his guilt." Implicit in these attributions is the assumption that emotions engender or include motivational states. Even though it might, in a reductionist sense, be more exact to say that the physiological and mental processes that induce people to experience emotions cause their behaviors, and to view emotional experiences as byproducts of these mechanisms, than to say that the emotions cause their behaviors, it seems permissible out of parsimony to attribute the behaviors to the emotional states. To account for the role played by emotions in the determination of prosocial behaviors, we need to identify the stimuli that activate the mental mechanisms that produce them, identify the neurological and hormonal processes in these mechanisms, and determine what kinds of thoughts and goals they engender. I will begin by extending the discussion of emotional sources of deference begun in Chapter 6, then turn to a more detailed discussion of emotional sources of altruism and cooperation.

Emotional Sources of Deference

In Chapter 6, I suggested that two types of emotions dispose people to behave in deferential ways—(1) feelings of fear and insecurity, and (2) feelings of admiration and awe. Fear is evoked by threatening stimuli. It is mediated by the autonomic nervous system and primitive brain mechanisms such as the amygdale, interacting with interpretive mechanisms in the prefrontal cortex. According to the neuroscientist Jorge Moll and his colleagues (2008), feelings of admiration and awe are evoked by accomplished people to whom observers are attached; however "the neuroanatomy of awe is still obscure" (p. 16).

In Chapter 6, I reviewed research demonstrating that hormones play an important role in the deferential dispositions displayed by humans and other animals and that status is correlated with androgen and serotonin levels in many species of primates. For example, researchers found that low-ranking members of vervet monkey groups had only half as much serotonin in their blood as their higher-ranking colleagues did.

Different mixtures of fear and awe engender different kinds of motivational states. Fear disposes people to show deference to powerful and intimidating authorities in order to avoid punishment, which seems psychologically selfish. In contrast, awe and admiration seem to give rise to more psychologically altruistic motives, disposing people to support those they look up to, to seek their approval, to curry their favor, and to get in their good books. Religious experiences that dispose "God-fearing" people to supplicate themselves to omnipotent and omniscient Gods ("Glory to God on the highest") seem to involve a synthesis of the two systems.

Emotional Sources of Altruism

Researchers have identified a wide array of emotional states that dispose people to help others—some positive in nature and others negative. With respect to negative emotional states, some investigators have concluded that people are motivated to help others when they feel bad in order to relieve their vicariously experienced distress and to elevate their mood (Cialdini, et al., 1987); whereas other investigators have concluded that experiencing the distress of others vicariously engenders the motivation to help them as an end in itself (Batson, 1991). With respect to positive emotional states, researchers have found that feelings of love, affection, attachment, loyalty, and solidarity motivate people to help others, as do mood-elevating experiences such as receiving unexpected favors and succeeding at a task (Isen & Levin, 1972). Within the suite of emotions that have been linked to altruism, the two that have received the most attention, by far, are sympathy and empathy, which will not be surprising to most people, based on their experience.

Sympathy and Empathy

Although sympathy and empathy are similar, especially when evoked by signs of distress in others, and although most of the research findings on each of these emotions apply to the other, sympathy differs from empathy in at least two ways. First, sympathy is evoked only by others' suffering and sorrow and involves an emotional state that is negative in nature. In contrast, empathy may involve positive and negative emotional states, depending one whether it is evoked by others' pleasures or their pains. Second, sympathy involves feeling *for* others; whereas empathy involves experiencing others' affective states vicariously and *sharing* their emotional states. People may feel sympathy for those who are blissfully ignorant of their plight. I argue that sympathy is an evolutionarily more advanced and cognitively more complex emotion than empathy is.

Frans de Waal (2008) has advanced a compelling model of the evolution of empathy and sympathy that mirrors a central assumption in the explanatory framework developed in this book. Agreeing with Darwin (1874), who said, "many animals certainly sympathize with each other's distress or danger" (p. 77), de Waal makes the point that "emotional connectedness in humans is so common, starts so early in life. . . . and shows neural and physiological correlates. . . . as well as a genetic substrate . . . that it would be strange indeed if no continuity with other species existed. Evolutionary continuity between humans and apes is reflected in the similarity of emotional communication . . . as well as similar changes in brain and peripheral skin temperatures in response to emotionally charged images" (p. 5). De Waal suggests that emotional empathy and primitive imitation stem from the same source.

Moll, di Oliveira-Sourza, Zahn, and Grafman (2008) have attempted to map the mental mechanisms that engender feelings of sympathy (that they call pity and compassion). They suggest that sympathetic reactions are activated when people recognize that a person or a group to whom they feel attached has experienced a negative outcome. Summarizing the findings from studies that have investigated areas of the brain that are activated when people experience sympathy, these neuroscientists report that "preliminary functional imaging results in normal subjects point to the involvement of the anterior PFC [prefrontal cortex], the dorsolateral PFC, the OFC [orbitofrontal cortices], the anterior insula, and the anterior temporal cortex" (pp. 15–16).

An important question about sympathy and empathy is, why are the mental mechanisms that produce these emotions activated by some people, but not by others? De Waal (2008, p. 16) cites research demonstrating that, "the empathic response is amplified by similarity, familiarity, social closeness, and positive experience with the other. . . . In human studies subjects empathize with a confederate's pleasure or distress if they perceive the relationship as cooperative." However, suggests de Waal, people tend to experience the opposite reaction when observing competitors experience pleasure and pain. He cites research showing that: "seeing the pain of a cooperative confederate activates pain-related brain areas, but seeing the pain of an unfair confederate activates reward-related areas, at least in men." De Waal concludes that, "the empathy mechanism is biased the way evolutionary theory would predict. Empathy is (a) activated in relation to those with whom one has a close or positive relationship, and (b) suppressed, or even turned into Schadenfreude, in relation to strangers and defectors." (p. 16).

The Empathy–Altruism Controversy

One of the longest-running debates in philosophy and in the social sciences pertains to the nature of the motivational state induced by sympathizing and empathizing with people in distress. Some scholars have argued that these emotions give rise to psychologically altruistic motives. Others scholars have questioned this conclusion, arguing that people help those with whom they empathize and for whom they feel sympathy to make themselves feel better or to achieve other self-serving goals.

As mentioned in Chapter 4, Darwin (1874) took a position on this issue in *The Descent of Man*. He questioned whether sympathetic behaviors are aimed at relieving "the sufferings of another, in order that our own painful feelings may be at the same time relieved," because this account fails to explain "the fact that sympathy is excited, in an immeasurably stronger degree, by a beloved, than by an indifferent person" (p. 103). More recently, the social psychologist, Dan Batson (Batson, 1991) has attempted to resolve the "altruism question" empirically. Batson argued that when people focus on the plight of others in need, they may react in one of two ways. First, they may experience a state of "personal distress," which they can reduce by helping the person in need, or by looking away, leaving the scene, and so on. Alternatively, people may experience "an other-oriented emotional response . . . [such as] empathy, sympathy, compassion, etc." (Batson, 2000, p. 208) that engenders "a motivational state with the ultimate goal of increasing another's welfare" (p. 207). When people are in this state, they seek to help those with whom they empathize, as an end in itself, as opposed to wanting to help them instrumentally in order to relieve their own vicariously experienced personal distress, or to achieve other egoistic goals. De Waal (2008) reviews evidence indicating that personal distress stems from the primitive core of empathy; whereas sympathetic and empathic concern stem from later-evolved layers of the brain.

To test the hypothesis that sympathy and empathy may engender altruistic motives, Batson and his colleagues have conducted more than two dozen experiments—some very ingenious—designed to determine whether individuals who observe others in distress are motivated to help them in order to relieve their own personal distress (rendering their behaviors egoistic) or to relieve the distress of the victims, as an end in itself (rendering their behaviors psychologically altruistic). As a general strategy, these researchers induced participants to empathize with victims (for example, by inducing them to take their perspective or by leading them to believe they were similar to them), then provided them with ways of achieving a variety of egoistic goals in less costly ways than by helping the victims.

Consider some examples described by Batson (1991). To determine whether people help others in order to reduce their own vicariously experienced aversive arousal, Batson and his colleagues offered them an opportunity to reduce their arousal by terminating their exposure to the victim rather than by helping him or her. To determine whether people help those with whom they empathize in order to gain social approval or to avoid disapproval, Batson and his colleagues determined whether people who empathized with victims were more likely to help in public than they were to help in private. To determine whether empathizing observers help victims in order to avoid self-censure, Batson and his colleagues offered them personally and socially acceptable reasons and justifications for not helping. To determine whether those in empathic states help in order to feel good about themselves, these researchers assessed the mood of participants after they learned that third parties helped victims. Without exception, the studies conducted by Batson and his colleagues supported the empathy–altruism hypothesis. Citing a review of the literature on prosocial behavior by the psychologists Piliavin and Charng (1990), Batson concluded that a "paradigm shift" is occurring in psychology, "away from the earlier position that behavior that appears to be altruistic must, under closer scrutiny, be revealed as reflecting egoistic motives. Rather, theory and data now being advanced are more compatible with the view that true altruism—acting with the goal of benefiting another—does exist and is a part of human nature" (p. 27).

In effect, Batson (1991) has challenged cynics who believe that empathy triggers a psychologically selfish motive to demonstrate that people help victims only when it enables them to achieve self-serving goals in the least costly manner. Some psychologists have claimed to have met this challenge, for example, by demonstrating that people help distressed victims with whom they empathize in order to relieve negative states of sadness (Cialdini et al., 1987; Schaller & Cialdini, 1988). However, Batson and others have disputed their conclusions (Batson et al., 1989; Dovidio, Allen, & Schroeder, 1990). Although it is not possible to prove that those who feel empathy for victims are not driven to help them by some unassessed selfish motive, Batson and his colleagues have been remarkably successful at demonstrating that people choose to help those with whom they empathize even when they can achieve selfish goals in more direct and less costly ways.

Evolutionary theory offers a context for understanding empathy. It alerts us to the fact that individual bodies are not the most appropriate unit of analysis when it comes to explaining human conduct. Inasmuch as individuals share genes and identify with others, they overlap genetically and psychologically. Because individuals' genetic and psychological selves include others, they can foster their inclusive fitness and help "themselves" by helping others.

Love

Like empathy and sympathy, love is a powerful emotion that disposes individuals to behave in caring, devoted, and altruistic ways. Among the many potential partners that individuals encounter, what causes them to fall in love with some, but not with others? No one knows for sure, but I believe that an important (albeit unromantic!) aspect of the answer to this question is, the perception that the recipient possesses relatively high reproductive value, compared to one's own.

To the dismay of some romantics, investigators are beginning to map the brain mechanisms and hormonal processes that produce feelings of love. Researchers have found that being in love is associated with the activation of the ventral tegmental and caudate nuculi of the brain (areas associated with experiences of pleasure), the production of neurochemicals such as dopamine, and the inhibition of neurochemicals such as serotonin (Fisher, 2004).

Feelings of Solidarity

There is a great deal of evidence that just as people are disposed to form attachments to other individuals, they also are disposed to form attachments to their groups as a whole, and to uphold their groups, even at great expense to themselves. As expressed by Richerson and Boyd (2001), "We are adapted to living in tribes, and the social institutions of tribes elicit strong—sometimes fanatical—commitment" (p. 215). Many studies have found that people are willing to sacrifice their own interests to promote the collective interests of their groups. The behaviors of soldiers during battle supply compelling examples. Quoting from the U.S. Army Field Manual, "While patriotism and sense of purpose will get American soldiers to the battlefield, the soldiers' own accounts (and many systematic studies) testify that what keep them there amid the fear of death and mutilation is, above all, their loyalty to their fellow soldiers" (Department of the Army, 1994; quoted by Brown & Brown, 2006, p. 38).

Social psychologists such as Tajfel and Turner (1985) have accounted for feelings of solidarity in terms of people's disposition to incorporate the group to which they belong into their self-concepts as aspects of their "social identities." These psychologists have found that people quickly identify with groups to which they have been assigned on an arbitrary basis, such as whether they prefer one or another form of abstract art, or whether they have blue eyes or brown eyes, and that they immediately feel disposed to favor the groups to which they have been assigned. The intensity of emotional identification with groups is readily apparent at sporting events, where "we" become "number 1," at least when "we" are winning (Cialdini, Borden, Thorne, Walker, Freeman, & Sloan, 1976).

Two questions arise with respect to the mental mechanisms that give rise to feelings of solidarity and group-upholding behaviors. First, how do people represent conceptions of their groups in their self-concepts; and second, how altruistic is the motivation to uphold one's group? Both of these questions are complex. With respect to the first one, consider the following summary by Batson (1998): "Concern for another's welfare may be a product of (1) a sense of we-ness based on cognitive unit formation or identification with the other . . . (2) the self expanding to incorporate the other . . . (3) the self–other distinction remaining and perhaps even being intensified . . . (4) the self being redefined at the group level, when me and thee become interchangeable parts of a self that is we . . . or (5) the self dissolving in devotion to something outside itself" (p. 306). Several investigators have made the point that in order for empathy to give rise to altruistic motives, people's sense of those they help must be distinct from their sense of themselves, else they would end up helping both themselves and others (Batson, 1998; de Waal, 2008; Hoffman, 2000).

With respect to the nature of the motivation to uphold one's group, although it is possible that people's willingness to sacrifice their lives for the sake of their groups is based on such selfish goals as enhancing their reputation or insuring their place in Heaven, several investigators have advanced evidence that people are naturally disposed to uphold the collective interests of their groups, as an end in itself, rather than upholding their groups' interests as a means of promoting their own interests (even if this effect occurs incidentally) (Dawes, van de Kragt, & Orbell, 1988).

As I discuss more fully in Chapter 14, some evolutionary theorists have argued that instincts to uphold large culturally defined groups evolved later than, and in a different way from, dispositions to help friends and relatives. For example, Richerson and Boyd (2005) have argued that relatively recently evolved tribal instincts evolved through cultural group selection, and "are laid on top of more ancient social instincts rooted in kin selection and reciprocal altruism" (p. 191). According to these theorists, "we are simultaneously committed to tribes, family, and self, even though our simultaneous and conflicting commitments very often cause us . . . great anguish" (p. 191). Richerson and Boyd see tribal instincts as similar to "the principles in the Chomskyan linguists' 'principles and parameters' . . . of language. . . . The innate principles furnish people with basic predispositions, emotional capacities, and social skills that are implemented in practice through highly variable cultural institutions, the parameters" (p. 191).

An Integrative Account of the Evolution
of Emotional Sources of Altruism

Faced with evidence that a suite of emotions disposes people to help those with whom they are associated in various ways, the daughter–father team of Stephanie and R. Michael Brown have advanced an integrative theory—social investment theory—that accounts for this process parsimoniously under one overriding principle, namely that individuals are naturally disposed to help those with whom they share fitness interdependence. Brown and Brown (2006) marshal a great deal of evidence in support of the idea that mental mechanisms have evolved in many species that give rise to emotionally mediated social bonds between and among mates, offspring, friends, and members of groups and that these bonds dispose them to treat one another in psychologically altruistic ways. Brown and Brown (2006) argue that their theory:

> complements and extends ultimate (biologically distal) contemporary gene-centered accounts of evolution by wedding the proximate motivation to help, provided by the social bond, to an ultimate condition that makes the evolution of altruism possible—fitness interdependence. . . . From the perspective of selective investment theory, the key to understanding the evolution of altruism is not whether a potential altruistic recipient carries copies of the altruist's genes, or whether the recipient is likely to be a reciprocal altruist, but rather the direction and magnitude of the correlation between the reproductive success of potential altruists and their recipients. (p. 9)

At a proximate level of analysis, Brown and Brown review evidence demonstrating that oxytocin and other hormones such as vasopressin, prolactin, and endogenous opioids structure social bonds, and that social bonds dispose humans and other animals to make costly long-term social investments in members of their groups with whom they share fitness interdependence (pp. 11–12).

In addition, Brown and Brown discuss the tension attended to by Darwin between psychologically selfish and altruistic dispositions. These theorists suggest that humans and other animals sometimes experience internal conflicts between emotional states that motivate them to behave in selfish, self-preserving ways, (i.e., to increase their fitness directly)—which involve one set of neuroendocrine responses—and emotional states that motivate them to help those on whom their fitness is dependent (i.e., to increase their fitness indirectly)—which involve another set of neuroendocrine responses. They argue that overarching regulatory mechanisms must have evolved to resolve such conflicts. Animals need such regulatory mechanisms to decide when to help themselves and when to help others, whom to help, and how much help to allocate to those with whom they have formed social bonds. However, Brown and Brown acknowledge that, "to our knowledge, the proximate machinery that would resolve self vs. other motivational conflicts, and activate and regulate emotions that facilitate costly long term investment— in ways that enhance fitness—has yet to be articulated" (p. 9).

Brown and Brown argue that social scientists have erred in characterizing costly long-term social investments as psychologically selfish, and accounting for them in terms of the proximate benefits they purvey. These theorists insist that selective investment theory "departs from reward-based theories . . . in its suggestion that consideration of another person's needs may be as important as consideration of our own in stimulating attraction or the desire for a relationship" (p. 47). According to these theorists, social bonds generate the desire to give, rather than the desire to receive, and the benefits people end up receiving from their friends are products of genuinely altruistic motivational states (Nesse, 2001).

With respect to the cognitive products of the mental mechanisms that dispose people to put others' needs ahead of their own, Brown and Brown suggest that the emotions engendered by social bonds induce people to make decisions that favor others by inducing them to overestimate the benefits of helping those on whom their fitness is dependent and to underestimate the costs. Studies have supported this idea (see Janicki, 2004).

Emotional Sources of Cooperation

Feelings of love, sympathy, and solidarity dispose people to uphold care-based forms of morality. In addition to the mental mechanisms that dispose humans and other animals to care for others, another suite of mental mechanisms have evolved in social species whose function is to dispose people to uphold systems of cooperation. These mechanisms uphold justice-based forms of morality.

As expressed by Kaplan, Gurven, and Lancaster (2007), "Natural selection has shaped our psychology to possess the following traits: (1) perceptual sensitivity to potential gains from cooperation; (2) motivation to take advantage of those gains; (3) perceptual sensitivity to opportunities for free-riding; (4) motivation to avoid being free-ridden; (5) motivation to take advantage of opportunities for free-riding; (6) perceptual sensitivity to the short- and long-term personal costs and benefits of social norms regarding cooperative behavior (from the perspective of both self and others); (7) motivation to negotiate social norms, so that personal benefits from cooperation and free-riding are maximized; and (8) motivation to obey and enforce social norms, so that punishment is avoided and those who disobey norms or fail to enforce them are punished" (p. 274).

Several emotions dispose individuals to uphold systems of cooperation. Some of the care-based emotions that I have discussed, such as sympathy, empathy, and feelings of solidarity, get cooperative exchanges started by motivating people to give goods and services to others. Feelings of pride reinforce such behaviors. Appreciation, gratitude, and a sense of indebtedness motivate those who have been helped to return the favors. Anger, indignation, and vindictiveness motivate those who have been cheated to punish those who cheated them, even if it is costly to do so in the short run. Guilt induces cheaters to regret exploiting others, and motivates them to make amends. Feelings of forgiveness induce people to reestablish cooperative relationships with those who have cheated them. Researchers have begun to map the design of the mental mechanisms that give rise to and structure the emotions that regulate cooperative behaviors, and to identify the areas in the brain that house them. Let us consider a sample of findings.

Pride

When I discussed the Seven Deadly Sins in Chapter 7, I distinguished between "hubristic pride" and "authentic pride" and suggested that the biological function of pride is to reinforce behaviors that elevate people's status. In Chapter 6, I reviewed evidence indicating that one of the main ways in which people elevate their status is by upholding the systems of cooperation in their groups. According to Moll et al. (2008), feelings of pride are evoked when people view themselves, and are viewed by others, as the agent of actions that produce good outcomes, that elevate their self-esteem, and that make them feel socially dominant. These investigators acknowledge that, "so far there is no clear evidence for the neural representation of pride, although it has been shown that patients with OFC [orbitofrontal cortex] lesions may experience this emotion inappropriately" (p. 14–15).

Gratitude

Moll and his colleagues (2008) assert that, "[Gratitude] is elicited by (1) detecting a good outcome to oneself, attributed to (2) the agency of another person, (3) who acted in an intentional manner to achieve the outcome. (4) Gratitude is associated with a feeling of attachment to the other agent and often promotes the reciprocation of favors. . . . Activated brain regions include the ventral striatum, the OFC, and the anterior cingulate cortex" (p. 16).

In support of these assertions, psychologists have found that feelings of gratitude are evoked by the perception that a benefactor has tried to improve one's well-being (McCullough, Kilpatrick, Emmons, & Larson, 2001). The intensity of gratitude is affected by the value of the benefit, the cost of giving the benefit, the perceived intentions of the benefactor, and the extent to which the beneficence was voluntary, expected, and normative (McCullough, Kimeldorf, & Cohen, 2008). In contrast to feelings of indebtedness, which are experienced as a negative state that motivates people to redress a perceived inequity, gratitude is experienced as a positive state that motivates people to help not only those who benefited them, but also to help third parties (Greenberg, 1980; McCullough et al., 2008). "The greater one's gratitude for a benefit, the greater one's desire to help, praise, and be near the benefactor. Conversely, the greater one's indebtedness, the greater one's distress and desire to avoid the benefactor" (McCullough et al., 2008, p. 283).

McCullough and his colleagues (2008) review research supporting Trivers' contention that the mental mechanisms that produce feelings of gratitude evolved to support reciprocity. These theorists go on to suggest that gratitude may have evolved "to stimulate not only direct reciprocal altruism, but also what [has been called] 'upstream reciprocity': passing benefits on to third parties instead of returning benefits to one's benefactors" (p. 283). This idea meshes well with Richard Alexander's model of the evolution of indirect reciprocity, which I discuss in Chapter 14.

Anger and Indignation

Being cheated and exploited, and seeing those with whom one identifies being cheated and exploited, may evoke anger and indignation, which in turn, may motivate people to retaliate. According to Moll et al. (2008), people experience these emotions when they observe people intentionally violating norms. "Indignation relies on . . . engagement of aggressiveness, following an observation of . . . bad outcomes to the self or a third party. [Researchers] have shown that indignation evokes activation of the OFC . . . the anterior PFC, anterior insula, and anterior cingulate contex" (p. 15).

Vindictiveness and the Desire for Revenge

It might seem that feelings of vindictiveness stem from the same kinds of mental mechanisms that produce feelings of anger and indignation, but several studies suggest that this is not the case. Instead, when people are in a vengeful state, areas of the brain such as the left prefrontal cortex and caudate nucleus, which are implicated in striving for desirable outcomes and pursuing rewarding goals, light up. Areas associated with feelings of satisfaction, such as the nucleus accumbens, light up when people achieve revenge or learn that those who have treated them unfairly are being punished. As expressed by McCullough (2008) in a book entitled *Beyond Revenge: The Evolution of the Forgiveness Instinct*:

> Mark Twain once wrote, 'Revenge is wicked, & unchristian & in every way unbecoming . . . (But it is powerful sweet, anyway).' A twenty-first-century paraphrase might read, 'Revenge pays neurochemical dividends.' People who have been harmed by another person are goaded into revenge by a brain system that hands them a promissory note certifying that revenge, when it comes, will make them feel good. . . . A hard truth of human nature is that it's often pleasant to watch our enemies suffer, and it's a pleasure that we'll sometimes go to great lengths to acquire. Natural selection's logic here seems pretty easy to comprehend: by paying us back with pleasure, our brains ensure that we'll go to the trouble of seeking the social advantages that come from returning harm for harm. Injustice, modern neuroscience tells us, can make sadists of us all.

Feelings of revenge and vindictiveness probably play a more significant role in human behavior than most people realize. Martin Daly and Margo Wilson (1988) surveyed the ethnographic records of 60 societies and found that revenge played an important role in the social relations of people from virtually all of them. People may hold grudges for long periods of time, waiting their chance to get even with those whom they believe have wronged them. In righting one wrong, people perpetrate another, which when righted, perpetrates another, and so on in the kind of self-defeating feedback circle that I discussed earlier with respect to negative forms of Tit-for-Tat reciprocity. Moral outrage fuels blood feuds that jeopardize the welfare of all parties involved.

In view of the maladaptive consequences of repeated, back and forth "get even" blood feuds, however, we might expect mechanisms designed to bring it all to an end to have evolved in humans and other animals. Frans de Waal and other primatologists have observed reconciliation behaviors in primates, and as pointed out by McCullough, in *Beyond Revenge*, anthropologists have found that when blood feuds become excessively costly to both sides, people may engage in elaborate reconciliation rituals designed to end them.

Emotional Sources of Reparation

As discussed with respect to the evolution of reciprocity, mistakes can destroy systems of cooperation. No one is perfect. Everyone occasionally harms others, breaks the rules, and violates the standards that govern cooperative exchanges in their groups. When this happens, it threatens the sanctity of the system and with it the benefits it produces. In view of the adaptive value of cooperation, it is not surprising that a set of emotional reactions that includes guilt, shame, and feelings of forgiveness has evolved to induce people to make amends, to repair damaged social relations, and to get mutually beneficial exchanges back on track.

Guilt and Shame

When people hurt and exploit others, free-ride, and otherwise violate the prosocial norms of their groups, they may feel guilty or ashamed. Researchers have found that feelings of guilt are evoked when people feel responsible for causing those to whom they feel attached to experience negative outcomes, especially as a result of behaviors that violate social norms (Baumeister, Stillwell, & Heatherton, 1994). Learning theorists tend to view guilt as a derivative of fear. The philosopher, Jesse Prinz (2007, p. 77), views it more as a derivative of sadness. Perhaps it is a blend of both. Moll et al. (2008) report that "recent neuroimaging data showed the involvement of the anterior PFC, the anterior temporal cortex, the insula, the anterior cingulated cortex, and the STS [superior temporal sulcus] regions in guilt experience" (p. 13). Punitive responses from others probably served as a selective force in the evolution of these emotions.

In contrast to guilt, suggest Moll et al. (2008), shame emerges when people violate social norms that produce bad outcomes to themselves, ("at least indirectly, such as damage to one's reputation"), and when they suffer a reduction in self-esteem and social dominance in their own eyes and in the eyes of others. Moll et al. (2008) suggest that "brain regions similar to those demonstrated for embarrassment should be involved [in the experience of shame]" (p. 14).[2] Prinz (2007) has suggested that people feel shame when they violate rules pertaining to the natural order and when they perpetrate transgressions against nature, such as when they engage in illicit sexual acts, violate food taboos, or engage in other "dirty" deeds.

Forgiveness

In *Beyond Revenge*, Michael McCullough reviews research on forgiveness, which he considers a social instinct. He cites evidence showing that this instinct mediates reconciliation in chimpanzees and other primates and that it constitutes a cultural universal in the human species. McCullough (2008) argues that forgiveness is activated by three main "if" conditions: (1) feeling close to, and prone to empathize with, a person who harmed you, (2) feeling anxious about losing a valued, potentially beneficial, relationship, and (3) feeling confident that the person who harmed you will not harm you again, and anticipating that forgiving him or her will enhance your security. To determine whether these conditions are met, people attend to information such as whether those who victimized

---

[2] The brain regions that have been found to be involved in embarrassment are the medial PFC, the anterior temporal cortex, the STS region, and the lateral division of the OFC.

them intended to inflict harm on them, could have avoided inflicting harm on them, regret their behavior, and are likely to repeat the offence.

The neurochemistry of forgiveness involves mechanisms that reduce the stress that humans and other animals experience when they are embroiled in social conflicts. Being mistreated activates stress hormones such as cortisol that generate unpleasant feelings of anger and anxiety. There are two basic ways of reducing such unpleasant states—by getting even, and by forgiving those who have harmed you. Holding a grudge entails holding on to the unpleasant feelings, which as we all know, may fester for long periods of time.

After reviewing research demonstrating that reconciliation reduces distress in other primates, McCullough (2008) argues that it is a mistake to assume that humans derive decisions about forgiving others in more rational ways: "As is the case with the nonhuman primates, it's our emotions that are central, and anxiety is one of the biggies, for kids and grown-ups alike" (pp. 127–128).

The Nature of Motives to Behave in Cooperative Ways

Sometimes—perhaps often—people behave in cooperative ways for psychologically selfish reasons. For example, people cooperate to maximize their gains in trade, and people forgive others to reduce their stress. However, the emotions that uphold cooperative behaviors—whether positive or negative in nature—need not necessarily give rise to selfish motives. To repeat a point I made earlier, there is no evolutionary reason that the proximate mechanisms that dispose people to feel like helping those who help them, or forgiving those who wrong them, as ends in themselves, could not have evolved, as long as such dispositions had the effect of increasing the frequency of genes that designed the mechanisms in ancestral environments. After asserting that, "for years, many biologists and social scientists alike viewed positive human characteristics—love, friendship, faithfulness, gratitude, honesty, altruism, cooperation, forgiveness, and so forth—as exceptions to the rule of human nature, as self-delusions, or as a whitewash that we've brushed on top of humanity's ruthless, competitive, aggressive, authentic nature," McCullough (2008) makes the following point with respect to forgiveness, "forgiveness, like other positive human attributes, isn't a pretty façade that we use to mask the ugly reality that we're vengeful brutes. *The capacity to forgive is every bit as much a product of natural selection as is our penchant for revenge; it is also an intrinsic feature of human nature—crafted by natural selection—that exists today because it was adaptive in the ancestral environment in which the human species developed*" (p. 13).

THE ADAPTIVE FUNCTIONS OF SOCIAL EMOTIONS

The ultimate adaptive function of all emotions is to dispose people to behave in inclusive-fitness-increasing ways. The emotions that some scientists have called "moral emotions" (e.g., Moll et al., 2008) help people foster their inclusive fitness by resisting the temptation to promote their short-term personal interests at the expense of their long-term biological and genetic welfare. In effect, moral emotions induce people to experience long-term biological costs and benefits as short-term pains and pleasures. Although it may be immediately costly to defer to authority, to help members of one's group, and to repay favors, behaving in these ways often pays off materially, psychologically, biologically, and genetically in the end. For example, feelings of emotional closeness, love, and empathy motivate people to foster the welfare of those who end up helping them survive and reproduce. Feelings of gratitude motivate people to behave in ways that end up producing gains in trade. Feelings of solidarity and other "tribal instincts" induce people to uphold groups that increase their long-term security.

Moll and his colleagues have suggested that when people are faced with decisions that affect their welfare, they unconsciously weigh the short-term benefits against the long-term consequences of the choices they are evaluating, and this process activates appropriate emotions. For example, "one considers attaining a selfish, short-term reward, but feels guilty and refrains from acting, foreseeing that the act would make another person suffer; or one acts in the first place but then realizes the possibility of adverse consequences to others" (Moll et al., 2008, p. 10).

The Value of Making and Keeping Commitments

Extending the idea that certain emotions help people reap the benefits of delayed rewards, several evolutionary theorists have suggested that an important function of such emotions is to motive people to keep their commitments even when it is costly to do so in the short run (Nesse, 2001, p. 13). When people make commitments, they say things like, "If you help me now, I will help you in the future," or "If you betray me, I will get even." Commitments are promises. Those who keep them come across as honest and trustworthy, and those who break them come across as dishonest and untrustworthy. Although it may be costly in the short-term to keep one's word, those who do so often come out ahead in the long run by inducing others to trust them, to seek them out as social partners, and to fear their reprisals. The long-term value of building a reputation as the kind of person who does what he or she says and who is as good as his or her word often outweighs the short-term costs of sustaining it.

According to Frank (1988):

> the commitment model is a tentative first step in the construction of a theory of unopportunistic behavior. It challenges the self-interest model's portrayal of human nature in its own terms by accepting the fundamental premise that material incentives ultimately govern behavior. Its point of departure is the observation that persons *directly* motivated to pursue self-interest are often for that reason doomed to fail. They fail because they cannot solve commitment problems. These problems can often be solved by persons known to have abandoned the quest for maximum material advantage. The emotions that lead people to behave in seemingly irrational ways can thus indirectly lead to greater material well-being. (p. 256)

CONCLUSIONS

Primitive forms of prosocial conduct stem from mental mechanisms that humans share with other animals, even though these forms of conduct may be affected in signigicant ways by mental capacities unique to humans. People sometimes help others impulsively, without concern for their own welfare. Like other animals, people can be taught to behave in prosocial ways by rewarding and punishing them. A suite of emotions dispose people to respect authority, to resist temptation, to help others, to uphold systems of cooperation, and to repair damaged relationships. These emotions may give rise to genuinely altruistic motivational states. The mechanisms that produce them evolved because they increased people's willingness to suffer short-term material, psychological, and biological costs in order to promote their long-term material, psychological, biological, and genetic interests.

This ends the discussion of how the primitive prosocial behaviors displayed by humans and other animals evolved and how the mental mechanisms that give rise to them are designed. It is now time to attend to Darwin's observation that although humans are basically similar to other animals, they also differ from them in significant ways. In the next part of this book (Part III), I review evidence that humans engage in forms of prosocial conduct that are unique to their species. I go on to present two quite different accounts of how the mental mechanisms that dispose people to emit uniquely human forms of conduct evolved, and end by discussing the ways in which the (uniquely human) mental mechanisms that give rise to these forms of conduct are designed, focusing on those that produce higher order mental abilities such as the ability to reason.

PART THREE

The Evolution of Uniquely Human Prosocial Behaviors

13

UNIQUELY HUMAN PROSOCIAL BEHAVIORS

Having offered accounts of how primitive deferential, altruistic, and cooperative dispositions evolved in humans and other animals, I now address Darwin's observation that in addition to these primitive dispositions, humans also are disposed to engage in forms of prosocial conduct unique to their species. If, as I have argued, one of the basic functions of prosocial behaviors is to uphold social orders that enable members of groups to reap the benefits of group living, then an appropriate first step toward accounting for the forms of conduct displayed by modern humans is to account for the kinds of social orders that they evolved to uphold. I open this chapter by dividing the history of human societies into four phases, beginning with small hierarchically organized groups similar to those formed by other primates, moving to the kinds of egalitarian groups formed by hunters and gatherers, progressing into tribal coalitions, and ending with the large complex societies formed by modern humans who live in urban environments. This account is derived primarily from the writings of Christopher Boehm, Peter Richerson, and Robert Boyd.

Following this, I describe the unique forms of deference, self-control, altruism, and cooperation that uphold the social structures of modern societies and review evidence that human are disposed to behave in these ways. Unlike other animals, humans show deference to abstract ideas such as laws and conceptions of God. They suppress selfish behaviors, control aggressive urges, plan for the future, and delay gratification over long periods of time. They donate to charity, pay their taxes, and devote significant portions of their lives to philanthropic activities. No other species practices the complex, indirect, and equitable forms of cooperation displayed by most contemporary humans.

In this chapter I review descriptive evidence pertaining to the evolution of human social systems and uniquely human prosocial behaviors. In the next chapter, I consider theoretical accounts of how large human societies and the prosocial behaviors that uphold them evolved. Do uniquely human forms of prosocial conduct stem from the same mechanisms that give rise to primitive forms of prosocial conduct, activated in different ways in modern environments, or do they stem from more recently evolved mechanisms? If from new mechanisms, did these mechanisms evolve in the same ways as those that regulate more primitive types of prosocial behavior, or did they evolve in different ways?

The groups formed by chimpanzees and other living primates have not changed much in thousands of years, and neither, I assume, have the kinds of prosocial behaviors that these primates employ to uphold their groups. In contrast, the groups formed by humans have changed dramatically during the past 100,000 years—indeed, even during the past 12,000 years—and so also have the forms of prosocial conduct they display. If one of the functions of prosocial behaviors is to uphold the social order of groups in order to reap the benefits of cooperative group living, then one of the keys to understanding how humans acquired the capacity to engage in the uniquely human forms of prosocial conduct that they display in contemporary societies is to explain how the uniquely human social systems that these forms of conduct are designed to uphold evolved. Put another way, if the mental mechanisms that dispose humans and other animals to behave in prosocial ways evolved to uphold the social orders of their groups, then an appropriate first step toward understanding how these mechanisms are designed is to examine the structure of the social orders they were designed to uphold. I will divide the evolution of human societies into four major stages. In the first stage, humans formed small hierarchically organized groups similar to those of other primates. In the second stage, they formed relatively small egalitarian groups similar to those of contemporary hunter–gatherer groups. In the third stage, they formed tribal coalitions, and in the final stage they formed city–states and the complex urban societies in which we now live.

EARLY HUMAN SOCIETIES

Comparisons between humans and primates with whom they share a common ancestor produce the following hypotheses about the social world of early humans. Early humans lived in relatively small mobile groups consisting of a few extended families. Although most of their food came from foraging, some came from hunting nutritionally rich game. There was a flexible sex-based division of labor. Males joined forces to hunt game and to defend their groups against predators. They also may have engaged in some intergroup combat (Wrangham, 1987). Females assumed primary responsibility for caring for offspring, probably with assistance from their mates, parents, and female relatives.

Early human groups were organized hierarchically (Boehm, 2000), but dominance and status were fluid, with subordinate members of groups seeking opportunities to climb the social ladder. Members of groups—especially males—formed coalitions to preserve and to elevate their status and power within groups. Early humans engaged in primitive forms of direct reciprocity (Tooby & DeVore, 1987). Like other primate groups, their societies were characterized by order without law, with at least some members intervening in conflicts and punishing those who violated social norms.

Early human males probably joined forces with members of their groups in much the same way that chimpanzees do to protect their territories, to raid competing groups, and to fight small "wars" (Richerson & Boyd, 2005, p. 90); however, relations among neighboring groups may not always have been hostile, because some members—either males or females, or both—must have left their groups when they reached sexual maturity to join neighboring groups. The migration rate was probably similar to that of other living primates—roughly 25%. Because early humans would have been related to some members of neighboring groups, we would expect them to have been disposed to interact with them in, at least, a "live and let live" manner.

As with other primates, we would expect the kinds of primitive mental mechanisms discussed in Part II of this book to have evolved in early humans, which would have disposed them to uphold the social orders of their groups. We also would expect modern humans to possess variations of these mechanisms. Deferential and dominant dispositions, as well as dispositions to assist kin and to uphold small groups, lie at the primitive core of human nature. But there is more.

HUNTER–GATHERER BANDS

During the late Pleistocene period, sometime between 45 and 150 thousand years ago, several major transformations occurred in groups of early humans in a remarkably short period of time that had significant implications for the evolution of morality. First, groups increased in size (Richerson & Boyd, 2005). Second, social orders became significantly more egalitarian than the social orders of earlier groups (Boehm, 2000). (Although there are prestige and status hierarchies in all groups, they are held in check in egalitarian groups. Males enjoy political parity and make decisions in relatively democratic ways.) Third, systems of direct reciprocity expanded into systems of indirect reciprocity in which members of groups voluntarily shared some of their resources with their groups as a whole, as communal or public goods (Alexander, 1987). Although early humans may have shared the food they obtained from foraging only with members of their immediate families, they almost certainly shared the food they obtained from hunting large game with other members of their groups and perhaps with members of neighboring groups as well (Ridley, 1996). Finally, designated members of groups, or the group as a whole, assumed responsibility for enforcing the norms of their groups, including norms that upheld egalitarian social orders and systems of indirect reciprocity. As explained by Boehm (2000), hunter–gatherer groups differ from the groups formed by other primates (1) because they are governed by explicitly articulated shared social norms aimed at upholding long-term social objectives, (2) because all members are sensitive to violations of social norms, and (3) because most, or all, members of the group unite to punish those who violate the norms and to suppress the dominance of high-ranking members.

TRIBAL COALITIONS

Following the transition to relatively egalitarian hunter–gatherer societies, another major transformation in the structure of human societies occurred. Neighboring bands united into tribal coalitions to protect themselves, to increase their security, to raid and battle other groups, to hunt game, to trade, to gain access to new mates, and to socialize. These tribal coalitions came to share a common language, customs, rituals, and norms that marked their identity and distinguished them from other groups (Richerson & Boyd, 2005). Following a review of the ethnographic evidence on the evolution of tribal societies, Richerson and Boyd (2005) concluded that, "many, if not most, Pleistocene societies were multilevel tribal formations in which small residential bands were nested within a larger society. . . . Most likely, the modal Pleistocene society living in relatively provident temperate environments was something like the Blackfeet, in which relatively limited tribal institutions organized many hundreds or perhaps a few thousand people to cooperate in subsistence and in warfare" (p. 229). In addition to, and on top of, the adaptations that enabled early humans to reap the benefits of living in small hierarchically organized groups and in somewhat larger egalitarian bands, humans who lived in the late Pleistocene period acquired adaptations that enabled them to reap the benefits of larger more complex coalitions. Following this, the structure of human societies changed again, becoming transformed into the kinds of societies familiar to us in the modern world.

MODERN SOCIETIES

Large, modern societies began with the advent of agriculture some 11,000–12,000 years ago. As expressed by Richerson and Boyd (2005), after people formed large groups, "the race was on. Larger societies can usually marshal larger military units and defeat smaller societies in military competition. Size allows economies of scale, and division of labor generates greater economic productivity. These also contribute to military success, and attract imitators and migrants. . . . The result was a steady increase in social scale complexity that continues today" (p. 230). Beginning approximately 5000 years ago, humans began to form large city–states marked by increasingly refined and complex divisions of labor. Members of these states gave goods and services to, and received goods and services from, people they did not know and would never meet. In contrast to hunter–gatherer bands, the political structure of these states was hierarchical, with leaders often possessing a great deal of power. Social classes emerged, creating groups that varied significantly in access to resources. The social order was upheld by designated authorities such as monarchs, nobles, military units, and police.

Comparing large, complex, modern city–states to hunter–gatherer groups and other groups in the animal kingdom, Richerson and Boyd note that, "human societies are a spectacular anomaly. . . . They are based on the cooperation of large, symbolically marked in-groups [that] complete with similarly marked out-groups. . . . Enormous bureaucracies like the military, political parties, churches, and corporations manage complex tasks, and . . . people depend on a vast array of resources produced in every corner of the globe" (p. 195). "The size, degree of division of labor, and degree of hierarchy and subordination of Rome and Los Angeles are orders of magnitude beyond the range of the most complex foraging societies" (p. 229).

THE NESTED SOCIAL STRUCTURE OF MODERN URBAN HUMAN SOCIETIES

Although the social structure of human societies has undergone at least four major transformations throughout history, new social structures did not displace the older social structures; they evolved around them and encompassed them, like concentric circles. Most modern humans live in large, complex groups that are defined by shared territories, languages, forms of dress, political and religious beliefs, customs, social norms, contractual agreements, and so on (the outer, most recently evolved ring of the circle). However, in addition, they "belong" to many other smaller groups, including coalitions with other groups, groups that are similar to the egalitarian groups of hunters and gatherers, and groups that are similar to the hierarchically ordered groups of other primates. Smaller groups are embedded, or nested, in larger groups.

Although most humans live in large societies with complex social orders, they spend most of their time interacting with members of smaller groups with flexible dominance hierarchies and relatively egalitarian social orders. In my own case, I live with members of my immediate family, which is organized in terms of a flexible hierarchy (with my wife and I exerting power over our young daughter). My daughter hangs out in a peer group with a status hierarchy (with plenty of competition for dominance). I interact with other members of my extended family in an egalitarian manner. I work at a university that is organized hierarchically at a formal level. It is headed by a president, followed by several vice presidents, associate vice presidents, deans, and chairs of departments. However, like most other members of the faculty, I rarely interact with members of the "senior" administration. I interact mainly with my peers in the Psychology Department, which is the size of a small hunter–gatherer band. Although my department is headed by a chair who has the authority to make certain decisions, the political structure of the department is more egalitarian than hierarchical. Chairs are elected for a limited period of time, and they must bring all significant decisions to the department for approval.

Modern humans are able to function in the nested sets of groups in their societies, because they possess a nested set of mental mechanisms that evolved to uphold the social orders of the groups to which they belong. According to Richerson and Boyd (2005), "cultural evolution . . . has produced institutions that conspicuously work around the constraints imposed by a psychology adapted to relatively small scale egalitarian societies." Further, "To function, humans construct a social world that resembles the one in which our social instincts evolved" (p. 230). Thus, "Institutions . . . evolve to take advantage of the progroup commitments [that social] instincts make possible, and finesse the conflict between egalitarian impulses and the stratification and command and control ubiquitous in complex societies" (pp. 212–213).

Richerson and Boyd point out that the kind of "institutionalized coercion" advocated by social theorists such as Thomas Hobbes is not sufficient to uphold large, complex, stratified social orders, because it creates "roles, classes, and subcultures with the power to turn coercion to their own advantage. Social institutions of some sort must police the police so they will act in the larger interest" (p. 231). As with the political structure of universities and other organizations, Richerson and Boyd argue that in modern societies, "top-down control is generally exerted through a segmentary hierarchy that is adapted to preserve nearly egalitarian relationships at the face-to-face level . . . Each level of the hierarchy replicates the structure of a hunting and gathering band. . . . New leaders are usually recruited from the ranks of subleaders . . . Even high-ranking leaders in modern hierarchies typically adopt much of the humble headman's deferential approach to leadership" (p. 232). Unfortunately, "the imperfect fit of institutions and social instincts often makes segmentary hierarchies painfully inefficient. Selfishness and nepotism— corrupt sergeants, incompetent aristocrats, vainglorious generals, power-hungry bureaucrats—degrade the effectiveness of social organizations" (p. 232).

To summarize the discussion to this point, the social structure of human societies evolved from relatively small hierarchically organized groups into larger, more egalitarian groups that joined other groups to form tribal coalitions, then finally into large scale societies. Different forms of prosocial conduct (and different kinds of moral norms) are necessary to uphold the social orders in each of these social systems. In previous chapters, I discussed the kinds of primitive prosocial behaviors that evolved to uphold families, small hierarchically organized groups, and somewhat larger, more egalitarian hunter–gatherer types of groups. It is time now to describe the kinds of behaviors necessary to uphold the social orders of tribal coalitions and large modern societies.

UNIQUELY HUMAN FORMS OF PROSOCIAL CONDUCT

Comparing the prosocial behavior displayed by humans with that of other primates reveals several basic differences: Humans help others more often and in a larger variety of ways than other primates do; the range of people that humans help is broader; and human prosocial behavior is more finely tuned and effective than the forms of prosocial conduct displayed by other primates. It produces more benefits for recipients at less cost.

Although humans may show deference to those in power in much the same way that other primates do when they interact with them in a face-to-face manner, people also express deference in more uniquely human ways. For example, people respect the authority of leaders such as kings, queens, presidents, and prime ministers whom they have never met. People obey the rules and laws that uphold their social orders, even when the probability of getting caught and punished for violating them is low. In addition, people show deference to entities they conceptualize as divine authorities, or gods.

Although other animals are able to delay gratification, humans stand out in their ability to persevere at tasks over very long periods of time in order to achieve long-term goals such as building monuments, painting pictures, and preparing for careers. In addition, people possess the capacity to behave in more disciplined ways than other primates do. For example, they may refrain from having sex until they are married, count to 10 before reacting to provocation, exercise to stay healthy, and watch their diets.

Like other primates, humans help their friends, relatives, and colleagues in face-to-face encounters, but in addition they assist people whom they do not know and will never meet. For example, people donate blood, give money to charity, contribute to food banks, help members of third world countries, risk their lives to overthrow oppressive governments in distant lands, devote time, energy, and resources to initiatives aimed at protecting the environment, and suffer personal costs to protect endangered species. In addition to the expansion in the range of those they help, humans are better than other primates at figuring out what others need and how best to help others meet their needs in appropriate ways.

Like other primates, humans engage in simple forms of cooperation; however, the balance between giving and receiving tends to be more refined and fairer. Observations of hunter–gathers suggest that they base their decisions about how to allocate the food they obtain from foraging on a principle that sustains a fair balance between effort expended and food received, taking into account their needs and abilities (Hill, 2002).

In addition, the delay between giving and receiving tends to be longer and more indirect; the number of people involved tends to be larger; and systems of exchange tend to be more impersonal. Modern societies are characterized by indirect systems of cooperation in which members contribute to groups such as unions, public broadcasting stations, and their societies as a whole that, in turn, assume responsibility for fostering their welfare. Their contributions pay off because large groups are able to produce and preserve products, or public goods, that individuals could not produce or preserve on their own, cheaper and more efficiently. The whole is greater than the sum of its parts.

Systems of cooperation in which people contribute to a common pool of goods and take their share give rise to social dilemmas. Although members of groups must contribute enough to produce the public goods from which they benefit, each member of the group may be able to gain more for himself or herself by not contributing to the public good, or by contributing less than his or her share, than by contributing his or her share—but only if enough other members contribute to produce the goods. In public goods dilemmas, "the payoff for each individual is higher for not contributing than for contributing, but if each individual follows this strategy, the outcome is one that no individual desires" (Caporael et al., 1989, p. 684). Consider contributions to public television, for example. As explained by Linnda Caporael and her colleagues (1989), for viewers to enjoy the programs offered through public television, someone must donate enough to fund them. If no one contributes, the programs will go defunct. However, except in the rare case where a single contribution will push funding over a critical level, it is in the personal financial interest of each member of the audience to withhold his or her contribution and let other viewers carry the burden. As long as a sufficient number of other viewers contribute, one's contribution is not necessary to ensure that the programs will be offered.

RESEARCH ON UNIQUELY HUMAN FORMS OF PROSOCIAL CONDUCT

Social scientists have used a variety of games to investigate uniquely human forms of prosocial behavior. They have been especially interested in studying people's willingness to help strangers anonymously and to uphold systems of indirect reciprocity by, for example, contributing to the public good. Let us review a sample of this research, then explore the implications of the findings, beginning with a game called Dictator.

The Dictator game is simple. One of two players is given a sum of money—usually somewhere in the neighborhood of 10 dollars, but sometimes much more—and asked to divide the money between himself or herself and the other player. That is it.

For those who are cynical about human nature, the choices made by people who have played the Dictator game, including those from non-Western countries, may be surprising. Although donors could keep all the money for themselves, virtually all donors from all countries donate some of the money to the other player. On average, adults from Western countries donate approximately half of the money that they are given; university students donate approximately 20%. The range of donations made by people from other cultures is greater. People from some non-Western countries give almost all the money to recipients, whereas people from other non-Western countries keep almost all of it for themselves. These findings suggest that all people from all cultures are disposed to share resources allotted to them but that cultural norms exert a strong influence on how much they feel obliged to share.

Other studies have found that people from the Western world are quite strongly disposed to behave in fair and equitable ways, even when they are able to advance their interests at the expense of others (Greenberg & Cohen, 1982). For example, in a classic study Adams (1965) found that workers performed better when they were paid more than they deserved, indicating that the workers were motivated to bring about a fair outcome rather than to maximize their benefits, relative to their costs. In addition, studies employing anonymous one-shot games have found that players assigned to "boss" roles compensate players assigned to "worker" roles in fair ways even when they could keep more for themselves with impunity.

Research employing another game, called Ultimatum, also suggests that people are more highly motivated to uphold norms of fairness than they are to maximize their monetary gains. Like the Dictator game, there are two players in the Ultimatum game, and one player is given a sum of money and asked to divide it between himself or herself and the other player. However, unlike the Dictator game, recipients are allowed to decide whether to accept the offer or to reject it. When recipients accept the offer, they receive the amount offered, and the donors receive the rest. However, if a recipient rejects the offer, neither the recipient nor the donor receives any money. Studies using this game have found that most donors make somewhat fair offers (between 30% and 50% of the money allotted to them), and most recipients reject extremely unfair offers (less than 20%), even though rejecting the offer means that they end up with less (i.e., nothing) than they would have if they had accepted the unfair offer (Henrich et al., 2001).

Social scientists also have used public goods games to investigate cooperative behaviors. In a typical game, each member of a group is given the same sum of money. Players are told that they may keep the money, or contribute all or some to a common pool (the public good) that will be divided equally among members of their group at the end of the game. Experimenters sweeten the pot by adding a substantial donation (a bonus) to the common pool—for example, by doubling it. In some experiments, this bonus is contingent on a portion of the group of players (usually more than half) making a contribution to the common pool. Each player ends up with the money he or she kept from the initial allotment (the money he or she did not contribute to the common pool), plus an equal share of the common pool. In some studies, players play a round of several games, sometimes with the same group and sometimes with other randomly formed groups.

When Caporael et al. (1989) examined people's choices in anonymous, one-shot public goods games among strangers, they found that a substantial number of players contributed to the common pool, even when they believed that their contributions were "redundant" because enough of the other players would contribute to enable them to get the bonus. When asked why, most of them attributed their behavior to a sense of equity or justice. Of the two reasons for not contributing, greed (attempting to obtain the bonus without suffering the cost of contributing) appeared to play a more important role than fear of not obtaining the bonus, or of being suckered.

One of the most interesting findings from this research was that when members of groups were allowed to talk to one another and to discuss strategies, virtually all groups ended up obtaining the bonus. Members of groups used three main methods to select donators—asking for volunteers, holding lotteries, and choosing the least needy members. Once selected, virtually all donators contributed to the common pool, to the benefit of all members of their groups. Caporael et al. (1989) accounted for these findings by suggesting that discussion increases individuals' tendency to identify with groups, to view themselves, not as individuals, but as a members of their groups (thus adopting a "social identity") and to place more value on the group's welfare than on their own welfare.

Many other studies have found that people are disposed to contribute a substantial share of their allotment to common pools anonymously in one-shot games and in the first rounds of repeated games (Fehr & Fischbacker, 2004). But the news is not all good. Studies also have found that as repeated games progress, the amount that players contribute to common pools tends to diminish, until in the end no one contributes anything. At first, players behave in generous or fair ways, but as the game progresses, they behave in increasingly self-serving ways (defined as keeping increasingly disproportionate amounts of money for themselves). The reason, apparently, is that small defections by self-serving players tend to evoke defections by other players in a snowballing manner. The lesson from these studies is a sad one. Although most people may be disposed to behave in cooperative ways, one self-serving cheater can launch a chain reaction that ends up costing everyone involved. However, there is still some hope, as demonstrated in a study conducted by Fehr and Fischbacker (2004).

This study began in the same way as traditional public goods studies do, but in a second stage, the experimenters posted the contributions made by each member of the group, without revealing his or her identity, and allowed the players to reduce the payoffs slated for any member of their group, at a cost to themselves. Fehr and Fischbacker found that most players used this opportunity to punish those who failed to contribute their share, even though it cost them to do so, in much the same way that players in Ultimatum games have been found to punish those who make unfair offers (by rejecting the offers). Other studies have produced similar findings. As summarized by Gächter and Herrmann (2006), "The majority of punishments are executed by above-average contributors and imposed on below-average contributors [and] punishment increases with the deviation of the free rider from other members' average contribution" (p. 297). The most hopeful aspect of the findings from the study by Fehr and Fischbacker is that punishing cheaters had a dramatic positive effect on cooperation, eventually inducing virtually all members of the group to contribute virtually all of their endowment to the common pool.

Dispositions to Punish Free-Riders

One of the ways in which members of modern societies uphold their complex systems of cooperation is by punishing those who free-ride by failing to do their share or by taking more than their share. As I discuss in the next chapter, punishment is important in the evolution of moral systems because it provides a way of increasing the costs of immoral behaviors that threaten the welfare of members of groups.

We know that members of many social species are disposed to punish those who disrupt the social order of their groups (de Waal, 1996; Flack, de Waal, & Krakauer, 2005). We also know that members of relatively small human groups are disposed to punish wrongdoers. For example, small coalitions of Ju'hoansi Bushmen from Botswana engage in escalating sanctions against those who violate moral norms, beginning with joking verbal insults, then more pointed criticisms, and finally physical attacks (Wiessner, 2005). Members of other tribal societies ostracize or execute deviant members of their groups, sometimes branding them as sorcerers (Knauft, 1987). And studies on people from the Western World have found that observers are willing to intervene to prevent third parties from littering, stealing others' possessions, assaulting them, and raping them (Chekroun & Brauer, 2002; Fischer, Greitemeyer, Pollozek, & Frey, 2006; Gelfand, Hartmann, Walder, & Page, 1973; Harari, Harari, & White, 1985; Latané & Nida, 1981). Based on such evidence, Gintis, Bowles, Boyd, and Fehr (2003) concluded that an other-regarding "predisposition to cooperate with others, and to punish those who violate the norms of cooperation, at personal cost, even when it is implausible to expect that these costs will be repaid" has evolved in the human species (p. 153). Gintis dubbed this disposition "strong reciprocity."

CONCLUSIONS

Early humans lived in relatively small hierarchically organized groups similar to those of other primates. During the course of evolution, they formed more egalitarian groups similar to those of contemporary hunter–gatherers, then tribal coalitions. Now, most of the people in the world live in large, complex urban societies.

The social behavior of modern humans stems from dispositions to behave in ways that uphold the kinds of social orders that have evolved in the species. In some contexts, people relate to one another in hierarchical ways. In other contexts, they behave in more egalitarian ways. A great deal of research indicates that the primitive prosocial dispositions that evolved in the human species have become refined and expanded in the course of human evolution. Modern humans customarily obey rules and laws. They suppress their selfish and aggressive urges, and delay gratification over long periods of time. They sacrifice their interests anonymously to help strangers, and extend their charity to people from other countries and other species. They display refined forms of equity, and they contribute to the public good, even when they could get away with cheating and doing less than their share. Modern humans also are disposed to punish free-riders and those who exploit members of their groups.

The evidence I have reviewed in this chapter is descriptive, meant to establish that although humans are similar to other primates in basic ways, they also differ from them in the range and quality of prosocial behaviors they display. When viewed from an evolutionary perspective, this evidence raises the question, how did the mental mechanisms that dispose people to behave in these ways evolve? When viewed from a psychological perspective, it raises the question, how are the mental mechanisms that give rise to uniquely human forms of prosocial conduct designed? In particular, do they motivate people to behave in biologically or psychologically altruistic ways? I address the first question in the next chapter and the second question in the chapter that follows it.

14

THE EVOLUTION OF UNIQUELY HUMAN
PROSOCIAL BEHAVIORS

Following the tradition of Thomas Hobbes, the anthropologist Christopher Boehm has asserted that morality originated when subordinate members of hierarchically ordered groups of early humans banded together to suppress the selfishness of dominant members. In place of Hobbes' Leviathan, Boehm suggests that at a critical point in the evolution of the human species, the group as a whole assumed responsibility for enforcing rules and norms that upheld egalitarian social orders. In this account, groups impose morality on their members by exerting external control.

It is easier to understand why subordinate members of groups join forces to suppress the selfishness and aggression of more dominant members than it is to explain how this process could produce an egalitarian group governed by rules that members are willing to enforce at a cost to themselves. To account for the evolution of dispositions to uphold egalitarian social orders, we must explain how early humans who were disposed to suppress their own antisocial urges and to suffer the costs of punishing those who behaved in antisocial ways could fare better genetically than those who were not, or how these dispositions could have evolved in the absence of genetic benefits.

The evolutionary biologist Richard Alexander has offered an account of how complex systems of cooperation evolved in the human species. He suggests that simple systems of direct reciprocity that originated in small groups became expanded into complex systems of indirect reciprocity in larger groups through the biological benefits of cooperating with cooperators and acquiring a reputation as an altruistic and cooperative person.

In recent years, a group of theorists has taken exception to the idea that dispositions to uphold the social orders of modern societies could evolve through individual-level selection. Building on Darwin's early ideas, these theorists argue that to account for uniquely human social systems and the prosocial behaviors that uphold them, we must recognize the role played by group-level selection of cultural norms. Two of these theorists, Peter Richerson and Robert Boyd, have suggested that humans inherit two sets of social instincts—ancient prosocial instincts that evolved through individual-level selection in the same way as the prosocial instincts inherited by other primates, and "tribal instincts" that evolved during the past 100,000 years through cultural group selection. The position advanced by Richerson and Boyd and other gene–culture coevolution theorists has been criticized by theorists who endorse more individual-level accounts of the evolution of altruism and cooperation.

Early in their evolutionary history, human groups were structured like the groups formed by contemporary primates: "There was no trade, little division of labor, and coalitions were limited to a small number of individuals" (Richerson & Boyd, 2005, pp. 196). However, "sometime between then and now, something happened that caused humans to cooperate in large, complex, symbolically marked groups. What caused this radical divergence with other social mammals?" (Richerson & Boyd, 2005, p.196). How did humans who live in urban societies get to where they are now from where they were 100,000 years ago, or even 10,000 years ago? Why did they form increasingly large and complex social systems? What rendered them willing to extend their assistance to strangers from other countries and members of other species, and to behave in increasingly fair and equitable ways? As I will explain, these questions have kindled a great deal of theoretical heat.

ACCOUNTING FOR THE EVOLUTION
OF EGALITARIAN SOCIAL SYSTEMS

Boehm (2000) has advanced an account of how early human groups that were structured hierarchically, like those of other primates, became transformed into the kinds of egalitarian groups characteristic of hunters and gatherers, and in the process, promoted the evolution of morality. Boehm begins by identifying several adaptive benefits of egalitarianism. First, he suggests that egalitarian social orders enable members of groups to maximize their gains from cooperative activities such as large-game hunting. Second, he suggests that suppressing dominance tends to promote group harmony, which improves the quality of everyone's life. Finally, and most importantly, he argues that it is in the interest of members of groups to promote egalitarianism in order to avoid being dominated by others: "In a despotic species given to strong status rivalry there is a natural propensity for adults to behave dominantly. This results in a dislike of being dominated oneself, and it makes for subordinate rebellion against superiors" (p. 97).

Boehm summarizes his theory as follows: "If resentful subordinates manage to collectivize and institutionalize their rebellion, you have a human type of politically egalitarian society, in which there is a major tension between the group and its more rivalrous individuals" (p. 84). "In effect, a large, *ad hoc*, community-wide political coalition serves as watchdog over individual behaviors that could lead to victimization of others, or to conflict within the group" (p. 80). "Moral communities arose out of group efforts to reduce levels of internecine conflict, as well as to avoid undue competition, domination, and victimization" (p. 85). How plausible is Boehm's account or the origin of morality?

It is easy to understand why subordinate members of groups would form coalitions to compete against more dominant members, and there is lots of evidence that they do. However, this in itself would not be enough to produce an egalitarian social order. It would simply replace a powerful individual with a powerful gang (which could compete with other powerful gangs). After all, coalitions of chimpanzees overthrow alpha males without producing egalitarian societies. To account for the evolution of egalitarian social orders, theorists must solve the selfishness problem. Why would members of groups be willing to suffer the costs of suppressing dominance in others if they were not rewarded by replacing them in the dominance hierarchy, or compensated in some other manner?

This question is a subset of a more general question, pertaining to the evolution of dispositions to punish third parties, which in turn is a subset of an even more general question pertaining to the ability of individual-level forms of natural selection to account for the evolution of uniquely human forms of prosocial conduct and large-scale systems of cooperation. As mentioned, dispositions to punish third party cheaters are significant in the evolution of moral systems because they induce members of groups to uphold norms and rules that promote harmony within groups, support systems of cooperation, and contribute to the welfare of the group as a whole. But how could such dispositions evolve? Revisiting fundamental social dilemmas, although such dispositions could create a "better life for all," each member of the group could avoid the costs of punishing those who dominate others, those who take more than their share, and those who violate group norms by engaging in second-order free-riding and by letting others do the dirty work. You have a bully in your group who pushes people around, or you have a cheater who exploits others and jeopardizes the social order of your group. It is in everyone's interest to put a stop to such selfish behaviors, but it is in no one's interest to be the one to pay the price. As pointed out by Robinson, Kurzban, and Jones (2007), the desire to see wrongdoers punished (at no cost to oneself) is quite different from the desire to punish wrongdoers (at a cost to oneself).

Boehm's account of the evolution of egalitarian societies emphasizes dispositions to control dominance, deviance, and free-riding from the outside—dispositions to exert external control and punish bad guys. This would not, of course, be necessary if members of groups were internally motivated to cooperate and to behave in prosocial ways—if they were good by nature. Alexander (1987), has advanced a model that accounts for the evolution of uniquely human forms of prosocial behavior and systems of cooperation in terms of both internal dispositions and external control.

ACCOUNTING FOR THE EVOLUTION OF SYSTEMS OF INDIRECT RECIPROCITY

Alexander (1987) hypothesizes that, early in the evolution of the human species, our ancestors formed small bands to cope with relatively harsh environments and that they were naturally inclined to help their mates, their offspring, and members of their extended families. He speculates that dispositions to engage in direct forms of reciprocity originated in this context either as mating effort (e.g., I give you food; you give me sex) or as an extension of altruism directed toward kin.

Like other theorists, Alexander notes that at a critical juncture in the evolution of the human species, humans began to form intermediate sized tribes. He suggests that when this happened, systems of direct reciprocity expanded into systems of indirect reciprocity, which were critically important to the evolution of morality.

In systems of indirect reciprocity, individuals who assist others and behave in cooperative ways are rewarded by third parties who, in effect, pay them back. In one form of indirect reciprocity, one person helps a second person who helps a third person who, in turn, helps the first person. In another form, one person helps another person who returns the favor, and a third person helps the person who returned the favor. In systems of indirect reciprocity, what goes around comes around with dividends, through third parties. Alexander suggests that systems of indirect reciprocity evolved because it is in the interest of third parties to initiate exchanges with those whom they observe behaving altruistically and cooperatively. Third parties may base their selections on information derived from their own observations or on information acquired from others.

Moving to the final stage of human evolution, Alexander suggests that humans developed large technological nations characterized by socially imposed monogamy, private property, laws, and so on. As these societies evolved, people invested more and more time and effort in systems of indirect reciprocity, which generated increasingly large returns. Alexander (1987) suggests that "in such a milieu ... a modicum of indiscriminate altruism would arise as social investments because of benefits to individuals being viewed as altruists." He goes on to argue that "general acceptance of indiscriminate altruism and general acceptance of its beneficial effects result in a society with high social utility. This encouragement and acceptance is expected to occur partly because of the likelihood, much of the time, that nearly everyone benefits from living in a unified society and partly because individuals gain from inducing indiscriminate altruism in others" (pp. 192–193).

Although systems of indirect reciprocity have the potential to generate significantly more benefits than systems of direct reciprocity do, because they are better equipped to maximize gains in trade, they tend to be more susceptible to free-riding. In most contexts, it is easier to determine whether someone has failed to pay you back than to determine whether he or she has failed to repay the debt by helping third parties, who in turn help you. However, Alexander suggests that this free-rider problem can be solved if members of groups interact with others in a selective manner, favoring cooperators and shunning cheaters. (Notice how this implies a solution to the cost-of-punishing-free-riders problem.) In addition, Alexander suggests that good guys may reap indirect benefits through the increased fitness of their collateral relatives and through the success of their groups. In contrast, free-riders and cheaters may suffer costs through losses in status, rejection as partners, ostracism from the group, and negative effects on the group that filter back to the cheater and his or her relatives. It follows that members of groups practicing indirect reciprocity should be vigilant for selfishness, should gossip about the social behaviors of others and should be concerned about their reputations and the reputations of others.

In support of Alexander's model, game theorists have demonstrated that altruistic strategies can evolve and become evolutionarily stable in systems of indirect reciprocity if they enhance individuals' reputations or social images and if members of groups discriminate in favor of those with good reputations (Nowak & Sigmund, 1998; Wedekind & Milinski, 2000). As Trivers writes:

> A subtlety of some importance is that an actor who is seen to fail to give to another can be so acting because the actor is stingy or because the recipient is unworthy (i.e., itself stingy in interactions with others). Likewise, punishing an unworthy individual may improve your image, while punishing a worthy one will have the opposite effect. But how is the observer to have this kind of detailed knowledge?

Opportunities for deception would seem to be rife, increasing further the cognitive complexity of reciprocal altruism, with associated selection on mental traits. (Trivers, 2006, p. 76)

Naturalistic studies have found that people evaluate the cooperativeness of members of their groups on the basis of their reputations, and show preference for those with good reputations. For example, anthropologists have found that members of small societies who contribute more than the average amount of food to communal projects and other aspects of the public good, and who are brave in battle, are held in higher esteem than their fellows (Chagnon, 1988; Hawkes, 1983; Price, 2006). Economists have found that the social status of employees in large business firms is positively related to their perceived generosity (Flynn, 2003). Game theorists have found that people are more prone to behave generously toward those whom they have observed treating others generously than toward those whom they have observed behaving selfishly (Wedekind & Milinski, 2000). And other studies have found that people behave more cooperatively in contexts in which their behavior will affect their reputations than in contexts in which it will not (Barclay, 2004).

Note that Alexander's model of the evolution of indirect reciprocity is, ultimately, rooted in mechanisms that evolved because they helped individuals propagate their genes, even though these mechanisms may give rise to psychologically unselfish behaviors. In addition to being disposed to help others in conditions in which helping others pays off genetically in the end, Alexander (1987) expects people to be disposed to exploit systems of indirect reciprocity and manipulate others in order to get more than their share. As expressed by Alexander (1987):

The long-term existence of complex patterns of indirect reciprocity may be seen as favoring the evolution of keen abilities, first, to make one's self seem more altruistic than is the case and, second, to influence others to be altruistic in such fashions as to be deleterious to themselves and beneficial to the moralizer, for example to lead others to invest too much, invest wrongly in the moralizer or his relatives and friends, or invest indiscriminately on a larger scale than would otherwise be the case. Thus, individuals are expected to parade the ideas of much altruism and of indiscriminate altruism as beneficial, so as to encourage people in general to engage in increasing amounts of social investment whether or not it is beneficial to their interests. They may be expected to locate and exploit avenues of genetic relatedness leading to nepotistic flows of benefits. . . . They may also be expected to depress the fitness of competitors by identifying them, deceptively or not, as reciprocity cheaters; to internalize rules or evolve the ability to acquire a conscience . . . and to self-deceive and display false sincerity as defenses against detection of cheating and attributions of deliberateness in cheating. (p. 190)

CRITIQUES OF INDIVIDUAL-LEVEL SELECTION ACCOUNTS OF HUMAN EVOLUTION

In recent years, a group of evolutionary theorists, whom I will label gene–culture coevolution theorists, has questioned models of the evolution of morality such as the one advanced by Alexander. These theorists have argued that it is implausible that dispositions to uphold large-scale systems of cooperation in which individuals contribute to the public good, refrain from free-riding, help strangers, repay their debts, and suffer the costs of punishing those who fail to do their share could have evolved through any form of individual-level selection (Gintis, Bowles, Boyd, & Fehr, 2008; Richerson & Boyd, 2005). Gene–culture coevolution theorists agree with other evolutionary theorists that "ancient" social instincts that evolved through kin selection and reciprocity dispose people to behave in prosocial ways in small groups. However, they argue, these ancient instincts, which evolved because they produced return benefits, cannot account for human's willingness to uphold large-scale systems of cooperation. "Each one of a thousand union members does not keep walking the picket line because she is afraid that her one defection will break the strike. . . . Nor do we recycle our bottles and newspapers because we fear our littering will doom the planet" (Richerson & Boyd, 2005, p. 200).

The primary evidence that gene–culture coevolution theorists advance in support of their position is evidence indicating that modern humans help others and make sacrifices to uphold their groups that do not increase their inclusive fitness. These theorists argue that members of large groups are not related to most of the people whom they help, so the prosocial dispositions could not have evolved through kin selection. Further, they argue that tit for tat forms of reciprocity would disintegrate in large groups, because it would be difficult to catch and punish cheaters and because free-riders would fare better than those who did their share. In addition, these theorists argue that uniquely human forms of prosocial conduct could not have evolved through indirect reciprocity, because people are disposed to contribute to the welfare of members of their groups when no one is watching and when it does not affect their reputation, and because the ability to cultivate a false reputation as a cooperator would undermine systems of indirect reciprocity in large groups. As expressed by Trivers (2006), according to these theorists, findings from research on prosocial behavior in large groups "prove that our sense of fairness cannot have a self-interested function, all possibility of return effects having been removed. Instead, it must have been selected to benefit the group or appeared by some process of cultural diffusion" (p. 79). Let us consider the most highly refined and elaborate model of gene–culture coevolution, advanced by Richerson and Boyd (2005), then review the debate between gene–culture coevolution theorists and individual-level selection theorists in more detail.

THE EVOLUTION OF LARGE-SCALE SYSTEMS OF COOPERATION THROUGH GENE–CULTURE COEVOLUTION AND CULTURAL GROUP SELECTION

Richerson and Boyd suggest that many thousands of years ago during the Pleistocene era the environments occupied by small bands of humans underwent rapid changes within and between generations, due in large part to frequent climatic changes. These changing environments increased the adaptive value of mental mechanisms that enabled early humans to learn how to solve the novel adaptive problems that the changing environments produced, and to share this information with members of their groups. Shared information that is passed from one generation to another constitutes culture. Richerson and Boyd review evidence demonstrating that although members of several species create and share cultural information, humans are the only species that creates and transmits increasingly effective forms of culture from one generation to another in a cumulative manner.

Cultural Evolution

Like genes, aspects of culture (which some theorists call memes) may evolve. Although people may produce a great deal of cultural information, they select, retain, and transmit only a sample of it to future generations. The remainder goes extinct. Like biologically designed adaptations, culturally designed ways of adapting to the environment may become increasingly refined over generations. However, in contrast to biological evolution, which occurs at a glacially slow rate, cultural change may occur very rapidly, which is why it offers an effective way of coping with changing environments.

Gene–Culture Coevolution

Genes guide the development of the mental mechanisms necessary to create, select, refine, and transmit culture. Early humans who inherited mental mechanisms that enabled them to copy the solutions to adaptive problems discovered by other members of their groups, to improve on them, and to share their insights with members of their families and in-groups were more likely to propagate their genes than early humans who did not inherit effective learning and social learning mechanisms. As early humans accumulated culture, the environments in which they lived (and died) came to be structured in increasingly pervasive ways by the cultures they created, and this affected the selection of genes. Individuals who inherited mechanisms (genotypes) that enabled them to adapt to new, culturally created environments fared better than those who did not, causing culture to affect biological evolution and the nature of the human species. Culture and the mental mechanisms that enabled people to acquire, to refine, and to transmit culture coevolved in a mutually supportive, snowballing manner. The adaptive value of culture increased the adaptive value of the mental mechanisms that enabled people to create and transmit it, which in turn produced increasing amounts of culture.

Group Expansion

Richerson and Boyd (2005) argue that culture paved the way for the creation of large groups by supplying a basis for sharing an identity through markers such as a common language or dialect, a form of dress, or a set of rituals. Such "symbolic markers" enable individuals to create large in-groups and distinguish them from out-groups without knowing all members of their in-groups personally—sort of the way travelers identify in-group members through their language and emblems of their countries on their clothes. Once symbolic markers exist, argue Richerson and Boyd, natural selection will favor the genetic evolution of mental mechanisms that induce individuals to interact selectively with members of their culturally defined in-groups, in the first instance because they are members of cooperative coalitions and, in addition, because it is more adaptive to interact with those who share similar beliefs, norms, and customs than those who do not.

The Evolution of Large-Scale Systems of Cooperation

Social norms that uphold systems of cooperation are an important aspect of culture. It is safe to assume that during the Pleistocene era, systems of direct and indirect reciprocity had evolved in relatively small groups. Toward the end of the Pleistocene, some groups developed cultural norms that promoted cooperation with neighboring groups, and others did not. Relations among neighboring bands are akin to relations among individuals within groups. In some conditions, a band can gain more for itself by competing and warring against neighboring bands, but in other conditions, it can gain more by cooperating with them. Like individuals within groups, bands may exchange goods and services to foster gains in trade. Like individuals within groups, bands that fare well and produce a surplus of goods can, in effect, invest in life insurance by sharing their goods with bands that are going through hard times.

More importantly, perhaps, in essentially the same way that it can be in the interest of subordinate members of groups to form coalitions to compete against dominant members, it can be in the interest of relatively weak bands to form coalitions to compete against stronger bands. Richerson and Boyd (2005) argue that cultural markers enabled integrated bands to establish a common identity. Competition among groups with different cultural norms favored the selection and cumulative evolution of the norms that increased group success. Relatively large symbolically marked tribes that adopted culturally created cooperative norms fared better than bands or tribes that adopted less cooperative norms, causing these norms to evolve through group selection at a cultural level. Not only were cooperative tribes able to defeat other groups during wars, the bands in such tribes also were able to maximize their gains through other forms of cooperation, such as trading and reciprocating assistance in times of scarcity. Cooperative, group-benefiting cultural norms spread even more when neighboring groups observed the success of tribes adopting them, and copied them themselves. Outsiders who migrated into cooperative groups accommodated to the cooperative norms, further favoring their expansion.

Sustaining Reduced Variation within Groups

Richerson and Boyd (2005) point out that although rapid cultural adaptation can dramatically decrease behavioral variation within groups and dramatically increase it between groups, such variation may be unstable due to the influx of new members (with different cultures) and the potential for members of groups to advance their own interests by violating the cooperative norms of their groups. "For group selection to be an important force, some processes that can *maintain* variation among groups must also operate" (p. 204).

Richerson and Boyd (2005) suggest that two processes, conformity and moralistic punishment (that is to say, the disposition to punish third-party cheaters and free-riders), are largely responsible for inducing members of large groups to uphold moral norms. "In a world where information is costly and individual learning therefore error prone, imitating common behaviors is a simple heuristic that will get you the correct behavior most of the time at a smaller cost than subjecting alternative behaviors to more rigourous tests" (p. 193). Mental mechanisms that dispose individuals to conform to the norms of their groups evolved because conformity is a quick and easy way of making adaptive choices and because those who fail to conform may be punished by members of their groups. Once a behavioral norm gets started, people's natural tendency to conform can cause it to spread and stabilize.

In addition, as discussed, social norms such as those that promote large-scale cooperation can be upheld by effective sanctions. However, to account for the evolution of dispositions to administer such sanctions, we must solve the second-order free-rider problem. How could such dispositions evolve if those who shirked their duties fared better than those who accepted them? Richerson and Boyd (2005) suggest that sanctions can be strengthened in large groups by imposing second-order sanctions on those who fail to punish those who violate group norms. However, these theorists acknowledge that such second-order sanctions could uphold any norm, leaving open the question of why they were evoked to uphold cooperative norms rather than other norms. In addition, anthropologists have noted that few, if any, foraging bands have norms prescribing punishment for those who fail to punish wrongdoers, and although some societies (such as Communist China) have developed norms that encourage citizens to report wrongdoers, I suspect that these norms are poorly enforced, at best, and are insignificant in the Western world. Indeed, people often conspire to help those who violate laws avoid punishment.

The Evolution of Tribal Instincts

Richerson and Boyd (2005) argue that the new, culturally based tribes and systems of cooperation created by humans during the Pleistocene era mediated the cultural group selection of qualitatively different prosocial dispositions from those that evolved through individual-level selection. These theorists call these recently evolved dispositions "tribal instincts." Richerson and Boyd assert that tribal instincts became "superimposed onto human psychology without eliminating those that favor friends and kin" (p. 215). Tribal instincts dispose people to identify with in-groups that are distinguished by symbolic markers, to abide by culturally created rules and norms that uphold their groups, and to punish those who violate the norms. In contrast to ancient instincts that evolved through kin selection and reciprocity, tribal instincts may be biologically and genetically altruistic. "Our social instincts hypothesis requires that cultural group selection be strong enough to counter individualistically motivated selfish decision making in order to favor tribal-scale cooperation" (Richerson & Boyd, 2005, p. 192).

Richerson and Boyd (2005) sum up their model in this way:

> Culturally evolved social environments favor an innate psychology that is suited to such environments. . . . a psychology which 'expects' life to be structured by moral norms and is designed to learn and internalize such norms, new emotions, such as shame and guilt, which increase the chance the norms are followed, and a psychology which 'expects' the social world to be divided into symbolically marked groups. Individuals lacking the new social instincts more often violated

prevailing norms and experienced adverse selection. They might have suffered ostracism, been denied the benefits of public goods, or lost points in the mating game. Cooperation and group identification in intergroup conflict set up an arms race that drove social evolution to ever greater extremes of in-group cooperation. . . . About one hundred thousand years ago, most people lived in tribal-scale societies. These societies were based on in-group cooperation when in-groups of a few hundred to a few thousand people were symbolically marked by language, ritual practices, dress, and the like. Social relations were egalitarian, political power was diffuse, and people were ready to punish transgressions of social norms, even when personal interests were not directly at stake. (p. 192)

COULD TRIBAL INSTINCTS HAVE EVOLVED THROUGH INDIVIDUAL-LEVEL SELECTION?

So we have two competing explanations for the evolution of large-scale systems of cooperation and the uniquely human forms of prosocial conduct that uphold them—one based in traditional forms of individual-level selection that produce return benefits and the other based in gene–culture coevolution that does not produce return benefits. Referring to their gene–culture account, Richerson and Boyd (2005) acknowledge that, "some of our evolutionist friends have complained to us that this story is too complicated" (p. 215). These (sometimes not so friendly) "friends" have questioned whether it is necessary to invoke group-level cultural selection to account for the evolution of "tribal instincts," arguing that the prosocial dispositions in question can be accounted for more parsimoniously through traditional individual-level processes such as kin selection, direct reciprocity, indirect reciprocity, and costly signaling.

Individual-level selection theorists have attempted to account for the evolution of dispositions to suffer the costs of behaving in uniquely human prosocial ways and punishing moral norm violators in two basic ways. First, they have attempted to establish that these forms of conduct reap net genetic gains, relative to alternative forms of conduct. Second, they have acknowledged that the behaviors in question are genetically costly in modern environments, but have argued that they paid off in the ancestral environments in which they evolved. Let us consider each of these arguments in turn.

Do the Benefits of Uniquely Human Forms of Prosocial Conduct Outweigh the Costs?

There are at least three ways in which the adaptive benefits of behaving in prosocial ways and punishing moral norm violators could outweigh the costs in contemporary human societies, relative to less socially responsible alternatives. To begin with, as expressed by Trivers (2006), dispositions to uphold fair systems of cooperation and punish those who violate them could "benefit us in everyday life by protecting us from unfair arrangements that harm our inclusive fitness. We [could] . . . react negatively to unfair offers by others . . . because . . . the unchallenged repetition of such behavior is expected in the future to inflict costs on our inclusive fitness" (p. 78). If people permit members of their groups to get away with cheating others, it may be only a matter of time before the cheaters cheat them.

Second, members of groups could reduce the costs of punishing cheaters by employing sanctions that were biologically cheap to administer, such as threats, disapproval, shunning, and gossip; by vesting responsibility in individuals who are able to administer sanctions at little cost to themselves (because for example, they are feared or respected), or by distributing the costs to the group as a whole.

Finally, as suggested by Alexander, the costs of assuming responsibility for upholding the social order of one's group could be compensated for by gains in power, status, reputation, social support, and the diminished probability that those who wrong others will attempt to wrong one's friends and relatives. In support of this idea, studies have found that people are more strongly disposed to punish third parties in public than in private, suggesting that the costs of administering such punishments may be compensated for by gains in reputation (Kurzban, DeScioli, & O'Brien, 2007).

Individual-level theorists have offered two solutions to the public goods free-rider problem. First, following Alexander, they have suggested that this problem can be solved through selective interaction (Kurzban et al., 2007). Cooperators could foster their mutual interests by joining with other cooperators to produce public goods that they share, excluding free-riders from the exchange. To guard against being fooled by free-riders who fake cooperation, cooperators could rely on honest signals of cooperation such as behavioral evidence of contributing one's share. In support of these ideas, studies—including those that involve cross-cultural comparisons—have found that members of groups tend to monitor and accurately assess others' contributions to their groups and that they take measures to foster exchanges with those who do their share, or more than their share. Clearly, however, it is more difficult to detect and punish free-riders in large groups than it is to detect and punish them in smaller groups.

Second, individual-level theorists have suggested that the public goods free-rider problem can be solved through conditional cooperation. Studies have found that cooperation can pay off if individuals contribute their share on the first move in public goods games, then adjust their contributions in accordance with the contributions made by others. When individuals behave in this manner, a high proportion of players end up contributing amounts equivalent to the average amount contributed by members of their groups (Kurzban & Houser, 2005). However, as discussed, it takes only one or two free-riders to launch an exponential decline in contributions (Kurzban, McCabe, Smith & Wilson, 2001).

Gene–culture coevolutionary theorists have not been persuaded by these arguments for at least three reasons. For openers, they have argued that there is evidence suggesting that people are willing to punish third party norm violators even when it is costly to do so. For example, in an interesting study conducted in the United States, Miller (1999) found that many people were willing to confront third parties who parked inappropriately in spaces reserved for handicapped drivers, even though, in some cases, these interventions evoked verbal attacks, physical assaults, and tire slashing. Even seemingly low-cost forms of punishment such as gossip may come back to bite people on their behinds if the objects of their disparagement find out and seek revenge (Kaplan & Hill, 1985).

Second, gene–culture coevolutionary theorists allude to evidence that people are disposed to behave in prosocial ways even when it could not possibly benefit them, citing studies such as those reviewed in the previous chapter that establish that many people are willing to help strangers who could not possibly repay them, even when their behavior is anonymous. Finally, these theorists point out that research comparing the willingness of members of groups that vary in size and complexity to allocate resources to anonymous partners in games such as Dictator and Ultimatum has found that members of large groups governed by market economies make significantly fairer and more altruistic decisions than members of smaller subsistence-level groups (Henrich et al., 2010).

Are Dispositions to Suffer the Costs of Uniquely Human Prosocial Behaviors Anachronistic?

Some individual-level theorists have accepted the evidence that modern humans are disposed to engage in biologically and genetically costly forms of prosocial conduct in some conditions, but they have argued that these behaviors can be accounted for in terms of the automatic, subconscious activation of mental mechanisms that evolved through individual selection in small groups of early humans. These theorists argue that there would not have been adequate opportunity in ancestral environments for natural selection to have designed mental mechanisms with decision rules that enabled people to discriminate between one-shot and repeated encounters or that enabled them to predict whether they would interact with strangers in the future. For example, Johnson, Price, and Takezawa (2008) argue that, "our psychology simply fails to optimize behavior in evolutionarily novel circumstances (such as laboratory experiments or big cities) and better reflects the constraints of the environments in which our psychological mechanisms for cooperation evolved, environments characterized by small groups of extended kin, few strangers, strong hierarchies and lasting reputations" (p. 335). What modern humans inherit, argue these theorists, are mechanisms designed in terms of decisions rules such as "help members of your group," and "help those who seem similar to you," which produced return benefits in early environments, and continue to produce return benefits on average in modern environments, even though they sometimes induce individuals to behave in biologically costly ways. Stimuli such as receiving assistance or perceiving that someone who seems similar to you is in need activate primitive emotional reactions such as sympathy, empathy, and gratitude that motivate people to engage in costly forms of prosocial conduct.

Individual selection theorists argue that early humans rarely, if ever, encountered the opportunity to make anonymous donations, and that they rarely, if ever, engaged in one-shot exchanges with strangers who were members of their in-groups. With respect to evidence from game theory research, Trivers (2006) points out that, "our responses were never selected to perform in the highly unusual, one-shot, anonymous interactions in a lab, with payoffs underwritten by a third party" (p. 79). Trivers questions whether participants in the research studies cited by gene–culture coevolutionary theorists really believe that their choices will be anonymous (especially to the experimenter, and maybe to God) or that they are involved in one-shot encounters. He goes on to argue that in the real world, interactions with strangers tend to lead to additional interactions (or at least to the possibility of, or expectation of, additional interactions), that even short interactions with strangers may involve more than one exchange, and that contemporary students view other students (in experiments) as in-group members (see Johnson et al., 2008).

It is difficult to derive criteria to evaluate individual-level versus group-level theories of how the prosocial behaviors that uphold large-scale systems of cooperation evolved.

Competing theorists tend to agree that if the social environments in which early humans evolved contained repeated opportunities to engage in one-shot exchanges anonymously with strangers, mental mechanisms that evolved through individual-level processes should be designed in ways that enable individuals to avoid making costly, fitness-reducing "mistakes" (which they are not). However, competing theorists disagree about the frequency of such opportunities in ancestral environments, with individual level theorists arguing that they were rare, and cultural group selection theorists arguing that they were frequent. In addition, evidence indicating that members of large-scale societies allocate resources in experimental games more fairly and altruistically than members of smaller-scale societies do seem less consistent with the idea that such behaviors stem from a misfiring of ancient mechanisms that evolved through individual-level selection than with the idea that they stem from other kinds of mechanisms that evolved in other ways, although the strangeness of such games to people from subsistence-level societies may reduce their ecological validity.

CONCLUSIONS

The societies formed by modern humans differ in significant ways from the societies formed by hunter–gatherers and by other primates. The systems of cooperation in modern societies involve large numbers of people who contribute to the welfare of others whom they will never meet, in highly indirect ways. Modern humans differ from other primates in the quantity and quality of the prosocial behaviors that they emit and their disposition to uphold egalitarian social systems. Some evolutionary theorists have suggested that these differences emerged because subordinate members of early human groups banded together to overthrow more dominant members, but it is unclear why such subordinates would not simply take the place of the dominant members they overthrew, as other primates do.

Alexander (1987) has suggested that the key determinant of the transition from small hierarchical groups to large, more egalitarian groups was also the key determinant of the evolution of altruistic dispositions and systems of morality—namely, indirect reciprocity. Alexander argues that it paid off biologically for early humans to help members of their groups because it enhanced their reputations, increased their attractiveness as exchange partners, and enabled them to avoid the costs of being viewed as selfish and uncooperative.

It is easy to understand how the willingness to suffer the costs of punishing third parties could mediate the evolution of egalitarian societies and large scale systems of cooperation. However, in view of the costs of punishing third parties and the benefits of letting some-one else do the dirty work, it is challenging to explain how such dispositions evolved. Some evolutionary theorists have argued that these dispositions evolved through individual-level selection, but other evolutionary theorists have disputed this claim, arguing that the only way in which such dispositions could have evolved is through cultural group selection.

Richerson and Boyd (2005) have advanced a complex model of cultural group selection. These theorists argue that humans evolved in much the same way as other primates did until relatively recently in their evolutionary history, when they acquired the capacity to create, transmit, select, and refine culture. Cultural markers enabled humans to expand their definitions of in-groups, and cultural norms enabled them to expand their systems of cooperation. Groups that created and enforced culturally transmitted moral norms outcompeted groups that did not, mediating the rapid expansion of such norms. The adaptive advantage of a capacity for culture mediated the selection of mental mechanisms that disposed early humans to create it, to transmit it, and to uphold it, which in turn mediated the expansion of culture, in an arms-race, snowballing manner. According to Richerson and Boyd (2005), culturally laden environments led to the selection of a uniquely human set of "tribal instincts" that evolved on top of the more ancient social instincts that humans share with other animals. It was these uniquely human instincts, argue these theorists, that enabled humans to create large, cooperative societies and to engage in the uniquely human forms of prosocial behavior necessary to uphold them.

Gene–culture coevolutionary models have not appealed to some evolutionary theorists, who have argued that we need look no further than basic evolutionary processes such as kin selection and reciprocity to account for the evolution of large-scale systems of cooperation and uniquely human prosocial behaviors. I believe that the evidence supports an integrative model that builds from a foundation of primitive inclusive-fitness-increasing forms of prosocial behavior, recognizes that the mechanisms that give rise to such behaviors may induce people to behave in fitness-reducing ways in modern environments, and acknowledges that culture came to play a significant role in the evolution and activation of moral dispositions. One way to look at the issue is in terms of the similarities and differences between the brains of humans and the brains of other primates. Evolutionarily ancient mechanisms give rise to primitive prosocial dispositions, but recently evolved mechanisms that endow humans with unique intellectual abilities, the ability to engage in symbolic communication, and the ability to create and refine culture endow them with the ability to create uniquely human societies and engage in the uniquely human types of prosocial behavior necessary to uphold them.

15

PSYCHOLOGICAL AND NEUROLOGICAL
SOURCES OF UNIQUELY HUMAN
FORMS OF PROSOCIAL CONDUCT

Darwin attributed the evolution of uniquely human forms of prosocial conduct to the evolution of higher mental abilities, especially those that enabled language and reason, but he acknowledged that his account was far from complete.

Because the unique forms of prosocial conduct displayed by humans stem from mechanisms that evolved in their brains and nervous systems, understanding how the brain evolved supplies a basis for understanding these forms of behavior. Human brains contain the same kinds of primitive mechanisms as the brains of other animals do. However, human brains are significantly larger than the brains of most other animals in proportion to their body size, and human brains contain more prefrontal cortex (in relation to body size) than the brains of any other animal.

Theorists have accounted for the evolution of the human brain in terms of different adaptive problems that large brains enabled early humans to solve—problems such as foraging for fruit, hunting large game, and adjusting to changes in climate. Of special significance to the evolution of morality, some theorists have suggested that the kinds of problems that played the most important role in the expansion of the human brain were social problems that arose when early humans banded together to foster their mutual interests. All theories of brain expansion may be partially correct because large brains could have helped early humans solve a suite of adaptive problems. In view of the rapidity with which the brain evolved during the Pleistocene era after remaining relatively stable for millions of years, it makes sense to expect one or more runaway "arms-race" process, such as those involved in sexual selection, the selection of social strategies, and the evolution of culture, to have mediated the expansion and refinement of the human brain.

Humans' large brains endow them with the ability to form and to manipulate images and ideas in their heads. This ability increases their capacity to learn, to remember, to plan, to predict, to perform mental simulations, to reason, and to engage in creative thinking, all of which enables people to expand and refine their prosocial behaviors. Social intelligence, especially the ability to represent the contents of other people's minds in one's own mind, which probably evolved as a tool in strategic social interactions, was instrumental in the refinement of prosocial behaviors.

The acquisition of symbolic language abilities contributed to the expansion and refinement of prosocial behaviors by increasing early humans' capacity for cumulative social learning, which enabled them to communicate their insights about adaptive forms of conduct to others, and to refine these insights through discussion. In addition, the ability to form social contracts, to make verbal commitments, to express approval and disapproval, and to gossip about the behavior of others mediated the expansion and refinement of large-scale systems of cooperation and egalitarian social norms. Finally, language improved early humans' ability to manipulate others into behaving in prosocial ways, and it enabled them to negotiate mutually beneficial solutions to conflicts of interest.

Prosocial behaviors are products of complex interactions among early-evolved and later-evolved mental mechanisms. Although sophisticated cognitive abilities may be necessary for some uniquely human prosocial behaviors, they are not sufficient. Advanced cognitive abilities endow people with the capacity to engage in the kinds of uniquely human prosocial behaviors discussed in the previous chapter, but they do not necessarily generate the motivation to enact them.

Humans sometimes act like apes, but that is not all bad, because apes sometimes behave in ways that humans deem good. Apes defer to authority, help their friends and relatives, console those who feel bad, make up after fights, and cooperate with members of their groups (de Waal, 2008; Flack & de Waal, 2000). However, as recognized by Darwin, and as discussed in the last chapter, humans also engage in forms of prosocial conduct that are unique to their species. To understand human nature, we must account for the ways in which humans are similar to and different from other primates.

THE EVOLUTION OF THE HUMAN BRAIN

The prosocial behaviors that animals emit stem from mechanisms that are housed in their brains. "Old brain" mechanisms such as those discussed in Chapter 12 that are possessed by humans and other animals are the root sources of primitive types of prosocial behavior. "New-brain" mechanisms that have evolved in the human species may activate old-brain mechanisms and modify their outcomes, enabling humans to behave in the uniquely human ways discussed in the previous two chapters.

Understanding how the brain evolved has important implications for our understanding of how the mechanisms that mediate uniquely human forms of prosocial conduct are designed. For example, if the brain evolved primarily to solve nonsocial problems, such as how to extract food from the environment, then we might expect uniquely human prosocial behavior to be by-products of nonsocial mental abilities. If, on the other hand, the brain evolved primarily to solve social problems—the so-called "social brain" hypothesis—then we would expect uniquely human prosocial behaviors to be products of mental mechanisms designed to solve social problems, such as negotiating beneficial cooperative exchanges and guarding against being cheated by members of one's group.

The average human brain is between 1250 and 1350 cubic centimeters in volume, compared to about 450 cubic centimeters for the average chimpanzee brain and for the brains of ancestors of humans who lived two million years ago. The human brain is a remarkable organ, containing some 20–30 billion neurons that can perform billions of operations per second. However, it is expensive to operate. Although it comprises only about 2% of adults' body mass, it takes approximately 20% of the calories people produce to run it. In addition, the large heads necessary to house large brains in newborn infants jeopardize mothers' welfare during the birthing process; and large brains render humans susceptible to psychiatric disorders such as depression, the schizophrenias, and bipolar disorder. We can safely assume that the adaptive benefits proffered by large brains during the course of their evolution were sufficiently large to outweigh these costs.

The size of the human brain increased rapidly during the Pleistocene era, peaking some 150,000 years ago. It is interesting to note that the brains of Neanderthals were about the same size as the brains of modern humans and that even though human brains have not changed much in 150,000 years, human societies have changed dramatically during the past 10,000 to 30,000 years.

Humans' brains evolved from the bottom up, and from the back to the front, expanding the cerebral cortex, especially in the prefrontal area, into the neocortex, while retaining the earlier-evolved structures. The volume of the neocortex is significantly larger in humans (and other primates) than it is in other animals, compared to the volume of the rest of the brain. The prefrontal cortex houses mechanisms that perform executive functions such as symbolic thinking, planning, working memory, and decision making.

What Caused the Expansion of the Human Brain?

The key questions we must answer to account for the evolution of the human brain, and therefore for the mental mechanisms that enable people to emit uniquely human forms of prosocial conduct, are (1) what kinds of adaptive problems did large neocortexes help early humans solve; (2) why didn't other animals acquire these problem-solving mechanisms; and (3) what caused the human brain to expand at such a rapid rate during the Pleistocene era, after millions of years of relatively slow growth? Did early humans encounter different kinds of adaptive problems from other animals during this era, or did humans acquire unique ways of solving the same kinds of adaptive problems that other animals were able to solve, in less costly ways? Ironically, perhaps, it is possible that other animals failed to acquire large brains because they were better equipped than early humans were to solve their adaptive problems without the costs of developing a large brain.

Some sort of runaway, arms race, expanding positive feedback loop, snowballing process must have mediated the rapid expansion of the human brain. As suggested by Mark Flinn and Kathryn Coe (2007), two front-running candidates for such "red queen"[1]

---

[1] The red queen metaphor comes from Lewis Carrol's book, *Through the Looking Glass*, in which the Queen responds to Alice's complaint that she is not getting anywhere, by saying, "Now, here, you see, it takes all the running you can do to keep in the same place" (p. 345). As explained by Flinn and Coe, "the [red queen] metaphor refers to the dynamic nature of adaptation when the

processes are the social selection of brain mechanisms that enabled early humans to prevail in within-group and between-group competitions and the selection of mechanisms that enabled early humans to create and transmit culture. Another obvious candidate is runaway sexual selection (Miller, 2007b). In all cases, individuals who inherited brain mechanisms that increased their ability to survive and reproduce would have changed the environments of members of their groups in ways that favored the selection of increasingly effective brain mechanisms. For example, strategic interactions among members of groups of early humans would have given rise to arms races that guided the rapid coevolution of the mental mechanisms that regulate the tactics they employed. Better offensive tactics would have created a selective pressure for better defensive tactics, which would have created a selective pressure for better offensive tactics, and so on (Duntley, 2005).

As expressed by Miller (2007b), "every possible mode, type, and level of selection has been identified as a possible cause of human brain expansion by someone, somewhere" (p. 288). Richerson and Boyd (2005) have focused on the selection of mental abilities necessary to adapt to variations in climate, and social learning abilities necessary for the transmission of cultural innovations that uphold tribal communities. Other theorists have argued that large brains evolved to enable early humans to obtain food and extract it from its sources, with some theorists focusing on the mental abilities necessary to find and calculate the nutritional value of fruit, others focusing on the invention of tools for cracking nuts and digging up roots and larva, and still others focusing on the mental abilities necessary to hunt large game (see Kaplan et al., 2007, for a review of the research).

Theories of brain evolution that emphasize the adaptive value to early humans of solving social problems are most relevant to the evolution of morality. Several theorists have argued that large brains evolved in the human species to enable them to maximize their gains from group living. The larger the group, the more complex the mental abilities required to reap the benefits of sociality.

Some "social brain" theorists have focused on the mental abilities necessary to win mating games (Miller, 2007a). Others have focused on the mental abilities necessary to compete for and maintain dominance in hierarchical social orders (Cummins, 2005). Still others have focused on the mental abilities necessary to uphold egalitarian and cooperative social relations (Kaplan et al., 2007, p. 272). As expressed by Kaplan et al., (2007), "the complexity and intensity of human cooperative relationships, especially among non-kin relationships such as spouses and friends, is unparalleled. Cooperation is risky and fragile given that the possibility of defection always looms in the background. As a result, choice of partners in contexts where cooperation can have profound effects on people's lives puts a large premium on intelligence" (p. 272).

competition is constantly changing and success is relative. [With respect to the selection of social strategies] the metaphor is further apt . . . because of the analogy with the 'looking glass' as a mental space for imaginary social scenarios, possibly even involving 'mirror neurons'. . . . used to experience social chess mentally."

Embedded within such theories are those that suggest that large brains evolved because they endowed early humans with "Machiavellian intelligence," which enabled them to outwit group members in within-group competitions for resources (Whiten & Byrne, 1997). For example, as discussed in Chapter 6, Cummins (2005) has suggested that the adaptive value of deception and other aspects of Machiavellian intelligence in strategic interactions aimed at elevating status played an important role in the evolution of the human brain. "Variation in intelligence is a trait on which natural selection can operate. This situation seems to produce a kind of evolutionary arms race in that species that show the greatest capacity for this type of deception (e.g., chimpanzees) also have the most unstable dominance hierarchies relative to those that have stable hierarchies (e.g., macaques). . . . It is difficult to dominate individuals who have the cognitive wherewithal to outwit you."

One way to evaluate theories of brain evolution is to determine whether a particular adaptive problem was more significant for early humans than it was for other species. As expressed by Miller (2007b), "It is not enough to identify some behavioral task that sounds computationally difficult but ancestrally useful, because almost all such tasks are already solved by many species of smaller-brained animals. Complex 'extended phenotypes' (animal architecture and tools) are constructed by spiders, termites, weaver-birds, bowerbirds, beavers, and chimpanzees. . . . Complex social intelligence is shown by hyenas, wolves, elephants, dolphins, whales, baboons, and great apes. . . . Complex social foraging for diverse, transient food sources is shown by many species, from pigeons to lions" (p. 289).

Another way to evaluate theories of brain evolution is to examine the correlation across relevant species between brain size, or more exactly, the ratio between the neocortex and the rest of the brain, and the presence or magnitude of the adaptive problem one believes large brains evolved to solve. An interesting finding from research that has employed this strategy is that brain size is highly correlated with group size across many species (Dunbar, 1996, 1998, 2007). Within groups, brain size is correlated with grooming behavior, the size of cliques, male mating strategies, social play, the frequency of tactical deception, and the length of juvenile socialization (Dunbar, 2007, p. 282).

Several theorists have suggested that it is misguided to try to identify "the" source of brain expansion in the human species, because the mental abilities housed in a large neocortex would have enabled early humans to solve many kinds of adaptive problems. According to Barbara Finlay (2007), "the problem of accounting for human brain evolution is not choosing which one of the many ways our behavior differs from our nearest relatives is the essential one, but developing an explanatory scheme that encompasses all of them" (p. 294). In this regard, Dunbar (2007) has asserted that:

> it is important to remind ourselves that the social hypothesis is itself . . . ultimately an ecological explanation. The evolution of the social brain did not take place merely to make group living for the sake of group living possible; rather, it occurred to enable animals to live in groups that were in turn designed to solve some ecological problem of day-to-day survival or reproduction. The issue is whether the ecological problems are solved directly by individuals acting alone (i.e., using their own powers of deduction and cause–effect learning) or socially by individuals collaborating to achieve a more effective solution. (p. 282)

Variations in climate and other sources of ecological uncertainty would have elevated the adaptive value of cooperative food gathering and hunting, which in turn would have elevated the adaptive value of the mental abilities necessary to coordinate efforts, to keep track of the resources obtained, to negotiate divisions of labor, to divide resources, and to prevail in strategic social interactions. Social learning abilities would have enabled early humans to solve social and nonsocial problems and to pass their insights on to future generations. Language abilities would have facilitated social learning and enabled early humans to coordinate cooperative social relations. "Forager children and adolescents have years of experience listening to others tell stories and anecdotes about different foraging activities, before ever engaging in these activities themselves. In nonhuman primates, the frequency of social transmission of information strongly predicts wide-ranging variation in primate brain size, and most of this information pertains to foraging" (Kaplan et al., 2007). As suggested by Finlay (2007), enlarged neocortexes endow people with the ability to shape the ways in which they solve the adaptive problems they experience in accordance with the opportunities, constraints, and guidance provided by the cultures in which their brains develop.

Although Darwin argued that the evolution of mental mechanisms that endowed humans with such intellectual abilities as expanded memory, reason, and language were instrumental in the expansion of their social instincts, he did not describe these abilities in any systematic way, or explain very thoroughly how they achieved this effect. It is worth delving into these issues in a little more detail, even though, in many cases, the explanations are obvious.

MENTAL MECHANISMS THAT MEDIATE UNIQUELY HUMAN FORMS OF PROSOCIAL CONDUCT

I believe that the key intellectual abilities that mediated the expansion and refinement of prosocial behaviors (and as I explain in Chapter 17, the expansion and refinement of the moral sense) in early humans were those that enabled them to construct portable symbolic representations of their physical and social worlds in their minds, to manipulate them imaginatively, and to communicate them to other people through the medium of language. Psychologists have mapped the relation between the stimuli that animals experience and the responses they emit with the symbols $S \rightarrow O \rightarrow R$ (stimuli, organism and response). The enlarged brains of humans enlarge the intervening "O" aspect of this relation. Although people may respond in relatively automatic, predictable ways to some stimuli, without thinking much about them (such as, for example, when they engage in impulsive helping), they also may code the information they receive from their environments, retain it in their minds, consult it repeatedly, manipulate it mentally, compare it with other information they have stored, and make considered decisions. In addition, they may generate ideas on their own, communicate them to other people, then refine them in response to the ideas they receive from others. The general ability to form mental representations of events and to operate on them in the mind affects a suite of more specific mental abilities that mediate the expansion and refinement of prosocial behaviors.

Social Learning Abilities

Although other animals may imitate some of the things that they see others doing, humans are unique in their capacity to categorize behaviors emitted by others in abstract ways (e.g., "she told the truth"), store cognitive representations of these abstractions in their minds, and imitate the general forms of conduct in appropriate contexts after long delays. As discussed in the previous chapter, humans possess the creative capacity to modify the forms of prosocial conduct they copy from others in ways that increase their effectiveness, and to pass these improvements on to future generations.

Memory

We know that Darwin placed a great deal of significance on the enduring nature of social instincts. Another way to interpret this aspect of human nature is in terms of people's expanded capacity to remember how they have behaved and to reflect on what they have done. When people store memories of how they have treated others, and of how others have treated them, they create a world in their minds that they can consult for guidance about how they should behave in the future.

Several theorists have argued that humans' sophisticated cognitive abilities are necessary for the evolution of complex systems of cooperation. To reap the benefits of delayed forms of cooperation, individuals must be able to remember who has helped them and whom they have helped. In addition, they must be able to detect when those they have helped are able to repay them, reckon the value of the goods or services given and received, delay gratification (avoid discounting the value of future rewards excessively), and perhaps most importantly, have some sense of the contingency between giving and receiving. According to Stevens et al. (2005), "[other] animals can easily implement [cooperative] strategies that yield immediate benefits, such as mutualism . . . because individuals do not have to track benefits over time. With a time delay between cooperating and receiving return benefits, however, individuals must invest in an uncertain future. Delayed benefits impede learning the consequences of cooperation, require more memory capacity for previous interactions, and trade off short-term fitness gains for long-term gains" (p. 507).

The Ability to Form Complex Cognitive Representations

The research on self-control discussed in Chapter 7 offers a good demonstration of how the ability to construct representations of events in one's mind mediates the expansion and refinement of prosocial behaviors. In studies in which children were given an opportunity to obtain a large, delayed reward if they resisted the temptation to take a less desirable immediate reward:

> the most important determinants of waiting time were not the particular external stimulus conditions, but instead the person's cognitive representations of the situation. . . . When the person mentally transformed the stimuli (e.g., by representing in imagination the actual reward as an abstract picture of the reward),

self-control behavior changed predictably. For example, when they focused on the arousing "hot" properties of the reward (e.g., the pretzel's crunchy, salty taste, or the fun of playing with the toy), delay became very difficult. But when they thought about the same stimulus with an abstract, "cool" focus (e.g., "the pretzels look like little sticks"), delay became easier for them. The stimuli themselves remained the same: it was their internal mental representations that mediated the children's goal-directed behavior. (Michel, Cantor, & Feldman, 1996, p. 332)

Mental Simulation, Prediction, and Planning

Humans' expanded brains enable them to avoid the costs of trial and error learning by performing mental simulations: "If I do this, it should produce this result; if I do that, it should produce that result." This ability is especially valuable during strategic social interactions and reciprocal exchanges. It may induce animals to suppress selfish tactics that evoke retaliation and employ cooperative tactics that reap greater returns.

Although other animals are able to make predictions about the immediate consequences of their behaviors in an implicit manner, humans are able to consider a vast array of information, weigh the pros and cons of various choices explicitly in their minds, and anticipate the long-term consequences of enacting them. This ability enables humans to understand that the long-term benefits of sacrificing their interests for others, investing in relationships, and doing their share to uphold their groups may outweigh the immediate costs of these strategies.

Researchers have found that the ways in which people construct plans affects their ability to achieve their goals. For example, in studies on delay of gratification, experimenters have found that "children's effectiveness at waiting is substantially improved if they are provided with self-regulatory plans in advance of being left along with the rewards, such as being instructed to 'think fun thoughts' or to think of the rewards in more abstract terms (e.g., think of marshmallows as clouds)" (Michel et al., 1996, p. 343).

Associated with the ability to form cognitive representations of phenomena and to produce mental simulations of events, humans are capable of putting ideas together in the kinds of creative ways that, for example, produce images of mythical creatures such as unicorns. In the social arena, people may imagine utopian societies based on ideal systems of cooperation that, if practiced by everyone, would maximize everyone's benefits.

Reason

Reason is a mental tool that enables people to organize ideas in their minds, draw inferences that go beyond the information given, create mental simulations, and test the validity of relations among ideas by evaluating their logical consistency. Although, like Darwin (1874), most people assume that the function of reason is to derive the truth, neo-Darwinian evolutionary theory encourages us to view reason as a tool that evolved to help people solve adaptive problems. As explained by Ghiselin (1974), fitness trumps truth, consistency, and logic: "Man's brain, like the rest of him, may be looked upon as a bundle of adaptations. . . . We are anything but a mechanism set up to perceive the truth for its own sake. Rather, we have evolved a nervous system that acts in the interests of our gonads. . . . If fools are more prolific than wise men, then to that degree folly will be favored by selection." We would expect people to engage in rational, logical decision making when these process contain the potential to foster their fitness (i.e., in appropriate "if" conditions) but not in conditions in which they do not. Viewed in this way, we would expect reasoning processes to dispose people to help one another when these processes support the conclusion that altruistic forms of conduct or strategies will produce the greatest returns. In addition, as discussed, after the capacity to reason evolved, it may have given rise to the ability to derive decisions that prescribed nonadaptive moral courses of action.

Mind Reading

Humans differ from other animals in their ability to represent the contents of other people's minds in their own minds, to view events from the perspective of others, and to imagine how others will respond to their behavior (Selman, 1980). Let me give a personal example. The other day, while I was out jogging, an elderly woman asked me for directions to a school in my community. I directed her to turn left at the next street, then follow the road until she was able to turn left again. "Two lefts" I reminded her as I jogged away. As I continued running, I reviewed mentally the route she would take, given my directions, and "saw" that if she followed them precisely, she would turn left down an alley, which would get her hopelessly lost. I pictured, in my imagination, this lady becoming increasingly distressed as she tried to find her way out of the maze of poorly organized streets and maybe even cursing me for misleading her. I turned around, caught her just as she was turning down the wrong street, apologized for my poor directions, and redirected her.

The ability to take the perspective of others is important to morality in two respects. First, in constructing mental images of others in our minds, we identify with them and, in effect, incorporate them into ourselves, which may induce us to empathize with them and feel what they feel. Psychologically, helping those with whom we identify is like helping ourselves. Second, when we internalize images of other people, we may experience these images as a sort of audience, making our private acts seem public and making us feel accountable. As I explain in Chapter 17, this has important implications for the evolution of conscience.

The mental mechanisms that enable people to read the minds of others must have evolved in the social arena. Early humans who acquired mental mechanisms that enabled them to understand what others were thinking, feeling, planning, and intending to do would have fared better in strategic social interactions than those who did not. Increasingly sophisticated perspective-taking and reasoning abilities enable people to derive increasingly complex arguments that tend to ratchet up during the give and take of negotiation and debate. As expressed by Dunbar (2007), "the social world requires an individual to imagine the future behavior of other organisms, and this in turn may require it to imagine the other organism's mental states. These aspects of the world cannot be observed or engaged with directly, but have to be constructed in the mind. The computational costs of doing so may be significantly increased if all the individuals concerned have to be factored into the relationships exhibited in a more direct sense by those individuals who are immediately present" (p. 289).

Although "mind-reading" abilities probably originated as tools, or weapons, in strategic social interactions, they came to play a significant role in the expansion and refinement of cooperative and altruistic behaviors, and in the evolution of morality. Understanding others' perspectives sensitizes perspective takers to alternatives and consequences that they would not otherwise have considered. For example, understanding that others want or need help may induce people to think of ways of helping them, and understanding exactly what others want or need may increase the effectiveness (i.e., degree of altruism) of the assistance people render.

Insight and Meta-cognitive Thinking

Humans' capacity to reflect on their own behavior, and their capacity for meta-cognitive thinking (critically examining their own ideas; planning to make plans, and so on) have been found to affect their ability to behave in prosocial ways. Again, this is well-exemplified in research on delay of gratification. "With age, children show a preference for increasingly sophisticated and effective delay strategies and a concomitant progression in metacognitive understanding of their impact on delay behavior . . . by age 5 or 6, most children recognize that waiting is facilitated by distraction from the rewards, and that attention to them would lead to frustration and difficulty waiting. . . . By sixth grade, most children know that abstracting the reward objects, as opposed to focusing on their consummatory properties, facilitates waiting" (Michel et al., 1996).

Language

Humans do not need to be able to take the perspective of others to determine what they are thinking. They need only ask them, though they might not receive an honest answer. Through language, people are able to communicate the contents of their minds to the minds of others, and incorporate the contents of other people's minds in their minds in return. There has been a great deal of debate about when early humans acquired the capacity for symbolic language, but genetic evidence (e.g., pertaining to the FOXP2 gene) indicates that there may have been an important punctuation point about 100,000 years ago.

As mentioned, language increases humans' capacity for adaptive social learning and the transmission of cumulative culture. It is the primary medium through which adults communicate cultural norms to children. It enables people to receive ideas from others, communicate their responses to them, send refined ideas back to others, receive refined ideas in return, and so on.

Language also is an invaluable tool in strategic social interactions. People use it to induce others to obey rules and defer to their authority, to manipulate them into behaving altruistically, and to persuade them to cooperate. Language enables people to coordinate their efforts and to develop the kinds of long-term plans that lead to the expansion of systems of cooperative exchange. In addition, it enables people to resolve their conflicts of interest through dialogue and negotiation, going back and forth until a mutually acceptable compromise is found.

The capacity for symbolic language would have enabled early humans to pass judgment on events that occurred in the past, to hold members of their groups accountable for how they behaved, and to influence how they would behave in the future. It would have enabled members of groups to transform primitive threats and promises into long-term commitments by persuading others that treating them (and others) in prosocial ways would pay off and that treating them in antisocial ways would not. As discussed, social contracts and other forms of commitment are important in the evolution of morality because they enable people to influence the immediate behavior of others by inducing them to believe that they will receive future outcomes. As discussed, it may be in people's long-term interest to honor their threats and promises, even when it is costly for them to do so, because the long-term benefits of upholding a reputation for keeping one's word may outweigh the short-term costs of honoring one's commitments (Nesse, 2001).

According to Boehm, the capacity for language was instrumental in history of the human species in precipitating the transition from hierarchically organized groups to egalitarian groups. Building on Darwin's early ideas, Boehm (2000) suggests that:

> abstract communication . . . permitted the articulation and refinement of group values having to do with morality, and it also facilitated the kind of highly specific gossiping (with displacement) that is universal in human groups. Gossiping serves as a means of building social networks. . . . but, perhaps more importantly, it also enables group members to arrive privately and safely at a negative consensus about dangerous deviants. Language also makes it possible for groups to conspire, and ambush even the most fearsome dominator and to execute him. (pp. 94–95)

COMPETENCE VERSUS PERFORMANCE

Explaining how the mental abilities acquired by humans endow them with the capacity to engage in expanded and refined forms of prosocial conduct is one thing. Explaining why people sometimes use these abilities, and sometimes do not, is another. Accounting for an ability, or capacity, does not equate to accounting for the motivation to employ it. Competence does not equate to performance.

I discuss the competence–performance issue with respect to moral reasoning in Chapter 17. Suffice it here to say that evolutionary theory leads us to expect people to be disposed to invoke the least-costly prosocial decision-making tools necessary to solve the problems they face. Simple problems require simple solutions. When activating stimuli and social contexts correspond to those experienced by early humans, people tend to derive prosocial decisions in relatively automatic ways from primitive mental mechanisms that are inexpensive to operate. If someone falls down in front of you, or if your child needs some help, you do not have to consider the long-term consequences of your decisions or their implications for society in order to derive a decision. People are disposed to invoke sophisticated mental abilities when these abilities are necessary to solve the problems they experience, and when the benefits of invoking these abilities exceed the costs.

INTERACTIONS BETWEEN "OLD BRAIN" AND "NEW BRAIN" MECHANISMS: THE EVOLUTION OF EMPATHY

If the human brain contains both primitive mechanisms and sophisticated, later-evolved mechanisms that are equipped to produce, regulate, and structure prosocial behaviors, two important questions arise. First, what causes one type of mechanism and not another to be activated or to control decision making, and second, if more than one mechanism is activated, how do they interact? De Waal's model of the evolution of empathy supplies a good example of how a sophisticated, recently evolved cognitive capacity—the capacity for sophisticated forms of perspective-taking—interacts with primitive emotional reactions to refine and expand people's capacity to behave in prosocial ways.

De Waal (2006) summarizes his model, which I introduced in Chapter 12, as follows:

> empathy covers all the ways in which one individual's emotional state affects another's, with simple mechanisms at its core and more complex mechanisms and perspective-taking abilities at its outer layers. Because of the layered nature of the capacities involved, we speak of the Russian doll model, in which higher cognitive levels of empathy build upon a firm, hard-wired basis. . . . The claim is not that [this basis] by itself explains [all forms of empathy], but that it underpins. . . . cognitively more advanced forms . . . and serves to motivate behavioral outcomes. (p. 11)

As discussed, the primitive core of empathy consists of emotional reactions that generate the motivation to allay one's personal distress, which is evoked by the distress of others. Animals that experience these primitive reactions fail to differentiate themselves from others. They experience others' distress as distressful to them, and are motivated to relieve their own, vicariously experienced distress.

According to de Waal, "the next evolutionary step ['cognitive empathy'] occurs when emotional contagion is combined with appraisal of the other's situation and attempts to understand the cause of the other's emotions" (p. 9). Cognitive empathy gives rise to sympathetic behaviors such as consoling those who have been harmed. De Waal cites evidence demonstrating that consolation is common in humans and apes (and interestingly, in some large-brained birds), but virtually nonexistent in monkeys.

With further brain evolution, humans (and maybe a few other species) acquired increasingly sophisticated abilities to understand how others are thinking and feeling, which endowed them with the capacity to refine their empathic reactions, converting them from feelings of personal distress to feelings of sympathetic concern. De Waal labeled the final step in the evolution of empathy "empathic perspective taking." He argued that the cognitive ability to distinguish oneself from others and to understand how others are feeling on their own terms is the crucial determinant of this mental ability: "For an individual to move beyond being sensitive to others toward an explicit other-orientation requires a shift in perspective. The emotional state induced in oneself by the other now needs to be attributed to the other instead of the self. A heightened self-identity allows a subject to relate to the object's emotional state without losing sight of the actual source of this state" (p. 9). de Waal cites evidence that apes, humans, elephants, and dolphins are able to recognize themselves in mirrors, that this ability is correlated with perspective-taking abilities in humans, and that animals that possess self-recognition abilities engage in "targeted helping," defined as "help that is fine-tuned to another's specific situation and goals" (p. 9).

In a recent review of neurological research on empathy, Decety (2005) presented evidence that supported the idea that empathic reactions in humans are produced by an interaction between primitive types of emotional contagion and more complex cognitive processes. In this review, Decety summarized research on the role of mirror neurons (which fire in identical ways when people observe others performing acts as they do when people perform the acts themselves) in the production of empathy, and concluded that "shared representations [that constitute] distributed patterns of neural activation in two individuals who socially interact . . . are widely distributed in the brain . . . . cognitive processes that exert a top-down control on these shared representations are mediated by specific subregions of the prefrontal cortex" (p. 153). According to Decety, the right inferior parietal cortex structures empathic reactions by helping people distinguish actions that they produce from actions produced by others.

De Waal's model accounts for the evolution of empathy in terms of the evolution of mental abilities in the human species mediated by the expansion of the human brain. Developmental psychologists have advanced complementary models based on the development of mental abilities in children as their brains expand from birth to adulthood. Consider, for example, the model advanced by the developmental psychologist, Martin Hoffman (2000). Hoffman begins by acknowledging that empathy stems from evolved dispositions, then goes on to describe four phases in its growth in children that are defined in large part by the development of perspective-taking abilities. In the first phase, infants experience empathic reactions as "global distress," triggered, for example, by the cries of other infants. In the second phase, infants display egocentric empathic reactions that motivate them to respond to others' distress by engaging in behaviors that make them (but not the others) feel better. In the third phase, children's empathic reactions are evoked by interpretations of the situations that others experience, and children make more finely tuned emotional attributions. In the final stage, children and adults are able to experience empathy for disadvantaged groups or classes of people that they have never observed directly. They might, for example, shed tears for starving people in third world countries. Mature adults also are able to engage in recursive perspective taking such as, "She will think that I will think that she will think . . . ." and view events from the perspective of "generalized others," groups, and even all of humanity.

CONCLUSIONS

The prosocial behaviors emitted by humans are products of mental mechanisms in their brains. After millions of years of relatively slow growth, the human brain expanded at an accelerated pace. In view of the high costs of possessing a human brain, we can safely assume that it evolved to solve significant adaptive problems. Identifying these problems has important implications for our understanding of the sources of the uniquely human forms of prosocial conduct that people with large brains are capable of emitting.

Theorists have attributed the expansion of the human brain to many sources, some ecological and some social. It is probably misguided to assume that there was only one source of brain expansion; many interacting sources probably contributed to it. In view of the rapidity with which the brain expanded during the Pleistocene era, one or more "red queen" process[es] must have been involved.

New brain structures enabled early humans to form and to manipulate ideas in their minds, which mediated the expansion and refinement of their ability to learn, to remember, to plan, to reason, to engage in creative thinking, to predict the behavior of others, and to understand what others are thinking and feeling. These abilities, in turn, endowed humans with the capacity to engage in the expanded and refined forms of prosocial conduct unique to their species.

The human brain contains both primitive mechanisms, located in relatively old and deep areas, and more recently evolved mechanisms, located in the outer parts of the brain, especially the neocortex. People may or may not derive decisions about prosocial behaviors from new-brain mechanisms. In addition to accounting for the evolution of sophisticated mental abilities, we must identify the stimuli that activate them and explain how they interact with more primitive mechanisms to generate the motives that guide human behavior. For example, understanding that others need help and how best to help them counts for little or nothing if one is not moved to action, and the impetus to act may stem from the primitive kinds of mental mechanisms that humans share with other animals.

This ends my account of the evolution of prosocial behaviors. As discussed in Chapter 2, people commonly view prosocial forms of conduct as moral in nature. I now want to distinguish between the kinds of mental mechanisms that dispose people to behave in prosocial ways, which I have been discussing, and the kinds of mental mechanisms that induce people to consider these behaviors moral, which I will now discuss. On the one hand, we have mechanisms that induce people to exert self-control, defer to authority, cooperate, and behave altruistically. On the other hand we have mechanisms that give rise to the sense that people are morally obliged to behave in these ways in some contexts, and that these forms of conduct are right. The first set of mechanisms regulates behavior. The second set of mechanisms gives rise to moral emotions and moral judgments. Things get complicated when we consider relations between behavioral dispositions and a sense of morality. Mechanisms that dispose people to behave in prosocial ways may, or may not, engender a sense of moral obligation, and mechanisms that produce a moral sense may, or may not, motivate people to behave in prosocial ways.

In the next chapter, I offer an account of the origin of the moral sense, evaluating Darwin's contention that the mechanisms that dispose individuals to behave in prosocial ways produce a primitive sense of moral obligation. In the ensuing chapter, I evaluate Darwin's contention that reason and language are primarily responsible for the expansion and refinement of the moral sense in the human species, and in the final chapter in Part IV, I refine Darwin's account of the evolution of moral norms.

PART FOUR

The Evolution
of the Moral Senses

16

THE ORIGIN OF THE MORAL SENSES

At this point in my account of the evolution of morality, I have explained how mental mechanisms that dispose animals to behave in ways that people usually consider good could have evolved. I have reviewed evidence that such mechanisms have evolved in a variety of species, and I have discussed the ways in which these mechanisms are designed. It is now time to bridge the gap between the evolution of behavioral dispositions that people consider moral and the evolution of the mental mechanisms that do the considering—the mechanisms that produce moral sentiments and moral judgments.

It is commonly assumed that people possess a sense of morality; however, it might be more accurate to say that people possess several qualitatively different senses of morality, or a suite of moral senses. The sense that we should respect authority is quite different from the sense that we should resist temptation, and this in turn is quite different from a sense of fairness or justice. Feeling morally obliged to behave in particular ways is different from feeling that others should behave in these ways. Passing judgment on oneself involves different psychological experiences from passing judgment on others. For example, we do not normally feel guilty about things that other people do, and we do not feel a sense of righteous indignation about our own misdeeds. Abstract, in-principle ideas, such as the Golden Rule and the cardinal moral principles espoused by philosophers of ethics, are different from concrete, contextualized moral attributions. And moral beliefs differ in significant ways from moral reasons and moral justifications.

In this chapter, I classify different aspects of the moral sense and offer a speculative account of how the most primitive aspects may have originated. I suggest that a sense of duty originated in the emotional and motivational states that induce people to behave in prosocial ways. A sense of rights originated in a consciousness of implicit social norms defining how members of groups are permitted to foster their welfare, and what they are owed by virtue of the contributions they make to their groups. Conscience originated in emotional reactions to social sanctions administered by others. Such moral sentiments as gratitude and indignation originated in emotional reactions to prosocial and antisocial behaviors emitted by others. A sense of justice originated as a means of counteracting cheating in cooperative exchanges. Abstract ideas about morality emerged when early humans acquired the ability to reflect on their moral intuitions. Although these accounts of the origin of the moral senses rise above "just so" stories, they are at best the first steps toward the development of a theory.

I close this chapter with a discussion of Jonathan Haidt's model of moral decision making, which contrasts rational sources of moral judgment with moral intuitions, reviewing research demonstrating that people often make moral judgments in irrational ways.

To say that you seek to explain how a sense of morality originated is to imply that you seek to account for one phenomenon—*a* sense of morality. However, this aspiration immediately encounters an obstacle, namely that people have quite different kinds of moral experiences. Although all aspects of people's sense of morality—or all moral senses—have something in common, because they are all moral, they differ in at least four systematic ways. First, some aspects consist of evaluative *feelings* such as pride, guilt and gratitude, whereas other aspects consist of evaluative *thoughts*, such as "people should respect the rights of others." Second, some aspects are *positive*; others are *negative*. Third, some aspects pertain to *oneself*—for example, feelings of moral obligation and feelings of guilt—whereas other aspects, such as gratitude and moral indignation, pertain to *others*. Finally, the thoughts and feelings people have *before* making moral decisions (such as feelings of moral obligation and ideas about what people should and should not do), differ from the thoughts and feelings people have *after* making moral decisions (such as pride, remorse, and positive and negative judgments about what people have done).

These aspects of the moral sense—or senses—can be classified in the $2 \times 2 \times 2 \times 2$ matrix outlined below. In this chapter, I focus on the hot, or emotional, aspects of the moral sense, which I argue are rooted in relatively primitive mental mechanisms that humans share with other primates. I discuss the colder, more rational and recently evolved aspects of the moral sense in the next chapter, along with relations between moral emotions and moral reasoning.

ANATOMY OF A SENSE OF MORALITY

To account for a sense of morality, we must explain what the aspects of this sense have in common that renders them moral, then we must explain how they differ from one another. What defines the body of a sense of morality, and what defines its components, or parts? What distinguishes the moral sense from other senses, and what distinguishes one aspect of this sense from other aspects of this sense?

Pondering these questions from an evolutionary perspective induces us to expect a sense of morality to have evolved because it solved some overriding adaptive problem with different aspects of this sense designed to solve different aspects of the problem. To understand what the aspects of the moral sense have in common, we need to identify the overriding adaptive problem that this sense evolved to solve; and to account for the ways in which the aspects differ, we need to break this problem down into its essential components or subproblems.

Self	Right	Prescriptive	Hot (a sense of duty)
			Cold ("I should" deontic judgments and justifications)
		Judgmental	Hot (a sense of self-approbation and pride)
			Cold ("I did wrong" judgments and justifications)
	Wrong	Prohibitive	Hot (resisting temptation, showing restraint)
			Cold ("I should not" deontic judgments and justifications)
		Judgmental	Hot (a sense of guilt, remorse, self-contempt, shame)
			Cold ("I did right" judgments and justifications)
Others	Right	Prescriptive	Hot (the sense that others should behave in prescribed ways)
			Cold ("You/he/she/they should" deontic judgments and justifications)
		Judgmental	Hot (feelings of moral approval)
			Cold ("You/he/she/they did right" judgments and justifications)
	Wrong	Prohibitive	Hot (the sense that others should not behave in prohibited ways)
			Cold ("You/he/she/they should not" judgments and justifications)
		Judgmental	Hot (a sense of moral disapproval, blame, disgust, righteous indignation)
			Cold ("You/he/she/they did wrong" judgments and justifications)

As a variation on one of the themes of this book, I believe that the overriding adaptive problem that a sense of morality evolved to solve was the same as the overriding adaptive problem that prosocial behavioral dispositions evolved to solve—the temptation for individuals to advance their short-term interests in ways that violate the social orders of their groups and jeopardize the welfare of other members who help them meet their needs. This idea is consistent with the notions that the central difference between moral emotions and other kinds of emotions is that moral emotions are associated with the welfare, or interests, of people and groups, and that they are usually evoked by behaviors that conform to, or violate, moral norms (Haidt, 2001).

Viewed in this way, all aspects of the moral sense should be designed to dispose members of groups to uphold social norms that support the social orders of their groups, with different aspects of this sense (or different moral senses) contributing to this function in different ways. For example, we would expect some aspects to dispose people to behave in prosocial ways (e.g., aspects designed to engender feelings of moral obligation, and aspects designed to make people feel guilty about harming others), with other aspects aimed at inducing others to behave in prosocial ways (e.g., aspects that induce people to admire those who cooperate and behave altruistically, to feel vengeful when others cheat them, and to feel indignant when they observe others behaving unfairly). In the ensuing sections of this chapter, I consider how the main aspects of a sense of morality could have originated, discussing in turn, the origin of a sense of moral obligation, the origin of conscience, the origin of a sense of rights, the origin of moral sentiments about others, the origin of a sense of justice, and the origin of abstract ideas about morality.

THE ORIGIN OF A SENSE OF MORAL OBLIGATION

It is commonly assumed that the moral sense guides moral behavior: Faced with a moral decision, people decide what they ought to do; then, if they are adequately motivated, they do the right thing (Kohlberg & Candee, 1984). There is no question that people sometimes make moral decisions in this way. For example, as cognitive-developmental psychologists have demonstrated, people sometimes think hard about how to solve moral problems, evaluate behavioral alternatives in terms of their moral merits, decide which course of action is most moral, then carry it out. As cognitive-developmental psychologists have noted, this process involves at least two kinds of mental mechanisms—one that does the deliberating, weighing, and selecting of alternatives and another that induces people to carry out the behavior (Kohlberg & Candee, 1983; Rest, 1983).

However, this is not the only way in which a sense of morality can be related to behavior, and it almost certainly is not the way in which it originally was related. People also may act first, then evaluate their behaviors in moral terms. This makes evolutionary sense because there is good reason to assume that prosocial dispositions evolved before a sense of morality. Many animals are disposed to behave in prosocial ways, but it seems implausible that they possess a sense of morality, at least like the one possessed by humans. If the mechanisms that produce prosocial behavioral dispositions evolved before the mechanisms that produce the kind of moral sense that humans possess, a good place to begin our search for the origin of a sense of morality is in these behavioral dispositions.

As mentioned in Chapter 4, Darwin (1874) suggested that the activation of social instincts—that is to say, the activation of mental mechanisms that induce animals to behave in prosocial ways—may engender a rudimentary sense of duty: "The imperious word ought seems merely to imply the consciousness of the existence of a rule of conduct, however it may have originated" (p. 112). When the proximate mechanisms that dispose people to behave in prosocial ways are activated, they produce emotional states that people experience as a primitive sense of moral obligation—a sense that they should behave in these ways. The function of these feelings is to induce people to behave in the kinds of altruistic, cooperative, temperate, and deferential ways that increased early humans' inclusive fitness. The crucial difference between feelings of obligation and feelings of moral obligation is that the latter pertain to shared standards about how members of groups ought to behave, which affect their welfare and are usually reinforced by sanctions.

THE ORIGIN OF CONSCIENCE

If you ask English-speaking people where their sense of morality is located, most of them would name a mental structure called conscience. In contrast to a sense of moral obligation, which gives rise to a forward-looking press to behave in moral ways, conscience gives rise to a backward-looking reaction to acts that one committed in the past, and to post hoc evaluations of one's intentions and motivational states. People's consciences "bother" them. (In addition, people may evaluate acts they intend to commit in an anticipatory way.) Conscience is a mechanism that induces people to pass judgment on themselves and their behaviors. It generates, or is associated with, moral emotions such as pride and guilt.

Darwin's account of conscience focused on the enduring nature of social instincts and people's negative reactions to violating them and behaving in selfish and antisocial ways. However, there is more to conscience than this. Choosing to satisfy a pressing but transient personal need that leaves a more enduring social need unsatisfied may well induce people to feel that they made the wrong choice, but it does not necessarily induce them to feel that the choice was immoral. Something more is needed. I think that Darwin sensed the main factor responsible for bridging the gap between regretting one's behavior and considering it morally reprehensible when he attended to the "deep regard" people feel for the "good opinion" of their fellows, and the recognition that, "man would be influenced in the highest degree by the wishes, approbation, and blame of his fellow-men" (p. 106).

Darwin's account of the acquisition of conscience can be reconceptualized in terms of social conditioning and the sanctions that uphold cooperative social orders (Aronfreed, 1968). Children evoke approval when they obey the rules, which makes them feel good, and they evoke disapproval when they disobey the rules, which makes them feel bad. Anticipating emitting behaviors that have been, and therefore could be, punished evokes fear. Children experience the psychological states associated with anticipating approval, disapproval, and other rewards and punishments as a primitive sense that it is right to behave in socially acceptable ways and that it is wrong to behave in socially unacceptable ways—that one should behave in ways that others condone, and that one should not behave in ways that others condemn.

Findings from contemporary research on the acquisition of conscience are easily incorporated in a Darwinian framework. Consider, for example, the following findings reported by Thompson, Meyer, and McGinley (2006) in a recent review. "Conscience development has its origins in infancy, where the sanctions (and rewards) of adults in response to the child's actions have emotional and behavioral consequences. . . .

experiences of approval and disapproval are important" (pp. 269–270). And, "One of the strong motivators for morally compliant behavior is the salient emotion that arises from cooperative and uncooperative conduct" (p. 277). And finally, "Young children are motivated to cooperate with the expectations of parents to enjoy the positive affectionate relationship that they enjoy. Viewed in this light, the parent–child relationship in early childhood can be conceived of as the young child's introduction into a relational system of reciprocity that supports moral conduct by sensitizing the child to the mutual obligations of close relationships" (p. 282).

Other animals, such as dogs, have been conditioned to display affective reactions akin to guilt by punishing them for their transgressions (Aronfreed, 1968). Fearful children develop particularly strong consciences (Kagan & Lamb, 1987). A team of researchers led by Grazyna Kochanska has concluded that children who are born with different temperaments may develop strong consciences in different ways (see Thompson et al., 2006 for a review). For example, as discussed in Chapter 7, some children may be naturally inclined to exert self-control. Other children may react strongly to punishment and disapproval, and still other children may behave themselves in order to maintain good relations with parents.

The neuroscientist Damasio (1994) and his colleagues have studied patients who have sustained brain injuries to an area of the prefrontal cortex (the "ventromedial" area, located behind and above the eyes) and made a fascinating set of discoveries. People with these injuries do not suffer any deficit in their logical reasoning abilities. For example, they respond to hypothetical moral dilemmas such as those on Kohlberg's test in much the same way as other people do, (and presumably in much the same way that they responded to them before they sustained their injuries). However, their real-life moral decision-making behavior is radically disrupted. Their judgment is impaired; they fail to abide by moral norms or make normal moral judgments, and they behave in selfish, irresponsible, uncaring, and immoral ways.

As explained by Damasio, the damage to these patients' sense of morality stems from a deficit in emotional responsiveness. People who have sustained these brain injuries understand the difference between right and wrong, but they do not *feel* the difference, because they do not experience emotions such as shame, guilt, gratitude, and moral outrage in the same way that normal people do. In a recent study, Young, Bechara, Tranel, Damasio, Hauser, & Damasio (2010) also found that such patients fail to take the intentions of those who perpetrate harmful acts into account when they make moral judgments, basing their judgments instead on the outcomes of the acts. For example, these patients judged characters in hypothetical scenarios who accidentally harmed or killed others more harshly than characters who tried to harm or kill others, but failed. According to the researchers, such patients "can process what people are thinking and their intentions, but they just don't respond emotionally to that information." "They can read about a murder attempt and judge it as morally permissible because no harm was done." These findings imply that making moral judgments requires at least two processes—a logical assessment of intention, and an emotional reaction to the assessment—with each of these processes mediated by different, but interacting, brain circuits.

Considered as a whole, the evidence supports a model of conscience in which experiences such as guilt stem from "the blending of elementary subjective emotional experiences, which are ubiquitous in mammals, with emotional and cognitive mechanisms that are typically human" (Moll et al., 2008, p. 4). An important implication of these findings is that "moral emotions might prove to be a key venue for understanding how phylogenetically old neural systems, such as the limbic system, were integrated with brain regions more recently shaped by evolution, such as the anterior PFC [prefrontal cortex], to produce moral judgment, moral reasoning, and behavior" (Moll et al., 2008, p. 17).

Although learning theory accounts of how children acquire a conscience, and models of how moral emotions such as guilt and shame are activated and represented in the brain contribute to our understanding of the moral sense, they are limited in at least two respects. First, there is more to conscience than conditioned responses and emotional reactions such as guilt and shame. There is, for example, the inner "voice" that people experience as approving and disapproving of their behavior. I offer an account of the origin of this inner voice in the next chapter and explain how it becomes transformed into a process that induces people to pass judgment on themselves.

Second, these accounts leave fundamental "why" questions unanswered. For example, establishing *that* people sometimes experience guilt when they harm other people does not explain *why* they experience this emotion. At a proximate psychological level of analysis, we need to identify the goals that the motives engendered by moral emotions help people achieve. At an ultimate level of analysis, we need to explain how achieving such goals increased the inclusive fitness of early humans. Darwin implied that one function of moral emotions is to help people obtain approval and avoid disapproval from members of their groups, which in turn increases their fitness. As discussed in Chapter 12, Frank (2001) and other theorists have argued that the function of moral emotions such as guilt and shame is to induce people to forgo immediate rewards in order to foster their long-term interests.

THE ORIGIN OF A SENSE OF RIGHTS

It is easy to account for the origin of the sense the one has the right to behave in certain ways because people are naturally inclined to feel entitled to behave in ways that enable them to meet their needs. The more basic the needs in question—for example, the need to survive and to reproduce (i.e., the right to life), the need for freedom, and the need for happiness—the more deeply seated people's endorsement of the idea that they have the right to pursue them. The challenge lies in accounting for the origin of people's sense that they do *not* have the right to satisfy their needs in any way they want and that *other people* have the right to satisfy their needs in certain ways.

Again, social sanctions must have played a crucial role in constricting early humans' sense of their rights and extending them to other members of their groups. Among the strategies adopted by early humans to meet their needs, strategies that promoted the welfare of others and upheld the social orders of their groups would have met with approval, and strategies that diminished the welfare of others and violated the social orders of their groups would have met with disapproval. In addition, early humans would have approved of others' prosocial behaviors, and disapproved of others' antisocial behaviors, and this would have narrowed down the forms of conduct that members of groups considered permissible. The idea that it is socially acceptable to foster one's survival and reproductive success in prosocial ways, but not in antisocial ways, came to be experienced as a sense of rights. Rights are linked to duties in systems of cooperation: Those who give earn the right to receive.

An evolutionary account of people's conception of rights is consistent with evidence that people from all cultures endorse the same basic rights, but that people from different cultures instantiate them in different ways (Helwig, 2006). Although evidence offered by cognitive-developmental psychologists that children's conceptions of rights becomes more cognitively sophisticated with development is not inconsistent with an evolutionary account, evolutionary theory leads us to expect significant differences between people's conceptions of their rights and people's conceptions of others' rights at all stages of development, which does not seem to have been investigated by researchers. Although it could be argued that the need for cognitive consistency is equipped to bridge the gap between people's sense that they have rights and the sense that others have (the same) rights, this process is, at best, a weak antagonist against self-serving biases in social cognition. As I will explain, public accountability constitutes a much stronger constraint on inconsistency than private rumination does.

THE ORIGIN OF MORAL SENTIMENTS ABOUT OTHERS

In addition to accounting for "self-praising" emotions such as pride and "self-critical" emotions such as guilt and shame, we must account for "other-praising" emotions such as admiration and gratitude, and for "other-critical" emotions such as contempt, disgust, and moral indignation (Moll et al., 2008). Early humans would have reacted positively when they were treated well by others, and negatively when they were treated poorly, just as contemporary humans do. Positive emotional reactions to being treated in respectful, altruistic, and cooperative ways would have evoked a primitive evaluative sense that these prosocial behaviors were right and that those who emitted them were good; and negative emotional reactions to being treated in selfish and harmful ways would have evoked a primitive sense that these behaviors were wrong and that those responsible for the behaviors were bad. Note that affective reactions such as these are directed at the people who evoke them, not just their behavior, and as such, they constitute trait attributions. We tend to approve of those who treat us right, and consider them good; and we tend to disapprove of those who wrong us, and consider them bad.

But there is more. Although the ways in which people are treated by others may be the most direct source of their positive and negative reactions to them, it is not the only source. Aspects of others such as their status, physical appearance, accomplishments, and cleanliness may affect the ways in which people feel about them. And, as irrational as it may seem, the emotional reactions evoked by such variables may affect people's moral judgments.

Disgust and Moral Contempt

Researchers have found that disgusting events that have little to do with morality can influence people's moral judgments. For example, one study found that people who were in a filthy, messy, room made harsher moral judgments than people who were in a tidy, clean room did (Schnall, Haidt, & Clore, 2005). Theorists such as Rozin, Haidt, and McCauley (2000) have suggested that moral disgust is an "embodiment" or extension of nonmoral disgust, which stems from digestive repulsion. Moll et al. (2008) report that "the neural representations of disgust . . . include the anterior insula, the anterior cingulated and temporal cortices, the basal ganglia, the amygdale, and the OFC" (p. 15).

Rozin and his colleagues (2000) have found that phenomena associated with the risk of harm due to germs evoke disgust—things such as bodily fluids, dead animals, garbage, and rancid smells—and that the forms of conduct and people associated with these kinds of events tend to be considered immoral. As these researchers have pointed out, sexual acts involve the exchange of bodily fluids, and many sexual prohibitions are structured by concepts associated with pollution and disgust—for example, prohibitions such as those associated with menstruation, anal sex, and bestiality. Rozin et al. (2000) and others have argued that reactions to physical impurity (and purity) may be transformed into ideas about spiritual impurity (and purity): acts that contaminate people's spirit are viewed as immoral, and pureness of spirit is viewed as moral.

The adaptive function of moral disgust is similar to the adaptive function of other forms of disgust—it motivates people to withdraw from, and reject, potentially harmful stimuli, whether physical or social in nature. People tend to steer clear of those who behave in impure ways (Prinz, 2007). Who would you rather have as a neighbor, a thief or a person who had sex with animals and never bathed?

THE ORIGIN OF A SENSE OF JUSTICE

Trivers (1985) suggested that "a sense of fairness has evolved in the human species as the standard against which to measure the behavior of other people, so as to guard against cheating in reciprocal relationships" (p. 388) and that "such cheating is expected to generate strong emotional reactions, because unfair arrangements, repeated often, may exact a very strong cost in inclusive fitness" (Trivers, 2006, p. 77). In a similar vein, in a discussion of primate social behavior, de Waal and Brosnan (2006) suggested that, "the squaring of accounts in the negative domain . . . may represent a precursor to human justice, since justice can be viewed as a transformation of the urge for revenge, euphemized as retribution, in order to control and regulate behavior" (p. 88). On the positive side of fairness, "the memory of a received service, such as grooming, induces a positive attitude toward the same individual, a psychological mechanism described as 'gratitude' by Trivers" (de Waal & Brosnan, 2006, p. 93).

In his early article on the evolution of reciprocal altruism, Trivers distinguished between gross and subtle cheating. Receiving help from those who have helped you would not have been enough to foster the evolution of reciprocity if the goods and services one received were worth less in fitness currency than the goods and services one gave. As discussed, reckoning the value of goods and services given and received, weighing the former against the latter, and evaluating them in terms of an appropriate standard of equity requires relatively sophisticated mental abilities (Hauser, 2006), and some theorists believe that the adaptive value of making such calculations played an important role in the evolution of the human brain (Byrne & Whiten, 1988).

Brosnan and de Waal (2003) conducted a study that seems to indicate that monkeys compare the rewards that they and others receive, and react negatively to inequities. These investigators allowed one capuchin monkey to observe another capuchin monkey receive a highly valued reward (a grape) for performing a task, then the researchers offered the observer a less desirable reward (a cucumber slice) for performing the same task. Brosnan and de Waal found that the monkeys that received the less desirable rewards refused to accept them and even threw them away. Such negative reactions were intensified when the monkeys that received the more highly valued rewards did not have to work for them. Brosnan and de Waal concluded that "capuchin monkeys thus seem to measure reward in relative terms, comparing their own rewards with those available and their own efforts with those of others" (p. 48).

Self-serving Biases in a Sense of Justice

Building on a theme introduced in the discussion of the origin of rights, Trivers has asserted that "an attachment to fairness or justice is self-interested and we repeatedly see in life . . . that victims of injustice feel the pain more strongly than do disinterested bystanders and far more than do the perpetrators" (Trivers, 2006, p. 77). In support of this assertion, there is a great deal of evidence that people are inclined to react more strongly to being treated unfairly by others than to treating others unfairly, to hold others to higher standards of fairness than they apply to themselves, to overestimate how much they deserve and are owed, to underestimate how much they owe others, and to reckon costs and benefits for themselves and others in different ways (Greenberg & Cohen, 1982). However, as discussed in the next chapter, we would not expect unconstrained self-serving biases in people's sense of justice to produce optimal outcomes, and the evidence suggests that self-serving biases are constrained by several factors.

Righteous Indignation

Although other primates react negatively when members of their troupes violate prosocial norms and take measures to punish norm violators, humans stand out in the animal kingdom in their disposition to punish free-riders and those who behave unfairly toward third parties. As expressed by J. Q. Wilson (1993), "Our sense of justice . . . involves a desire to punish wrongdoers, even when we are not the victims, and that sense is a 'spontaneous' and 'natural' sentiment" (p. 40). Interpreting findings from the kinds of economic games discussed in earlier chapters, Gächter and Hermann (2006) conclude, "Overall, the results suggest that free riding causes negative emotions . . . [which is] consistent with the hypothesis that emotions trigger punishment" (p. 297). According to Moll et al. (2008), "Indignation evokes activation of the OFC . . . the anterior PFC, anterior insula, and anterior cingulate contex" (p. 15).

THE ORIGIN OF ABSTRACT IDEAS ABOUT MORALITY

The positive and negative feelings that early humans experienced when they behaved in prosocial and antisocial ways would have converged with the positive and negative feelings that they experienced when others behaved in prosocial and antisocial ways to contribute to a more general sense that prosocial forms of conduct are right, and constitute virtues, that antisocial forms of conduct are wrong, and constitute vices—that those who behave in prosocial ways are good, and that those who behave in antisocial ways are bad. This is why people from all cultures consider altruistic, cooperative, honest, respectful, and temperate forms of conduct right; and all people consider selfish, aggressive, uncooperative, dishonest, disrespectful, and self-indulgent forms of conduct wrong, even though there are significant differences between and within cultures in how these forms of conduct are defined.

INTUITIVE AND RATIONAL ASPECTS OF THE MORAL SENSES

The social psychologist, Jonathan Haidt (2001) has advanced a model of how people make moral judgments that meshes nicely with the framework for the origin of a sense of morality that I have derived from evolutionary theory. Haidt suggests that people may derive moral judgments from two qualitatively different sources—moral intuitions and moral reasoning. Haidt defines moral intuitions as "the sudden appearance in consciousness of a moral judgment, including an affective valence (good–bad, like–dislike), without any conscious awareness of having gone through steps of searching, weighing evidence, or inferring a conclusion" (p. 818). Moral intuitions are like "gut feelings in the mind." Haidt suggests that, ultimately, they stem from the kinds of innate evolved dispositions discussed in the previous chapter.

Haidt endorses Damasio's (1994) somatic marker account of moral decision making, which suggests that moral judgments and moral behaviors are structured by classically conditioned emotional (autonomic nervous system) responses to mental representations of cues in the physical and social environment. In addition, Haidt endorses Rozin's ideas about "embodied cognition," suggesting, for example, that feelings of disgust evoked by physically impure phenomena such as rotting food may become generalized to, and "embodied" in, metaphors about moral impurity (e.g., a rotten scoundrel), giving rise to moral beliefs and judgments such as those that uphold dietary and sexual restrictions (Rozin, Haidt, & McCauley, 2000).

In Haidt's model, people are born with the capacity to experience all kinds of specific moral intuitions just as they are born with the capacity to produce the sounds of all languages. However, as with language, their cultural experiences narrow down the range of moral intuitions that they end up acquiring and in part determine what evokes them. Haidt argues that it is less the case that children are taught the norms of their cultures explicitly by adults, and more that they learn them implicitly (especially from peers) as they are immersed in the complex of customs of their groups. Haidt sums up his model as follows, "Moral development is primarily a matter of maturation and cultural shaping of endogenous intuitions. People can acquire explicit propositional knowledge about right and wrong in adulthood, but it is primarily through participation in cultural complexes. . . . involving sensory, motor and other forms of implicit knowledge. . . . shared with one's peers during the sensitive period of late childhood and adolescence. . . . that one comes to feel, physically and emotionally. . . . the self-evident truth of moral propositions" (Haidt, 2001, p. 828). Although Haidt does not deny that people may derive moral judgments in rational ways, he claims that people usually derive moral judgments from moral intuitions; moral intuitions are the default.

Haidt (2001) and his colleagues have evaluated his model of moral intuitions by giving participants in their studies scenarios such as the following one:

> Julie and Mark are brother and sister. They are traveling together in France on summer vacation from college. One night they are staying alone in a cabin near the beach. They decide that it would be interesting and fun if they tried making love. At the very least it would be a new experience for each of them. Julie was already taking birth control pills, but Mark uses a condom too, just to be safe. They both enjoy making love, but they decide not to do it again. They keep that night as a special secret, which makes them feel even closer to each other. What do you think about that? Was it OK for them to make love? (p. 814)

Other scenarios assessed people's ideas about the moral permissibility of engaging in acts such as cleaning a toilet with one's country's flag, or eating one's dog after it died.

Researchers using such scenarios have found that virtually all participants view the behaviors in question as wrong—often very wrong—but have difficulty explaining why. When pressed to give reasons, they tend to give invalid reasons (e.g., Julie could get pregnant; Mark and Julie would feel bad.). When the invalidity of their reasons is pointed out, they become lost for words, saying things like, "I can't explain it; I just know it's wrong." Haidt dubbed this phenomenon "moral dumbfounding."

MORAL HEURISTICS

The overriding theme of Haidt's research is that people may derive moral judgments from sources other than moral reasoning, and because these other sources are not structured by reason, they may induce people to form moral judgments that they are unable to justify in rational ways. Research on moral heuristics and moral grammar offers additional support for the idea that people may derive moral judgments in automatic, irrational ways. Consider the following examples from a review of research on moral heuristics published by Sunstein (2005).

People tend to judge acts of commission more harshly than they judge acts of omission, even thought the committed and omitted acts produce exactly the same negative consequences. For example, people think it is worse to kill someone than to let someone die on purpose, and people make harsher judgments about actively starving others than they do about passively letting people starve. In addition, people pass harsher judgments on those who unintentionally harm others in the process of trying to help them than they do on those who fail to intervene when they could prevent others from harming themselves. People tend to feel that punishment should be proportionate to the outrageousness of an act (Hauser, 2006), and they tend to consider direct acts that produce harmful consequences more immoral than indirect acts that produce the same consequences. For example, participants in one study judged the behavior of an evil-intentioned wrongdoer more harshly when he directly stabbed his enemy than when he was bumped by a jogger and did the dirty deed (Pizzaro, Uhlmann, & Bloom, 2003).

People also tend to judge moral transgressions more harshly when they involve physical contact than when they do not. Consider the following famous moral dilemma, called the Trolley Problem. Five people are walking along a set of railway tracks, and one person is walking along an adjacent set of railway tracks. A trolley, or train, that they cannot see or hear is coming down the tracks behind the five people. A bystander is standing beside a switch that, if pulled, will divert the train onto the adjacent tracks, killing the single person walking on them. The question people must answer is, what should this bystander do? What is the most moral decision—to throw the switch, or not to throw the switch? If you are like the vast majority of people who have responded to this dilemma, you will say "throw the switch," reasoning that the most permissible course of action in this no-win situation is to sacrifice one life to save five lives. Note that this decision is utilitarian in nature; it fosters the greatest good (welfare) for the greatest number.

Now consider another dilemma, called the Footbridge Problem. This dilemma is similar to the Trolley Problem, except there is no side track. Instead, there is a footbridge that spans the train tracks, which contains a very heavy person. When people are asked whether it is permissible to push the heavy person onto the tracks to save five people, the vast majority say no. In this context, they do not believe it is right to sacrifice one life in order to save five. The question is, what is the source of the difference between people's moral judgments about the Trolley Problem and about the Footbridge Problem? One possibility is that pushing someone to his death is much more direct and personal than throwing a switch to divert a train.

Other research employing these kinds of dilemmas has found that people judge harmful acts initiated as a means to an end more harshly than they judge harmful acts that occur as a foreseen byproduct of another act. For example, people think it is more permissible to pull a switch to divert a train onto a sidetrack that (1) contains a heavy person, and (2) loops back to the main track than it is to push the heavy person onto the main track. People's judgments become more permissive when the loop contains a large weight in addition to the heavy person (Hauser, 2006).

Philosophers of ethics have invested a great deal of effort arguing that intuitions such as these are rational and morally justifiable—derived from moral reasoning—but I think that they are barking up the wrong tree. With Haidt and other psychologists, I believe that these intuitions are derived from irrational sources and that these aspects of the moral sense are fundamentally irrational. Most people are unable to offer rational explanations for why aspects of moral issues such as whether bad consequences are produced directly or indirectly, though omission or commission, and in personal or impersonal ways affect their moral judgments; indeed, they are usually unaware that these variables are affecting their judgments. And even when participants (and philosophers) are able to offer justifications for the effect of these variables on their moral judgments, they could be post hoc rationalizations of judgments that originally were formed in irrational ways. People may form moral judgments in intuitive ways, then support them with reasons after the fact. I explore the implications of this idea for the nature of morality in Chapter 19.

So where does the revulsion associated with ideas such as pushing people onto railway tracks come from? With one of the most eminent researchers in this area, Joshua Greene (2008), I believe that the mechanisms that produce such reactions evolved in ancestral environments because they induced early humans to behave in adaptive ways: "Our most basic moral dispositions are evolutionary adaptations that arose in response to the demands and opportunities created by social life" (p. 60). I discuss this issue further in the next chapter.

CONCLUSIONS

All normal people in all cultures possess a sense of morality that induces them to feel obliged to behave in certain ways and not in other ways. All people pass judgment on themselves and others when they behave in ways that violate the moral standards of their communities. As suggested in the 18th century by the philosopher David Hume, people's sense of morality is rooted deeply in their emotional experiences, or passions. The mechanisms that give rise to moral emotions were selected in ancestral environments because they induced early humans to behave in ways that increased their inclusive fitness. A sense of moral duty probably originated in the emotions and motivational states that disposed early humans to behave in prosocial ways. This sense helped them reap the long-term benefits of group living. A sense of pride and guilt probably originated in reactions to the social approval and disapproval of others. These senses reinforced prosocial dispositions, helped people resist temptation, and induced them to repair damaged social relations. A sense of justice probably evolved to uphold systems of cooperative exchange.

Other primates experience emotions that serve these functions. However, as I explain in the next chapter, the emotions experienced by early humans became refined and expanded as their brains evolved, and the emotions experienced by human infants become refined and expanded as they develop.

17

THE EXPANSION AND REFINEMENT OF THE
MORAL SENSES IN THE HUMAN SPECIES

Other animals may experience something akin to the primitive moral sentiments discussed in the previous chapter, but humans are the only species capable of forming beliefs about right and wrong, reflecting on moral matters, engaging in moral reasoning, and expressing moral judgments in words. Humans are unique in the animal kingdom in their ability to derive moral attributions, to pass judgment on themselves and others, to evaluate alternatives in terms of the extent to which they meet moral standards, and to categorize behaviors, states, traits, and people as moral and immoral. We are the only animals capable of consciously thinking that it is right to behave in some ways and that it is wrong to behave in other ways, and of giving reasons to justify our beliefs.

To account for the proximate sources of moral beliefs and moral judgments, we need to delve into people's heads, identify the mental mechanisms that produce them, and map their design. What should we expect to find when we search in this manner—one general-purpose mechanism, such as a structure of moral reasoning, or many different moral-belief-forming and moral-judgment-making mechanisms? Should we expect to find mechanisms that induce people to deliberate about moral issues in rational and impartial ways, or mechanisms that induce people to make moral decisions in intuitive and self-serving ways? Answers to these questions have important implications for models of human nature. Are humans inherently rational or irrational, fair or unfair, by nature?

Evolutionary theory leads us to expect people to possess a suite of mental mechanisms that induce them to make moral judgments in a variety of ways, and this expectation is supported by a great deal of evidence. In the previous chapter, I focused on mental mechanisms that produce moral feelings. In this chapter, I consider those that produce "colder" and more rational moral decisions. Refining Darwin's account of the evolution of moral reasoning, I suggest that the mental mechanisms that endow people with the capacity to derive moral judgments in rational ways evolved in the context of strategic social interactions. I suggest that several structures of moral reasoning evolved in the human species, which are most gainfully viewed as tools that people use to achieve social goals. To understand the nature of these structures, we must understand the goals that people use them to achieve.

Although moral reasoning is susceptible to a variety of self-serving biases, these biases may be minimized during strategic social interactions when people invoke impartial standards to resolve their conflicts of interest and reach optimal decisions. In addition, when people preach morality to others, they may persuade themselves that their judgments are valid, and others may insist that they abide by them themselves.

There is a great deal of adaptive value in the ability to anticipate the moves of others in social games—to figure out what they are thinking, what they intend to do, whether they will cooperate, pay you back, detect your deception, and so on. One of the ways in which humans accomplish this is through a process that psychologists call mind-reading or perspective-taking. When people take the perspectives of others, they construct portable cognitive representations of them, store them in their minds, view events from their perspectives, and imagine how they will respond to their behavior. I theorize that perspective-taking processes that were selected because they enabled early humans to advance their interests in strategic social interactions by anticipating how others would respond to their behaviors mediated the expansion and refinement of the human conscience.

If people are able to derive moral beliefs and moral judgments from several mental mechanisms, the central challenge facing those who seek to explain how people make moral decisions is to identify the factors that activate one mechanism and not others, and if more than one mechanism is activated, to explain how they interact. Attending to the adaptive functions that moral beliefs, moral judgments, and moral reasoning served in the social environments in which they evolved provides a basis for meeting this challenge.

Dual-processing theorists have demonstrated that people derive beliefs in two quite different ways—first, by processing information quickly, automatically, effortlessly, unconsciously, holistically, contextually, and "mindlessly;" and second, by processing information in slower, more effortful, intentional, controlled, considered, reflective, conscious, analytic, and context-independent ways (Chaiken, 1987; Haidt, 2001; Petty & Cacioppo, 1986). The distinction between automatic and controlled ways of forming beliefs—probably more a matter of degree than of kind—offers a helpful way of organizing the mental mechanisms that have been found to produce moral ideas. Moral judgment-making mechanisms that operate automatically are mediated mainly by structures in the old brain that are shared with other animals. I offered an account of their origin in the previous chapter. Mechanisms that operate in a more controlled manner, which I will now discuss, tend to be mediated by more recently evolved structures in the brain, and they are especially prominent in the human species.

MORAL REASONING

Like Darwin (1874), most philosophers and psychologists believe that moral reasoning is the most significant source of moral judgments. Indeed, ethicists have argued that the only kind of judgments that qualify as moral are those that stem from moral reasoning (see Kohlberg, 1984). In contrast to the relatively direct S-R link between activating stimuli and moral judgments in primitive, intuitive moral decision-making mechanisms, rational moral decision making involves significantly more intervening "O" cortical mediation, interpretation, and cognitive construction. For this reason, moral judgments that are derived from moral reasoning seem to say more about the people who make them than moral judgments derived in more automatic ways do.

As I acknowledged earlier in this book, there is no question that humans are unique in their capacity to reflect on moral issues, to deliberate about them, to process relevant information in rational ways, and to derive moral decisions from structures of moral reasoning. People possess the capacity to behave like scientists, processing evidence systematically, evaluating it in terms of impartial standards, and deducing logical conclusions. People also possess the capacity to behave like judges, considering the arguments of interested parties, evaluating their claims in terms of principles of justice, and deriving fair decisions (Haidt, 2001). In addition, as Darwin (1874) said, people are able to anticipate "the more remote consequences of [their] actions" (p. 129) and use such considerations to derive utilitarian moral judgments. However, as everybody knows, people often fail to behave in such rational ways, and the most sophisticated forms of moral reasoning available to people are not the only ones they possess.

The Domain Specificity of Moral Reasoning

An issue that has attracted a great deal of attention from social scientists pertains to the domain-specificity of moral reasoning. Some theorists have suggested that moral reasoning is a byproduct of general purpose reasoning abilities: People derive moral judgments from the same kinds of reasoning processes that they use to draw logical inferences about relations in the physical and social world (Williams, 1989). Other theorists have argued that people possess one dominant structure of moral reasoning that they use to make moral decisions (Colby & Kohlberg, 1987), and still other theorists have suggested that people possess several different structures of moral reasoning that they invoke to solve different kinds of moral problems (Damon, 1977; Fiske,1992).

Although Darwin seemed to assume that people use general reasoning abilities to derive moral judgments, there is good reason to expect this to be, at best, only part of the story. When considered from an evolutionary perspective, we would expect general-purpose moral decision-making mechanisms to evolve if the kinds of moral problems that early humans experienced were structured in ways that were best solved by general reasoning abilities. However, early humans must have faced a variety of qualitatively different kinds of moral problems, which would have differed in significant ways from the nonmoral problems they faced. For these reasons, we would expect early humans to have acquired a variety of moral decision-making mechanisms specialized for solving different kinds of moral problems. Evolutionary theory leads us to expect modern humans to be disposed to make moral decisions in the ways that best promoted the inclusive fitness of early humans in the social environments in which early humans evolved. If moral problems are like locks that early humans opened in order to survive and to reproduce, then moral decision-making mechanisms are like the keys that natural selection designed to open the locks.

Although some forms of moral reasoning may well "borrow" operations such as deductive forms of logical inference that helped early humans solve nonsocial problems, it is as plausible to assume that nonsocial reasoning borrowed aspects of social reasoning as it is to assume the reverse. Consider, for example, the tendency for people to impute human qualities to inanimate objects. When my wife, a highly intelligent woman, cuts herself in the kitchen, she can be heard to mutter, "Stupid knife." In addition, some forms of moral reasoning are dependent on processes such as perspective-taking and the attribution of intentions that are specially designed to solve social problems.

Domain-Specific Cognitive Schemata

The anthropologist, Fiske (1992) has amassed evidence that people from all cultures are innately disposed to develop four types of cognitive "schemata" that organize information about four types of social relations: (1) affectionate relations among people who share social bonds; (2) hierarchical relations among people who differ in social rank; (3) egalitarian exchanges among equals; and (4) economic relations aimed at maximizing cost/benefit ratios across different commodities. Primate researchers have found that chimpanzees develop the first three schemata. The fourth appears to be unique to the human species (Cheney & Seyfarth, 1990; Haslam, 1997). Cognitive schemata are activated by certain kinds of information, and they structure the ways in which people process the information, supplying interpretive frameworks, or frames of reference. In order, the schemata identified by Fiske give rise to moral beliefs and judgments that uphold the altruistic, deferential, and cooperative forms of conduct discussed in earlier chapters of this book.

THE SOCIAL EVOLUTION OF MORAL JUDGMENT AND MORAL REASONING

Implicit in the idea that people use, or "exapt," structures of reasoning that evolved to solve nonmoral problems to solve moral problems is the assumption that the mental mechanisms that mediate moral reasoning evolved in the same way as the mental mechanisms that mediate nonmoral reasoning, but this assumption could not be valid. People undoubtedly invoke general-purpose reasoning mechanisms to solve some kinds of moral problems; however, because most of the moral problems that people experience in their everyday lives are social in nature, it makes sense to expect the structures of moral reasoning that people invoke to solve them to have evolved in different ways from the structures of reasoning they invoke to solve nonsocial problems. In particular, it makes sense to expect structures of moral reasoning to have evolved through social selection, especially as it occurred during strategic social interactions.

Moral Judgments as Tactics in Strategic Interactions

Before early humans acquired language, they probably used tactics similar to those used by chimpanzees and other apes to induce others to behave in ways that fostered their interests—tactics such as begging, administering physical and material rewards and punishments, issuing threats, and signalling their approval and disapproval through facial expressions, body language, and auditory signals that conveyed respect, gratitude, anger, disgust, and so on (de Waal, 1991). However, as discussed earlier, the dynamics of strategic social interaction would have changed dramatically when early humans acquired the capacity to transmit ideas symbolically through language. In particular, as George Williams (1989) has pointed out, "the unparalleled human capability for symbolic communication has an incidental consequence of special importance for ethics. In biological usage, communication is nearly synonymous with attempted manipulation. It is a low-cost way of getting someone else to behave in a way favorable to oneself" (p. 211).

Ironically, moral judgments probably originated in the human species as tools of social influence and tactics in strategic interactions. Endowed with symbolic speech, early humans could express their approval of prosocial behaviors and people and express their disapproval of antisocial behaviors and people with words such as "good" and "bad;" and they could buttress their moral judgments with reasons, explanations, and justifications designed to increase their persuasive power. The acquisition of language would have extended early humans' ability to hold others accountable for their moral and immoral behaviors by enabling them to share their impressions with other members of their groups, and to gossip (Alexander, 1987; Dunbar, 1966). Because moral judgments pertain to forms of social conduct that affect people's welfare, and because they are associated with positive and negative social sanctions, they tend to evoke strong affective reactions from those to whom they are directed (Kagan & Lamb, 1987).

It is commonly assumed that people form moral beliefs, then express them in moral judgments—that moral judgments are explications of people's moral beliefs. However, this in not the only possible relation between moral beliefs and moral judgments. People could make moral judgments that they do not believe—for example, in order to exert social influence or to create a good impression—and making such judgments could induce people to form moral beliefs that correspond to the judgments that they made. People could persuade themselves in the process of persuading others.

The Adaptive Value of Moral Reasoning

Symbolic language also could have mediated the expansion and refinement of morality by enabling people to resolve their conflicts of interest through negotiation. Moral reasoning is a powerful tool in the resolution of social conflicts, enabling people to buttress their moral judgments with arguments designed to increase their persuasive power (Haidt, 2001). When people negotiate with one another and engage in moral argumentation, they implicitly attempt to activate each others' moral intuitions and prosocial emotions by appealing to one another's rational faculties (Saltzstein & Kasachkoff, 2004).

If structures of moral reasoning evolved in the social area, and if their original function were to influence others, then we would expect them to be activated in social contexts and designed in ways that enable people to achieve social goals. Viewed in this way, it is not surprising that people invoke different forms of moral reasoning to solve different kinds of moral problems, or that the forms that they invoke in response to the kinds of hypothetical moral dilemmas that cognitive-developmental psychologists employ in their research and that philosophers of ethics analyze are different from the forms of moral reasoning that they invoke in their everyday lives.

Self-serving Biases in Moral Reasoning

Although people possess the capacity to think logically about moral issues and to derive moral judgments from general-purpose reasoning abilities, evolutionary theory leads us to question whether people are disposed to derive moral judgments in rational ways, as an end in itself. Inasmuch as reason is a tool that evolved to help early humans advance their adaptive interests, and inasmuch as these interests were self-serving (which, as explained in Chapter 3, they need not necessarily be at an individual level), then moral reasoning should be biased in self-serving ways. Indeed, one of the central assumptions of game-theory models of the evolution of social strategies is that it is rational to behave in ways that advance one's interests. Although moral reasoning is widely viewed as a process for deriving fair and valid moral decisions, we would, from the perspective of evolutionary theory, expect people to engage in impartial moral reasoning only when it contains (or more exactly, contained) the greatest potential to solve the adaptive problems they face; and we would expect people to be inclined to delude themselves when illusions and biased moral reasoning better serve their needs (Alexander, 1987; Krebs, Denton & Higgins, 1988; Trivers, 2000). To account for the role that general purpose reasoning plays in moral decision making, we must explain why people would use it to achieve moral, rather than immoral, ends, which boils down to explaining what motivates people to want to uphold morality.

Building on a theme introduced in earlier chapters, if the original function of moral reasoning were to help people maximize their benefits from strategic interactions, we also would expect the mental mechanisms that produce it to be susceptible to self-serving biases. In particular, we would expect people to be disposed to invoke the kinds of moral reasoning that most effectively enabled them to achieve their goals. A great deal of research on social cognition supports this expectation. Haidt (2001) has supplied a good summary of the evidence:

> People show a strong tendency to search for anecdotes and other "evidence" exclusively on their preferred side of an issue, a pattern that has been called the 'my-side-bias.' Research on social cognition . . . indicates that people often behave like "intuitive lawyers" rather than like "intuitive scientists" . . . directional goals (motivations to reach a preordained conclusion) work primarily by causing a biased search in memory for supporting evidence only. . . . self-serving motives bias each stage of the hypothesis-testing sequence, including the selection of initial hypotheses, the generation of inferences, the search for evidence, the evaluation of evidence, and the amount of evidence needed before one is willing to make an inference. (p. 821)

With respect to moral judgments, we would expect people to be more inclined to exhort others to sacrifice their interests for their sake than the reverse, to hold others to higher moral standards than the standards that they apply to themselves, to overestimate how much they deserve (their rights) and to underestimate how much they owe (their duties), while underestimating how much others deserve, and overestimating how much others owe. In addition, we would expect them to be inclined to attempt to induce others to overvalue their contributions in social exchanges, while undervaluing the contributions of others (Chadwick-Jones, 1976; Greenberg & Cohen, 1982). In support of these expectations, "when hypotheses involve one's moral commitments. . . . the empirical findings generally show bias and motivated reasoning" (Haidt, 2001, p. 822). Studies have found that moral reasoning is susceptible to framing, directional, motivational, nepotistic, and group-serving biases (Chaiken, Giner-Sorolla, & Chen, 1996; Kunda, 2000; Lerner & Miller, 1978; Pyszczynski & Greenberg, 1987). People also may use moral judgments and moral reasoning to manage their impressions in order to maximize their gains from social exchanges, inducing others to believe that they are more cooperative and altruistic than they really are (Alexander, 1987; Goffman, 1959).

On the antisocial side of the coin, people may use moral judgments to justify their immoral behavior and to deflect responsibility onto others (Bandura, 1991; Haidt, 2001). For example, they may use moral judgments to diminish their transgressions, to excuse their misdeeds, and to avoid responsibility, as well as to exaggerate the blameworthiness of adversaries' immoral behavior (Snyder & Higgins, 1988). Krebs & Laird, (1998) found that people tend to minimize the magnitude of the misdeeds they commit in their everyday lives by attributing them to situational pressures ("he provoked me"), whereas they magnify the wrongness of the misdeeds of others by attributing them to internal traits ("he is untrustworthy").

Antidotes to Self-serving Biases

Fortunately for the sake of morality, however, there are at least two constraints on self-serving biases in moral reasoning. First, manipulating others into advancing one's personal interests could diminish one's genetic interests, or inclusive fitness, for reasons discussed in Chapter 3 (because personal interests may not equate to genetic interests). Second, we would not expect unconstrained self-serving biases in moral reasoning and moral judgment to advance people's goals effectively in the social arena. Biased forms of moral reasoning face the same evolutionary obstacles in real life as selfish tactics do in Prisoner's Dilemma games: It is not in people's interest to let others exploit them, and if both parties invoke selfish strategies, they may end up in mutually self-defeating exchanges. Although we would expect people to be evolved to exhort others to perform more altruistic and self-sacrificial acts than they are inclined to perform (which may be why so many people preach the praises of altruism), we would not expect extremely biased exhortations such as, "you should always sacrifice your interests for me" to have much persuasive impact because we would expect natural selection to hone receiving mechanisms in ways that reduced receptiveness to costly types of moral judgment and moral reasoning.

Inasmuch as early humans were able to gain more by coordinating their efforts with the efforts of others and engaging in mutually beneficial social exchanges than they were by attempting to exploit others, we would expect mechanisms that enable and dispose people to find common ground and to mesh with others to have evolved. In support of this expectation, my colleagues and I found that people tend to adapt their moral judgments to the moral orientations they impute to others. For example we found that students made significantly more philosophical moral judgments when they directed them to a Professor of Philosophy than they did when they directed them to a Professor of Business Administration (Carpendale & Krebs, 1992). We also found that when couples were engaged in moral conflicts, each tailored his or her judgments to the kinds of moral judgments made by the other (Krebs et al., 2002). More generally, studies have found that people tend to modify their attitudes to produce a good fit with those of people with whom they are interacting in cooperative ways. Indeed, there is evidence that when two people engage in a social interaction, they coordinate their mannerisms and body language—a phenomenon that has been dubbed the "chameleon effect"(Chartrand & Bargh, 1999).

THE EXPANSION AND REFINEMENT OF MORAL REASONING

An important general impetus for the expansion and refinement of moral reasoning in the human species must have been the adaptive value of resolving inconsistencies. There are at least two private and two public sources of inconsistency in moral judgments. To begin with, people may reflect on their moral beliefs in private and become aware of logical inconsistencies among them. For example, they may sometimes believe it is right to tell the truth, to obey the law, and to be faithful to their spouses but sometimes not. (I am reminded of Saint Augustine's infamous pronouncement to the effect, "Oh Lord, help me resist my lustful urges, but not just yet.") In addition, people may experience inconsistencies between what they say (their moral judgments) and what they do (their moral behaviors). More publicly, people may find themselves making different kinds of moral judgments to different people, as discussed above, and people may be exposed to inconsistent moral judgments from others. For example, some people say that abortion and capital punishment are wrong; other people say that these practices are right. Some people say that we should help those who are less fortunate than ourselves; other people say that we should make needy people fend for themselves.

Studies have found that discrepancies among internal moral standards and between moral standards and behaviors may evoke negative affective reactions such as guilt, which motivate people to take measures to resolve the inconsistencies (Baumeister, Stillwell, & Heatherton, 1994; Higgins, 1987). However, although some philosophically oriented people may reflect on their moral judgments and standards in private, become aware of inconsistencies, and take measures to resolve them, I question how prevalent this process is. Most people become aware of inconsistencies in their moral reasoning in social settings, when other people point them out to them, often in the context of moral argumentation, and they are motivated to resolve them in order to prove themselves right, to protect their social image, or to preserve positive social relations.

Hoist on One's Own Petard: Moral Argumentation and the Generation of Impartial Moral Standards

When people use reason and logical consistency as weapons against others in moral arguments, they may end up hoisting themselves on their own petards. As suggested earlier, the process of justifying moral judgments may induce people to believe that they are valid (Festinger, 1964), and believing the prescriptive judgments one makes may reap adaptive benefits by increasing their persuasive power (Trivers, 2000). In addition, recipients of logical arguments may turn them back on those who advance them: What is good for the goose is good for the gander. Finally, people may be inclined to believe the moral judgments and moral standards that they evoke during moral negotiations because the judgments and standards are supported by good arguments, because the negotiators participated in generating them, and because they work—they help them achieve desirable goals and advance their interests in optimal ways. Several theorists have suggested that moral dialogues are equipped to generate "emergent" ideas and preferences (Elster, 2000; Habermas, 1993).

Expanding the Circle

As discussed in Chapter 4, Darwin (1874) suggested that during the course of evolution, our "sympathies became more tender and widely diffused, so as to extend to men of all races . . . and [even] to the lower animals" (p. 121). One way to account for this expansion of the range of those whom people feel obliged to treat morally is to argue that people's social circles are significantly larger than they were in earlier eras and that people are exposed to many more people, either directly or indirectly (for example, through the media). However, as writers such as Paul Bloom have pointed out, this account does not explain why so many modern humans think that practices that were once considered morally permissible, such as slavery, burning heretics at the stake, discriminating against people on the basis of their race, gender, or sexual orientation, are wrong, or why so many modern humans feel morally obliged to help unfortunate people they know they will never meet—for example by donating money to charity, giving blood, and helping people from other countries who have been victimized by natural disasters. Bloom (2004) argues that deliberative persuasion has played an important role in the expansion of people's moral circles, suggesting that people influence one another through the stories they tell and the opinions they advance. The key aspect of this process lies in the "deliberative" aspect of persuasion.

Like Darwin, the philosopher Peter Singer (1981) attributed the expansion of the circle of those equipped to activate moral judgments to humans' capacity to reason, especially as invoked in moral argumentation: "Ethical reasoning, once begun, pushes against our initially limited ethical horizons, leading us always toward a more universal point of view. . . . If I claim that what I do is right, while what you do is wrong, I must give some reason other than the fact that my action benefits me (or my kin, or my village) while your action benefits you (or your kin or your village)" (pp. 118–119). In a similar vein, Bloom (2004) has argued that "once a creature is smart enough, impartiality—and an appreciation of moral codes such as the Golden Rule—will emerge as a consequence of this smartness" (p. 139). However, reason is not the only process equipped to expand the circle of those whom people treat in prosocial ways. As discussed in earlier chapters, kin-selected altruistic dispositions may be activated by those who look like kin; people may identify with groups to which they have been assigned on an arbitrary basis; and small groups may unite to pursue a common cause.

The account of the expansion of contemporary humans' moral circle that is most consistent with the model I have been advancing attributes it to the expansion of systems of cooperation in the modern world, which in part is mediated by the expansion of reason, social identity, and perspective-taking. When children grow up in safe and secure environments in which their needs are met, and when they receive good educations, they come to consider themselves part of a vast system of cooperation that includes, in principle, everyone in the human race. When such people have plenty, when it does not cost them a lot to give, and when they are prodded, they are disposed to help those in need. Implicitly, they expect be helped in return by those who have plenty when they suffer some misfortune. When people are comfortable and secure, and when all their needs are met, it is easy to empathize with the plight of the oppressed and to understand that it is right to help them.

However, identification with humanity and charitable dispositions are highly conditional. Many children are raised in hostile environments in which they are oppressed by, or in conflict with, out-groups. Such children learn from an early age that it is futile to cooperate with members of these out-groups, and however intelligent these children may become as adults, they come to view these outsiders as enemies, hate them, and feel disposed to discriminate against them and harm them. In a similar vein, highly intelligent people who normally are disposed to fight oppression and to help members of disadvantaged groups will turn against those they classify as outsiders and treat them in the most inhuman ways when they feel threatened by them.

THE EXPANSION AND REFINEMENT OF CONSCIENCE

In addition to mediating the expansion and refinement of moral reasoning abilities, the process of strategic social interaction also may have mediated the expansion and refinement of conscience. Alexander (1990) has suggested that the adaptive value of the ability to "see ourselves as others see us so that we may cause competitive others to see us as we wish them to" (p. 7) played a pivotal role in the rapid expansion of the human brain. Perspective-taking abilities enable people to consider imaginatively how others will react to their transgressions, and the *imagined* approval and disapproval of others, which people may experience as the "voice of conscience," may activate emotions such as pride, fear, shame, and guilt (Aronfreed, 1968; Freud, 1925; Higgins, 1987).

When viewed from an evolutionary perspective, an important aspect of the human conscience is internalized images of others reacting to one's behavior. In imagining the negative reactions of others, people feel anticipatory fear, sadness, or embarrassment, which they experience as guilt or shame. As people internalize an increasingly broad array of imaginary audiences, and as they integrate them in their minds, the judgments of others become increasingly abstract, general, and impartial. In the end, people end up passing judgment on themselves (Selman, 1980). As expressed by J. Q. Wilson (1993), "at first we judge others; we then begin to judge ourselves as we think others judge us; finally we judge ourselves as an impartial, disinterested third party might" (p. 33).

We would expect highly developed perspective-taking processes to give rise to fairer and more altruistic decisions than more primitive perspective-taking processes do. As expressed by Bloom (2004), "Our enhanced social intelligence allows us to reason about how other people will act and react in situations that do not yet exist, so as to plan and assess the consequences of our own actions. It is adaptive to be capable of imagining hypothetical situations and to view these situations from another person's point of view . . . one perverse side effect of this is increased empathy" (pp. 141–142).

THE ACTIVATION OF MORAL
DECISION-MAKING MECHANISMS

In this and the previous chapter, I advanced evidence demonstrating that a suite of mental mechanisms equipped to produce moral judgments and moral beliefs has evolved in the human species. Some mental mechanisms produce moral judgments in relatively hot and automatic ways. Others produce moral judgments in colder and more controlled ways. The brain structures that enable people to derive moral beliefs and judgments from reflective reasoning and sophisticated perspective-taking abilities evolved later than, in addition to, and on top of structures that induce people to derive moral judgments and beliefs in automatic ways. Although the most recently evolved mechanisms may be equipped to modify more primitive mechanisms, they have not replaced them. If these ideas are valid, it becomes important to identify the factors that determine which mechanisms are activated, and when more than one is activated, how they interact. When, for example, do people derive moral decisions from sophisticated forms of moral reasoning, and when do they derive them from other sources?

The Activation of Automatic Moral Decision-Making Processes

Because the mental mechanisms that mediate complex forms of moral decision making are more costly in time and effort to operate than the ones that produce simpler forms are, we would expect people to invoke simple, automatic decision-making processes as their default (Gigerenzer, 2000; Gilovich, Keltner, & Nisbett, 2006). As suggested by Frank (1988), decisions mediated by emotional reactions are often "strategically superior to those based on rational calculation." We would expect people to make moral decisions automatically in contexts in which the costs of deliberation are high (Piliavin et al., 1981) and to make simple judgments when such judgments constitute the most effective forms of persuasion and impression-management (such as, for example, when they are directed toward children). We would expect people to adopt and to preach the moral norms of their cultures without thinking much about them, as long as it enables them to get by in a reasonably effective manner (Simon, 1990). We would expect people to use mental shortcuts in contexts in which heuristics generate acceptable moral decisions (Chaiken, 1987; Gigerenzer, 2000; Sunstein, 2005), and when people engage in moral reasoning, we would expect them to invoke the simplest forms necessary to solve the moral problems they face.

In response to the question, "Why should our adaptive moral behavior be driven by moral emotions as opposed to something else, such as moral reasoning?" Greene (2008) offers the following answer:

> Emotions are very reliable, quick, and efficient responses to recurring situations, whereas reasoning is unreliable, slow, and inefficient in such contexts . . . Nature doesn't leave it to our powers of reasoning to figure out that ingesting fat, sugar,

and protein is conducive to our survival. Rather it makes us hungry and gives us an intuitive sense that things like meat and fruit will satisfy our hunger. . . . and Nature doesn't leave it to us to figure out that saving a drowning child is a good thing to do. Instead, it endows us with a powerful "moral sense" that compels us to engage in this sort of behavior (under the right circumstances). In short, when Nature needs to get a behavioral job done, it does it with intuition and emotion whenever it can. Thus, from an evolutionary point of view, it is no surprise that moral dispositions evolved, and it is no surprise that these dispositions are implemented emotionally. (p. 60)

The Activation of Domain-Specific Structures of Moral Reasoning

Having reviewed a great deal of evidence that humans are naturally disposed to behave in prosocial ways, it remains only to explicate the obvious, namely that the moral belief-forming and moral judgment-making mechanisms that induce people to think and feel that they and others *should* behave in deferential, altruistic, and cooperative ways are activated by opportunities to achieve the adaptive goals that these forms of conduct enable people to achieve. Put another way, the four kinds of cognitive schemata described by Fiske (1992), which are activated by four kinds of social problems, give rise to, or structure, corresponding kinds of moral judgments.

The Activation of Controlled Moral Decision-Making Processes

In general, we would expect people to derive moral decisions from reflective, rational moral decision-making processes when these processes offer the most effective ways of solving problems and achieving adaptive goals. We would expect people to engage in complex, controlled, and reflective forms of moral reasoning when the adaptive costs of deliberation are low and the adaptive benefits of making a rational decision are high. We would expect people to invoke sophisticated forms of moral reasoning to solve complex moral problems that cannot be solved in simpler ways—problems such as those that involve conflicts among moral intuitions and moral norms (Haidt, 2001), conflicts between the rights and duties of people participating in embedded systems of cooperation (Kohlberg, 1984; Rest, 1983), and complex contemporary problems such as those that relate to the ethics of cloning and stem cell research (Pizarro & Bloom, 2003). People should be inclined to invoke these decision-making processes when they possess ample cognitive processing capacity, and when they have sufficient time to think things through. And people should be inclined to invoke impartial forms of moral reasoning when there are no negative consequences to making impartial moral decisions, such as when the dilemmas they are considering are abstract and hypothetical in nature.

We also would expect people to invoke sophisticated forms of moral reasoning in the context of moral argumentation when, like lawyers, they are attempting to persuade people who are receptive to rational argument, and when they are in the role of third person arbitrators, mediators, judges, and so on. In a similar vein, we would expect people to invoke sophisticated forms of moral reasoning to concoct complex (and sometimes convoluted) justifications for their immoral acts, and to show off their intellectual abilities. Finally, and most hopefully, we would expect people to invoke sophisticated forms of moral reasoning when attempting to derive ideal moral principles that best govern moral decision making in ideal social systems designed to maximize everyone's benefits from group living.

BRAIN RESEARCH ON MORAL DECISION MAKING

Research by brain scientists supports the evolutionary model of moral decision making that I have been describing. Neuroscientists have used a technique called functional magnetic resonance imaging, or fMRI, to determine which areas of the brain light up when normal people consider moral dilemmas that are structured in different ways. Remember the Trolley Problem discussed in the last chapter? Researchers have found that when people conclude that it is permissible to pull a switch that diverts a train onto a track containing one person in order to save five people, relatively recently evolved parts of their brains that are implicated in mental processes such as deductive reasoning light up (such as the inferior parietal lobe and the dorsolateral surfaces of the prefrontal cortex). However, when people conclude that it is not right to push a heavy person from a footbridge in order to save five people walking on a train track, older, more emotionally based areas of people's brains light up (for example, the amygdala and the medial prefrontal cortex) (Greene, 2008).

These findings suggest that people may make some moral decisions, such as those about the Trolley Problem, in controlled, rational, ways, and other moral decisions, such as those about the Footbridge Dilemma, in automatic, emotional, intuitive ways. If this is the case, we need to determine why. To derive an explanation, we must identify the crucial differences between the Trolley Problem and the Footbridge Problem. What is it about the former that activates rational processes, and what is it about the latter that activates more emotional processes? Joining others who have attempted to answer this question, I believe that the key difference between the two moral dilemmas lies in the difference between pulling a switch that will indirectly cause the death of a person in a relatively impersonal way and directly pushing a person to his death (Greene, 2008). This difference is similar to the difference between pressing a button that releases a bomb that kills people and bayoneting another person to death. As indicated in brain research, the latter scenario evokes much stronger emotional revulsion than the former scenario does, and this emotional revulsion affects moral decisions. It is difficult for people to believe that it is right to behave in ways that make them sick to their stomachs. It is sobering and frightening to contemplate that we may be naturally disposed to feel that it is worse, morally, to kill one person with our bare hands than to kill hundreds of people by pushing a button or pulling a switch.

MAPPING INTERACTIONS AMONG MORAL
DECISION-MAKING MECHANISMS

Stimuli that emanate from the external world or from people's minds may activate different decision-making mechanisms located in different areas of their brains, simultaneously or sequentially. Jointly activated mechanisms may interact in complementary or antagonistic ways.

Popular conceptions of human nature posit a conflict between evolved dispositions to behave in immoral ways and rational decisions to behave in moral ways—in Freud's terms, between the id and the ego (Campbell, 1978). However, as Darwin (1874) recognized, this is not the only type of internal conflict that people may experience. Prosocial desires may conflict with antisocial desires; altruistic motives may conflict with egoistic motives (Batson, 1991; Sober & Wilson, 1998), and instincts may conflict with habits. In addition, people's natural desire to do the right thing may conflict with their rational calculation of self-interest; people may invoke rational thinking to figure out ways of shirking their heart-felt duties; and one line of rational thought may conflict with another line of rational thought.

Although some theorists have implied that reason is the only process qualified to resolve conflicts between conflicting dispositions (Saltzstein & Kasachkoff, 2004), this is not necessarily the case. Animals that lack sophisticated reasoning abilities are able to resolve conflicts between prosocial and antisocial dispositions. Recent research on the neurological correlates of decision making suggests that the "brain's neural circuitry actually makes choices by internally representing the payoffs of various alternatives as neural firing rates, and choosing a maximal such rate" (Gintis, 2007).

As modeled by Haidt (2001), the process of moral decision making may involve complex, iterative, interactions among automatic and controlled processes. For example, on the one hand, people may impulsively intervene in emergencies, help those for whom they feel sorry, and obey powerful authorities, then rationalize their decisions on a post hoc basis. On the other hand, the ways in which people interpret their primitive affective reactions may affect the kinds of emotions and intuitions they experience (Pizarro & Bloom, 2003; Schachter & Singer, 1962). Factual information, interpretive processes, perspective-taking, and moral reasoning may generate, structure, and change moral intuitions. As discussed in Chapter 15, perspective-taking may activate empathic reactions, engender altruistic motives, and expand the circle of those considered in moral decisions. Rational considerations may overpower intuitions. Encouraging people who are engulfed in various affective states to reflect on the moral issues they face before making a decision, either in private or in interaction with other people, may modify the emotions they experience. Most hopefully, moral reasoning may engender affective reactions and motivational states that dispose people to behave in moral ways. For example, people may decide that "violations of reciprocity or justice, like violations of logic, 'shouldn't be' [and] the inference of unfairness [may] generate a motivation to restore the 'necessary' reciprocity or equality" (Gibbs, 2003, p. 36).

Some theorists have argued that moral reasoning may become automatic if repeated sufficiently often (Bargh, 1996; Pizarro & Bloom, 2003): "Having learned (or decided) how to respond to certain moral situations and having responded subsequently to like situations in the same way over and over again, we now no longer have to deliberate before responding" (Saltzstein & Kasachkoff, 2004, p. 279). Although this idea may be valid for some forms of moral reasoning, I have argued that it is implausible that the structures of moral reasoning that define the highest stages of moral development described by cognitive-developmental theorists could become automatic (Krebs & Denton, 2006; but see also Gibbs, 2006, for opposing arguments).

Some theorists have pointed out that rational people may take measures in advance to control the kinds of affective reactions and intuitions they experience in situations they anticipate encountering (Pizarro & Bloom, 2003). For example, people may resolve to think before they act, or to consider everyone's perspective before making a decision. Viewed from an evolutionary perspective, however, there is not much reason to be optimistic about people's ability to abide by such resolutions in strong situations (Zimbardo, 2005), and sadly, this reflects my own experience. I have never been very good at avoiding feeling jealous, angry, upset, or aroused in strong situations by resolving in advance not to, and I doubt that I am much different from most other people in this respect.

But all is not lost. When people anticipate encountering compelling temptations, they can take preventative measures to avoid them (Burnham & Phelan, 2000). For example, alcoholics can take measures to avoid bars, and sex addicts can take measures to avoid pornography. Even when encounters with temptations are inevitable, people can attend to their least activating aspects, or follow Ulysses's lead when he tied himself to the mast of his ship to avoid the lure of the Sirens, and bind themselves in advance (Elster, 2000). The mental mechanisms necessary for such long-term planning are located in the newest parts of the brain, the frontal lobes.

CONCLUSIONS

Humans' capacity to take the perspective of others imaginatively and to engage in moral reasoning endows them with the ability to derive moral judgments in rational ways. Perspective-taking, moral reasoning, and the disposition to express moral judgments in words probably evolved in ancestral environments as tools in strategic social interactions. They enabled early humans to resolve their conflicts of interest in adaptive ways. Although moral reasoning is susceptible to self-serving biases, these biases are constrained by logical consistency and the give and take of moral argumentation. When people advance rational arguments in support of the positions they are promoting, they tend to become bound by them themselves.

It is plausible to postulate that the human conscience was refined in the context of strategic social interactions. Early humans who inherited mental mechanisms that enabled them to "read the minds" of others and to understand what they were thinking, feeling, and intending to do would have fared better than those who did not. Perspective-taking abilities would have enabled early humans to imagine how others would react to their transgressions, which eventually would have given rise to the voice of conscience. Developmental psychologists have shown that this voice becomes increasingly abstract and general with development, eventually endowing people with the ability to pass judgment on themselves.

If people inherit a suite of mental mechanisms that enable them to make moral judgments in different ways, we need to figure out what causes each mechanism to be activated; and if two or more mechanisms are activated, we need to figure out how they interact. Evolutionary theory leads us to attend to the adaptive costs and benefits of invoking different moral-decision-making mechanisms, and to predict that people will usually derive moral decisions in automatic ways, without giving them much thought. In some conditions, automatic and controlled processes give rise to similar moral judgments. In other conditions, they produce internal moral conflicts. As demonstrated by research mapping brain regions that are activated by moral problems, moral judgments may be influenced by a complex array of mental mechanisms interacting in wide variety of ways.

18

THE EVOLUTION OF MORAL NORMS

Some moral norms are universal. Others are unique to particular cultures. Although many people assume that universal moral norms are products of innate processes and that culturally relative moral norms are acquired though social learning, both types of norms are products of interactions between evolved information-processing mechanisms and the types of information that they process.

Although some theorists have suggested that social learning mechanisms are designed in ways that render people susceptible to all forms of social influence, the evidence suggests that these mechanisms are designed in discriminating ways. People are selective about the kinds of moral judgments they accept and repeat, and this selectivity plays an important role in the evolution of moral norms.

Darwin suggested that universal moral norms uphold evolved social instincts that increase people's welfare and that they are supported by social sanctions and reason. In contrast, he argued that culturally relative moral norms are acquired mainly through habit, or social learning. Contemporary evolutionary theorists have suggested that universal norms evolve through interactions between species-specific evolved mechanisms and commonalities in the environments of all cultures. Culturally relative norms may stem from differences in the environments of different cultures, from misguided ideas, from alternative but equally effective ways of solving the same adaptive problems, from biases in social learning (such as imitating high-status members of one's group), and from random aspects of the evolutionary process.

Although Darwin attributed irrational moral norms to the poor powers of reasoning of aboriginal people, highly intelligent people from all cultures may espouse irrational moral norms; and seemingly irrational moral norms may serve subtle adaptive functions.

Even though it might seem that people from the same culture endorse the same moral norms, each individual may interpret the norms of his or her culture in different ways. In addition, different people may invoke different norms in the same social contexts. The key to understanding this variation lies in understanding the adaptive functions of preaching and upholding particular moral norms in particular conditions.

A great deal of evidence suggests that people are more sensitive to violations of moral norms than they are to violations of other norms, and that they are especially strongly disposed to punish those who violate moral norms. Developmental psychologists have found that children acquire these dispositions at an early age.

Moral norms have been defined in two main ways (Krebs & Janicki, 2004). First, they have been defined behaviorally as prosocial forms of conduct practiced by most members of a group (which probably constitute evolutionarily stable social strategies). Norms upholding reciprocity, deference to authority, honesty, and helping those in need are prominent examples (Berkowitz, 1972; Gouldner, 1960). I discussed the evolution of such behavioral norms in earlier chapters. Second, moral norms have been defined as *shared beliefs* about which forms of conduct are right and which forms of conduct are wrong—beliefs adopted by most members of a culture pertaining to how people should and should not behave; what they are permitted to do and what they are prohibited from doing; the "thou shalts" and the "thou shalt nots" of societies. It is these norms that I seek to explain in this chapter—those that reflect the sense of morality shared by members of groups, and that manifest themselves in the moral judgments that they preach to one another.

As discussed in Chapter 2, anthropologists and other social scientists have found that all cultures contain moral norms prescribing that people should help others, cooperate, fulfill their responsibilities, behave fairly, keep promises, respect authority, and do their share to uphold their groups. In addition, all cultures contain moral norms prohibiting rape, theft, lying, cheating, free-riding, harming others unnecessarily, violating others' rights, treating others unfairly, and in general, behaving in ways that diminish the welfare of their groups. However, these moral norms may be interpreted, instantiated, and organized in different ways in different cultures. For example, although all people may believe that it is wrong to cheat and to harm others unnecessarily, people from different cultures may possess different conceptions of what constitutes cheating and harm, and people from different cultures may have different ideas about when it is permissible to violate these norms. In addition, there may be considerable variation in people's moral beliefs within particular cultures, and the moral norms of cultures may change over time.

LEARNING MORAL NORMS FROM OTHERS

I have asked students in my classes how they think people acquire moral beliefs. Here are some typical answers. "People acquire their moral beliefs from the people around them when they are growing up." "Moral beliefs are taught to us at a young age by society indirectly and by our parents directly. They are passed on to us via overt direction (e.g., be kind to others, or do not bully other children) and less overt means; for example we may learn by imitating adults." "People learn social customs and conform to group norms, values, and objectives. People are influenced by role models, books, or religions." As mentioned in Chapter 1, early in my career, I also thought that people acquire their morals through social learning.

For those who view evolutionary theory as antagonistic toward learning theory, it will come as a surprise that the renown evolutionary biologist, Richard Dawkins (1989) has endorsed the idea that moral norms evolve culturally through social learning. Dawkins suggests that genes have built social learning machines (i.e., brain mechanisms) that have freed themselves from the selective forces that designed them, much like computers, once programmed, can acquire the ability to think for themselves. Dawkins labeled the phenomena that these social learning mechanisms copy "memes." In contrast to the units of biological evolution—genes—memes constitute the unit of cultural evolution. Dawkins suggested that memes compete against each other for space in people's minds. Some are selected, transmitted to other minds, increase in frequency and evolve; others are rejected and go extinct. In contrast to biological evolution (the selection of genes), which progresses very slowly, cultural evolution (the selection of memes) may occur with great rapidity, as manifest in the spread of slang expressions and changes in fashion. Because Dawkins believes that cultural evolution has become uncoupled from biological evolution, he believes that it is a waste of time to search for the fitness-increasing sources or effects of cultural memes.

Although social learning plays an important role in the transmission of moral norms, it cannot, as I have pointed out, account for the origin of these norms. When people engage in social learning, they copy the beliefs of others. Although the people whom they copy may have acquired their beliefs by copying others, and so on, someone had to create the beliefs that were copied in the first instance. In addition, as discussed, people do not copy others indiscriminately, and people often alter the ideas they copy from others. For a moral judgment to become a "meme," or a moral norm, those to whom it is preached must attend to it, accept it, copy it, and reiterate it. When recipients accept and reject moral judgments, they serve as agents of selection, determining which judgments succeed, get repeated, develop into moral norms, and contribute to their culture. Dawkins recognizes that people are selective in the memes they copy, but he does not account for people's preferences except to say that they are rooted in their psychology. Although Dawkins's contention that people may copy memes that do not increase their fitness may be valid with respect to fads and fashions such as hula hoops, baseball caps worn backwards and sideways, and culturally specific moral norms, I do not think it is valid with respect to universal moral norms, which I think were selected because of their adaptive value.

NATURE VERSUS NURTURE? GENES VERSUS CULTURE?

Many people assume that universal moral norms stem from innate, species-specific evolved dispositions, whereas culturally relative norms are products of social learning. Even though Darwin seemed to endorse this distinction, I think that it is misguided. I believe that culturally universal and culturally relative moral norms are shaped by innate, species-specific dispositions and by social learning. Social learning has played as significant a role in the evolution of universal moral norms as it has in the evolution of culturally relative moral norms.

The idea that universal norms stem from innate processes and that culturally relative norms are learned is implicitly rooted in a spurious nature versus nurture, either–or dichotomy. Nature and nurture are not opposing forces; they are complementary. As expressed by the father of social learning theory, Albert Bandura (1989), "Both experiential and physiological factors interact, often in intricate ways, to determine behavior. . . . Action patterns regarded as instinctual, because they draw heavily on inborn elements, require appropriate experience to be developed. Sensory systems and brain structures are alterable by environmental influences. . . . Dichotomous thinking, which separates activities neatly into innate and acquired categories is seriously inaccurate" (p. 47).

To account fully for the evolution of moral norms, we must account for the ways in which genes and culture interact. Genes guide the creation of mental mechanisms that induce people to create moral norms and other aspects of culture and to transmit them to others. Moral norms originate in, and are shaped by, the evolved minds (biology) of people. Evolved mechanisms produce preferences for particular types of moral ideas and determine which ideas people copy and repeat. Outputs from these evolved mental mechanisms produce moral beliefs and judgments, and these aspects of culture affect the probability that the genes that helped design the mechanisms that produced them will be propagated. For example, moral norms that constrain reproduction, induce people to ostracize cheaters, and uphold capital punishment may become agents of natural selection.

ACCOUNTING FOR THE EVOLUTION OF CULTURALLY UNIVERSAL AND CULTURALLY SPECIFIC MORAL NORMS

A challenge faced by those who seek to account for the evolution of moral norms is to explain why certain kinds of norms evolve in all cultures; whereas other kinds evolve only in particular cultures. Darwin (1874) identified four features of universal moral norms: They "are founded on the social instincts" (p. 118); they increase people's welfare; they are "supported by the approbation of our fellow-men," (p. 118), and they are supported by reason.

I have argued that dispositions to behave in deferential, self-controlling, altruistic, and cooperative ways have evolved in the human species because they increased the welfare of early humans. As a result, people from all cultures display these forms of conduct, feel that they are right, and are receptive to moral judgments that uphold them in appropriate contexts. Inasmuch as prosocial behaviors reap rewards and inasmuch as antisocial behaviors evoke punishments, it is in people's interest to copy the (normative) prosocial behaviors emitted by others. Inasmuch as preaching prosocial norms pays off, it is in people's interest to repeat the (normative) prosocial judgments expressed by others. Finally, as Darwin implied, people are prone to accept universal moral norms such as the norm of reciprocity and the Golden Rule because they make sense to them, because they seem logical, and because, if adopted by everyone, they are equipped to produce the greatest benefits. As discussed, people tend to evaluate (either consciously or unconsciously) the moral prescriptions issued by others in terms of the costs and benefits of complying with them.

Tooby and Cosmides (1992) have labeled universal aspects of culture metaculture. They have suggested that metaculture evolved through an interaction between the evolved mechanisms possessed by our hominid ancestors and the regularities in the social and physical environments of human societies that existed during the Pleistocene era. Universal moral norms evolve because they solve universal moral problems such as those created by conflicts of interest and the temptation to renege on commitments.

This said, it is important to recognize that even though people from all cultures may endorse the same set of moral norms, people from different cultures may conceptualize these norms in different ways. For example, people from different cultures may have different conceptions of what it means to help and to harm others and what it means to treat others justly and unjustly; and people from different cultures may harbor different ideas about what makes these forms of conduct right and wrong. There also may be cultural differences in conceptions of the range of others to whom moral obligations apply. For example, most people from Western cultures see nothing wrong with killing and eating other animals, but Brahmin Indians believe that it is wrong to destroy any living thing, and that people are morally obliged to practice vegetarianism (Vasudev & Hummel, 1987).

Accounting for the Evolution of Culturally Relative Moral Norms

People tend to take universal moral norms for granted because it seems obvious that people should help one another, pay their debts, keep their promises, uphold their groups and so on. What tends to stand out to people are the dramatic differences among the moral norms of different cultures. For example, homosexuality is permitted in some cultures, but it is condemned and severely punished in others. Bestiality is considered an abomination in most cultures, but it permitted in some. Although polygamy is a crime in the United States, it is normative in many cultures, and some groups within the United States believe that they are morally obliged to practice it. People in the Western world believe it is wrong to kill children, but people from other cultures condone the killing of female infants. And, as discussed, people from different cultures may harbor very different beliefs about the kinds of food it is right and wrong to eat.

Earlier I mentioned that Darwin (1874) believed that virtues he classified as "self-regarding" are culturally relative because they arise primarily from social learning (or as Darwin put it, "public opinion, matured by experience and cultivation"[p. 118], and because they uphold forms of conduct that do not affect the welfare of groups directly. Darwin felt that although culturally relative norms are generally guided by ideas about what is best for the community, these ideas "will not rarely err from ignorance and weak powers of reasoning" and that they often give rise to "the strangest customs and superstitions, in complete opposition to the true welfare and happiness of mankind" (p. 118).

Haidt (2001) has advanced an insightful account of the origin of culturally relative moral norms. He suggests that children from all cultures inherit mechanisms that produce a large number of culturally universal, species-specific moral intuitions, just as children from all cultures inherit mechanisms that produce language. However, as with language, the particular moral beliefs that children develop are determined by the moral beliefs to which they are exposed. Haidt suggests that the process of socialization is more appropriately characterized as a process of selecting ideas and intuitions from the huge set children originally possess than of putting ideas into their heads. "A culture that emphasized all of the moral intuitions that the human mind is prepared to experience would risk paralysis as every action triggered multiple conflicting intuitions. Cultures seem instead to specialize in a subset of human moral potential" (p. 827). Haidt emphasizes the integrated nature of cultural ideas, or "cultural complexes." "Cultural knowledge is a complex web of explicit and implicit, sensory and propositional, affective, cognitive, and motoric knowledge" (p. 827). Children learn the norms of their cultures implicitly by being immersed in them, especially when they interact with their peers.

But how do such integrated systems of moral norms originate, and why do they assume different forms in different cultures? We could attribute some cross-cultural variation in moral norms to stupidity, arguing as Darwin did, that ignorant members of some cultures derive misguided ideas about customs that are best for their communities and misjudge the long-term consequences of adopting particular moral norms (see also Richerson & Boyd, 2005); however, at best, this account of cultural differences in moral norms is incomplete. Although the normative systems of some cultures may well be more rational than the normative systems of other cultures are, cultural differences in moral norms may stem from sources other than variations in the reasoning power of those who create and uphold them.

To begin with, different norms may evolve in different cultures because different environmental inputs impinge on the same evolved mental mechanisms of their members (Tooby & Cosmides, 1992). As explained by many theorists, in the inherently unpredictable social environments in which early humans evolved, we would expect natural selection to have designed flexible, context-sensitive ("facultative") mental mechanisms that enable people to accommodate to variations in the forms that adaptive problems assume in different environments (Gangestad & Simpson, 2007). "Because evolved psychological mechanisms are functionally flexible, they are responsive to differences in local ecologies—to the unique opportunities, threats, and constraints afforded by the physical and social world around them—and so different ecologies afford superficially different cultural solutions to the same underlying adaptive problems" (Schaller, 2007, p. 369).

On this line of thought, cross-cultural differences in the content of moral norms stem from cultural differences in the structure of adaptive problems. For example, cultures with a surplus of women may develop norms that support a polygamous marriage system. Cultures that have access to different foods may develop different dietary norms and food prohibitions (Durham, 1991). For example, moral norms upholding cooperative food-sharing may evolve in hunter–gatherer societies in which the probability of success on a hunt is variable, but not in societies in which the probability of each individual obtaining food by gathering is more consistent. And moral norms sanctioning infanticide and suicide in elders tend to evolve in harsh environments such as those occupied by the Inuit, to ensure the preservation of some of their relatives. Note how the same abstract moral norm (for example, maximize the preservation and quality of life; preserve as many members of your group as possible) may be instantiated in very different ways in different environments.

Different moral norms also may evolve in different cultures because they constitute equally effective ways of solving the same adaptive problem—because there is more than one way to skin the same cat. For example, as pointed out by Maynard Smith (1982), it does not really matter whether one drives on the right side of the road or the on the left side of the road, as long as everyone adopts the same convention. And as pointed out by Richerson and Boyd (2005), once an arbitrary convention becomes adopted by most members of a group, it may be in the adaptive interest of other members to adopt it as a signal that they belong to the group and that they fit in.

In addition, culturally relative moral norms may by shaped by the biases built into evolved social learning mechanisms. For example, people may copy the idiosyncratic beliefs of high status models and influential members of their groups, and powerful models may manipulate members of their groups into adopting peculiar norms that advance their interests. Finally, as demonstrated by Kenrick, Li, and Butner (2006), random aspects of the dynamic process of strategic social interaction may produce culturally relative moral norms. Consider, for example, a group that contains a random distribution of individuals with cooperative and aggressive traits. Kenrick and his colleagues have shown that if members of such groups adopt the strategies of the majority of their neighbors, norms favoring either cooperation or aggression may emerge depending on the (random) assortment of individuals within the population. In addition, Kenrick et al. (2006) demonstrated that individual differences in thresholds for cooperation and aggression may exert profound effects on the evolution of norms, and that a small number of uncooperative individuals may quickly corrupt cooperative groups.

Accounting for the Evolution of Irrational and Arbitrary Moral Norms

Although Darwin attributed the irrationality of some of the moral norms he observed among the aboriginal people he encountered to deficiencies in their powers of reasoning, we do not have to look very far among the most intelligent of our friends to find irrational moral beliefs, especially those espoused in their religions. What sense is there in the belief that it is morally wrong to eat certain foods, to have certain kinds of sex, to utter profanities, and to take the name of the Lord in vein? What sense is there in believing that it is wrong to cut one's hair, to display one's breasts, or to show one's face?

One way of accounting for irrational moral norms is to establish that the behaviors they prescribe were adaptive in the environments in which the norms originated and have endured even though the environments have changed. As examples, it might once have made sense not to eat a particular food, because eating it rendered people vulnerable to some disease; or it once may have made sense for everyone to eat fish on Fridays because it guarded against the depletion of other food resources (Janicki & Krebs, 1997).

Another way of accounting for arbitrary moral norms is to establish that they serve indirect adaptive functions, such as marking group membership and unifying groups. It might not matter much what the content of some norms is; what might matter is that upholding it serves as a sign that one is a member of a particular group.

VARIATIONS IN MORAL NORMS WITHIN CULTURES

People tend to assume that all, or virtually all, members of a culture accept and preach the moral norms of their culture. Indeed, this assumption is implicit in the very definition of a moral norm. However, this assumption is valid, at best, only at an abstract level. If you ask people to identify the moral norms of their culture, most people would probably give similar answers. However, if you observed these people in their everyday lives, I am quite sure that you would witness significantly less consistency.

For example, although virtually all people believe that it is right for individuals to obey rules and to abide by moral norms, the particular content of the rules and norms may vary dramatically across cultures and within cultures, and people from different cultures may base their moral beliefs on different reasons. People from different cultures may have different conceptions of what it means to help and to harm others and what it means to treat others justly and unjustly; and people from different cultures may harbor different ideas about what makes these forms of conduct right and wrong. There also may be cultural differences in conceptions of the range of others to whom moral obligations apply. Darwin (1874) was sensitive to this issue, offering examples of cultures that contained norms prescribing that its members should help members of their groups, but exploit, harm, and kill members of other groups.

As mentioned, cultures contain many moral norms, which can be interpreted and instantiated in many ways. From an evolutionary perspective, we would expect people to interpret moral norms in ways that were biologically beneficial in the environments in which they reside and for them to invoke the moral norms that contain the greatest potential to foster their biological interests. Consider, for example, norms of fairness. The developmental psychologist, William Damon (1977), found that children faced with the task of distributing a resource such an extra piece of pizza tended to invoke norms that favored their interests, and the social psychologists, Leventhal and Anderson (1970) found that adults who contributed the most to tasks tended to invoke norms of equity that justified dividing resources in proportion to the magnitude of contributions, whereas those who contributed least tended to argue that the resources should be divided equally.

Points made in the previous chapter about the evolution of moral judgments also apply to the evolution of moral norms. We would expect people to tailor the moral norms they preach to others in ways that enhance their persuasive impact, and there is lots of evidence to support this expectation. We would not expect recipients to conform passively to the moral norms preached by others when the norms in question do not advance their interests. When people's interests differ, we would expect arguments and negotiations to occur, with each partner modifying his or her position in an attempt to find mutually beneficial common ground.

If people invoke moral norms as tools to resolve the conflicts that arise when self-interested individuals seek to maximize their gains in social exchanges, the moral norms (tools) that people preach and accept (use) should vary in accordance with the types of relationships they have with recipients, and the accompanying confluences and conflicts of interest (the structure of the adaptive problems people use moral norms to solve). So, for example, we would expect children to adopt different norms in relations with adults than they do in relations with peers, as developmental psychologists have found (see Krebs & Van Hesteren, 1994, for a review). We also would expect people to invoke different norms in different kinds of relationships. In support of this idea, social psychologists have found that friends tend to invoke norms of equality (Austin, 1980), whereas marital partners tend to invoke norms upholding mutual gratification of needs (Greenberg & Cohen, 1982). Clark, Mills, and Powell (1986) have distinguished between "exchange relationships" that are upheld by equity norms that enable people to balance their costs and benefits, and "communal relationships," that are upheld by more altruistic and needs-based norms. Social psychologists have accounted for variations in the norms people invoke to variations in the "outcome interdependencies" (i.e., confluences and conflicts of interest) of the types of relationship in question. Like social psychological accounts, an evolutionary account of moral norms implies significantly more situational variation in the moral norms that people invoke than expected in psychological theories such as those espoused by cognitive-developmental theorists, and many studies have supported this expectation (e.g., Krebs, Denton, Vermeulen, Carpendale, & Bush, 1991; Krebs, Denton, & Wark, 1997).

SENSITIVITY TO MORAL NORMS

Moral norms are a special variety of norm. Social psychologists have found that people are more vigilant to violations of moral rules and norms than they are to violations of other kinds of norms, at least when perpetrated by others, and that people are strongly disposed to punish those who violate moral norms, as discussed in earlier chapters (see Tooby & Cosmides, 2005). Developmental psychologists have found that children acquire these dispositions early in life: "Children are significantly better at detecting violations of rules in the social domain, such as those dealing with permissions, prohibitions, promises, obligations, and warnings, than they are at detecting violations of rules in other domains" (Cummins, 2005, p. 698). Studies have found that "children as young as 16 months look longer at visual displays depicting violations of arbitrary social rules than at similar displays that do not constitute violations of social rules" (Cummins, 2005, p. 688). By age three, children distinguish between moral rules and rules that uphold social conventions. "When asked to test compliance with social rules, 3-year-olds have been found to spontaneously seek out potential rule violations just as adults do. . . . readily distinguish rule-violating behavior from compliant behavior. . . . and give cogent explanations as to why violating instances constitute violations of the rule. . . . The average 3-year-old appears to have as firm a grasp on the implications of socially prescriptive rules as the average adult" (Cummins, 2005, p. 689). It is important, however, to note that this research does not establish that children are motivated to obey rules, to detect violations of rules in themselves, or to assume responsibility for inducing others to obey the rules at a cost to themselves.

CONCLUSIONS

Moral norms are abstract beliefs about how people should and should not behave that are shared by most members of a culture. They are products of complex interactions between shared experiences and evolved belief-producing, belief-selecting, and belief-maintaining mental mechanisms. Genes guide the creation of these mechanisms, which produce aspects of culture that, in turn, affect the selection of the genes that design the mechanisms. Universal moral norms stem from beliefs upholding evolved, species-specific prosocial dispositions that increase the welfare of members of groups, are supported by social sanctions, and are reasonable. Several factors may produce cultural differences in moral norms, including differences in the form that adaptive problems assume in different cultures, equally effective ways to solve the same adaptive problems, biases in social learning mechanisms, and random evolutionary processes.

Moral norms that were adaptive in ancestral environments may be maladaptive in modern environments, and maladaptive norms may evolve in a variety of ways. However, some moral norms that seem irrational and maladaptive may benefit people in subtle ways.

There is a great deal of evidence that humans are evolved to distinguish moral rules and norms from other kinds of rules and norms, to pay special attention to moral rules and norms, to detect violations of them more easily than they detect violations of other rules and norms, and to punish moral norm violations.

PART FIVE

Implications and Applications

19

HUMAN NATURE AND THE NATURE
OF MORALITY

So, after all this, can we answer the question that people have pondered for so long—how moral are humans by nature? In earlier chapters, I advanced arguments against the idea that humans are born bad, or immoral, by nature and refined Darwin's account of the evolution of morality. In this chapter, I consider four conceptions of what it means to be moral, and take a position on the extent to which people are naturally inclined to meet the criteria for each conception of a moral person. In the first conception, morality is defined in terms of dispositions to behave in prosocial ways. In the second conception, morality is defined in terms of virtue. In the third conception, morality is defined in terms of moral knowledge or wisdom, and in the final conception, morality is defined in terms of honor and integrity.

I conclude that humans are naturally disposed to help others, to obey rules, and to behave in virtuous ways. All normal people possess the ability to make moral decisions and to use them to guide their conduct. However, these natural inclinations are activated only in conducive conditions, and people also are naturally disposed to behave in immoral ways. Contemporary humans are as good as their early human ancestors had to be to reap the benefits of sociality, and a little more.

Revisiting an idea introduced earlier in this book, I close this chapter by defining morality in terms of the functions that it evolved to serve, and I argue that in optimal conditions, there is no necessary inconsistency between behaving in accordance with lofty, humanitarian, moral principles and propagating one's genes.

I have made the point that people's answers to questions about how altruistic and moral humans are by nature depend on how they define altruism and morality. When people say that someone is moral, they could mean at least four things. First, they could mean that the person is *well behaved*—someone who exhibits self-control, resists temptation, obeys the rules, does his or her share, and helps others when they are in need. Second, they could mean that the person is *virtuous*—someone who possesses internal character traits such as honesty, altruism, courage, conscientiousness, compassion, loyalty, and a sense of fairness. Third, they could mean that the person is *wise*—someone who understands the difference between right and wrong, has developed a sophisticated conception of morality, and is able to solve complex moral problems. Finally, they could mean that the person is *honorable,* or *upright*—that the person possesses integrity and is disposed to behave in accordance with acceptable moral standards. In the first case, people base their moral attributions primarily on what people do. In the second case, they base their attributions on the type of person an individual is. In the third case, they base their attributions primarily on what people think and say, and in the final case, they base their attributions on the extent to which people abide by moral principles. Social learning theorists implicitly harbor the first conception of a moral person, and cognitive-developmental theorists harbor the third. The evolutionary framework I have developed in this book supplies a basis for evaluating them all.

HOW WELL-BEHAVED ARE HUMANS BY NATURE?

Guided by Darwin's assumption that humans inherit (pro)social instincts that dispose them to aid their fellows and to uphold their groups, I have advanced a great deal of evidence that humans are naturally disposed to behave in deferential, altruistic, and cooperative ways in certain conditions and that they possess the capacity to control their antisocial urges, to resist temptation, and to delay gratification. We can safely conclude from this evidence that humans are conditionally good by nature, in the sense in which parents use the word when they say, "You are a good girl," or "You are a good boy." However, because people also behave in ways that people consider bad, it also is clear that people are conditionally bad by nature. There is not anything surprising in these conclusions—we are exposed to evidence supporting them every day.

Humans differ from other primates in the magnitude and effectiveness of the prosocial behaviors they emit because the deferential, altruistic, and cooperative dispositions that have evolved in the human species can be activated by a significantly broader array of stimuli than comparable dispositions in other primate species can—especially stimuli emanating from inside their minds— and because humans are better than other primates at understanding what others need and how best to help them. Although evolutionary theorists disagree about the nature of the mechanisms that dispose people to emit uniquely human prosocial behaviors—with some theorists arguing that the expansiveness of human altruism and cooperation stems from a "misfiring" of mechanisms that evolved in ancient environments, and other theorists arguing that this expansiveness stems from mechanisms that were designed to induce modern humans to uphold tribal communities—everyone accepts the evidence that humans are unique among primates in their magnanimity. Whatever the original source, as humans evolved, changes in environments and the expansion and reorganization of the human brain increased significantly the range of stimuli equipped to activate prosocial dispositions, rendering humans increasingly altruistic and cooperative by nature.

Alexander (1987), has suggested that "complete and indiscriminate beneficence, as in the utilitarian system of philosophers, would not always be a losing strategy for individuals [who live in large, complex societies], even in evolutionary terms," and that our evolving species might be heading toward "a utilitarian or idealized model of morality" (p. 100). Systems of indirect reciprocity based on divisions of labor that enable large numbers of individuals to make low-cost contributions in return for high-value returns may be equipped to increase the welfare of all members of a society more than any other social system is—especially, as Alexander has suggested, when groups are threatened by other groups. However, as discussed, for such systems to evolve, they must contain ways of controlling cheating, and the beneficence in question is limited to in-group members.

There is a parallel between the evolution of mental mechanisms that expanded the range of stimuli equipped to activate prosocial dispositions, which occurred over hundreds of thousands of years of evolutionary time and the "additive-inclusive" expansion of the range of these stimuli that occurs during the human life span of children, as they develop into adults.

How Moral Are Well-Behaved People?

There can be no question that humans are naturally disposed to behave in prosocial ways and that prosocial dispositions usually induce people to behave in ways that seem moral to most people. However, prosocial dispositions do not always induce people to behave in moral ways. For example, they could induce them to obey Nazi types of authorities, tell the truth when it leads to atrocities, permit others to exploit them, and so on.

As discussed, Darwin argued that the morality of prosocial behaviors could be assessed by determining the extent to which they produce utilitarian consequences such as fostering the greatest good for the greatest number. I have questioned this idea, arguing that the morality of acts, and even more so the morality of people, is rooted more in the motives and intentions that guide behaviors than in the consequences they produce. In my view, in order to assess the morality of prosocial behaviors, we need to determine the extent to which evolved prosocial dispositions engender moral motives such as the desire to maximize the amount of good in the world.

Viewed from the perspective of evolution, there is little reason to expect people who behave in prosocial ways to be driven by the motive to foster the greatest good for the greatest number or by any other lofty moral goal, because prosocial dispositions did not evolve to enable people to achieve such goals—they evolved to enable people to maximize their long-term genetic gains by delaying gratification, upholding their groups, and joining with others to advance their adaptive interests. Although it is possible that people are occasionally moved by lofty motives, I do not believe that people are motivated to pursue humanitarian goals on a consistent basis. The research findings that come closest to supporting the idea that people possess such dispositions are those that suggest that people are motivated to uphold principles of fairness; however, as discussed, such motives are highly conditional and susceptible to a variety of biases.

Even if people were motivated to maximize the amount of good in the world, they would immediately face a stifling obstacle, namely that there are billions of people in the world, and no one can help them all. Good-hearted people must decide how much of the goodness at their disposal they should allocate to themselves, how much they should allocate to their friends and relatives, how much they should allocate to needy people from other counties, and so on. In addition to trying to foster the greatest amount of good, a truly moral person would have to distribute his or her efforts in fair and impartial ways, without discriminating against anyone. Although one might argue that maximizing the amount of good in the world entails directing one's beneficence to those who would benefit most from it, this goal is hopelessly unrealistic.

I believe that it is safe to conclude that although evolved prosocial dispositions dispose people to behave in ways that most people consider moral, they do not render humans consistently moral, because these dispositions are conditional and activated only in some contexts. Although humans may possess the capacity to promote the welfare of a broad range of recipients, people are not naturally disposed to allocate their beneficence in impartial ways. People are naturally inclined to allocate their altruism in ways that increased the inclusive fitness of their early human ancestors—discriminating in favor of themselves, their relatives, those with whom they have formed cooperative relations, members of their in-groups, and others on whom their fitness is dependent, which, entails discriminating against members of out-groups and those with whom they do not identify. The challenge for those who seek to maximize the amount of goodness in the world is to figure out how to lower the threshold for the activation of people's prosocial dispositions and increase the threshold for the activation of people's antisocial dispositions.

HOW VIRTUOUS ARE PEOPLE BY NATURE?

We know that, like Darwin, most people consider such virtues as altruism, self-control, honesty, and fairness moral. I have presented Geoffrey Miller's argument that sexual selection played an important role in the evolution of moral virtues. To review briefly, Miller suggested that because early humans were disposed to select virtuous people as mates, the genes that guided this preference and the genes that coded for virtuous traits were passed on to their offspring, who passed them on to their offspring, and so on in a runaway fashion. The reason that people who inherited mental mechanisms that induced them to value virtues produced more viable offspring than those who did not inherit these mechanisms was not only because they selected mates who were disposed to treat them and their relatives in virtuous ways, but in addition, because these people produced offspring with virtues that were attractive to members of the opposite sex and because virtues constitute honest signals of fitness. Note how Miller's application of sexual selection theory helps account for the value that people attach to virtues and the role that attributions of virtue play in people's moral sense.

The conclusions about how virtuous people are by nature that follow from an evolutionary analysis of morality are the same as the conclusions about how well-behaved people are by nature because virtuous people behave in prosocial ways. Although humans possess the capacity to behave in virtuous ways, virtuous dispositions are conditional, activated only by a limited set of stimuli.

How Moral Are Virtuous People?

Even though there is a close correspondence between moral virtues and moral behaviors (you cannot *be* compassionate, honest, or fair without *behaving* in these ways), I think that virtues are more relevant than forms of conduct are to the question of how moral people are by nature because virtues are located inside people, where their natures reside, and because virtues constitute general, stable, person-defining, and species-defining traits. Like dispositions and social strategies, virtues can be considered sources of moral behavior. Rooting morality in virtues rather than in behaviors helps us get around the "good acts for bad reasons" problem. When we ask how moral humans are by nature, we are asking about the kinds of stable, internal qualities that give rise to good intentions, not to the consequences of the acts they emit (although, of course, the two are usually related).

In our everyday lives, we are often concerned less about the fallout from the specific acts that people emit than we are with why they did what they did and whether they will do it again in the future. What we really want to know is what kinds of people we are dealing with. Are they the kind of people with whom we want to associate and in whom we want to invest, or are they the kind of people whom we want to avoid or punish. As expressed by Miller (2007a, p. 103), "it seems unlikely that our prehistoric ancestors made moral judgments about isolated behavioral acts. Rather, as in other domains of person perception. . . . they probably interpreted the behavioral acts as cues of stable individual traits (virtues or vices). In small-scale hunter–gatherer bands, morality came in person-sized units, not act-sized units. Ancestral hominids had to choose their lovers, friends, and allies as integrated moral packages—good or bad, hero or villain, lover or stalker, reciprocator or cheat." Miller goes on to say, "the moral person and moral act levels of description show some other key differences. . . . First, 'morality' means something different at the person level compared to the act level. A moral act may be one that obeys some rationally defensible, universal, deontic, or consequentialist [i.e., utilitarian] principle. However, from the point of view of a standard prehistoric hunter–gatherer, a moral person is someone who embodies prosocial virtues that make them a good mate, friend, relative, or trading partner." I am not sure that Miller's claim that people do not make moral attributions about acts is correct. People do, on occasion, make judgments about the morality and immorality of acts, saying things such as "You did the right thing," and "That was unfair," and people base their trait attributions on the things people do. However, I think Miller's claim that people are more concerned with how moral people are than with how moral the specific behaviors they emit are is valid.

In Miller's (2007a) paper on the sexual selection of moral virtues, he makes some skeptical comments about the philosophy of ethics. For example, he asserts that:

> normative ethics is supposed to help us distinguish right from wrong and good from evil. . . .The hope is that normative ethicists can articulate a set of universal, coherent, consistent moral principles that yield intuitively acceptable moral implications across all possible situations, thereby embodying a rational distillation of human moral sensibility. Almost all moral philosophers accept that this is the legitimate goal of normative ethics, though debates still rage between consequentialists and deontologists, act ethicists and virtue ethicists. However, if moral virtues rose through sexual selection, this reflective equilibrium approach to normative ethics will probably continue to fail, as it has for 2,500 years. (p. 116)

Miller defends his skepticism with three arguments. First, he argues that if people's moral intuitions stem from primitive "hot" emotional reactions, then there is little reason to expect these intuitions to correspond to universal principles derived from reason: "Moral philosophers are trying to do ethical alchemy: trying to refine unconscious, domain-specific, person-perception adaptations (the base metal) into verbally articulated, domain-general, universal moral principles (the gold)" (p. 116). Second, Miller argues "if our person-perception system relies on social-inference heuristics that are fast, frugal, and pragmatic, then our moral judgments will often violate procedural norms of rationality derived from logic, statistics, and rational choice theory, such as consistency, transitivity, and completeness" (p. 116). And finally, Miller argues that if the function of the mental mechanisms that induced early humans to assess others' virtue was to help them make decisions about whether to mate with them, to form friendships with them, to cooperate with them, and so on, then we would not expect these mechanisms to be activated by "evolutionary novel moral dilemmas that involve isolated, hypothetical, behavioral acts by unknown strangers who cannot be rewarded or punished through any normal social primate channels" (p. 116). As mentioned, the findings from research that my colleagues and I have conducted support this expectation. Miller concludes that "normative ethics seems likely, at best, to become a discipline like higher mathematics—a small world of like-minded geniuses pursuing consensual moral truths that remain forever beyond the moral imagination of most humans" (p. 116).

The validity of Miller's arguments notwithstanding, they leave an important question about the relation between virtues and morality unanswered, which I raised, but left unresolved, in Chapter 2—namely whether all virtues are equally moral, or whether some are more moral than others. Are there cardinal virtues? Do some virtues trump others? Are altruistic people more moral than honest people are? Are courageous people more moral than fair people are? What should people do when they are required to violate one virtue to uphold another one? If you, as an altruistic and honest person, were asked by a Nazi whether you were hiding a Jew, should you behave honestly or altruistically? If you promised someone you would return a gun he had lent you but knew that he intended to use it to kill innocent people, should you keep your promise?

One way of answering these questions is to organize virtues hierarchically, and establish that some virtues qualify as cardinal virtues that trump others when they come into conflict with them. Among the many virtues, the one that has been given greatest precedence by evolutionary theorists is altruism. As mentioned, evolutionary theorists such as Alexander (1987) have asserted that the concept of morality implies altruism. As much as I like altruistic people, and as much as I value altruism, I believe it is misguided to equate altruism and morality, to assume that altruism is a cardinal virtue, or to assume that all altruistic acts are moral. To begin with, the question, "Is altruism moral?" implies that altruism and morality are different and that there are standards by which the morality of altruistic acts (and therefore the morality of other virtues) can be evaluated. Second, the only place an ideally altruistic person who always helped others at his or her own expense and always put the needs of others above his or her own needs could exist is in our imaginations. People must satisfy some of their needs in order to survive.

Third, when we consider the outcomes of social exchanges between altruistic and selfish people, none of them seems moral. It is obvious that exchanges between selfish people and altruistic people produce outcomes that are unfair to the altruists, who end up exploited. Somewhat less obvious, permitting oneself to be exploited may end up damaging other people, including the exploiters, in the long run, because turning the other cheek may reinforce people's selfishness, which eventually may end up making them self-indulgent and disliked by others. Even less obvious, perhaps, is that exchanges between two unconditional altruists also may be dysfunctional: "You go first." "No, you go first. . . ."

Fourth, when principles that prescribe that people are morally obliged to sacrifice their interests for others unconditionally are universalized, they produce logical inconsistencies. If I should sacrifice my interests for you, then on the same principle, you should sacrifice your interests for me, but I can't really exhort you to do this, because that would entail promoting my interests. Finally, and perhaps most importantly, unconditional altruism fares poorly as a cardinal virtue because it violates principles of fairness. Without some sort of qualification, altruism creates an imbalance; one person suffers a cost and another person gains a benefit. In contrast, justice, as symbolized by the blindfolded woman holding scales, involves a balance.

So where does this leave us with respect to the morality of virtues such as altruism? In most of the situations people encounter in their lives, they can behave morally by behaving virtuously without really thinking much about it. When called upon to be altruistic, they can be altruistic; when called upon to be honest, they can be honest; when called upon to be fair, they can be fair, and so on. However, in some situations, such as when one virtue conflicts with another virtue, or when people must decide how to allocate their virtuous behaviors, more is needed. And this, I think, is where moral wisdom and overriding principles of morality enter the picture. If there is a cardinal virtue, I think it must lie in the knowledge necessary to resolve conflicts among moral prescriptions in principled ways, which brings us to the role of moral reasoning in defining a moral person.

HOW MORALLY WISE ARE PEOPLE BY NATURE?

Cognitive-developmental psychologists have established that people tend to acquire increasing amounts of moral wisdom as they mature. For example, in contrast to other primates and to young children, all normal adults are able to understand how moral principles such as the Golden Rule, Kant's categorical imperatives ("act only on that maxim through which you can at the same time will that it should become a universal law"; "treat all people as ends, not means"), and utilitarian principles that promote the greatest good for the greatest number are equipped to resolve a broader range of moral conflicts more effectively than other principles are. Based on the data collected by cognitive-developmental psychologists on the distribution of stages of moral development (and therefore the proportion of the population capable of engaging in highly sophisticated forms of moral reasoning), we could conclude that young children are deficient in moral wisdom, most adults are moderately wise, and a few highly intelligent people possess a great deal of moral wisdom. As an illustration of what cognitive-developmental theorists consider moral wisdom, let us consider the following sample of ("Stage 6") moral reasoning—a response to Kohlberg's Heinz dilemma made by "Joan" ("a 32-year-old woman with graduate training in philosophy").

If I were Heinz I, you know, would keep trying to talk with the druggist . . . I have a hard time thinking of any decision as being static, and it seems to me that dialogue is very important and a continuing dialogue in this kind of situation. But if it came to a point where nothing else could be done, I think that in consultation with his wife, if he and his wife decided that that would be an acceptable alternative for Heinz, then yes he should [steal the drug to save his wife]. Because I think that ultimately it comes down to a conflict of duties. . . . I hate to put it this way, but I really tend to think of things in a Kantian sense—I don't think that Heinz should do anything that he would not be willing to say that everyone should do. And breaking into a store and stealing is not an action that can be prescribed for humanity, for our societal group as a whole. On the other hand, Heinz, I think as, just by virtue of being a member of the human race, has an obligation, a duty to protect other people—I guess that's a way to put it. And when it gets down to a conflict between those two, I think that the protection of human life is more important. (Colby & Kohlberg, 1987, pp. 33–34)

How Moral Are Morally Wise People?

Some psychologists have questioned whether highly sophisticated forms of moral reasoning such as the ones displayed by Joan reflect moral wisdom. For example, Haan, Aerts, and Cooper, (1985) characterized the forms of moral reasoning that define the highest stages in Kohlberg's sequences as "nothing more than reified adulterations of intellectualized restatements of interactional morality, preferred or more persistently used by problem solvers with special intellectual training. . . . Platonic morals are the intellectual's phobic reactions to social uncertainty" (p. 246). However, let us grant that a few highly intelligent people, such as Joan, Kohlberg, and some philosophers of ethics, possess a certain type of moral wisdom. If I were faced with a complex moral problem, I might appeal to these sages for advice, and I would expect them to derive more ideal solutions than I, who possess less moral wisdom, could think of. The question is, how moral does this kind of wisdom, demonstrated by the academic ability to understand morality and to solve complex moral problems, render people? Is Joan more moral than the average person? How about Kohlberg; was he more moral than, say, eminent social learning theorists or eminent evolutionary theorists? In one sense perhaps but not in others. I would not expect experts in moral philosophy to behave any differently from people who possess less moral knowledge when they make common moral decisions in their everyday lives, for two reasons.

First, as I have argued, people do not usually invest the intellectual energy necessary to puzzle out all the implications of real-life moral decisions because it is not usually necessary to do so. Second, to qualify as a moral person, an individual must possess more than moral wisdom. He or she also must possess the qualities necessary to apply this wisdom appropriately in his or her everyday life. People who understand clearly what they ought, morally, to do, but fail to do it may well be less moral than people who do not possess sophisticated conceptions of what they are morally obliged to do in the first place.

When viewed from an evolutionary perspective, moral wisdom is a tool that can be used for good or for bad purposes. On the good side, people can use moral wisdom to produce ideal solutions to moral conflicts and to create utopian social orders, which if everyone upheld them, would maximize everyone's benefits. But how much moral wisdom do we need to accomplish this? It does not take a rocket scientist to understand how much people's lot could be improved if everyone followed a principle like the Golden Rule, which Darwin considered the foundation of morality. Consider a specific example—doing unto others as you would have them do unto you while driving on congested roads. If everyone conformed to the Golden Rule and resisted the temptation to cheat—that is to say, if everyone drove at the posted speed, took turns merging, refrained from passing, cutting in, and so on, everyone would get home in the shortest period of time with the least danger of getting in an accident. Cars would move in unison in a well-organized, effective manner. And sometimes this happens. It is sort of blissful to be part of a pattern of cooperative drivers; there is a harmony to it, a sense of serenity and connectedness that feels good. It is easy to understand what people need to do to produce such results.

I should make it clear that I am not saying that the Golden Rule is a completely adequate moral principle. In fact, I do not believe it is because it exhorts people to project their preferences onto others ("as you would have them do unto you"), rather than accommodating to the preferences of others,[1] or evaluating people's preferences in terms of a more general principle, such as the greatest good. In addition, the Golden Rule does not prescribe a method for adjudicating between the conflicting claims of others. How do you decide whom to treat as you would want to be treated if two people require your assistance and you can help only one of them? This said, the Golden Rule is well equipped to produce good results in most contexts. If everyone followed it, the world would be a much better place. People would help and support each another, whatever their race, nationality, or in-group affiliation. There would be no rapes, assaults, thefts, or wars; no need for armies or police; no occasion to suffer the costs of punishing cheaters. And we could invest all the money we saved from police, jails, and military support in improving the quality of everyone's life.

However, as we all know only too well, this is not the way things are because although most people understand the wisdom of the Golden Rule, and although most people may obey it in some contexts, people are not evolved to follow the Golden Rule in a consistent manner, and it takes only one cheater to destroy a cooperative system in which people are doing unto others as they would have them do unto themselves. Thus, you are driving home from work in rush hour. Someone is late, so he speeds up and cuts in front other drivers, or he refuses to let someone merge. Other drivers speed up to keep pace or refuse to let others merge, and on it goes in a chain reaction until someone gets into an accident, and you all sit in gridlock.

Understanding deeply and fully why one moral choice is morally superior to other choices may, as cognitive-developmental theorists have argued, engender some motivation to behave accordingly. People may feel motivated to carry out the decisions that make most sense to them, and they may be motivated to avoid logical

---

[1] For example, a disturbed person could do a lot of damage by treating others as he or she wants to be treated.

(and psychological) inconsistency. People may sometimes behave in ways that are consistent with lofty (Stage 6) principles, and they may even derive moral decisions from such principles and use them to guide their behavior in some contexts. However, at best, this occurs only rarely. As demonstrated in earlier chapters, the motivation generated by moral wisdom is weak in many real-life contexts when pitted against the motives generated by more emotional and self-interested sources. On my reading, the evidence suggests that moral reasoning needs to be buttressed by other qualities to engender the motivation to behave in accordance with the moral decisions it produces. In addition, as discussed, people may use their moral wisdom for immoral purposes.

You might argue that the kinds of moral principles invoked by very wise people are not equipped to justify immoral acts, and there is a sense in which this is true, because the principles are designed to produce fair decisions. However, my point is that there is a difference between possessing the wisdom to make fair moral decisions and using this wisdom to guide actual choices that matter. I do not consider cerebral people who indulge themselves day in and day out inspecting their moral belly-buttons very moral.

"The Secret Joke of Kant's Soul"

The neuroscientist Greene (2008) has advanced an interesting argument pertaining to the evolved sources of moral wisdom and their relation to the normative theories advanced by philosophers of ethics. To review, philosophers have advanced two main types of moral principles—those that are consequential and those that are deontological. Utilitarian principles such as those derived by Mills and Darwin are consequential—they prescribe that people should strive to produce the best consequences for those affected by moral decisions. In contrast, deontological principles such as those derived by Kant prescribe that people should act in accordance with moral rules and principles even if this practice does not produce the most beneficial results. For example, Kant argued that people should keep their promises, even if it ends up hurting others.

Like Kohlberg, most deontological philosophers believe that people derive moral decisions from reason. Such philosophers invoke their well-cultivated reasoning abilities to derive the best possible moral principles—those that are most universal, prescriptive, reversible, and so on—then they evaluate the adequacy of these principles in terms of their ability to account for behaviors that normal people consider moral. However, in an article entitled, "The Secret Joke of Kant's Soul," Greene (2008) presents evidence from brain imaging research that, in fact, people (including philosophers of ethics) do not derive deontological moral judgments in the way that deontological philosophers and cognitive-developmental psychologists think they derive them. According to Greene, "what deontological moral philosophy really is, what it is essentially, is an attempt to produce rational justifications for emotionally driven moral judgments, and not an attempt to reach moral conclusions on the basis of moral reasoning"(p. 39).

Appealing to findings from the Trolley Dilemma research I discussed earlier, Greene and his colleagues demonstrated that when people make deontological moral judgments such as "It is wrong to push a heavy person off a footbridge even though it would save the lives of five people on a railway track," emotional areas in their brains that produce automatic moral intuitions light up, which the people then justify in rational terms.

In contrast, when people make consequential, utilitarian decisions, such as those that prescribe sacrificing the life of one person to save the lives of five people, the areas in their brains that mediate higher level rational processes override their initial emotional reactions: "The parts of the brain that exhibit increased activity when people make characteristically consequentialist judgments are those that are most closely associated with higher cognitive functions such as executive control. . . . complex planning. . . . deductive and inductive reasoning. . . . taking the long view in economic decision making . . . and so on. . . . These brain regions are among those most dramatically expanded in humans compared with other primates" (Greene, 2008, p. 47).

Greene sums up his conclusions as follows:

> What turn-of-the millennium science is telling us is that human moral judgment is not a pristine rational enterprise—that our moral judgments are driven by a hodgepodge of emotional dispositions, which themselves were shaped by a hodgepodge of evolutionary forces, both biological and cultural. Because of this, it is exceedingly unlikely that there is any rationally coherent normative moral theory that can accommodate our moral intuitions. Moreover, anyone who claims to have such a theory, or even part of one, almost certainly does not. Instead, what that person probably has is a moral rationalization. (p. 72)

In conclusion, although humans undoubtedly are more morally wise than any other animal is, although people generally become increasingly wise as they develop, and although some people may well possess a great deal of moral wisdom, moral wisdom is neither necessary nor sufficient to render a person moral. In the end, people's morality is determined by what they do, and why—not by how they think, or what they know. To qualify as moral, a morally wise person must use his or her moral wisdom in moral ways to derive moral decisions that guide his or her behavior; and the evidence suggests that other, more emotional and heuristic mechanisms usually structure moral judgments and dispose people to behave in moral ways. People who acquire Stage 6 structures of moral reasoning may well possess more moral wisdom than those who have not reached this level of cognitive development, but more is needed to induce such people to use their wisdom to guide the moral decisions they make in their everyday lives.

HOW HONORABLE ARE PEOPLE BY NATURE?

One way to bridge the gap between conceptions of moral personhood rooted in moral knowledge and conceptions rooted in dispositions to behave in moral ways—that is to say, to behave in ways that meet acceptable standards of morality—is to make both moral knowledge and the qualities that induce people to behave in moral ways prerequisites for morality. On these criteria, to qualify as moral, a person must possess the knowledge necessary to derive sound moral decisions, the motivation to behave in accordance with such decisions, and the strength to stick to his or her convictions. We would call such a person honorable, upright, and principled—a person with an integrated moral fiber, or a person of integrity. Although this standard sets the bar for morality very high, I think that it corresponds to the standards that people implicitly evoke when they make moral evaluations of others. For example, although we might assume that a person who possessed a great deal of moral knowledge was moral when he or she engaged in philosophical debates about morality, we would revise this assumption if we observed this person behaving in a dishonest or uncharitable manner. Although we might consider altruistic people moral, we would modify our attributions if they behaved unfairly. Everyone has experienced a sense of disillusionment when people whom they considered moral lost self-control, succumbed to temptation, made a stupid decision, or folded under pressure. Lots of people's hearts are in the right place, but they fail to anticipate the negative consequences of their kind-hearted behaviors. People who have been awarded heroes medals do not tend to be any more principled, or kind, or conscientious than other people are (Huston, Geis, & Wright, 1976).

Developmental psychologists Anne Colby and William Damon (1992) conducted an interesting study on "moral exemplars" that supports the idea that the essence of morality lies in integrity. These investigators asked a group of 22 experts to develop a set of criteria for moral exemplars, then to nominate people they believed met the criteria. The experts selected the following five criteria, which mesh well with the idea that to qualify as moral, a person must be honorable:

1. A sustained commitment to moral ideals or principles that include a generalized respect for humanity
2. A disposition to act in accord with one's moral ideals or principles
3. A willingness to risk one's self-interest for the sake of one's moral values
4. A tendency to be inspiring to others and thereby to move them to moral action
5. A sense of realistic humility about one's own importance relative to the world at large, implying a relative lack of concern for one's own ego (p. 29)

Although all nominated moral exemplars whom Colby and Damon interviewed possessed all five qualities, each exemplar displayed the qualities in a different manner. For example some exemplars (following the ideal displayed by Mother Theresa) were inspired to do humanitarian work for religious reasons; whereas others (following the ideal displayed by Martin Luther King Jr.) were inspired to redress social injustices. Interestingly, when Colby and Damon gave their moral exemplars Kohlberg's Moral Judgment Interview, only a few of them scored at the highest level. Consistent with the model I derived from evolutionary theory, most moral exemplars did not need sophisticated conceptions of morality to guide their behavior; a moderate amount of moral wisdom was sufficient. It is interesting to speculate whether, if these people were faced with a moral problem that required sophisticated forms of moral reasoning to solve, they would lose some of their moral luster.

The key characteristics that distinguished moral exemplars from other people were the importance they attached to their moral ideals and the significance of morality to their personal identities. Being moral—achieving the goals that they considered moral—was at the core of their sense of self. They were highly motivated to do good and willing to make the sacrifices necessary to accomplish it. The source of their moral behavior was their moral principles, which in the eyes of some theorists, is the only valid source of morality.

I think that humans are evolved to behave in honorable ways in some contexts. Virtually all people develop moral principles and behave in accordance with them, as long as it is not too costly. However, people may differ greatly in the strength of their convictions. When viewed through an evolutionary lens, we would expect to find biologically and developmentally based individual differences in the qualities that endow people with moral intelligence, the motivation to behave in moral ways, and the determination, courage, and will power, or ego strength, to achieve their moral goals; and research indicates that the heritability of these qualities is high (see Miller, 2007, for a review). Some people are wise, other people are kind-hearted, and still others are courageous. A few people may possess all these qualities, at least to a moderate degree.

EVOLUTIONARY ETHICS

We have come to the part where I take a shot at the philosophy of ethics. As may soon become apparent, I have no training in this discipline. However, at the end of this long exploration of the evolution of morality, I feel motivated to give it a go. I am familiar with the "naturalistic fallacy" of attempting to derive "ought" prescriptions from "is" statements of fact. However, I believe that science (the "is") and ethics (the "ought") intersect in two ways. First, in the end, people's "ought" judgments stem from the evolved mental mechanisms in their brains—their psychology. So understanding the "is" of how these mechanisms are designed and how they operate, as I have attempted to do in this book, supplies a basis for understanding the source of "ought" judgments. Second, there are important senses in which "ought" implies "is." It makes little sense to set the standards of morality so high that no one is capable of meeting them, and as I hope I have demonstrated, science is equipped to assess people's capacity for morality. Although it might be interesting, as an intellectual exercise, to derive ideal standards of morality that no one could ever meet, it seems to me that when we say that people are morally obliged to behave in certain ways, we imply that this goal is at least potentially achievable by some people in some conditions.

It will come as no surprise that I believe that the approach to normative ethics that meshes most comfortably with the model of morality I have derived from evolutionary theory is functional in nature. The basic assumptions underlying a functional approach to evolutionary ethics are that morality evolved for a reason—to help people solve adaptive problems and to achieve adaptive goals—and the better a moral idea, judgment, emotion, principle, behavior, strategy, or disposition fulfills this function, the more morally adequate it is.

Viewed in this way, the challenge is to identify the function or functions morality evolved to serve. I have presented a great deal of evidence that prosocial behaviors, virtues, and structures of moral reasoning can help people survive, reproduce, and foster their inclusive fitness. However, it is clear that these ultimate goals do not qualify as criteria for morality. People can promote their biological and genetic welfare in moral or in immoral ways. As discussed, it also does not make sense to conclude that the function of morality is to promote the welfare of the human species or the greatest biological good for the greatest number, as Darwin did, because promoting inclusive fitness is a zero sum game. Promoting the inclusive fitness of some members of the species entails not promoting, or diminishing, the inclusive fitness of other members of the species. Morality pertains to the means people adopt to achieve the ultimate goals they are evolved to strive to achieve, which correspond to proximate goals. The function of morality is to induce people to strive to increase their inclusive fitness in certain (moral) ways, and not in other (immoral) ways, which implies pursuing certain proximate goals in certain ways, and not pursuing other proximate goals in other ways.

I have argued that the mental mechanisms that endow people with a moral sense evolved to help them resist the temptation to foster their immediate adaptive interests at the expense of other people's adaptive interests and to induce them to foster their long-term interests in ways that foster the interests of other members of their groups, by doing their share and by taking their share, by maintaining mutually beneficial social relations, by resolving conflicts of interest in adaptive ways, and by upholding (and improving) the systems of cooperation and social orders of their groups. As expressed by Miller (2007), "In evolutionary theory, a moral person is simply one who pursues their ultimate genetic self-interest through psychological adaptations that embody a genuine, proximate concern for others"(p. 103).

Defined functionally, moral people possess the qualities that induce them to go about the long-term business of surviving, reproducing, and propagating their genes in fair and altruistic ways. These qualities include all of the qualities I have been discussing—proso-cial behavioral dispositions, self-control, a strong will, moral virtues, moral knowledge, moral principles, integrity, and so on. On this line of thought, the reason that people consider moral exemplars so moral is because moral exemplars are exceptional in the extent to which they achieve the functions that morality evolved to serve.

But you do not have to be a moral exemplar to behave morally. Ordinary people customarily pursue their interests by behaving in ways that advance the welfare of others. They treat others to dinner; they help their friends when they are in need; they pay their debts; they obey rules; they respect legitimate authority; they help people in emergencies; they donate to charity; they do their jobs, and so on. In most situations, simple behavioral strategies, such as those based on concrete reciprocity are adequately moral, because they work—they fulfill the functions morality evolved to serve. Simple strategies lose their moral status only when they fail to fulfill these functions—such as, for example, when they give rise to blood feuds or are invoked instead of more adaptive principles, such as those that uphold the kinds of long-term social investments that people make in their friends. On functional criteria, the reason that "Stage 3" strategies such as the ideal forms of reciprocity prescribed by the Golden Rule are better (more moral) than "Stage 2" Tit-for-Tat strategies is because they do a better job of helping people foster their welfare in ways that foster the welfare of others—when the conditions are right.

If moral dispositions and a sense of morality evolved because they disposed early humans to behave in ways that achieved ultimate adaptive goals by supporting those on whom their fitness was dependent, including upholding their groups, it might seem that, on a functional criterion, people's moral obligations would extend only to those on whom their fitness is dependent. Clearly, most people feel a stronger moral obligation to help their relatives, friends, and members of their in-groups than they do to help strangers and members of out-groups. However, after we have derived a functional criterion for morality (an "ought"), it can take on a life of its own, independent of current "is" constraints. If the function of morality is to enable people to promote their long-term welfare in ways that promote the welfare of others, then it need not be constrained by the psychological mechanisms that evolved to fulfill this function in ancestral environments. As human groups increase in size, and as the world develops into a global community, everyone's fate becomes increasingly dependent on everyone else's fate. Indeed, as signaled by global warming concerns, people's fates are becoming increasingly connected to the fates of other plants and animals.

In the end—and I will end this chapter with this thought—I do not believe that there is a necessary inconsistency between pursuing one's ultimate biological interests and behaving in ways that maximize the amount of good in the world. Like other animals, humans are evolved to behave in ways that increased the inclusive fitness of their early ancestors. The question is, what are the most optimal routes? Although moral strategies may not be optimal in all circumstances, they could be optimal if the conditions were right. If all people agreed to attempt to foster their interests in moral ways, everyone could come out ahead in the end. Like drivers on congested roads, if everyone adopted a moral strategy, what goes around could come around, and everyone could arrive at his or her destination in the best possible shape. If!

CONCLUSION

There are at least four qualitatively different conceptions of what it means to be moral—behaving in prosocial ways, possessing virtues, possessing moral wisdom, and possessing integrity. Although most people are naturally inclined to meet the criteria inherent in all four conceptions of morality, moral traits are highly conditional and people are naturally inclined to behave in immoral ways in ancestral conditions in which bad behaviours paid off better than good behaviours. Research indicates that utilitarian moral judgments stem from higher-order cognitive processes than deontological moral judgments do, and that the latter are more highly influenced by emotional reactions than the former are. The evolutionary account of morality presented in this book implies a functional approach to ethics. In conducive conditions there is no necessary inconsistency between optimizing one's ultimate biological welfare and behaving in accordance with the kinds of cardinal moral principles derived by philosophers of ethics.

20

REFRAMING PSYCHOLOGICAL MODELS
OF MORAL DEVELOPMENT

Morality is a puzzle that many psychologists have attempted to solve. Psychological theories of moral development tend to attribute morality to one particular kind of mental mechanism. For example, psychoanalysts attribute it to the superego; cognitive–developmental theorists attribute it to structures of moral reasoning, and social learning theorists to the mental mechanisms that mediate social learning. Such theories offer accounts of how their featured mechanisms originate in childhood, how they change with development, how they give rise to moral decisions, and how they regulate behavior.

There is a tendency for psychologists to assume that the mental mechanisms featured in their preferred accounts of moral development are the only, or the most important, sources of morality, and to criticize the accounts advanced by others. Although I may have fallen into this trap myself, I believe that a more constructive strategy is to acknowledge that morality may stem from many mechanisms, as Darwin implied, and to attempt to organize them in meaningful ways. In this chapter, I review the insights about moral development derived from two of the grand theories in psychology—social learning theory and cognitive-developmental theory—and explain how they can be integrated, refined, and reconceptualized by viewing them from an evolutionary perspective. I argue that evolutionary theory offers a framework equipped to situate these, and other, accounts of morality in the big picture, illuminate relations among them, and supply a basis for resolving their differences.

Social learning theory is not incompatible with evolutionary theory. The mental mechanisms that mediate social learning evolved because they helped animals survive and reproduce. These mechanisms are more domain specific than traditional learning theorists assumed. Viewing social relations within families as strategic social interactions among individuals motivated to behave in ways that increase their inclusive fitness helps account for the data on parenting and peer relations produced by research on social learning.

Although Kohlberg's model explains why children's capacity to engage in sophisticated forms of moral reasoning increases with development, it fails to explain why people often fail to perform at their level of competence. Evolutionary theory accounts for performance in terms of the adaptive goals that different kinds of moral judgments enable people to achieve, and it accounts for stages of moral development in terms of the prominence of adaptive problems that people experience at different times in their lives. An evolutionary approach to morality is equipped to account for the domain specificity of moral judgment, sex differences in moral reasoning, self-serving and nepotistic biases in moral judgment and moral behavior, the effects of social contexts and emotional states, and differences between moral judgments about self and others.

In the opening chapter of this book, I described my attempts to understand how people become moral. Coming full circle, I now want to tell this story in more detail and in the process make and defend a bold claim, namely that the evolutionary account of morality I have presented in this book is equipped to subsume, integrate, and refine the models of moral development advanced by psychologists. It would take another volume to explain where all the minimodels advanced by psychologists fit in the big picture and how they can be improved by viewing them through an evolutionary lens, so I will focus on the models of moral development derived from two grand psychological theories, social learning theory and cognitive-developmental theory.

Let me emphasize at the outset that I do not believe that the psychological approaches to morality that I will review are wrong, even though they may not appeal to many evolutionary psychologists. My claims are that these approaches are limited, because they are equipped to account for only some aspects of moral development, and that their explanatory power can be improved by viewing their insights through an evolutionary lens.

REFRAMING SOCIAL LEARNING MODELS OF MORAL DEVELOPMENT

I alluded to social learning in several chapters of this book. I mentioned that most people from the Western world harbor an implicit social learning model of morality, that Darwin was attentive to the role of habits in the moralization of children and the transmission of culturally relative moral norms, and that Darwin recognized that approval and disapproval (i.e., social reinforcement) play an important role in the evolution of conscience. I discussed the role of cumulative social learning in the expansion of culture and the evolution of moral norms. I argued against nature versus nurture conceptions of the relation between evolved dispositions and learning. In more than one place, I explained why acknowledging that social learning plays an important role in the acquisition of morality is not incompatible with evolutionary theory.

The first step in reconciling social learning accounts of morality with evolutionary accounts is to recognize that the mental mechanisms that mediate social learning are evolved mechanisms. In his book, *The Selfish Gene*, Richard Dawkins (2006) explained why learning mechanisms have evolved in so many species. He began by pointing out that genes are not able to adjust rapidly to changes in the environment, but they are able to "oversee" the construction of brains, and equip them with programs that enable animals to adjust their behavior in response to changing environments.

One way for genes to solve the problem of making predictions in rather unpredictable environments is to build in a capacity for learning. Here the program may take the form of the following instructions to the survival machine [i.e., to the animal]: "Here is a list of things defined as rewarding: sweet taste in the mouth, orgasm, mild temperature, smiling child. And here is a list of nasty things: various sorts of pain, nausea, empty stomach, screaming child. If you should happen to do something that is followed by one of the nasty things, don't do it again, but on the other hand repeat anything that is followed by one of the nice things." The advantage of this sort of programming is that it greatly cuts down the number of detailed rules that have to be built into the original program; and it is also capable of coping with changes in the environment that could not have been predicted in detail. (p. 57)

The same point applies to mental heuristics, imitation, and conformity.

Viewing social learning from the perspective of evolution enables us to integrate and reconceptualize the insights of social learning theorists in ways that increase their explanatory power. To begin with, evolutionary theory encourages us to view social learning in terms of adaptive strategies. Bandura (1989) was attentive to the adaptive value of social learning: "Because people can learn approximately what to do through modeling before they perform any behavior, they are spared the costs and pain of faulty effort. The capacity to learn by observation enables people to expand their knowledge and skills on the basis of information exhibited and authored by others" (p. 47). When game theorists attribute strategic choices to conditional decision rules such as, "if your choice pays off, repeat it; if it does not, choose another alternative," and when they program computers to play strategies such as "tit for tat," "win–stay, lose–change," and "Pavlov," they are invoking principles of learning. Richerson and Boyd (2005) have developed mathematical models outlining the conditions under which social learning pays off better biologically than individual learning does. For example, social learning tends to pay off when environments stay relatively stable, but individual learning tends to pay off when environments change rapidly.

Social learning theorists tend to report findings pertaining to characteristics of models and contexts that facilitate social learning in a piecemeal, descriptive manner. Evolutionary theory enables us to organize and explain these findings in terms of their adaptive functions. For example, the reason that people are disposed to imitate success-ful, competent, powerful, famous, and high-status people is because the forms of con-duct displayed by these people offered more effective ways of surviving, reproducing, and propagating genes in early environments than the forms of conduct displayed by people who do not possess these qualities. The reason that people are more strongly disposed to copy normative behaviors than they are to copy deviant behaviors (in most circumstances) is because it usually pays off to go along with the crowd.

I argued that social learning theory is not equipped to account for the origin of the forms of conduct and cultural norms that people copy. In contrast, evolutionary theory is. I devoted Part II of this book to explaining how prosocial behavioral dispositions originated, and in Part IV I offered an account of how early humans came to believe that these forms of conduct were right and how these beliefs came to constitute universal cultural norms.

Early learning theorists insisted that the mental mechanisms governing learning, or more exactly the mental mechanisms that regulate classical and operant conditioning, are general purpose mechanisms that govern all forms of learning, and that they function in essentially the same way in all animals (and in some plants!). Viewing learning mechanisms as evolved mechanisms leads us to expect them to be designed in different ways in animals that face different types of adaptive problems and to be more domain specific than traditional learning theorists assumed. Over the years, researchers have accrued a great deal of evidence in support of these evolutionary expectations, which has been well summarized by Gaulin and McBurney (2004, pp. 194–195).

Gaulin and McBurney present data demonstrating that "selection has favored a wide array of learning mechanisms . . . In many cases a very precise form of environmental input is required and a very narrow aspect of the behavioral phenotype is modified." These authors explain that although learning mechanisms are species-typical traits that are possessed by all normal members a particular species, the things that these animals learn vary in accordance with their experiences. For example, "individual human children will grow up speaking different languages because they will have extracted different sets of rules depending on the language their parents spoke." Gaulin and McBurney (2004) conclude that "the most useful way to think about learning is not as an alternative to evolved behavior patterns. Learning occurs not because evolution has left some behavior to chance, but because some kinds of behavior lead to higher fitness if they are molded to fit current environmental conditions."

With respect to socialization, evolutionary theory encourages us to view the family contexts in which parents teach children to behave morally as microcosms of larger social groups. Because parents and children need each other to propagate their genes, it is in their genetic interest to help one another and to uphold familial systems of cooperation. However, it is often in each member's interest to favor himself or herself and those with whom he or she shares the largest complement of genes. Conflicts of interest precipitate strategic social interactions in which members of families attempt to induce one another to behave in ways that maximize their biological and genetic benefits (although usually not consciously). The ways in which members of families resolve their conflicts of interest affect the ways in which their conceptions of morality are structured and calibrated.

Evolutionary theory leads us to expect the learning that takes place in the family to be conditional. It offers an explanation for why children behave differently when their parents are absent from how they behave when they are present and why children behave in one way in the presence of their mothers and another way in the presence of their fathers. In addition, evolutionary theory alerts us to the reason that certain events are rewarding and others are punishing. For example, the effectiveness of love withdrawal in disciplining children makes sense from an evolutionary perspective in view of the dependency of children on their parents for survival. Evolutionary theory also helps explain why some kinds of rewards and punishments are notoriously ineffective. As an example, neglected children may find the attention they evoke from their parents more rewarding than the punishments that accompany it.

In attending to strategic social interactions within families, evolutionary theory sensitizes us to the fact that social learning is often a two-way process—an insight embraced by contemporary social learning theorists (Grusec, 2006). Children are agents as well as objects, sending as well as receiving persuasive communications. The reciprocal relations between the evolved learning mechanisms of parents and the evolved learning mechanisms of children become apparent when we contemplate the reason that parents find their infants' cries aversive and their infants' smiles rewarding.

Piaget (1932) recognized that moral argumentation among peers fostered their moral development; however, children also argue with their parents. As irritating as these arguments may be to parents, they may benefit children in significant ways. Researchers have found that socialization practices that involve rational exchanges and discussions between parents and children are especially effective in fostering moral development (Baumrind, 1989). Contemporary accounts of the acquisition of conscience that portray the child "as an agent in moral socialization who actively processes parental moral messages" and engages in "discourse" with his or her parents (Kochanska & Aksan, 2004, p. 303) are consistent with evolutionary accounts that emphasize the role of strategic interactions in the inculcation of morality.

REFRAMING COGNITIVE-DEVELOPMENTAL MODELS OF MORAL DEVELOPMENT

I introduced Kohlberg's cognitive-developmental model of moral development early in this book, referred to it in several chapters, and explained why I once found it appealing but eventually decided to abandon it in favor of an evolutionary approach. I would now like to justify this decision in more detail. Although recounting how I came to believe that evolutionary theory contains greater explanatory potential than cognitive-developmental theory entails telling the beginning of a story after disclosing its ending (explaining what led me to reach many of the main conclusions that I have already presented in this book), I think this exercise is worthwhile, because it explicates ways in which cognitive-developmental approaches to morality can be gainfully reframed within an evolutionary framework.

The strongest support for Kohlberg's model stems from data that Kohlberg and his colleagues collected from a 20-year longitudinal study on a group of male participants who made moral judgments every 3 or 4 years in response to a sample of the hypothetical moral dilemmas from Kohlberg's *Moral Judgment Interview*. On final testing, virtually all the moral judgments made by participants from this study corresponded to the expectations of his model of moral development, up to Stage 5. (Lacking empirical support, Kohlberg cut Stage 6 from his sequence, redefining it as a theoretical possibility.) The boys in the sample began by making structurally simple ("Stage 1" and "Stage 2") moral judgments (outlined in Table 2.2). As they grew older, the form of their moral reasoning became more sophisticated, changing qualitatively in ways that defined, first "Stage 3" moral reasoning, then "Stage 4" moral reasoning, and finally "Stage 5" moral reasoning. Most of their judgments were structurally consistent, defined as conforming to the structure of the stage of moral development they were in or the new stage they were moving into. In addition, Kohlberg and his colleagues presented evidence that people who were in relatively high stages of moral development (that is to say, displayed relatively advanced forms of moral reasoning on Kohlberg's *Moral Judgment Interview*) were more likely than people at lower stages to behave in ways that people commonly consider moral (Colby & Kohlberg, 1987).

As mentioned in the introductory chapter, Kohlberg's model of moral development has a lot to recommend it. It offers a definition of morality that goes beyond conformity to cultural norms. It accounts for the organization of people's ideas about morality and the tendency for children to develop increasingly sophisticated conceptions of morality as they develop. It offers an active and constructive model of the mind that accounts for the role that children and adults play in creating their own moral standards. It offers an explanation for differences between the moral standards that adults preach to children and the moral standards that children espouse. It accounts for people's tendency to be selective in the moral norms they accept and for children's tendency to resist some forms of social influence. And it suggests an account of the origin of moral norms.

However, as Kohlberg's model gained popularity, some of his colleagues began to question some of the key assumptions on which it was founded. Most sensationally, Kohlberg's colleague, Carol Gilligan (1982), argued that Kohlberg's model is biased against women. In particular, she argued that women tend to possess a care-based moral orientation that is (mis)classified as Stage 3 in Kohlberg's hierarchy, whereas men tend to possess a justice-based moral orientation that is classified as Stage 4.

Evaluating Kohlberg's Cognitive-Developmental Model of Moral Development

My main concern about Kohlberg's model of moral development was that most of the data supporting it were derived from people's moral judgments to the hypothetical dilemmas on his test, obtained in academic settings, in response to "why questions." I suspected that people process the information in the hypothetical dilemmas on Kohlberg's test in different ways from how they process the information in other kinds of moral dilemmas. In particular, I suspected that they process it in colder, more rational, impartial, analytic, and academic ways. Because the dilemmas on Kohlberg's test contain complex conflicts between moral norms, the dilemmas challenge people to do their best thinking. The reason that people's moral judgments to these dilemmas are structurally consistent may be because Kohlberg's dilemmas are similar in form and pull for the same forms of logical thought, especially when people respond to them in an academic context. In addition, it seemed to me that the post hoc justifications that people offer for the moral decisions they make in response to the probes following Kohlberg's dilemmas could well be different from their original reasons for making them (Haidt, 2001; Krebs & Denton, 2005). In the extreme, asking people to explicate their principles of ethics may constitute an intellectual exercise that bears no more relation to their practical sense of morality than the musings of philosophers of ethics bear on whether they cheat on their income taxes. (Alternatively, the human mind may naturally synthesize overriding principles from practical experiences, giving rise to ever-improved conceptions of what it means to be moral, as cognitive-developmental psychologists have asserted.)

To explore these possibilities, my colleagues and conducted a set of studies designed to determine whether people make moral judgments about other kinds of moral dilemmas, in other contexts, in the same ways as they do on Kohlberg's test. We found that although participants in our studies tended to make structurally similar (i.e., same stage) moral judgments to hypothetical moral dilemmas similar to those on Kohlberg's test when tested in academic settings, they tended to make different (stage) moral judgments to other kinds of hypothetical moral dilemmas in other settings. For example, participants made significantly lower-stage moral judgments to hypothetical moral dilemmas about whether or not to help others in need (Krebs, Denton et al., 1991), to drive after drinking (Denton & Krebs, 1990), to foster their interests in business transactions (Carpendale & Krebs, 1995), and to support free trade (Carpendale & Krebs, 1995) than they did on Kohlberg's test. Based on these data, we concluded that moral reasoning is not as structurally consistent as Kohlberg asserted, which challenged Kohlberg's claim that people go through stages of moral development that are defined by "structures of the whole."

In further support of this conclusion, when my colleagues and I examined the consistency of moral reasoning across different kinds of moral dilemmas, we found considerable variation in the forms people evoke (see Krebs, 2005, and Krebs & Denton, 2005, for reviews of the research). For example, participants in our research tended to invoke instrumental ("Stage 2") forms of moral reasoning to derive moral judgments about business deals, care-oriented ("Stage 3") forms to derive moral judgments about interpersonal conflicts, and society-upholding ("Stage 4") forms to derive judgments about issues such as free trade. In Chapters 17, I presented evidence that people from a wide array of cultures process moral information in terms of four social schemata that are structurally similar to the structures of moral reasoning that define Kohlberg's first four stages of moral development.

Another notable finding from the studies we conducted was that the social contexts and psychological states in which people made moral judgments affect the form of their judgments. For example, university students made lower-stage moral judgments when they were drinking at bars and parties than they did in academic contexts (Denton & Krebs, 1990); and they made lower-stage moral judgments when they believed they were directing them to someone who they believed would be receptive to low-stage moral judgments than they did when they were directing them to someone who they believed would be receptive to higher-stage judgments (Carpendale & Krebs, 1992). We also found that people's emotional reactions to moral dilemmas affect the kinds of moral judgments they make (Krebs, Vermeulen et al., 1991). Considered as a whole, our findings demonstrated that adults do not usually invoke the highly sophisticated forms of moral reasoning they invoke to resolve the hypothetical dilemmas on Kohlberg's test to solve other kinds of moral problems because, consistent with conclusions reached in previous chapters, other less sophisticated moral decision-making processes enable them to solve these problems in more efficient ways.

When it came down to it, we did not consider people's moral judgments about hypothetical moral dilemmas very important. What we really wanted to know was whether people make moral judgments about real-life dilemmas that have actual consequences to them and to others in the same ways in which they make moral judgments about hypothetical moral dilemmas. To examine this issue, we compared the moral judgments that people made to Kohlberg's dilemmas to the moral judgments that they made to moral dilemmas they were experiencing in their lives, such as dilemmas that involve conflicts between parents and their children (Krebs, Vermeulen et al., 1991), conflicts experienced by couples in close relationships (Krebs et al., 2002), decisions by female juvenile delinquents about whether or not to engage in prostitution (Bartek, Krebs, & Taylor, 1993), and dilemmas that involve resisting temptation, reacting to social pressure, deciding whether to help someone in need, and responding to transgressions (Krebs et al., 2002; Wark & Krebs, 1997).

Based on the findings from these studies, we concluded that people do not usually make real-life moral decisions in the same ways in which they make hypothetical moral decisions. When we stage-typed people's real-life moral judgments, we found that these judgments tended to stem from the structures of moral reasoning that define lower stages than the judgments they made on Kohlberg's test. We found that people hardly ever invoke "Stage 5" or "Stage 6" forms of moral reasoning in their everyday lives, except when they philosophize about morality or engage in arguments about abstract moral issues. Other investigators reported similar findings (see Krebs, Vermeulen et al., 1991, for a review of the research).

When we compared the real-life moral judgments made by women to those made by men, we found, as Gilligan (1982) claimed, that women tend to make more Stage 3 care-based moral judgments than men do, and men tend to make more Stage 4 justice-based moral judgments than women do (Wark & Krebs, 1997). However, we did not conclude that these trends supported Gilligan's claims about sex bias in Kohlberg's model of moral development for two reasons. First, men also made more low-stage (Stage 2) justice-based moral judgments than women did, and more importantly, the reason that women tended to make more Stage 3 care-based moral judgments was because they tended to report more care-based real-life moral conflicts than men did. When we asked men to make moral judgments about the care-based moral conflicts reported by women, they made as many Stage 3 moral judgments as the women did, and when we asked women to make moral judgments to the justice-based moral conflicts reported by men, they made as many Stage 4 moral judgments as the men did. These findings are important because they suggest that the forms of moral reasoning labeled "Stage 3" and "Stage 4" by Kohlberg and other cognitive-developmental psychologists are best viewed as domain-specific forms of moral reasoning designed to solve different kinds of moral problems, and that the questions asked (the types of moral problems that people face) exert a strong effect on the answers given (the ways in which they process information).

The moral judgments that people make to hypothetical dilemmas are third-person moral judgments about others. When people make moral judgments in their everyday lives, they also make second-person judgments about others, and first-person judgments about themselves. We found that the real-life moral judgments that people made about themselves differed in significant ways from the real-life judgments they made about others (Krebs et al., 2002; Krebs & Laird, 1998). Other researchers have reported similar results. For example, following a review of relevant studies, MacDonald (1988) concluded that, "reasoning about oneself, one's relatives, and significant others is done with a different calculus than is reasoning about hypothetical situations" (p. 148).

Our findings also suggested that the relation between moral judgment and moral behavior is more complex than Kohlberg and other cognitive-developmental theorists assume. As postulated by cognitive-developmental theorists, in some contexts, people may invest considerable energy figuring out what they ought to do, then act on their decisions. However, in most real-life contexts, the ways in which people think about moral issues are influenced by the outcomes they seek to achieve. People often act without engaging in moral reasoning, then invoke moral judgments to justify their decisions (Krebs, 2005). Findings from our research and the research of others support MacDonald's (1988) conclusion that "individuals who are adept at moral reasoning (i.e., who perform at the higher stages) are better able to provide reasons which rationalize their self-interested actions in a manner that would justify their behavior to other individuals" (p. 143).

Attempting to Repair a Leaking Ship

Our first reaction to findings that failed to support Kohlberg's model of moral development was to revise his model within a cognitive-developmental framework in ways that rendered it consistent with the data that we and others had obtained. Other cognitive-developmental theorists have invoked this revisionist strategy. We began by replacing Kohlberg's assumption that moral reasoning is organized in one overriding structure of the whole with the assumption that people possess several domain-specific structures of moral reasoning, and we replaced the assumption that new structures of moral reasoning transform and displace earlier-acquired structures with the assumption that structures of moral reasoning develop in an additive-inclusive manner.

We accounted for the data that Kohlberg and his colleagues presented in support of the structural consistency of stages of moral judgment by pointing out that the moral dilemmas on Kohlberg's test involve complex conflicts between different moral norms that challenge people to perform at their level of competence, that different issues are salient to people at different stages in their lives, and that the system that Kohlberg and his colleagues used to stage-type moral judgments overestimated the amount of consistency by disregarding judgments that were inconsistent with the dominant pattern. We accounted for the difference between the kinds of moral judgments made by children and adults by concluding that when children consider the moral dilemmas on Kohlberg's test, they not only interpret them in cognitively less sophisticated ways than adults do, they also attend to different issues from those attended to by adults.

After patching up and repairing Kohlberg's model for several years, we concluded that we would be better off abandoning it in favor of another approach. Others have reached a similar conclusion. For example, following the assertion that "the history of science will record the latter decades of the twentieth century as the apotheosis of the cognitive-developmental approach," Lapsley (2006) acknowledged that, "to speak of an apotheosis that is now past, and of an era in moral psychology that is post-Kohlberg, is to suggest that something has happened to the status of moral stage theory. Indeed, the claim that moral psychology is at an important crossroad is now being voiced with increasing frequency. . . . One senses, given the slight and perfunctory treatment of moral stage theory in contemporary textbooks, and its relative obscurity at professional meetings, that the topic is more a matter of faint historical interest than a source of animated research activity on the cutting edge of developmental science" (pp. 37–38).

Reframing Kohlberg's Model of Moral Development

I believe that it would be a mistake to conclude that Kohlberg's *Moral Judgment Interview* and other similar measures used by cognitive-developmental researchers are not equipped to assess any aspect of moral development. I believe that the evidence supports the conclusion that these tests constitute valid measures of moral reasoning competence, or capacity. Although Colby & Kohlberg (1987) reached a similar conclusion, they did not seem to recognize the threat it constitutes for Kohlberg's model of moral development. Of what significance to morality is people's capacity to make highly sophisticated moral judgments if people rarely invoke this capacity? To account for the kinds of moral judgments and moral behaviors that people emit in their everyday lives, we must identify the factors that affect people's performance and find or create a theory equipped to account for them. As implied by earlier discussions, my colleagues and I came to see that, to answer these questions, we need to attend to the kinds of problems that people use moral judgments to solve and the kinds of goals that people use them to achieve, which led us to adopt a functional approach to morality.

Although evolutionary approaches to morality may seem to have little or nothing in common with cognitive-developmental approaches, the two approaches are similar in several significant ways. Both approaches assume that the mental mechanisms that give rise to moral decisions are designed in different ways from the mental mechanisms that give rise to other kinds of decisions. Both approaches assume that moral decision-making mechanisms are activated by moral problems such as those that involve conflicts of interest, and that they are designed in ways that enable people to solve these problems in effective ways. Both approaches assume that the form or pattern of the judgments and behaviors produced by moral decision-making mechanisms (the output) reflects the ways in which the mechanisms are designed, and that the primary challenge for researchers is to map the design of these mechanisms by deciphering the operating principles, or decision rules, implicit in their output. Finally, both approaches attempt to account for how mental structures and mechanisms originate and change over time.

However, these similarities notwithstanding, evolutionary approaches are based in significantly different assumptions from those made by cognitive-developmental approaches about how mental structures originate, how they develop, what activates them, and the goals they are designed to achieve. Whereas cognitive-developmental theorists assume that structures of moral reasoning develop through the cognitive processes of assimilation and accommodation, and that people use them to deduce the most moral solution to moral problems, evolutionary theorists assume that structures of moral reasoning originated from genetic variations in mental mechanisms selected in ancestral environments, and that people use them to solve the kinds of real-life social problems faced by early humans.

Reconceptualizing Stages of Moral Development

Evolutionary theory accounts for developmental changes in people's minds (and bodies) in significantly different ways from the ways in which cognitive-developmental psychologists account for them. Members of many species undergo qualitative structural transformations as they develop. For example, caterpillars change into butterflies, and human females develop breasts at puberty. Evolutionary theory accounts for such changes in terms of the adaptive problems that animals encounter at different phases in their life cycles. Like other mammals, the problems faced by young children pertain mainly to survival. When children reach sexual maturity, they face problems pertaining to reproduction. As parents, they face problems pertaining to the survival and reproduction of members of their families. As elders, they face problems pertaining to upholding their extended families and groups.

Evolutionary theory leads us to expect people to develop structures of moral reasoning in a sequence determined by the types of social problems their early ancestors faced at different phases in their life cycle. Viewed from this perspective, the reason that young children develop Stage 1 structures that dispose them to believe it is right to obey authority is because obeying authority is an adaptive strategy for relatively small, weak, and vulnerable people, as discussed in Chapter 6. The reason that older children develop Stage 2 structures that dispose them to believe that it is right to engage in concrete forms of reciprocity with their peers is because making deals with one's peers is more adaptive than showing deference to them, as discussed in Chapter 11.

It is worth noting that Piaget was more sensitive than Kohlberg was to the influence of social relations on moral reasoning. Whereas Kohlberg attributed moral development almost exclusively to cognitive development, Piaget (1932) attributed the change from the "heteronomous" moral orientation of young children to the more autonomous and egalitarian moral orientation of older children to an interaction between the growth of cognitive sophistication and the increasing prominence of peer relations. Several eminent contemporary developmental psychologists have concluded that the research evidence supports Piaget's account (Carpendale, 2000; Damon & Hart, 1992; Youniss & Damon, 1992). Viewed from an evolutionary perspective, the reason that older children are disposed to value concepts such as reciprocity is because these concepts enable them to solve the kinds of social problems they experience when interacting with peers.

Continuing through the life span, adolescents enter new social worlds to which they adapt by forming coalitions, long-term friendships, and pair bonds, and in which they are expected to do their part to uphold their groups. Care-oriented, Stage 3 structures of moral reasoning become prominent during this era of the life span because they help adolescents achieve these goals in effective ways. The function of Stage 3 forms of moral reasoning is to induce people to do their part to uphold the social relationships and systems of indirect reciprocity that foster their long-term interests. Striving to cultivate a good social reputation, and believing it is right to help one's friends and to do one's part to uphold one's group, improved early humans' survival and reproductive success (Brown, Lohr, & McClenahan, 1986; Krebs & Van Hesteren, 1994).

Finally, as adolescents grow into adults, they enter social worlds that present the kinds of social problems that guided the selection of structures that produce Stage 4 moral judgments. The function of Stage 4 forms of moral reasoning is to induce people to support the rules, laws, and norms that uphold the social order of their societies. As expressed by Alexander (1987), "I see Kohlberg's Stage 4 as representing a transition from being primarily a rule follower to being also concerned with rule enforcement. This interpretation is consistent with the idea that after having learned and followed the rules one's self, having invested in the system, and having produced and instructed relatives with whose welfare one is ultimately concerned, there is reproductive value in ensuring that one's investment is safe, i.e., that the rules do not change" (p. 134).

With respect to the impartial and reversible forms of moral reasoning that define the pinnacles of Kohlberg's hierarchy of moral judgment (Stages 5 and 6), an evolutionary reconceptualization of Kohlberg's stages of moral development leads to the same conclusion reached by one of Kohlberg's colleagues, Gibbs (2003), namely that these forms of thinking are "meta-cognitive" and rarely used by people in their everyday lives.

When viewed through an evolutionary lens, Kohlberg's contention that new structures of moral reasoning incorporate or integrate older structures within them makes some sense, because in general, new structures evolve from variations in older structures, and because more complex types of social relations are built upon and include less complex types. For example, it is difficult to imagine how Stage 4 systems of indirect reciprocity could have evolved and could have been maintained without support from Stage 1 obedience strategies, Stage 2 instrumental exchange strategies, and Stage 3 impression-management strategies. Reconceptualized in evolutionary terms, the reason that high-stage structures are "better" or more adequate than low-stage structures are is because they prescribe strategies that contain the potential to solve a wider array of social problems and to produce an expanded range of benefits than lower-stage strategies do.

Viewed from an evolutionary perspective, the acquisition of new structures of moral reasoning increases the number of tools available to people, and endows them with an increased capacity for flexibility. From this perspective, it seems misguided to assume that people are "in" stages of moral development—except perhaps young children who have neither the cognitive sophistication nor the incentive to make high-stage moral judgments. It seems more reasonable to assume that people acquire an increasingly broad range of strategies that enable them to adapt to an increasingly broad range of social contexts.

Accounting for the Activation of Structures of Moral Reasoning

I discussed the issue of activation in Chapter 17. In revising Kohlberg's model, we came to see that if normal adults possess a set of domain-specific structures of moral reasoning that they acquire at different stages of their lives, we need to explain what activates one and not another, which entails explaining why people perform, or fail to perform, at their level of competence. Kohlberg and his colleagues did not really offer a solution to this problem other than to assert that such "performance factors" as the low-level moral atmosphere of traditional prisons induce people to make immature moral judgments. In contrast, evolutionary theory suggests a clear explanation for the activation of structures of moral reasoning: Each structure is activated by the kinds of adaptive problems it was designed to solve. Moral decision-making mechanisms are activated and regulated by stimuli that meet the "if" conditions in the decision rules designed by natural selection and calibrated during development. The reason that prisoners make low-stage moral judgments about the dilemmas they experience in prison is because these kinds of judgments help them survive in prison.

Accounting for Multiple Sources of Moral Judgment

Kohlberg and other cognitive-developmental theorists assume that people derive their moral decisions from structures of moral reasoning. However, as discussed in earlier chapters, evolutionary theory leads us to expect people also to derive moral decisions from other mental mechanisms, including those that produce automatic, "hot" reactions; and there is a great deal of evidence to support this expectation. Recognizing that people may derive moral judgments from many sources—some primitive and some sophisticated; some rational and others irrational—induces us to recognize that the set of moral decision-making mechanisms that people possess is much larger and more complex than most cognitive-developmental theorists assume, and this, in turn, increases the challenge of accounting for them.

Reconceptualizing the Functions of Moral Judgment

As discussed, cognitive-developmental accounts of moral development focus on intellectual functions of making moral judgments, such as solving complex moral problems. When people use moral judgments to achieve these kinds of goals, they tend to perform at their level of competence, making the kinds of sophisticated and structurally consistent moral judgments that cognitive-developmental theorists expect them to make. However, consistent with the evolutionary account discussed in earlier chapters, we found that people use moral judgments for other purposes in their everyday lives, such as exerting social influence, praising, blaming, justifying, excusing, winning arguments, and managing impressions (Denton & Krebs, 1990; Krebs et al., 2002; Krebs & Laird, 1998). Even when people make moral judgments about the hypothetical dilemmas on Kohlberg's test, they may be motivated to achieve social goals such as meeting the expectations of interviewers and making a good impression.

When viewed from the perspective of evolutionary theory, the main functions that moral judgments evolved to achieve can be divided into two categories—influencing the behavior of others and guiding one's own behavior. When people make deontic ("should") judgments to others, they are rarely trying to explicate their ideal conceptions of morality; rather, they are trying to induce those to whom they are directing the judgments to behave in the ways they are prescribing. When people support such judgments with reasons such as, "because you will cultivate a good reputation" and "everyone will benefit in the end," they are trying to induce recipients to form cognitive representations of the "if" conditions that activate the behaviors they are attempting to evoke.

In contrast to the third-person judgments that people make on cognitive-developmental tests, and in contrast to the second-person and third-person judgments that they make to influence others in their everyday lives, people make first-person judgments privately to guide their own behavior. (People also may make first person judgments publicly to influence others.) Although there is no reason, in Kohlberg's model, to expect these three kinds of moral judgments to stem from different sources, there is every reason, in evolutionary theory, to expect the mental mechanisms that produce them to be designed in different ways. As discussed in earlier chapters, evolutionary theory leads us to expect moral judgments to be biased in self-serving ways and for the magnitude of such biases to vary across a variety of conditions.

CONCLUSIONS

The acquisition of morality is a complex, many-faceted process. Although the models derived from the major theories in psychology help account for part of the picture, evolutionary theory offers an overriding framework that integrates the insights from these models, ties them together in meaningful ways, resolves their inconsistencies, supplies a basis for expanding and refining them, and increases their explanatory power. It supplies a basis for taking the pieces obtained by psychologists, putting them together in coherent ways, and modifying them, when necessary, to produce better fits with the pieces obtained by others. I focused on social learning and cognitive-developmental theory in this chapter, but I believe that evolutionary theory is equipped to organize and refine all psychological models of morality. Other evolutionary theorists have explained how psychoanalytic models of morality can be profitably reconceptualized in evolutionary terms (Badcock, 1998; Nesse, 2001; Wright, 1994).

Viewing morality from an evolutionary perspective illuminates issues overlooked in psychological approaches. Whereas psychological approaches attempt to account for the origin and development of morality in children, evolutionary approaches explain how the mental mechanisms featured in psychological approaches originated and evolved in the human species. Evolutionary approaches direct us to attend to the order in which the mechanisms that give rise to morality evolved in the brain, and to attend to the interaction between old brain and new brain structures. They guide us to search for the adaptive benefits that these mechanisms helped early humans obtain, which in turn directs us to attend to the adaptive functions of making moral judgments and behaving in moral ways in contemporary environments. Attending to the adaptive functions of making moral judgments and behaving in moral ways induces us to recognize the inherently social nature of morality. Recognizing that the mental mechanisms that give rise to conscience, that guide social learning, and that produce moral reasoning are *evolved* mechanisms leads us to expect them to be designed in certain ways and to be activated by certain stimuli. It directs our attention to the proximate goals that they help people achieve, and it offers a basis for organizing these goals in terms of their ultimate functions.

When viewed from the perspective of evolution, an important reason that children and adults resist the temptation to behave in selfish and aggressive ways is because these forms of conduct evoked fitness-reducing consequences in ancestral environments, just as they do today. The reason that people punish antisocial behaviors is because it was not, and is not, in their interest to permit others to behave in these ways. The reason that people copy the moral behavior of some people and not of other people is because being selective paid off in ancestral environments, just as it does today. The reason that people engage in different forms of moral reasoning when considering different kinds of moral issues is because different structures of moral reasoning enabled early humans to solve different kinds of social problems, just as they do today. The reason that people make different kinds of moral judgments in their everyday lives from those they make when considering hypothetical, philosophical dilemmas is because people adapt the moral judgments they make to the goals they use them to achieve. Although psychological models of morality are equipped to account for some aspects and some functions of morality, the only theoretical perspective that is equipped to integrate these accounts under one overriding framework and supply a basis for refining them in gainful ways is the theory of evolution.

REFERENCES

Adams, J. S. (1965). Inequity in social exchange. In L. Berkowitz (Ed.), *Advances in experimental social psychology* (Vol. 2) (pp. 266–300). New York: Academic Press.

Ainslie, G. (1975). Specious reward: A behavioral theory of impulsiveness and impulse control. *Psychological Bulletin, 82,* 463–496.

Alcock, J. (1998). *Animal behavior: An evolutionary approach* (6th ed.). Sunderland, MA: Sinauer Associates.

Alcock, J. (2001). *The triumph of sociobiology.* Oxford: Oxford University Press.

Alexander, R. D. (1961). Aggressiveness, territoriality, and sexual behavior in field crickets. *Behaviour, 17,* 130–223.

Alexander, R. D. (1985). A biological interpretation of moral systems. *Zygon, 20,* 3–20.

Alexander, R. D. (1987). *The biology of moral systems.* New York: Aldine de Gruyter.

Alexander, R. D. (1990). How did humans evolve? Reflections on the uniquely unique species. *Museum of Zoology, Special Publication No. 1.* Ann Arbor: University of Michigan Press.

Alvard, M. S., & Nolin, D. A. (2002). Rousseau's whale hunt: Coordination among big-game hunters. *Current Anthropology, 43,* 533–559.

Anderson, J. (1974). Bystander intervention in an assault. Paper presented at the meeting of the Southeastern Psychological Association. Hollywood, FL, May 3.

Armon, C. (1995). Moral judgment and self-reported moral events in adulthood. *Journal of Adult Development, 1,* 49–62.

Aronfreed, J. (1968). *Conduct and conscience.* New York: Academic Press.

Atran, S. (2004). *In gods we trust.* Oxford: Oxford University Press.

Austin, W. (1980). Friendship and fairness: Effects of type of relationship and task performance on choice of distribution rules. *Personality and Social Psychology Bulletin, 6,* 402–408.

Axelrod, R. (1988). The further evolution of cooperation. *Science, 242,* 1385–1389.

Axelrod, R., & Hamilton, W. D. (1981). The evolution of cooperation. *Science, 211,* 1390–1396.

Badcock, C. (1998). PsychoDarwinism: The new synthesis of Darwin and Freud. In C. Crawford & D. L. Krebs (Eds.), *Handbook of evolutionary psychology* (pp. 431–456). Mahwah, NJ: Lawrence Erlbaum Associates.

Bandura, A. (1989). Social cognitive theory. *Annals of Child Development, 6,* 1–60.

Bandura, A. (1991). Social cognitive theory of moral thought and action. In W. M. Kurtines & J. L. Gewirtz (Eds.), *Handbook of moral behavior and development* (Vol. 1) (pp. 54–104). Hillsdale, NJ: Lawrence Erlbaum Associates.

Barclay, P. (2004). Trustworthiness and competitive altruism can also solve the "tragedy of the commons." *Evolution and Human Behavior, 25,* 209–220.

Bargh, M.A. (1996). Automaticity in social psychology. In E. T. Higgins & A. W. Kruglanski (Eds.), *Social psychology: Handbook of basic principles* (Vol. 1) (pp. 1–40). New York: Guilford Press.

Barinaga, M. (1996). Social status sculpts activity of crayfish neurons. *Science, 271,* 290–291.

Barrett, H. C. (2007). Modules in the flesh. In S. W. Gangestad & J. A. Simpson (Eds.), *The evolution of mind: Fundamental questions and controversies* (pp. 161–168). New York: Guilford Press.

Barrett, L., Dunbar, R., & Lycett, J. (2002). *Human evolutionary psychology*. Princeton, NJ: Princeton University Press.

Bartek, S., Krebs, D. L., & Taylor, M. (1993). Coping, defending, and the relations between moral judgment and moral behavior in prostitutes and other female juvenile delinquents. *Journal of Abnormal Psychology, 102*, 65–73.

Batson, C. D. (1991). *The altruism question: Toward a social-psychological answer*. Hillsdale, NJ: Lawrence Erlbaum Associates.

Batson, C. D. (1998). Altruism and prosocial behavior. In D. T. Gilbert, S. T. Fiske, & G. Lindzey (Eds.), *The handbook of social psychology* (4th ed.) (pp. 282–315). Boston: McGraw-Hill.

Batson, C. D. (2000). Unto others: A service . . . and a disservice. *Journal of Consciousness Studies, 7*, 207–210.

Batson, C. D., Batson, J. G., Griffitt, C. A., Barrientos, S., Brandt, R. J., Sprengelmeyer, P., & Bayly, M. J. (1989). Negative-state relief and the empathy-altruism hypothesis. *Journal of Personality and Social Psychology, 56*, 922–933.

Baumeister, R. F., Stillwell, A. M., & Heatherton, T. F. (1994). Guilt: An interpersonal approach. *Psychological Bulletin, 115*, 243–267.

Baumrind, D. (1989). Rearing competent children. In W. Damon (Ed.), *Child development today and tomorrow* (pp. 349–378). San Francisco: Jossey-Bass.

Bercovitch, F. B. (1988). Coalitions, cooperation and reproductive tactics among adult male baboons. *Animal Behavior, 36*, 1198–1209.

Berkowitz, L. (1972). Social norms, feelings, and other factors affecting helping behavior and altruism. In L. Berkowitz (Ed.) *Advances in experimental social psychology* (Vol. 6) (pp. 63–106). New York: Academic Press.

Bjorklund D. F., & Pellegrini, A. D. (2002). *The origins of human nature: Evolutionary developmental psychology*. Washington DC: American Psychological Association.

Bloom, P. (2004). *Descartes' baby: How the science of child development explains what makes us human*. New York: Basic Books.

Boehm, C. (1999). *Hierarchy in the forest: The evolution of egalitarian behavior*. Cambridge, MA: Harvard University Press.

Boehm, C. (2000). Conflict and the evolution of social control. *Journal of Consciousness Studies, 7*, 79–101.

Boehm, C. (2008). Purposive social selection and the evolution of human altruism. *Cross-cultural Research, 24*, 319–352.

Bornstein, G., & Ben-Yossef, M. (1994). Cooperation in intergroup and single-group social dilemmas. *Journal of Experimental Social Psychology, 30*, 52–67.

Boyd, R., & Richerson, P. J. (1992). Punishment allows the evolution of cooperation (or anything else) in sizable groups. *Ethology and Sociobiology, 13*, 171–195.

Boyer, P. (2001). *Religion explained: The human instincts that fashion Gods, spirits, and ancestors*. London: William Heinemann

Brosnan, S. F., & de Waal, F. B. M. (2003). Monkeys reject unequal pay. *Nature, 425*, 297–299.

Brown. B. B., Lohr, M. J., & McClenahan, E. L. (1986). Early adolescents' perceptions of peer pressure. *Journal of Early Adolescence, 6*, 139–154.

Brown, D. E. (1991). *Human universals*. New York: McGraw-Hill.

Brown, R. (1984). *Social psychology: A second edition*. New York: Free Press.

Brown, S. L., & Brown, M. (2006). Selective investment theory: Recasting the functional significance of close relationships. *Psychological Inquiry, 17,* 30–59.

Burnham, T., & Phelan, J. (2000). *Mean genes.* New York: Perseus Publishing.

Burnstein, E. (2005). Altruism and genetic relatedness. In D. Buss (Ed.), *The handbook of evolutionary psychology* (pp. 528–551). Hoboken, NJ: John Wiley & Sons.

Burnstein, E., Crandall, C., & Kitayama, S. (1994). Some neo-Darwinian decision rules for altruism: Weighing cues for inclusive fitness as a function of the biological importance of the decision. *Journal of Personality and Social Psychology, 67,* 773–789.

Burton, R. V., & Kunce, L. (1995). Behavioral models of moral development: A brief history and integration. In W. M. Kurtines & J. L. Gewirtz (Eds.), *Moral development: An introduction* (pp. 141–172). Boston: Allyn and Bacon.

Buss, D. (1999). *Evolutionary psychology: The new science of the mind.* Boston: Allyn and Bacon.

Buss. D. (2004). *Evolutionary psychology: The new science of the mind* (2nd ed.). Boston: Allyn & Bacon.

Buss, D. (Ed.) (2005). *The handbook of evolutionary psychology.* New York: John Wiley & Sons.

Buss, D. (2008) *Evolutionary psychology: The new science of the mind* (3rd ed). Boston: Pearson Education.

Byrne, R. W., & Whiten, A. (Eds.). (1988). *Machiavellian intelligence: Social experience and the evolution of intellect in monkeys, apes, and humans.* Oxford: Oxford University Press.

Calvin, J. (1995). *Creation of the sacred.* Cambridge, MA: Harvard University Press. (Original work published 1559).

Campbell, D. (1978). On the genetics of altruism and the counterhedonic components of human nature. In L. Wispe (Ed.). *Altruism, sympathy, and helping* (pp. 39–58). New York: Academic Press.

Caporael, L., Dawes, R. M., Orbell, J. M., & van de Kragt, A. J. C. (1989). Selfishness examined: Cooperation in the absence of egoistic incentives. *Behavioral and Brain Sciences, 12,* 683–739.

Carpendale, J. I. M. (2000). Kohlberg and Piaget on stages and moral reasoning. *Developmental Review, 20,* 181–205.

Carpendale, J., & Krebs, D. L. (1992). Situational variation in moral judgment: In a stage or on a stage? *Journal of Youth and Adolescence, 21,* 203–224.

Carpendale, J., & Krebs, D. L. (1995). Variations in moral judgment as a function of type of dilemma and moral choice. *Journal of Personality, 63,* 289–313.

Cashdan, E. (1983). Territoriality among human foragers: Ecological models and an application to four Bushman groups. *Current Anthropology, 24,* 47–66.

Chadwick-Jones, J. K. (1976). *Social exchange theory: Its structure and influence in social psychology.* London: Academic Press.

Chagnon, N. A. (1988). Life histories, blood revenge, and warfare in a tribal population. *Science, 239,* 985–992.

Chaiken, S. (1987). The heuristic model of persuasion. In M.P. Zanna, J.M. Olson, & C.P. Herman (Eds.), *Social influence: The Ontario Symposium* (pp. 3–39). Hillsdale, NJ: Lawrence Erlbaum Associates.

Chaiken, S., Giner-Sorolla, R., & Chen, S. (1996). Beyond accuracy: Defense and impression motives in heuristic and systematic information processing. In P. M. Gollwitzer & J. A. Bargh (Eds.), *The psychology of action: Linking cognition and motivation to behavior* (pp. 553–578). New York: Guilford Press.

Chartrand, T. L., & Bargh, J. A. (1999). The chameleon effect: The perception–behavior link and social interaction. *Journal of Personality and Social Psychology, 76*, 893–910.

Chekroun, P., & Brauer, M. (2002). The bystander effect and social control behavior: The effect of the presence of others on people's reaction to norm violations. *European Journal of Social Psychology, 32*, 853–866.

Cheney, D. L., & Seyfarth, R. M. (1990). *How monkeys see the world: Inside the mind of another species*. Chicago: University of Chicago Press.

Cialdini, R. B., Borden, R.J., Thorne, A., Walker, M. R., Freeman, S., & Sloan, L. R. (1976). Three (football) field studies. *Journal of Personality and Social Psychology, 34*, 366–375.

Cialdini, R. B., Schaller, M., Houlihan, D., Arps, J., Fultz, J., & Beaman, A. L. (1987). Empathy-based helping: Is it selflessly or selfishly motivated? *Journal of Personality and Social Psychology, 52*, 749–758.

Clark, M. S., & Mills, J. (1993). The difference between communal and exchange relationships: What it is and is not. *Personality and Social Psychology Bulletin, 19*, 684–691.

Clark, M. S., Mills, J., & Powell, M. C. (1986). Keeping track of needs in communal and exchange relationships. *Journal of Personality and Social Psychology, 51*, 333–338.

Clark, R. D. III, & Word, L. E. (1974). Where is the apathetic bystander? Situational characteristics of the emergency. *Journal of Personality and Social Psychology, 29*, 279–287.

Colby, A., & Damon, W. (1992). *Some do care*. New York: Free Press.

Colby, A., & Kohlberg, L. (Eds.) (1987). *The measurement of moral judgment* (Vols. 1–2). Cambridge: Cambridge University Press.

Conner, R. C., Smolker, R. A., & Richards, A. F. (1992). Dolphin alliances and coalitions. In A. H. Harcourt & F. B. M. de Waal (Eds.), *Coalitions and alliances in humans and other animals* (pp. 415–443). Oxford: Oxford University Press.

Cosmides, L. (1989). The logic of social exchange: Has natural selection shaped how humans reason? Studies with the Wason selection task. *Cognition, 31*, 187–276.

Cosmides, L., & Tooby, J. (2005). Neurocognitive adaptations designed for social exchange. In D. Buss (Ed.), *The handbook of evolutionary psychology* (pp. 584–627). Hoboken, NJ: John Wiley & Sons.

Crawford, C. B., & Anderson, J. L. (1989). Sociobiology: An environmentalist discipline? *American Psychologist, 44*, 1449–1459.

Cummins, D. D. (1998). Social norms and other minds: The evolutionary roots of higher cognition. In D. D. Cummins & C. A. Allen (Eds.), *The evolution of mind* (pp. 30–50). New York: Oxford University Press.

Cummins, D. (2005). Dominance, status, and social hierarchies. In D. Buss (Ed.), *The handbook of evolutionary psychology* (pp. 676–697). Hoboken, NJ: John Wiley & Sons.

Daly, M., & Wilson, M. (1983). *Sex, evolution, and behavior*. Boston: Willard Grant Press.

Daly, M., & Wilson, M. (1988). *Homicide*. New York: Aldine de Gruyter.

Damasio, A. R. (1994). *Decartes' error: Emotion, reason, and the human brain*. New York: Grosset/Putnam.

Damon, W. (1977). *The social world of the child*. San Francisco: Jossey-Bass.

Damon, W., & Hart, D. (1992). Self understanding and its role in social and moral development. In M. H. Bornstein & E. M. Lamb (Eds.), *Developmental psychology: An advanced textbook* (2nd ed.) (pp. 421–465). Hillsdale, NJ: Lawrence Erlbaum Associates.

Darwin, C. (1874). *The descent of man and selection in relation to sex*. New York: Rand, McNally & Company.

Dawes, R., van de Kragt, A. J. C., & Orbell, J. M. (1988). Not me or thee but we: The importance of group identity in eliciting cooperation in dilemma situations: Experimental manipulations. *Acta Psychologica, 68,* 83–97.

Dawkins, R. (1989). *The selfish gene* (2nd ed.). Oxford: Oxford University Press.

DeBruine, L. M. (2002). Facial resemblance enhances trust. *Proceedings of the Royal Society of London Series B. Biological Sciences, 269,* 1307–1312.

Decety, J. (2005). Perspective taking as the royal avenue to empathy. In B. F. Malle & S. D. Hodges (Eds.), *Other minds: How humans bridge the divide between self and others* (pp. 143–157). New York: Guilford Press.

Denton, K., & Krebs, D. L. (1990). From the scene to the crime: The effect of alcohol and social context on moral judgment. *Journal of Personality and Social Psychology, 59,* 242–248.

Denton, K., & Zarbatany, L. (1996). Age differences in support processes in conversations between friends. *Child Development, 67,* 1360–1137.

de Waal, F. B. M. (1982). *Chimpanzee politics.* London: Jonathan Cape.

de Waal, F. B. M. (1991). The chimpanzee's sense of social regularity and its relation to the human sense of justice. *American Behavioral Scientist, 34,* 335–349.

de Waal, F. B. M. (1996). *Good natured: The origins of right and wrong in humans and other animals.* Cambridge, MA: Harvard University Press.

de Waal, F. B. M. (2006). *Primates and philosophers: How morality evolved.* Princeton, NJ: Princeton University Press.

de Waal, F. B. M. (2008). Putting the altruism back in altruism. *Annual Review of Psychology, 59,* 279–300.

de Waal, F. B. M., & Brosnan, S. F. (2006). Simple and complex reciprocity in animals. In P. M. Kappeler & C. P. van Schaik (Eds.), *Cooperation in primates and humans* (pp. 85–105). New York: Springer-Verlag.

de Waal, F. B. M., & Luttrell, L. M. (1988). Mechanisms of social reciprocity in three primate species: Symmetrical relationship characteristics or cognition? *Ethology and Sociobiology, 9,* 101–118.

Dovidio, J. F., Allen, J. L., & Schroeder, D. A. (1990). The specificity of empathy-induced helping: Evidence for altruistic motivation. *Journal of Personality and Social Psychology, 59,* 249–260.

Dugatkin, L. A. (1997). *Cooperation among animals: An evolutionary perspective.* New York: Oxford University Press.

Dugatkin, L. A., & Reeve, H. K. (1994). Behavioral ecology and levels of selection: Dissolving the group selection controversy. *Advances in the Study of Behavior, 23,* 101–133.

Dunbar, R. I. M. (1966). *Grooming, gossip, and the evolution of language.* London: Faber and Faber.

Dunbar, R. I. M. (1996). Determinants of group size in primates: A general model. In G. Runciman, J. Maynard Smith, & R. I. M. Dunbar (Eds.), *Evolution of social behavior patterns in primates and man* (pp. 33–58). Oxford: Oxford University Press.

Dunbar, R. I. M. (1998). The social brain hypothesis. *Evolutionary Anthropology, 6,* 187–190.

Dunbar, R. (2007). Evolution of the social brain. In S. W. Gangesad & J. A. Simpson (Eds.), *The evolution of mind: Fundamental questions and controversies* (pp. 280–286). New York: Guilford Press,

Duntley, J. D. (2005). Adaptations to dangers from humans. In D. Buss (Ed.), *The handbook of evolutionary psychology* (pp. 224–254). Hoboken, NJ: John Wiley & Sons.

Durham, W. H. (1991). *Coevolution: Genes, culture and human diversity.* Stanford, CA: Stanford University Press.

Eisenberger, N. I., Lieberman, M. D., & Williams, K. D. (2003). Does rejection hurt? An fMRI study of social exclusion. *Science, 302,* 290–292.

Elkind, D., & Weiner, I. B. (1978). *Development of the child.* New York: John Wiley & Sons.

Ellis, B. J. (1998). The partner-specific investment inventory: An evolutionary approach to individual differences in investment. *Journal of Personality, 66,* 383–442.

Elster, J. (2000). *Ulysses unbound.* London: Cambridge University Press.

Essock-Vitale, S., & McGuire, M. (1985). Women's lives viewed from an evolutionary perspective II: Patterns of helping. *Ethology and Sociobiology, 6,* 155–173.

Fehr, E., & Fischbacker, U. (2004). Third-party punishment and social norms. *Evolution and Human Behavior, 25,* 63–87.

Fehr, E., & Gächter, S. (2003). Reply. *Nature, 421,* 912.

Festinger, L. (1964). *Conflict, decision, and dissonance.* Stanford, CA: Stanford University Press.

Finlay, B. L. (2007). *E pluribus unum*: Too many unique human capacities and too many theories. In S. W. Gangesad & J. A. Simpson (Eds.), *The evolution of mind: Fundamental questions and controversies* (pp. 294–301). New York: Guilford Press

Fischer, P., Greitemeyer, T., Pollozek, F., & Frey, D. (2006). The unresponsive bystander: Are bystanders more responsive in dangerous emergencies? *European Journal of Social Psychology, 36,* 267–278.

Fischer, R. A. (1930). *The genetical theory of natural selection.* Oxford: Clarendon Press.

Fisher, H. (2004). *Why we love: The nature and chemistry of romantic love.* New York: Henry Holt.

Fiske, A. P. (1992). Four elementary forms of sociality: Framework for a unified theory of social relations. *Psychological Review, 99,* 689–723.

Flack, J. C., & de Waal, F. B. M. (2000). "Any animal whatever": Darwinian building blocks of morality in monkeys and apes. *Journal of Consciousness Studies, 7,* 1–29.

Flack, J. C., de Waal, F. B. M., & Krakauer, D. C. (2005). Social structure robustness and policing cost in a cognitively sophisticated species. *American Naturalist, 165,* 126–139.

Flinn, M. V., & Alexander, R. D. (1982). Culture theory: The developing synthesis from biology. *Human Ecology, 10,* 383–400.

Flinn, M. V. & Coe, K. (2007). The linked red queens of human cognition, coalitions, and culture. In S. W. Gangesad & J. A. Simpson (Eds.), *The evolution of mind: Fundamental questions and controversies* (pp. 339–347). New York: Guilford Press.

Flinn, M. V., & Low, B. S. (1986). Resource distribution, social competition, and mating patterns in human societies. In D. I. Rubenstein & W. Wrangham (Eds.), *Ecological aspects of social evolution: Birds and mammals* (pp. 217–243). Princeton, NJ: Princeton University Press.

Flynn, F. J. (2003). How much should I give and how often? The effects of generosity and frequency of favor exchange on social status and productivity. *Academy of Management Journal, 46,* 539–553.

Frank, R. H. (1988). *Passions within reason: The strategic role of the emotions.* New York: W. W. Norton.

Frank, R. H. (2001). Cooperation through emotional commitment. In R. Nesse (Ed.), *Evolution and the capacity for commitment* (pp. 57–76). New York: Russell Sage Foundation.

Frankena, W. K. (1973). *Ethics.* Englewood Cliffs, NJ: Prentice-Hall.

Frankena, W. K. (1980). *Thinking about morality.* Ann Arbor: University of Michigan Press.

Freud, A. (1963). The infantile instinct life. In H. Herma and G. M. Karth (Eds.), *A handbook of psychoanalysis.* New York: World Publishing Company.

Freud, S. (1925). *Collected papers*. London: Hogarth Press.

Gächter, S., & Herrmann, B. (2006). Human cooperation from an economic perspective. In P. M. Kappeler & C. P. van Schaik (Eds.), *Cooperation in primates and humans* (pp. 275–302). New York: Springer-Verlag.

Gangestad, S. W., &. Simpson, J. A. (Eds.) (2007). *The evolution of mind: Fundamental questions and controversies*. New York: Guilford Press.

Gardner, P. (1991). Foragers' pursuit of individual autonomy. *Current Anthropology, 32,* 543–558.

Gaulin, S. J. C., & McBurney, D. H. (2004). *Evolutionary psychology* (2nd ed.). Englewood Cliffs, NJ: Pearson Prentice Hall.

Geary, D. C. (2000). Evolution and proximate expression of human paternal investment. *Psychological Bulletin. 126,* 55–77.

Gelfand, D. M., Hartmann, D. P., Walder, P., & Page, B. (1973). Who reports shoplifters? A field-experimental study. *Journal of Personality and Social Psychology, 23,* 276–285.

Ghiselin, M. T. (1974). *The economy of nature and the evolution of sex*. Berkeley, CA: University of California Press.

Gibbs, J. C. (2003). *Moral development and reality: Beyond the theories of Kohlberg and Hoffman*. Thousand Oaks, CA: Sage.

Gibbs, J. C. (2006). Should Kohlberg's cognitive developmental approach to morality be replaced with a more pragmatic approach? Comment on Krebs and Denton (2005). *Psychological Review, 113,* 666–671.

Gigerenzer, G. (2000). *Adaptive thinking: Rationality in the real world*. New York: Oxford University Press.

Gilligan, C. (1982). *In a different voice: Psychological theory and women's development*. Cambridge, MA: Harvard University Press.

Gilovich, T., Keltner, D., & Nisbett, R. E. (2006). *Social psychology*. New York: W. W. Norton.

Gintis, H. (2000). *Game theory evolving: A problem-centered introduction to modeling strategic interaction*. Princeton, NJ: Princeton University Press.

Gintis, H. (2007). A framework for the unification of the behavioral sciences. *Behavioral and Brain Sciences, 30,* 1–16.

Gintis, H., Bowles, S., Boyd, R., & Fehr, E. (2003). Explaining altruistic behavior in humans. *Evolution and Human Behavior, 24,* 153–172.

Gintis, H. Bowles, S., Boyd, R. & Fehr, E. (2008). Gene-culture coevolution and the emergence of altruistic behavior in humans. In C. Crawford & D. L. Krebs (Eds.), *Foundations of evolutionary psychology* (pp. 313–329). New York: Taylor & Francis.

Goffman, E. (1959). *The presentation of self in everyday life*. New York: Anchor Books.

Gould, S. J., (1978). Sociobiology: The art of storytelling. *New Scientist, 80,* 530–533.

Gouldner, A. W. (1960). The norm of reciprocity: A preliminary statement. *American Sociological Review, 25,* 161–178.

Graziano, W. G., Jensen-Campbell, L. A., Todd, M., & Finch, J. F. (1997). Interpersonal attraction from an evolutionary perspective: Women's reactions to dominant and prosocial men. In J. A. Simpson & D. T. Kenrick (Eds.), *Evolutionary social psychology* (pp. 141–167). Hillsdale, NJ: Lawrence Erlbaum Associates.

Greenberg, J. (1980). A theory of indebtedness. In K. Gergen, M. S. Greenberg, & R. H. Willis (Eds.), *Social exchange: Advances in theory and research*. New York: Plenum Press.

Greenberg, J., & Cohen, R. L. (1982). *Equity and justice in social behavior*. New York: Academic Press.

Greene, J. (2008). The secret joke of Kant's soul. In W. Sinnott-Armstrong (Ed.), *Moral psychology* (Vol. 3): *The neuroscience of morality: Emotion, brain disorders, and development* (pp. 35–80). Cambridge MA: MIT Press.

Grueneich, R. (1982). Issues in the developmental study of how children use intention and consequence information to make moral evaluations. *Child Development, 1,* 29–43.

Grusec, J. (2006). The development of moral behavior and conscience from a socialization perspective. In M. Killen & J. Smetana (Eds.), *Handbook of moral development* (pp. 243–266). Mahwah, NJ: Lawrence Erlbaum Associates.

Haan, N., Aerts, E., & Cooper, B. (1985). *On moral grounds.* New York: New York University Press.

Habermas, J. (1984). Interpretive social science vs. hermeneutics. In N. Haan, R. B. Bellah, P. Rabinow, & W. Sullivan (Eds.), *Social science as moral inquiry.* New York: Columbia Univeristy Press.

Habermas, J. (1993). *Justification and application.* Cambridge, MA: MIT Press.

Hagen, E. H., & Symons, D. (2007). Natural psychology: The environment of evolutionary adaptedness and the structure of cognition. In S. W. Gangestad & J. A. Simpson (Eds.), *The evolution of the mind: Fundamental questions and controversies* (pp. 38–44). New York: Guilford Press.

Haidt, J. (2001). The emotional dog and its rational tail: A social intuitionist approach to moral judgment. *Psychological Review, 108,* 814–834.

Haidt, J. (2007). Moral psychology and the misunderstanding of religion. Edge Foundation. www.edge.org/3rd_culture/haidt07/haidt07_index.html.

Haidt, J., & Joseph, C. (2004). Intuitive ethics: How innately prepared intuitions generate culturally variable virtues. *Daedalus, (Fall),* 55–66.

Hamilton, W. D. (1964). The evolution of social behavior. *Journal of Theoretical Biology, 7,* 1–52.

Harari, H., Harari, O., & White, R. V. (1985). The reaction to rape by American male bystanders. *Journal of Social Psychology, 125,* 653–658.

Harms, W. (2000). The evolution of cooperation in hostile environments. In L. D. Katz (Ed.), *Evolutionary origins of morality* (pp. 308–312). Exeter, UK: Short Run Press.

Hart, B. L. & Hart, L. A. (1992). Reciprocal allogrooming in impala *Aepyceros melampus. Animal Behavior, 44,* 1073–1083.

Hartshorne, H., & May, M. A. (1928). *Studies in the nature of character.* New York: Macmillan.

Haslam, N. (1997). Four grammars for primate social relations. In J. A. Simpson & D. T. Kenrick (Eds.), *Evolutionary social psychology* (pp. 297–316). Mahwah, NJ: Lawrence Erlbaum Associates.

Hauser, M. D. (2006). *Moral minds: How nature designed our universal sense of right and wrong.* New York: HarperCollins Publishers.

Hauser, M. D., Chen, M. K., Chen, F., & Chuang, E. (2003). Give unto others: Genetically unrelated cotton-top tamarin monkeys preferentially give food to those who altruistically give food back. *Proceedings of the Royal Society, 270,* 2363–2370.

Hawkes, K. (1983). Kin selection and culture. *American Ethnologist, 10,* 346–363.

Hawkes, K., Bliege, K., & Bird, R. (2002). Showing off, handicap signaling, and the evolution of men's work. *Evolutionary Anthropology, 11,* 58–67.

Heinsohn, R., & Packer, C. (1995). Complex cooperative strategies in group-territorial African lions. *Science, 269,* 1260–1262.

Helwig, C. (2006). Rights, civil liberties, and democracy across cultures. In M. Killen & J. Smetana (Eds.), *Handbook of moral development* (pp. 185–210). Hillsdale, NJ: Lawrence Erlbaum Associates.

Henrich, J., Boyd, R., Bowles, S., Camerer, C., Fehr, E., Gintis, H., & McElreath, R. (2001). In search of homo economicus: Behavioral experiments in 15 small-scale societies. *American Economic Review, 91,* 73–78.

Henrich, J., Ensminger, J., McElreath, R., Barr, A., Barrett, C., Bolyanatz, A., ... Ziker, J. (2010). Markets, religion, community size, and the evolution of fairness and punishment. *Science, 19,* 1480–1484.

Higgins, E. T. (1987). Self-discrepancy theory: A theory relating self and affect. *Psychological Review, 94,* 319–340.

Hill, K. (2002). Altruistic cooperation during foraging by the Ache, and the evolved human predisposition to cooperate. *Human Nature, 13,* 105–128.

Hoffman, M. (2000). *Empathy and moral development: Implications for caring and justice.* Cambridge: Cambridge University Press.

Høgh-Olesen, H. (Ed.) (2010). *Human morality and society: Evolutionary & comparative perspectives.* Houndmills, UK: Palgrave Macmillan.

Huston, T. L., Geis, G., & Wright, R. (1976). The angry Samaritans. *Psychology Today, 85,* 61–64.

Huxley, T. (1893). *Evolution and ethics. The second Romanes Lecture.* London: Macmillan.

Isen, A. M., & Levin, P. F. (1972). Effect of feeling good on helping: Cookies and kindness. *Journal of Personality and Social Psychology, 21,* 384–388.

Janicki, M. (2004). Beyond sociobiology: A kinder and gentler evolutionary view of human nature. In C. Crawford & C. Salmon (Eds.), *Evolutionary psychology: Public policy and personal decisions* (pp. 51–72). Mahwah, NJ: Lawrence Erlbaum Associates.

Janicki, M. G., & Krebs, D. L. (1997). Evolutionary approaches to culture. In C. Crawford & D. L. Krebs (Eds.), *Handbook of evolutionary psychology: Ideas, issues, and applications* (pp. 163–208). Hillsdale, NJ: Lawrence Erlbaum Associates.

Jankowiak, W., & Diderich, M. (2000). Sibling solidarity in a polygamous community in the USA: Unpacking inclusive fitness. *Evolution and Human Behavior, 21,* 125–139.

Johnson, D. D. P., Stopka, P., & Knights, S. (2003). The puzzle of human cooperation. *Nature, 421,* 911–912.

Johnson, D. D. P., Price, M. E., & Takezawa, M. (2008). Renaissance of the individual: Reciprocity, positive assortment, and the puzzle of human cooperation. In C. Crawford & D. L. Krebs (Eds.), *Foundations of evolutionary psychology* (pp. 331–352). New York: Taylor & Francis.

Kagan, J., & Lamb, S. (1987). *The emergence of morality in young children.* Chicago: University of Chicago Press.

Kaplan, H. S., Gurven, M., & Lancaster, J. B. (2007). Brain evolution and the human adaptive complex: An ecological and social theory. In S. W. Gangestad & J. A. Simpson (Eds.), *The evolution of mind: Fundamental questions and controversies* (pp. 269–279). New York: Guilford Press.

Kaplan, H. S., & Hill, K. (1985). Food sharing among Ache foragers: Tests of explanatory hypotheses. *Current Anthropology, 26,* 233–245.

Kappeler, P. M., & van Schaik, C. P. (2006). *Cooperation in primates and humans: Mechanisms and evolution.* Berlin: Springer-Verlag.

Kenrick, D. T., Li, N. P., & Butner, J. (2006). Dynamical evolutionary psychology: How social norms emerge from individual decisions rules. In P. A. M. van Lange & A. Kruglanski (Eds.), *Bridging social psychology: The benefits of transdisciplinary approaches* (pp. 285–292). Hillsdale, NJ: Lawrence Erlbaum Associates.

Knauft, B. M. (1987). Reconstructing violence in simple human societies: Homicide among the Gebusi of New Guinea. *Current Anthropology, 28,* 457–500.

Kochanska, G., & Aksan, N. (2004). Conscience in childhood: Past, present, and future. *Merrill-Palmer Quarterly, 50*, 299–310.

Kohlberg, L. (1976). Moral stages and moralization: The cognitive-developmental approach. In T. Lickona (Ed.), *Moral development and behavior: Theory, research, and social issues* (pp. 31–53). New York: Holt, Rinehart & Winston.

Kohlberg, L. (1984). *Essays in moral development: The psychology of moral development* (Vol. 2). New York: Harper & Row.

Kohlberg, L., & Candee, D. (1984). The relationship of moral judgment to moral action. In L. Kohlberg (Ed.), *Essays in moral development* (Vol. 2). *The psychology of moral development* (pp. 498–581). New York: Harper & Row.

Korchmaros, J. D., & Kenny, D. A. (2001). Emotional closeness as a mediator of the effect of genetic relatedness on altruism. *Psychological Science, 12*, 262–265.

Krebs, D. L. (1970). Altruism: An examination of the concept and a review of the literature. *Psychological Bulletin, 73*, 258–303.

Krebs, D. L. (1979). Piaget's theory of moral development: A reconsideration. *Human Nature, 2*, 93–95.

Krebs, D. L. (2003). Fictions and facts about evolutionary approaches to human behavior: Comment on Lickliter and Honeycutt (2003). *Psychological Bulletin, 129*, 1–6.

Krebs, D. L. (2005). An evolutionary reconceptualization of Kohlberg's model of moral development. In R. Burgess & K. MacDonald (Eds.), *Evolutionary perspectives on human development* (pp. 243–274). Thousand Oaks, CA: Sage Publications.

Krebs, D. L., & Denton, K. (1997). Social illusions and self-deception: The evolution of biases in person perception. In J. A. Simpson & D. T. Kenrick (Eds.), *Evolutionary social psychology* (pp. 21–47). Hillsdale, NJ: Lawrence Erlbaum Associates.

Krebs, D. L., & Denton, K. (2005). Toward a more pragmatic approach to morality: A critical evaluation of Kohlberg's model. *Psychological Review, 112*, 629–649.

Krebs, D. L., & Denton, K. (2006). Explanatory limitations of cognitive-developmental approaches to morality. *Psychological Review, 113*, 672–675.

Krebs, D. L., & Denton, K. (2009). Benign folie à deux: The social construction of positive illusions: Commentary on Mckay & Dennett. *Behavioral and Brain Sciences, 32*, 525–526.

Krebs, D. L., Denton, K., & Higgins, N. (1988). On the evolution of self-knowledge and self-deception. In K. MacDonald (Ed.), *Sociobiological perspectives on human behavior* (pp. 103–139). New York: Springer-Verlag.

Krebs, D. L., Denton, K., Vermeulen, S. C., Carpendale, J. I., & Bush, A. (1991). The structural flexibility of moral judgment. *Journal of Personality and Social Psychology, 61*, 1012–1023.

Krebs, D. L., Denton, K., & Wark, G. (1997). The forms and functions of real-life moral decision-making. *Journal of Moral Education, 20*, 131–145.

Krebs, D. L., Denton, K., Wark, G., Couch, R., Racine, T. P., Krebs, D. L. (2002). Interpersonal moral conflicts between couples: Effects of type of dilemma, role, and partner's judgments on level of moral reasoning and probability of resolution. *Journal of Adult Development, 9*, 307–316.

Krebs, D. L., & Janicki, M. (2004). The biological foundations of moral norms. In M. Schaller & C. Crandall (Eds.), *Psychological Foundations of Culture* (pp. 25–148). Hillsdale, NJ: Lawrence Erlbaum Associates.

Krebs, D. L., & Laird, P. (1998). Judging yourself as you judge others: Perspective-taking, moral development, and exculpation. *Journal of Adult Development, 5*, 1–12.

Krebs, D. L., & Van Hesteren, F. (1994). The development of altruism: Toward an integrative model. *Developmental Review, 14*, 103–158.

Krebs, D. L., Vermeulen, S. C., Carpendale, J. I., & Denton, K. (1991). Structural and situational influences on moral judgment: The interaction between stage and dilemma.

In W. Kurtines & J. Gewirtz. (Eds.), *Handbook of moral behavior and development: Theory, research, and applications* (pp. 139–169). Hillsdale, NJ: Lawrence Erlbaum Associates.

Kruger, D. L. (2003). Evolution and altruism: Combining psychological mediators with naturally selected tendencies. *Evolution and human behavior, 24*, 118–125.

Kunda, Z. (2000). *Social cognition: Making sense of people.* Cambridge MA: MIT Press.

Kurland, J. A., and Gaulin, S. J. C. (2005). Cooperation and conflict among kin. In D. Buss (Ed.), *The handbook of evolutionary psychology* (pp. 447–482). New York: John Wiley & Sons.

Kurzban R. (2010). Grand challenges of evolutionary psychology. *Frontiers in Psychology, 1* (3), 1–3. doi:10.3389/fpsyg.2010.00003.

Kurzban, R. & Aktipis, C. A. (2007). On detecting the footprints of multilevel selection in humans. In S. W. Gangestad & J. A. Simpson (Eds.). *The evolution of the mind: Fundamental questions and controversies* (pp. 226–232). New York: Guilford Press.

Kurzban, R., DeScioli, P., & O'Brien, E. (2007). Audience effects on moralistic punishment. *Evolution and Human Behavior, 28*, 75–84.

Kurzban, R., & Houser, D. (2005). Experiments investigating cooperative types in humans: A complement to evolutionary theory and simulations. *Proceedings of the National Academy of Sciences of the U.S.A. 102* (5), 1803–1807.

Kurzban, R., McCabe, K., Smith, V. L., & Wilson, B. J. (2001). Incremental commitment and reciprocity in a real time public goods game. *Personality and Social Psychology Bulletin, 27*, 1662–1673.

Lancaster, J. G., & Lancaster, C. S. (1987). The watershed: Change in parental-investment and family-formation in the course of human evolution. In J. B. Lancaster, J. Altman, A. S. Rossi, & L. R. Sherrod (Eds.), *Parenting across the life span: Biosocial dimensions* (pp. 187–205). New York: Aldine de Gruyter.

Lapsley, D. K. (2006). Moral stage theory. In M. Killen & J. Smetana (Eds.), *Handbook of moral development* (pp. 37–66). Mahwah, NJ: Laurence Erlbaum Associates.

Latané, B., & Nida, S. (1981). Ten years of research on group size and helping. *Psychological Bulletin, 89*, 308–324.

Latané, B., Nida, S. A., & Wilson, D. W. (1981). The effects of group size on helping behavior. In J. P. Rushton & R. M. Sorrentino (Eds.), *Altruism and helping behavior: Social, personality, and developmental perspectives* (pp. 287–314). Hillsdale, NJ: Lawrence Erlbaum Associates.

Leakey, R. E., & Lewin, R. (1977). *Origins.* New York: Dutton

Lerner, M. J., & Miller, D. T. (1978). Just world research and the attribution process: Looking back and ahead. *Psychological Bulletin, 85*, 1030–1051.

Leventhal, G. S., & Anderson, D. (1970). Self-interest and the maintenance of equity. *Journal of Personality and Social Psychology, 15*, 57–62.

Lickliter, R., & Honeycutt, H. (2003). Developmental dynamics: Toward a biologically plausible evolutionary psychology. *Psychological Bulletin, 129*, 819–835.

Lieberman, D., & Linke, L. (2007). The effect of social category on third party punishment. *Evolutionary Psychology, 5*, 289–305.

Littlefield, C. H., & Rushton, J. P. (1986). When a child dies: The sociobiology of bereavement. *Journal of Personality and Social Psychology, 51*, 797–802.

Lorenz, K. Z. (1966). *On aggression.* London: Methuen.

Lovejoy, C. O. (1981). The origin of man. *Science, 211*, 341–350.

MacDonald, K. B. (1988). Sociobiology and the cognitive-developmental tradition on moral development research. In K. B. MacDonald (Ed.), *Sociobiological perspectives on human development* (pp. 140–167). New York: Springer-Verlag.

MacDonald, K. B. (1997). The coherence of individual development: An evolutionary perspective on children's internalization of values. In J. E. Grusec & L. Kuczynski (Eds.), *Parenting and children's internalization of values: A handbook of contemporary theory* (pp. 362–397). New York: John Wiley & Sons.

Maynard Smith, J. (1982). *Evolution and the theory of games.* Cambridge: Cambridge University Press.

McCullough, M. E. (2008). *Beyond revenge: The evolution of the forgiveness instinct.* San Francisco: Jossey-Bass.

McCullough, M. E., Kilpatrick, S, D., Emmons, R. A., & Larson, D. B. (2001). Is gratitude a moral affect? *Psychological Bulletin, 127,* 249–266.

McCullough, M. E., Kimeldorf, M. B., & Cohen, A. D. (2008). An adaptation for altruism? The social causes, social effects and social evolution of gratitude. *Current Directions in Psychological Science, 17,* 281–285.

Milgram, S. (1974). *Obedience to authority.* New York: Harper.

Miller, D. T. (1999). The norm of self-interest. *American Psychologist, 54,* 1053–1060.

Miller, G. F. (1998). The history of passion: A review of sexual selection and human evolution. In C. Crawford & D. L. Krebs (Eds.), *Evolution and human behavior: Ideas, issues and applications* (pp. 87–130). Hillsdale, NJ: Lawrence Erlbaum Associates.

Miller, G. F. (2007a). The sexual selection of moral virtues. *The Quarterly Review of Biology, 82,* 97–125.

Miller, G. F. (2007b). Brain evolution. In S. W. Gangesad & J. A. Simpson (Eds.), *The evolution of mind: Fundamental questions and controversies* (pp. 287–293). New York: Guilford Press

Miller, J. P. (2006). Insights into moral development from cultural psychology. In M. Killen and J. G. Smetana (Eds.), *Handbook of moral development* (pp. 375–398). Mahwah, NJ: Lawrence Erlbaum Associates.

Miller, J. G., & Bersoff, D. M. (1992). Culture and moral judgment: How are conflicts between justice and interpersonal responsibilities resolved? *Journal of Personality and Social Psychology, 62,* 541–554.

Mischel, W., Cantor, N., & Feldman, S. (1996). Principles of self-regulation: The nature of willpower and self-control. In E. T. Higgins & A. W. Kruglanski (Eds.), *Social psychology: Handbook of basic principles* (pp. 329–360). New York: Guilford Press.

Moll, J., di Oliveira-Sourza, R., Zahn, R., & Grafman, J. (2008). The cognitive neuroscience of moral emotions. In Sinnott-Armstrong, W. (Ed.) *Moral psychology: The neuroscience of morality: Emotion, brain disorders, and development* (pp. 1–18). Cambridge, MA: MIT Press.

Moller, A. P. (2008). Sex and sexual selection. In Crawford, C., & Krebs, D. L. (Eds.), *Foundations of evolutionary psychology* (pp. 71–90). New York: Taylor & Francis.

Murphy, J. G. (1982). *Evolution, morality, and the meaning of life.* Totowa, NJ: Rowman and Littlefield.

Nesse, R. M. (2000). How selfish genes shape moral passions. In L. D. Katz (Ed.), *Evolutionary origins of morality: Cross-disciplinary perspectives* (pp. 227–231). Thorverton, UK: Imprint Academic.

Nesse, R. M. (Ed.) (2001). *Evolution and the capacity for commitment.* New York: Russell Sage Foundation.

Nowak, M. A., & Sigmund, K. (1998). Evolution of indirect reciprocity by image scoring. *Nature, 393,* 573–577.

Nunez, M., & Harris, P. L. (1998). Psychological and deontic concepts: Separate domains or intimate connection? *Mind and Language, 13,* 153–170.

Oliner, P. M., Oliner, S. P., Baron, L., Krebs, D. L., & Smolenska, M. Z. (Eds.) (1992). *Embracing the other: Philosophical, psychological, and historical perspectives on altruism*. New York: New York University Press

Osherow, N. (1995). Making sense of the nonsensical: An analysis of Jonestown. In E. Aronson (Ed.), *Readings about the social animal* (7th ed.) (pp. 68–86). San Francisco: W. H. Freeman.

Packer, C. (1977). Reciprocal altruism in *Papio anubis*. *Nature, 265*, 441–443.

Petty, R. E., & Cacioppo, J. T. (1986). The elaboration likelihood model of persuasion. In L. Berkowitz (Ed.), *Advances in experimental social psychology* (pp. 123–205). New York: Academic Press.

Piaget, J. (1932). *The moral judgment of the child*. London: Routledge & Kegan Paul.

Piliavin, J. A., Dovidio, J. F., Gaertner, S. L., & Clark, R. D. (1981). *Emergency intervention*. New York: Academic Press.

Piliavin, J., & Charng, H. (1990). Altruism—A review of recent theory and research. *Annual Review of Sociology, 16*, 27–65.

Pizarro, D. A., & Bloom, P. (2003). The intelligence of the moral intuitions: A reply to Haidt (2001). *Psychological Review, 110*, 193–196.

Pizarro, D. A., Uhlmann, E., & Bloom, P. (2003). Causal deviance and the attribution of moral responsibility. *Journal of Experimental Social Psychology, 39*, 653–660.

Platek, S. M., Burch, R. L., Panyavin, I. S., Wasserman, B. H., & Gallup, G. G. (2003). How much paternal resemblance is enough? Sex differences in hypothetical investment decisions but not in the detection of resemblance. *Evolution and Human Behavior, 24*, 81–87.

Price, M. E. (2006). Monitoring, reputation, and "greenbeard" reciprocity in a Shuar work team. *Journal of Organizational Behavior, 27*, 201–219.

Prinz, J. (2007). *The emotional construction of morals*. New York: Oxford University Press.

Pyszczynski, T., & Greenberg, J. (1987). Toward an integration of cognitive and motivational perspectives on social inference: A biased hypothesis-testing model. *Advances in experimental social psychology, 20*, 297–340.

Rachlin, H. (2002). Altruism and selfishness. *Behavioral and Brain Sciences, 25*, 239–296.

Rapoport, A. C. (1965). *Prisoner's dilemma*. Ann Arbor: University of Michigan Press.

Rawls, J. (1999) *A theory of justice* (rev. ed.). Cambridge, MA: Harvard University Press.

Reeve, K., & Sherman, P. W. (2007). Why measuring reproductive success in current populations is valuable: Moving forward by going backward. In S. W. Gangestad & J. A. Simpson (Eds.), *The evolution of the mind: Fundamental questions and controversies* (pp. 90–91). New York: Guilford Press.

Rest, J. F. (1983). Morality. In J. H. Flavell & E. M. Markman (Eds.), *Handbook of child psychology* (Vol. 3): *Cognitive development* (4th ed.) (pp. 556–629). New York: John Wiley & Sons.

Richards, R. J. (1982). Darwin and the biologizing of moral behavior. In W. R. Woodward & M. G. Ash (Eds.), *The problematic science: Psychology in nineteenth-century thought* (pp. 43–64). New York: Praeger.

Richerson, P. J., & Boyd, R. (2001). The evolution of subjective commitment: A tribal instincts hypothesis. In R. Nesse (Ed.), *Evolution and the capacity for commitment* (pp. 186–219). New York: Russell Sage Foundation.

Richerson, P. J., & Boyd, R. (2005). *Not by genes alone: How culture transformed human evolution*. Chicago: University of Chicago Press.

Ridley, M. (1996). *The origins of virtue: Human instincts and the evolution of cooperation*. New York: Viking.

Ridley, M. (2003). *Nature via nurture*. New York: HarperCollins.

Robinson, P. H., & Darley, J. M. (1995). *Justice, liability, and blame: Community views and the criminal law.* Boulder, CO: Westview Press.

Robinson, P., Kurzban, R., & Jones, O. D. (2007). The origins of shared institutions of justice. *Vanderbilt Law Review, 60,* 1631–1688.

Rozin, P., Haidt, J., & McCauley, C. R. (2000). Disgust. In M. Lewis & J. M. Haviland-Jones (Eds.), *Handbook of emotions* (2nd ed.) (pp. 637–653). New York: Guilford Press.

Rushton, J. P. (1999). Genetic similarity theory and the nature of ethnocentrism. In K. Thienpont & R. Cliquet (Eds.), *In-group/out-group behavior in modern societies: An evolutionary perspective* (pp. 75–107). The Netherlands: Belgium Vlaamse Gemeenschap/CBGC.

Rushton, J. P., Russell, R. J. H., & Wells, P. A. (1984). Genetic similarity theory: Beyond kin selection *Behavior Genetics, 14,* 179–193.

Sachs, J. L., Mueller, U. G., Wilcox, T. P., & Bull, J. J. (2004). The evolution of cooperation. *Quarterly Review of Biology, 79,* 135–160.

Saltzstein, H. D., & Kasachkoff, T. (2004). Haidt's moral intuitionist theory: A psychological and philosophical critique. *Review of General Psychology, 8,* 273–282.

Schachter, S., & Singer, J. E. (1962). Cognitive, social and psychological determinants of emotional state. *Psychological Review, 69,* 379–399.

Schaller, M. (2007). Turning garbage into gold: Evolutionary universals and cross-cultural differences. In S. W. Gangestad & J. A. Simpson (Eds.), *The evolution of mind: Fundamental questions and controversies* (pp. 363–369). New York: Guilford Press.

Schaller, M., & Cialdini, R. B. (1988). The economics of empathic helping: Support for a mood management motive. *Journal of Experimental Social Psychology, 24,* 163–181.

Scheel, D., & Packer, C. (1991). Group hunting behavior of lions: A search for cooperation. *Animal behavior, 41,* 711–722.

Scheyd, G. J., Garver-Apgar, C. E., & Gangestad, S. W. (2008). Physical attractiveness: Signals of phenotypic quality and beyond. In C. Crawford & D. L. Krebs (Eds.), *Foundations of evolutionary psychology* (pp. 239–260). New York: Taylor & Francis.

Schnall, S., Haidt, J., & Clore, G. L. (2005). Disgust as embodied moral judgment. Unpublished manuscript, Department of Psychology, University of Virginia.

Segal, N. L. (1984). Cooperation, competition, and altruism within twin sets: A reappraisal. *Ethology and Sociobiology, 5,* 163–177.

Selman, R. L. (1980). *The growth of interpersonal understanding.* New York: Academic Press.

Shackelford, T. K., & Buss, D. M. (1996). Betrayal in mateships, friendships, and coalitions. *Personality and Social Psychology Bulletin, 22,* 1151–1164.

Shweder, R. A., Much, N. C., Mahapatra, M., & Park, L. (1997). The "big three" of morality (autonomy, community, divinity), and the "big three" explanations of suffering. In A. Brandt & P. Rozin (Eds.), *Morality and health* (pp. 119–169). New York: Routledge.

Siegel, E., & Rachlin, H. (1995). Soft commitment: Self-control achieved by response persistence. *Journal of the Experimental Analysis of Behavior, 64,* 117–128.

Sime, J. D. (1983). Affiliative behavior during escape to building exits. *Journal of Experimental Psychology, 3,* 21–41.

Simon, H. (1990). A mechanism for social selection of successful altruism. *Science, 250,* 1665–1668.

Simpson, J. A., & Campbell, L. (2005). Methods of evolutionary sciences. In D. M. Buss (Ed.), *The handbook of evolutionary psychology* (pp. 119–144). New York: John Wiley & Sons.

Singer, P. (1981). *The expanding circle: Ethics and sociobiology.* New York: Farrar, Straus and Giroux.

Skyrms, B. (2000) Game theory, rationality, and evolution of the social contract. *Journal of Consciousness Studies, 7,* 269–284.

Smith, M. S., Kish, B. J., & Crawford, C. B. (1987). Inheritance of wealth as human kin investment. *Ethology and Sociobiology, 8,* 171–182.

Snyder, C. R., & Higgins, R. L. (1988). Excuses: Their effective role in the negotiation of reality. *Psychological Bulletin, 104,* 23–35.

Sober, E., & Wilson, D. S. (1998). *Unto others: The evolution and psychology of unselfish behavior.* Cambridge, MA: Harvard University Press.

Sober, E., & Wilson, D. S. (2000). Summary of *Unto Others: The Evolution and Psychology of Unselfish Behavior.* In L. D. Katz (Ed.), *Evolutionary origins of morality: Cross disciplinary perspectives* (pp. 185–206). Exeter, UK: Imprint.

Staub, E. (1979). *Positive social behavior and morality.* New York: Academic Press.

Strayer, F. F., & Strayer, J. (1976). An ethological analysis of social agonism and dominance relations among preschool children. *Child Development, 47,* 980–989.

Strayer, F. F., & Trudel, M. (1984). Developmental changes in the nature and function of social dominance among young children. *Ethology and Sociobiology, 5,* 279–295.

Stereley, K. (2007). An alternative evolutionary psychology? In S. W. Gangestad & J. A. Simpson (Eds.). *The evolution of the mind: Fundamental questions and controversies* (pp. 78–185). New York: Guilford Press.

Stevens, J. R., Cushman, F. A., & Hauser, M. D. (2005). Evolving the psychological mechanisms for cooperation. *Annual Review of Ecology and Systematics, 36,* 499–518.

Sunstein, C. R. (2005). Moral heuristics. *Behavioral and Brain Sciences, 28,* 531–573.

Tajfel, H., & Turner, J. C. (1985). The social identity theory of intergroup behavior. In S. Worchel & W. G. Austin (Eds.), *Psychology of intergroup relations* (pp. 7–24). Chicago: Nelson-Hall.

Tetlock, P. E., Visser, P. S., Singh, R. Polifroni, M., Scott, A., Elson, S. B., . . . Rescobar, P. (2007). People as intuitive prosecutors: The impact of social-control goals on attributions of responsibility. *Journal of Experimental Social Psychology, 43,* 195–209.

Thaler, R. H., & Shefrin, H. M. (2005). An economic theory of self-control. In M. H. Bazerman (Ed.), *Negotiation, decision making and conflict management* (Vols. 1–3) (pp. 577–591). Northampton, MA: Edward Elgar Publishing.

Thompson, R., Meyer, S., & McGinley, M. (2006). Understanding values in relationships: The development of conscience. In M. Killen & J. Smetana (Eds.), *Handbook of moral development* (pp. 267–298). Mahwah, NJ: Lawrence Erlbaum Associates.

Tooby, J., & Cosmides, L. (1992). The psychological foundations of culture. In J. Barkow, L. Cosmides, and J. Tooby (Eds.), *The adapted mind: Evolutionary psychology and the generation of culture* (pp. 19–136). New York: Oxford University Press.

Tooby, J., & Cosmides, L. (1996). Friendship and the banker's paradox: Other pathways to the evolution of adaptations for altruism. *Proceedings of the British Academy, 88,* 119–143.

Tooby, J., & Cosmides, L. (2005). Conceptual foundations of evolutionary psychology. In D. Buss (Ed.), *The handbook of evolutionary psychology* (pp. 5–67). New York: John Wiley & Sons.

Tooby, J., & Devore, I. (1987). The reconstruction of hominid behavioral evolution through strategic modeling. In W. G. Kinzey (Ed.), *The evolution of human behavior: Primate models* (pp. 183–237). Albany, NY: SUNY Press.

Tracy, J. L., Cheng, J. T., Robins, R. W., & Trzesniewski, K. H. (2009). Authentic and hubristic pride: The affective core of self-esteem and narcissism. *Self and Identity, 8,* 196–213.

Trivers, R. L. (1971). The evolution of reciprocal altruism. *Quarterly Review of Biology, 46,* 35–57.

Trivers, R. (1974). Parent–offspring conflict. *American Zoologist, 14,* 249–264.

Trivers, R. (1985). *Social evolution.* Menlo Park CA: Benjamin Cummings.

Trivers, R. (2000) The elements of a scientific theory of self-deception. In D. LeCroy & P. Moller (Eds.), *Evolutionary perspectives on human reproductive behavior* (pp. 114–131). New York: The New York Academy of Sciences.

Trivers, R. L. (2002). *Natural selection and social theory: Selected papers of Robert Trivers.* Oxford: Oxford University Press.

Trivers, R. (2006). Reciprocal altruism: 30 years later. In P. M. Kappeler & C. P. van Schaik (Eds.), *Cooperation in primates and humans* (pp. 67–84). New York: Springer-Verlag.

Turiel, E. (1983). Domains and categories in social-cognitive development. In W. Overton (Ed.), *The relationship between social and cognitive development.* Hillsdale, NJ: Lawrence Erlbaum Associates.

Turiel, E. (2006). Thought, emotions, and social interactional processes in moral development. In M. Killen & J. Smetana (Eds.), *Handbook of moral development* (pp. 7–36). Mahwah, NJ: Lawrence Erlbaum Associates.

van den Berghe, P. L. (1983). Human inbreeding avoidance: Culture in nature. *Behavioral and Brain Sciences, 6,* 91–123.

Vasudev, J., and Hummel, R. C. (1987). Moral stage sequence and principled reasoning in an Indian sample. *Human Development, 30,* 105–118.

Walker, L. J., Pitts, R. C., Hennig, K. H., & Matsuba, M. K. (1995). Reasoning about morality and real-life moral problems. In M. Killen & D. Hart (Eds.), *Morality in everyday life: Developmental perspectives* (pp. 371–407). Cambridge: Cambridge University Press

Wallace, G., & Wallace, A. D. M. (Eds.) (1970). *The definition of morality.* London: Methuen & Co.

Wang, X. T. (2002). A kith-and-kin rationality in risky choices: Empirical examinations and theoretical modeling. In F. Salter (Ed.), *Risky transactions: Trust, kinship, and ethnicity* (pp. 47–70). Oxford: Berghahn.

Wark, G., & Krebs, D. L. (1996). Gender and dilemma differences in real-life moral judgment. *Developmental Psychology, 32,* 220–230.

Wark, G., & Krebs, D. L. (1997). Sources of variation in real-life moral judgment: Toward a model of real-life morality. *Journal of Adult Development, 4,* 163–178.

Webster, G. D. (2003). Prosocial behavior in families: Moderators of resource sharing. *Journal of Experimental Social Psychology, 39,* 644–652.

Wedekind, C., & Milinski, M. (2000). Cooperation through image scoring in humans. *Science, 288,* 850–852.

Whiten, A., & Bryne, R. W. (Eds.) (1997). *Machiavellian intelligence II: Extensions and evaluations.* Cambridge: Cambridge University Press.

Wiessner, P. (2005). Norm enforcement among the Ju/hoansi Bushmen: A case of strong reciprocity? *Human Nature, 16,* 115–145.

Wilkinson, G. S. (1990). Food sharing in vampire bats. *Scientific American, February,* 76–82.

Williams, G. C. (1989). A sociobiological expansion of "Evolution and Ethics," *Evolution and Ethics* (pp. 179–214). Princeton, NJ: Princeton University Press.

Wilson, J. Q. (1993). *The moral sense.* New York: The Free Press.

Wrangham, R. W. (1987). African apes: The significance of African apes for reconstructing social evolution. In W. G. Kinzey (Ed.), *The evolution of human behavior: Primate models.* Albany: SUNY Press.

Wright, R. (1994). *The moral animal.* New York: Pantheon Books.

Young, L., Bechara, A., Tranel, D., Damasio, H., Hauser, M., & Damasio, A. (2010). Damage to ventromedial prefrontal cortex impairs judgment of harmful intent. *Neuron, 65,* 845–851.

Young, L. Camprodon, J. A., Hauser, M., Pascual-Leone, A., & Saxe R. (2010). Disruption of the right temporo-parietal junction with transcranial magnetic stimulation reduces the role of beliefs in moral judgments. *Proceedings of the National Academy of Sciences of the U.S.A., 107,* 6753–6758.

Youniss, J., & Damon, W. (1992). Social construction in Piaget's theory. In H. Beilin & P. Pufall (Eds.), *Piaget's theory: Prospects and possibilities.* Hillsdale, NJ: Lawrence Erlbaum Associates.

Zahavi, A. (1995). Altruism as a handicap—the limitations of kin selection and reciprocity. *Journal of Avian Biology, 26,* 1–3.

Zahavi, A., & Zahavi, A. (1997). *The handicap principle.* New York: Oxford University Press.

Zajonc, R. B. (1968). Attitudinal effects of mere exposure. *Journal of Personality and Social Psychology Monograph Supplement, 9,* 2–27.

Zimbardo, P. (2005). A situationalist perspective on the psychology of good and evil: Understanding how good people are transformed into perpetrators. In A. G. Miller (Ed.), *The social psychology of good and evil* (pp. 21–50). New York: Guilford Press.

Zimbardo, P. G., Hane, C., Ganks, W. C., and Jaffe, D. A. (1973, April 8). Pirandellian prison: The mind is a formidable jailer. *New York Times Magazine,* pp. 38–60.

INDEX

Page numbers followed by "n" indicate footnotes.